TimeOut

Vancouver

timeout.com/vancouver

Published by Time Out Guides Ltd, a wholly owned subsidiary of Time Out Group Ltd.
Time Out and the Time Out logo are trademarks of Time Out Group Ltd.

© **Time Out Group Ltd 2006**

10 9 8 7 6 5 4 3 2 1

This edition first published in Great Britain in 2006 by Ebury Publishing
Ebury Publishing is a division of The Random House Group Ltd,
20 Vauxhall Bridge Road, London SW1V 2SA

Random House Australia Pty Limited 20 Alfred Street, Milsons Point, Sydney, New South Wales 2061, Australia
Random House New Zealand Limited 18 Poland Road, Glenfield, Auckland 10, New Zealand
Random House South Africa (Pty) Limited Isle of Houghton, Corner Boundary
Road & Carse O'Gowrie, Houghton 2198, South Africa

Random House UK Limited Reg. No. 954009

Distributed in USA by Publishers Group West
1700 Fourth Street, Berkeley, California 94710

Distributed in Canada by Penguin Canada Ltd
10 Alcorn Avenue, Toronto, Ontario, Canada M4V 3B2

For further distribution details, see www.timeout.com

ISBN 1-904978-72-X (until 31 December 2006)
ISBN 978-1-904978-72-5 (after 1 January 2007)

A CIP catalogue record for this book is available from the British Library

Colour reprographics by Icon, Crowne House, 56-58 Southwark Street, London SE1 1UN

Printed and bound in Germany by Appl

Papers used by Ebury Publishing are natural, recyclable products made from wood grown in sustainable forests

Time Out Guides Limited
Universal House
251 Tottenham Court Road
London W1T 7AB
Tel + 44 (0)20 7813 3000
Fax + 44 (0)20 7813 6001
Email guides@timeout.com
www.timeout.com

Editorial

Editors Tom Charity, Fiona Morrow
Deputy Editor Edoardo Albert
Listings Editor Alisma Perry
Proofreader Marion Moisy
Indexer Anna Norman

Editorial/Managing Director Peter Fiennes
Series Editor Ruth Jarvis
Deputy Series Editor Lesley McCave
Business Manager Gareth Garner
Guides Co-ordinator Holly Pick
Accountant Kemi Olufuwa

Design

Art Director Scott Moore
Art Editor Tracey Ridgewell
Senior Designer Josephine Spencer
Graphic Designer Henry Elphick
Digital Imaging Dan Conway
Ad Make-up Jenni Prichard

Picture Desk

Picture Editor Jael Marschner
Deputy Picture Editor Tracey Kerrigan
Picture Researcher Helen McFarland

Advertising

Sales Director Mark Phillips
International Sales Manager Ross Canadé
International Sales Executive Simon Davies
Advertising Sales (Vancouver) West Coast Media
Advertising Assistant Kate Staddon

Marketing

Marketing Director Mandy Martinez
Marketing & Publicity Manager, US Rosella Albanese

Production

Production Director Mark Lamond
Production Controller Marie Howell

Time Out Group

Chairman Tony Elliott
Managing Director Mike Hardwick
Group Financial Director Richard Waterlow
Group Commercial Director Lesley Gill
Group General Manager Nichola Coulthard
Group Circulation Director Jim Heinemann
Group Art Director John Oakey
Online Managing Director David Pepper
Group Production Director Steve Proctor
Group IT Director Simon Chappell

Contributors

Introduction Tom Charity. **History** Michael Kluckner (*Going green* Charles Campbell; *The shipping news* Terence Tate).
Vancouver Today Heather Watson (*West vs East* Steve Burgess; *Rain city* Nancy Lanthier). **West Coast Art** Craig Burnett
(*'X' marks the spot* Nancy Lanthier). **Where to Stay** Eve Gabereau. **Sightseeing Introduction** Tom Charity, Matthew Mallon.
Downtown Matthew Mallon (*Dogville* Charles Demers; *The space man* Heather Watson). **Stanley Park** Charles Campbell.
The West Side Justin Smallbridge (*Skinny dipping* Camilla Pickard; *Blooming marvellous* Alison Appelbe). **East Vancouver**
Nancy Lanthier. **Restaurants & Cafés** Alexandra Gill, additional reviews Judith Adam, Fiona Morrow, Jane Mundy, Stephen
Wong (*Introduction* Fiona Morrow; *Know your noodles* Stephen Wong; *Izakaya time, Korea moves* Steve Burgess; *Caffeine fix,
Something fishy* Elaine Corden; *Cheap eats* Chris Eng). **Bars** David Gayton (*Napa of the north* Murray Bancroft). **Shops &
Services** Sarah Bancroft, additional reviews Judith Adam, Chris Eng (Comics), Lucy Hyslop (Sport), Camilla Pickard (Classical
music), Curtis Woloschuk (Popular music). **Festivals & Events** Fiona Morrow. **Children** Fiona Morrow. **Film** Tom Charity.
Galleries Craig Burnett. **Gay & Lesbian** Meita Winkler. **Music & Nightlife** *Rock and folk* Curtis Woloschuk; *Classical and jazz*
Camilla Pickard; *Nightclubs* Nancy Lanthier. **Performing Arts** Tim Carlson; *Dance* M David Dinesen. **Sport & Fitness** Lucy
Hyslop. **Getting Started** Tom Charity. **Excursions** *Bowen Island* Nancy Lanthier; *Steveston* Justin Oppelaar; *Fraser Valley*
Chris McBeath; *Expeditions* Nancy Lanthier (*On the ocean wave* Nancy Lanthier; *Sea to sky* Tom Charity). **Victoria &
Vancouver Island** Tom Charity, Fiona Morrow (*Southern Gulf Islands, Spa around* Chris McBeath; *Thar she blows!* Tom
Charity). **The Okanagan** Alison Appelbe. **Whistler** Tom Charity, Julia McKinnell, Fiona Morrow (*Seeking powder, Bro-speak:
lessons in the local lingo* Julia McKinnell). **Directory** Tom Charity, Fiona Morrow, Alisma Perry, Terence Tate.

Maps by JS Graphics (john@jsgraphics.co.uk). Maps are based on material supplied by ITMB Publishing Ltd (Vancouver).
Whistler Map based on material supplied by Tourism Whistler.

Photography Shannon Mendes (p54 courtesy: Adam with pillar by Rodin, from a collection of Iris and B.Gerald Cantor
Foundation and the Vancouver Art Gallery); page 10 Private Collection, The Stapleton Collection/ Bridgeman Art Library;
page 13 City of Vancouver Archives; page 26 courtesy of the artist and Catriona Jeffries Gallery, Vancouver; page 27 Trevor
Mills; page 29 Robert Keziere; page 30 Masterfile/ Sherman Hines; page 61 Tourism Vancouver; page 189 Corbis; page
192 Alamy; pages 213, 215 (left) Tourism Whistler; page 215 (right) Dean Thomson Photography; page 223 Dean Cote.
The following images were provided by the feautured establishments/ artist: pages 14, 167

The Editor would like to thank Marion Bancroft, David Beers, Julian Beder, Laurence Boxhall, Charles Campbell, Meg Charity,
Joe Charity, Alan Franey, Eve Gabereau, Matthew Mallon, Katherine Monk, Michael Scott, Mia Stainsby and Carlyn Yandle.

Contents

Introduction   6

In Context   9

History   10
Vancouver Today   19
West Coast Art   26

Where to Stay   33

Where to Stay   34

Sightseeing   49

Introduction   50
Downtown   53
Stanley Park   60
  Map: Stanley Park   63
The West Side   67
East Vancouver   76
North Shore   81

Eat, Drink, Shop   87

Restaurants & Cafés   88
Bars   113
Shops & Services   121

Arts & Entertainment   137

Festivals & Events   138
Children   142
Film   146
Galleries   150
Gay & Lesbian   155
Music & Nightlife   159
Performing Arts   167
Sport & Fitness   173

Trips Out of Town   183

Getting Started   184
  Map: Trips Out of Town   186
Excursions   188
Victoria & Vancouver Island   195
  Map: Victoria   196
The Okanagan   207
  Map: The Okanagan   209
Whistler   213
  Map: Whistler   217

Directory   225

Getting Around   226
Resources A-Z   230
Further Reference   238
Index   240
Advertisers' Index   244

Maps   245

Greater Vancouver   246
Street Maps   248
Street Index   254
Local Transport   256

Introduction

Picture a sandy beach just steps from a bustling downtown shopping district and ten minutes stroll from the largest city park in North America. Turn around and admire the gleaming glass spires that have shot up like bamboo over the last decade, framed by the snowcapped peaks of Grouse, Seymour and Cypress mountains. Breathe in and savour the light breeze rolling off the Pacific.

All around you, people are running, biking, swimming and sailing, or they're taking time out at the nearest café, drinking in the most spectacular city in the northern hemisphere. Throw in some umbrellas – yes, it does rain sometimes – and the picture is complete.

Canada's third largest city, Vancouver feels a world away from the metropolitan rush of Toronto – indeed, 3,366 kilometres (2,091 miles) separates them. This is the West Coast – Lotusland according to the easterners – and Vancouverites have as much in common with the people of (relatively) nearby Seattle, Portland and San Francisco as they do with the prairie folk to the east. There is enterprise and industry here (notably timber, movies and tourism) but the careerists tend to move on. To feel at home in Vancouver, eat well, play hard and work less.

Even so, and to some locals' consternation, Vancouver is being held up as a model for urban development – one day all cities will be designed this way! – and, as Canada's gateway to the Pacific Rim, it is attracting a massive influx of immigrants from across Asia. Not only that, the world's attention will focus even more on the north-west when the city co-hosts (with Whistler) the Winter Olympics in 2010.

The Olympic impetus can be felt everywhere: the federal and provincial governments are stumping up hundreds of millions of dollars for new facilities, improved transport links and an environmentally sustainable athletes' village (destined to become a mixed-use housing project when the Games are over). Real estate is booming, there is a projected shortfall in the workforce and even the region's previously under-resourced cultural institutions are stretching their muscles: the Vancouver Art Gallery, Vancouver Museum and the Maritime Museum all have refurbishment and expansion plans, and the brand new Vancouver International Film Centre opened for business in January 2006.

With all these advantages, both geographic and political, Vancouver has no problem attracting newcomers, either as tourists or immigrants. However, once they get here the city sometimes seems not entirely sure what to do with them. While readers of *Condé Naste Traveler* voted Vancouver the best city in the Americas in 2004 and 2005, *Canadian Business* magazine recently rated it the very worst city in the country to set up in business – citing prohibitive costs and the relatively poor crime statistics.

But maybe all this is to be expected as the normal growing pains of a city that has only begun to put itself firmly on to the world stage. Vancouver is a young place, incorporated as recently as 1866, that is changing fast – and if some die-hards wax nostalgic for the quiet provincial outpost of their youth, few will deny the excitement in the air, or fail to appreciate the cultural (and culinary) diversity that is thriving here.

ABOUT TIME OUT CITY GUIDES

This is the first edition of *Time Out Vancouver,* one of an expanding series of Time Out guides produced by the people behind the successful listings magazines in London, New York and Chicago. Our guides are all written by resident experts who have striven to provide you with all the most up-to-date information you'll need to explore the city or read up on its background, whether you're a local or a first-time visitor.

THE LIE OF THE LAND

Surrounded by sea and bordered by mountains, Vancouver has not sprawled as much as other North American cities. Couple this with another unusual feature for the continent, an efficient public transport system, and you have a city that is easy to get around on foot, bicycle, boat or bus. And if all else fails remember one simple rule: look for the mountains. Find them and you'll know where north lies. To make both book and city even easier to navigate, we've divided Vancouver into areas and assigned each one its own chapter in our Sightseeing section. For consistency, the same areas are used in addresses throughout the guide. We've also included cross-streets, phone numbers, website addresses, zip codes for those venues to which you might want to write and map

references that point to our street maps at the back of the guide. For further orientation information, *see p50*.

ESSENTIAL INFORMATION

For all the practical information you might need for visiting the area – including visa and customs information, details of local transport, a listing of emergency numbers, information on local weather and a selection of useful websites – turn to the Directory at the back of this guide. It begins on page 226.

THE LOWDOWN ON THE LISTINGS

We have tried to make this book as easy to use as possible. Addresses, phone numbers, bus information, opening times and admission prices are all included in the listings. However, businesses can change their arrangements at any time. Before you go out of your way, we'd strongly advise you to phone ahead to check opening times and other particulars. While every effort and care has been made to ensure the accuracy of the information contained in this guide, the publishers cannot accept responsibility for any errors it may contain.

PRICES AND PAYMENT

We have noted where venues such as shops, hotels, restaurants and theatres accept the following credit cards: American Express

(AmEx), Diners Club (DC), Discover (Disc), MasterCard (MC) and Visa (V). Many will also accept travellers' cheques, and/or other cards such as Carte Blanche.

The prices we've listed in this guide should be treated as guidelines, not gospel. If prices vary wildly from those we've quoted, ask whether there's a good reason. If not, go elsewhere. Then please let us know. We aim to give the best and most up-to-date advice, so we want to know if you've been badly treated or overcharged.

TELEPHONE NUMBERS

Vancouver and much of the Lower Mainland (including Whistler) share the area code 604. Although Vancouver businesses often place the prefix in brackets or drop it altogether, you must dial the code no matter where you are calling from. Accordingly, we include the area code in all telephone numbers listed in the guide.

MAPS

The map section at the back of this book includes a map of Greater Vancouver, street maps of the most visited parts of the city and a transport map showing bus, ferry and SkyTrain routes in the downtown area. The maps start on page 246, and now pinpoint the specific locations of hotels (❶), restaurants and cafés (❶), and bars (❶).

LET US KNOW WHAT YOU THINK

We hope you enjoy the *Time Out Vancouver Guide*, and we'd like to know what you think of it. We welcome tips for places that you consider we should include in future editions and take note of your criticism of our choices. You can email us at guides@timeout.com.

There is an online version of this book, along with guides to over 100 international cities, at **www.timeout.com**.

In Context

History	**10**
Vancouver Today	**19**
West Coast Art	**26**

Features

West Side vs East Side	12
Going green	15
The shipping news	16
West vs East	20
Rain city	25
Off the Wall	28
'X' marks the spot	32

Museum of Anthropology. *See p74.*

Vancouver's early days.

History

The end of the road spells endless new beginnings for Canada's terminal city.

Location, location, location: what's true for real estate is doubly so for cities. From our 21st-century perspective, Vancouver is a great city because of its beautiful setting and easy access to pristine wilderness. To 19th-century settlers it was ideal for a different reason: its large, ice-free port with easy access to the ocean and the necessary raw materials to feed its sawmills and canneries. Add in the other requirements: not just a railway, but a railway terminus; enough land for the city to grow into; and a hinterland – the Fraser River delta – for dairying and vegetable-growing. And in Vancouver's case, perhaps an additional *raison d'être*: the international border only a few miles to the south. If there were no border, would there be major cities at both Seattle and Vancouver?

Location had also made the site of Vancouver significant to Natives for 6,000 years before the arrival of European explorers and settlers. For the Stó:lo – the 'people of the river' – the important corridor was the Fraser River, along which were fishing grounds and gathering places they used on their seasonal rounds. There were permanent settlements at Khwaykhway in today's Stanley Park, at Mahli near the mouth of the Fraser River and at Cheechilwhik on the North Vancouver shoreline. As with the other 'Pacific Northwest' nations, the Stó:lo were blessed with a natural bounty, most notably the western red cedar (*Thuja plicata*) which was easily crafted into ocean-going canoes, split into planks for the construction of sophisticated post-and-beam dwellings and carved into totem poles. Their hunters and gatherers easily produced a surplus of food for the community, allowing people of artistic talent to enrich the culture to an incredible extent.

European diseases devastated the Native communities before any Europeans arrived. Two-thirds of the Stó:lo died in the first great smallpox epidemic of 1782, which apparently had spread north through intertribal trading networks from Mexico City, where it had spread from the Spanish two years earlier. Although subsequent epidemics also took their toll, it was the governmental policy of assimilation, including the banning of the potlatch ceremony, the building of individual family homes on reserves rather than the previous communal clan dwelling, and the introduction of residential schools, that almost wiped out Native cultures. The recent renaissance of totem-pole carving and jewellery making has helped First Nations all along the coast to recover pride in their culture, while lengthy land claims negotiations continue with the provincial government. Supreme Court decisions confirmed that Aboriginal title was never extinguished in BC and the treaty process is leading First Nations towards a form of self-government in their traditional territories across the province.

The first Europeans to reach western Canada were explorers working for the Hudson's Bay Company (HBC) and its competitors in the 1790s. They began to trade with the Natives, tapping into their long-established trading networks and using their trails.

By sea, the coastline had been 'discovered' in 1791 by the Spanish navigator Jose Maria Narvaez. The following year, Royal Navy Captain George Vancouver, confirming and expanding on the information from James Cook's Pacific voyages of the 1780s, charted the future harbour and coincidentally met with another Spanish expedition off Point Grey.

The name Spanish Banks, for a beach near the University of BC, commemorates this meeting, and local and regional place names such as Langara, Valdez and Galiano recall Spanish attempts to expand their empire northward from its California outpost. Vancouver named Burrard Inlet after a British admiral and Point Grey after a fellow officer. A subsequent survey in 1859 noted the strategic potential of the peninsula at the first narrows and reserved it for military purposes. Like the Presidio base at San Francisco's Golden Gate, it later became parkland – Stanley Park, named for the governor general who is mainly remembered today as the namesake of a hockey trophy. A number of Native names, in anglicised form, stayed on the landscape or

were added to it: Siwash Rock in Stanley Park, for example. The Capilano River recalls a chief of the Squamish band, as does the ultra-trendy Kitsilano neighbourhood.

SETTING THE STAGE

The HBC, which had been trading along the coast since the 1820s and had established Fort Vancouver (that is, Vancouver, Washington) at the mouth of the Columbia River, began to clash with American migrants moving westward over the Oregon Trail. By the early 1840s, America's 'Manifest Destiny' was its dominant political issue. Militant American expansionists thought the USA should extend north as far as Russian Alaska, while the HBC believed the HBC had established a claim to Washington through its trading posts and farms. In the event, the 49th parallel, already accepted as the international boundary across the great central plain of North America, was extended to the western shore. As the HBC had wisely established Fort Victoria in 1843, Vancouver Island remained British, and became a colony in 1849. On the mainland, Burrard Inlet was the nearest harbour north of the border.

A few years later, gold was discovered in California, triggering the first of the frantic rushes that moved a rabble of humanity westward. Prospectors then moved north, discovering gold and silver in the 1850s along the Fraser River. The British administration in Victoria moved quickly to establish a new colony on the mainland, naming it British Columbia. A city, imaginatively named New Westminster, was established on the Fraser River at the strategic point where it widens into a delta, thus ensuring control of river traffic attempting to get to the gold fields.

The gold rush had little immediate impact on the Vancouver area. However, disillusioned gold seekers soon returned to the coast. By the mid-1860s there were sawmills operating on Burrard Inlet, one – Stamp's Mill – near the foot of modern Main Street. The loggers, like their compatriots in Oregon and Washington, had discovered the extraordinary stands of Douglas fir (*Pseudotsuga menziesii*), a tree second only to the California redwood in size, and were soon exporting timber from Burrard Inlet.

THE INVENTION OF VANCOUVER

Partly in response to the American Civil War and concerns that the violence might spread north of the border, the eastern British colonies confederated and became Canada. Before long, the government was negotiating to bring the isolated west-coast colony into the Canadian fold. The inducement was a railway that would connect the west coast with the settled east.

Meanwhile, late in the summer of 1867, while far-away Canada was celebrating its nationhood, a barkeeper named John Deighton came ashore just west of Stamp's Mill with, it is said, a barrel of whisky and another of nails, and invited the mill workers to help him build a saloon near a large native maple tree. Deighton was garrulous, bearing the nickname 'Gassy Jack'. Additional stores and saloons soon sprang up along the shore just west of the 'maple tree square'. Sleepy little Gastown, as it was commonly known, officially became Granville in 1870 when it was surveyed into a grid of six square blocks from Maple Tree Square at Carrall west to Cambie, and Water Street south to Hastings.

Little happened for a decade while far-off financiers and politicians haggled over the railway and its proposed route. Eventually, the Canadian Pacific Railway (CPR) decided on the difficult southern route – mainly to ensure that perfidious Americans would not sneak spur lines into the province to ship away all the goods – with a terminus at Burrard Inlet. Suddenly, Gastown woke up to its new destiny.

CPR general manager William Van Horne visited his future terminal city in 1884, met with local businessmen and land speculators (losing heavily at poker with them) and was delighted with everything he saw. Except the name. According to legend, he reached back into his stock of historical lore and intoned, 'I name thee Vancouver.' After a little arm-twisting, everyone fell into line, and the new city was incorporated in April 1886.

Land clearing crews – clearcutting as opposed to the selective logging typical of the 1860s and 1870s – pushed south and west during the exceptionally dry May of 1886. On June 13, a slash fire got out of hand and swept across the land, burning everything in its path, sparing only the sawmill and one Water Street hotel whose occupants soaked blankets and beat out the sparks. In retrospect a fine example of urban renewal, the fire forced Vancouverites to adopt safety codes and begin to rebuild their downtown buildings with more permanent materials. Before the ground cooled, buildings were rising again.

The following 23 May the city was truly born, for on that day the first through train from eastern Canada reached Vancouver. The CPR had been busy, laying out grand streets in its new downtown centred on the corner of Granville Street and Georgia Street, building the Hotel Vancouver and an opera house there, and launching ships that would connect Vancouver with the Far East.

Transport brought first-class tourists – mainly English, travelling the world to see the Empire – and more colonists. Cargos of tinned salmon from canneries on the Fraser River went the other way. Flatcars left the city loaded with 'Vancouver toothpicks' – beams a metre square

West Side vs East Side

Why is Vancouver's east side poorer, more ethnically diverse and more architecturally jumbled than the city's west side? Partly because the working (class) port is east of downtown, and pretty English Bay and its beaches on the west side have always acted as lures to the affluent bourgeoisie. But the real key is the land grant that the provincial government gave to the Canadian Pacific Railway in return for its 'founding' of Vancouver in the 1880s. Most of this 16 million square metres (174 million square feet) was south of False Creek, between Ontario and Trafalgar streets on the west side of the old Municipality of South Vancouver.

The railway's land department ensured that neighbourhoods like Kitsilano and Kerrisdale were well laid-out and provided with modern services. On the east side, however, speculators and builders made it up as they went along. Streets often didn't line up, odd lots crowded narrow blocks, and there were few of the amenities, such as street trees, that kept property values high on the west side. So disgruntled were the west-siders that they seceded from South Vancouver in 1908 and founded their own municipality, Point Grey, which enforced strict development rules. Both municipalities ended up amalgamating with Vancouver in 1929.

A visit to Main Street around King Edward Avenue (25th) is instructive, as well as inviting for exploring galleries and coffee houses. East of Main, and on the two blocks to the west as far as Ontario Street, there is a jumble of interesting houses. Along Ontario Street – the boundary with the CPR lands – the roads don't line up with the ones to the west. And as you look west along King Edward Avenue from Ontario, you can see a broad prospect as the road widens into a grand boulevard towards ritzy Shaughnessy Heights, which was named, of course, for CPR President Sir Thomas Shaughnessy.

The way the city was.

by 30 metres long (10.7 square feet by 98 feet) – the kind of timber that supported the floors of brick warehouses, including those on the site of the razed saloons and hotels of Gastown. One load of beams left Burrard Inlet in 1884 for Beijing's Imperial Palace.

Vancouver's port quickly became the hub of the western economy. A state-of-the-art electric interurban (tram) system connected the agricultural Fraser Valley with the city. By 1900 there were about 25,000 inhabitants, and boosters erected banners on the streets proclaiming (poetically if not accurately in terms of gender) that 'In 1910 Vancouver Then Will Have 100,000 Men!' They just made it.

THE EDWARDIAN BOOM

The first dozen years of the 20th century defined the city's form. In the downtown, landmark buildings – those that today define 'old Vancouver' – sprang up along the main commercial streets of Hastings and Granville. In the streetcar suburbs, middle-class families pursued the dream of a bungalow with a garden on a quiet street far from the city's factories. The wealthy abandoned their fine homes on so-

called Blueblood Alley (today's West Hastings Street), first for new mansions above Sunset Beach in the West End, then for the curving streets of the CPR's Shaughnessy Heights.

'The soggy Shangri-la was white and overwhelmingly British.'

Along the streetcar loop of Davie-Denman-Robson in the West End, shops lined the streets and apartments began to appear. New satellite cities in North and West Vancouver started ferry services for their commuters. In the summer, throngs of people went to English Bay in the West End or took the streetcar across False Creek to the new beach at Kitsilano.

Ethnically, the soggy Shangri-la was white and overwhelmingly British. Where it wasn't English it tended to be Scottish rather than Irish. (There's an old saying that England gave Canada its institutions and Scotland gave it its people.) It was church-going and predominantly Protestant but not church-building, at least

The arrival of Canadian Pacific Railway's first train in Vancouver. *See p12.*

compared with older Canadian cities such as Victoria and Toronto. Non-Anglo immigrant groups packed into the workers' community named Strathcona, just south of the Hastings sawmill and the port: a Jewish street here, an Italian one there. Natives still lived on reserves in Kitsilano and North Vancouver.

There were Asians, too: Chinese, Japanese and Indians. As the Union Pacific Railroad in the US had done in the 1860s, the CPR brought Chinese workers to BC to lay its tracks. When construction ended in 1885 they drifted to the coast, but few had enough money to return home. Vancouver's Chinatown adjoined the city's red-light district on low-lying, swampy land between the Hastings Street commercial district and False Creek. It was overwhelmingly male, as a head tax made it all but impossible to bring in wives or concubines. Formed into tongs (family societies), the Chinese built some substantial brick buildings along Pender Street, and tenements on the side streets and in narrow

alleyways. Legally manufactured opium and illegal gambling occupied many of them, and the police, and fascinated the public.

Unlike the Chinese, who had come to 'Gold Mountain' to make a fortune and then return home, the Japanese came as settlers and, because of Britain's military alliance with Japan, were not subject to head taxes. Highly organised and disciplined, and proud of their country's defeat of Russia in 1905, they attracted the enmity of the mainstream due to their success in fishing and market gardening, and began early in the 20th century to insist on the right to vote. Their community occupied the blocks of Powell Street east of Main.

In 1907, a hiccup in the economic boom caused disaffected whites to rampage through Chinatown, breaking windows, destroying businesses, and beating anyone who couldn't get out of the way. But when the mob tried to do the same to the Japanese, they were met with armed resistance and were forced to retreat.

Going green

Vancouver is a natural locus of environmental activism, located as it is on the verge of so much wilderness waiting to be spoiled. Travel north from the city along British Columbia's mainland coast, and you won't find another settlement of more than 15,000 people until you reach Alaska.

And it is this location so near so much pristine nature that was certainly one of the keys to the emergence of Greenpeace in Vancouver in 1970 and '71.

'We had the biggest concentration of tree-huggers, radicalised students, garbage-dump stoppers, shit-disturbing unionists, freeway fighters, pot smokers and growers, ageing Trotskyites, condo killers, farmland savers, fish preservationists, animal rights activists, back-to-the-landers, vegetarians, nudists, Buddhists, and anti-spraying, anti-pollution marchers and picketers in the country, per capita, in the world,' wrote the late, great Bob Hunter (1941-2005), Greenpeace member 000 and the central genius in the organisation's early years.

There were also ex patriate Americans – Vietnam-era draft dodgers and others looking for a kinder, gentler version of the United States. Dorothy and Irving Stowe brought the Quaker tradition of bearing witness to the anti-war and emerging 'ecology' movements in the early '70s. Their Don't Make a Wave Committee opposed nuclear testing on Alaska's Amchitka Island. In 1970, Marie Bohlen suggested sailing a protest boat to the island. That same year, after Irving Stowe concluded a meeting with the salutation 'peace', Bill Darnell fatefully replied, 'Make it a green peace.'

In the fall of 1971, an old halibut trawler renamed the *Greenpeace* was sailing through the Gulf of Alaska's gales and into history.

A variety of ad-hoc Greenpeace offices were soon established around the world on the strength of the media-savvy Vancouver activists. Anti-whaling and anti-sealing campaigns followed, and in 1979 Greenpeace International was formed, based in Amsterdam and headed by Vancouverite David McTaggart, who had been beaten by the French military while protesting against French nuclear testing in the South Pacific.

Today, Greenpeace is a £100-million enterprise. Original member Paul Watson decries its ubiquitous door-to-door fund-raisers as the Fuller Brush salesmen of the environmental movement. Yet while some see Greenpeace as a neutered bureaucracy, the organisation can negotiate for environmental interests with the mere threat of a protest, and it is still seen as radical in places such as Brazil and Russia.

Today, a host of British Columbia-bred groups use a wide variety of strategies to raise the profile of environmental concerns. Watson's Sea Shepherd Society takes a confrontational approach, mainly on whaling. The Western Canada Wilderness Committee and the Raincoast Conservation Society adopt the harder line on forestry issues. More moderate groups such as the Rainforest Action Network and the David Suzuki Foundation work the public- and corporate-policy development front.

Vancouver's internationally renowned Adbusters Media Foundation, whose *Adbusters* magazine founder Kalle Lasn calls 'the Greenpeace of the mental environment', has brought Greenpeace's satirical savvy to the issue of consumerism. And the Green party – which emerged in Europe in tandem with Greenpeace – is finally edging towards becoming a political force in British Columbia. One in ten voters supported it in the last two provincial elections.

There's no shortage of issues, from the damaging effect of fish farms on the wild salmon population, to the depletion of boreal forests, to the renewed spectre of offshore drilling. Whaling is becoming prominent again, as aboriginal populations around the world assert their heritage for good and ill, and thus pose a real quandary for environmental groups: do animal rights take precedence over human rights, or vice versa? Notwithstanding the quaint, official City of Vancouver signs that declare Vancouver a 'nuclear weapons free zone', and the demise of annual anti-war protests that once routinely drew 50,000 people, nuclear weapons – which goaded Greenpeace into existence – remain a critical concern.

The world, along with the environmental movement, is growing more complicated by the day. But the principles remain simple, and they matter more to British Columbians now than they did when a motley crew of protestors set out to change the world some 35 years ago.

The third Asian group were Indians, mainly Sikhs although referred to as 'Hindoos' in those days, whose presence in Vancouver again reflected Britain's far-flung empire and alliances. Typically in the early years they worked in the sawmills along False Creek and lived in small houses nearby. For most Vancouverites, the Sikhs were out-of-sight, out-of-mind, but they were nevertheless disenfranchised in 1907. Things hadn't improved seven years later when the *Komagata Maru*, a chartered Japanese ship filled with Indian passengers, arrived in Vancouver harbour but, after a lengthy and ugly stand-off, it was refused landing.

WAR, DEPRESSION, WAR AGAIN

Vancouver lost a generation of its youth in World War I, while not benefiting as eastern cities did from munitions manufacturing and shipbuilding. Then, the roaring twenties merely squeaked along for several years, picking up as the city began to ship grain through the Panama Canal. The must-see landmark from that era is the art deco Marine Building at Burrard and Hastings.

But no sooner had prosperity returned than the Great Depression began. Drought on the prairies and industrial collapse in the east put thousands of men on the road, and the majority of them hopped freights west to the Terminal

The shipping news

It is not possible to explore downtown Vancouver without noticing a veritable flotilla of private boats moored in the many inlets and marinas of the city. Whether it be recreational sailing, commercial cruise shipping, or supertankers laden with cargo, visitors to Vancouver cannot fail to understand the important role maritime activity has played, and continues to play, in the evolution of the city.

The Port of Vancouver is the largest on the western seaboard of North America. Its deep-water, ice-free environment enables it to generate an economic output of $8.9 billion a year, including $1.5 billion in wages for its 62,000 employees. Trading with over 90 countries, particularly the emerging markets of the Pacific Rim, the port processes 70 million tonnes of cargo annually. In addition to trade, the Port is also a starting point for cruises to Alaska. Approximately one million passengers a year use the Port's cruise terminals and each sailing, of which there are 300 annually, generates a revenue of $1.5 million. Complete with modern day navigational aids, gamma ray scanning and a dedicated team of environmentalists the Port of Vancouver is one of the safest and cleanest in the world. These measures were sadly lacking in March 1945, when the freighter *Greenhill Park* went up in flames and became the worst disaster in the Port's history. The blast killed eight dockers, injured 19 other workers and shattered hundreds of windows in downtown. The cause: a match, a barrel of contraband liquor and a cargo of sodium chlorate.

All this is a far cry from the late 1700s, when the waters off Vancouver were

populated by nothing more demonstrative than the canoes and kayaks of the Salish Indians. Despite Captain James Cook landing at Nootka Sound in 1778, the Salish enjoyed another 14 years of peace and quiet before Captain George Vancouver entered Burrard Inlet in 1792, setting in motion successive waves of European exploration that culminated with the westward expansion of Canadian nationhood. Although the city was named after him, Captain Vancouver was more interested in locating the western end of the Northwest Passage than he was in lending his name to what would become one of the great cities of the world.

During World War II Vancouver's shipyards built minesweepers, corvettes and cargo ships for service in the Atlantic Ocean. Around half of Canada's naval contribution to the Allied war effort came from Vancouver. Another significant contribution to the eventual victory was made by the Royal Canadian Mounted Police vessel *St Roch*, built in North Vancouver in 1929, and currently residing in the A-frame annexe to the Maritime Museum in Vanier Park. Originally designed as a patrol vessel, its legendary World War II voyages across the Arctic made it the first ship to sail the Northwest Passage in both directions, an achievement that asserted Canada's sovereignty over its northern borders during the time of war. At a modest 31 metres (104 feet) in length the *St Roch* really does not look capable of withstanding the rigours of the Arctic but it does seem to embody the spirit of those intrepid pioneers who tamed the vast expanses of Canada's endless rivers, lakes, bays and coastal waters.

City. A makeshift relief system helped for
a time, but once the heavy-handed federal
government forced the unemployed into remote
work camps their militancy increased. A near-
riot at Victory Square in 1935 began the On-to-
Ottawa trek to demand work and wages. Three
years later, the unemployed occupied the art
gallery, the main post office (now Sinclair
Centre) and the Hotel Georgia until police
forced them out on 'Bloody Sunday'.

Depression-era bargains in Vancouver
coincided with the rise of fascism in Europe,
prompting the Guinness company to invest far
from the potential fray. It bought the Marine
Building in 1932, then several thousand acres
of forest on West Vancouver's Hollyburn
Mountain for an exclusive development called
the British Properties. To connect their land
with the city, the company completed the Lions
Gate Bridge in 1938 with a roadway through
Stanley Park. But its vision of a car-oriented
future would have to wait.

In 1939 when World War II began,
Vancouver was once again far from the
action. But two-and-a-half years later, after
the Japanese attack on Pearl Harbor, the city
mobilised. As in the western USA, Japanese
Canadians were stripped of their property and
forced into internment camps in the BC interior,
only beginning to return to the coast after
restrictions were lifted in 1949. A handful of
wartime buildings, including a former seaplane
hangar, survive today on the army base at
Jericho. Two of these buildings have new roles
as a youth hostel and a theatre. The wartime
shipbuilding operations on the North Shore
and False Creek have disappeared.

MODERN TIMES
By the mid 1950s, with a rapidly growing
population again, Vancouver was finally able to
dream of itself as a modern city. A Los Angeles,
in fact. In rapid succession, the ageing streetcar
and interurban systems were dismantled, and
the government began to plan for more cars. A
new highway bridge crossed the harbour at the
Second Narrows, a tunnel under the Fraser
River opened up suburban lands to the south,
and the public was captivated by the idea of a
family home on a cul-de-sac in the Fraser
Valley. The city's old residential areas were
rezoned for apartments, and blocks of houses
near downtown were demolished and paved
over for parking. Shopping malls opened in
West Vancouver, Burnaby and Richmond.
Radical post-and-beam houses by young,
cutting-edge architects like Ron Thom and
Arthur Erickson began to dot the rugged
slopes of West Vancouver, harbingers of
a new West Coast lifestyle.

Downtown desolation.

Hastings Street suffered the most. It lost thousands of daily visitors when the interurban line closed and the North Shore ferries were cancelled. The old warehouses on Gastown's narrow streets became obsolete as businesses migrated to the suburbs with their 18-wheelers. Plans were drafted for a waterfront freeway system, coming into downtown from the east and razing historic Gastown, Chinatown, and Strathcona, all home to poor people with little political voice. Urban renewal – the demolition of old housing and its replacement by towers set in greenspace – completed the package.

'Downtown is young, hip and vibrant.'

But then Vancouver got lucky again. Its position way out on the edge of the plate, both geographically and politically far from the Ottawa power centre, made it slow to get the freeway and urban renewal money that had already disfigured Toronto and Montreal. Meanwhile, it could observe what had been happening in the USA, especially in nearby Seattle. Accordingly, by the end of the 1960s when the government machinery was finally in place to transform downtown Vancouver, the times they had a-changed.

Like San Francisco's Haight-Ashbury, Kitsilano was a declining neighbourhood awaiting redevelopment – the perfect venue for communal living in cheap old houses. Fourth Avenue blossomed in 1967 and '68 with head shops and coffee houses. At the same time, young entrepreneurs were fixing up Gastown and opening art galleries and boutiques. The arch-conservative civic government, with its hippie-baiting mayor Tom Campbell, was a perfect target for the poets, folkies and American Vietnam war protestors who read and wrote for Dan McLeod's *Georgia Straight* newspaper. Militant cyclists found common cause with antipoverty activists in the fight against urban renewal and the freeway. The Amchitka nuclear test galvanised Vancouver environmentalists into founding Greenpeace (*see p15* **Going green**).

The watershed came in 1972. Sustained protests persuaded the federal government to withdraw its support from the freeway plan. That summer, the 20-year-old conservative provincial government was defeated and replaced by a democratic socialist one. And in the autumn voters turfed out the civic governing party, replacing it with a group of liberals and academics with new ideas.

Modern Vancouver really began that year. The south side of the old False Creek industrial area was replaced with co-op and middle-income housing. The federal government turned its Granville Island property over to a trust which guided its transformation into an area of markets and galleries. In 1976, the city hosted the United Nations Habitat conference, concurrently holding a people's forum at Jericho Beach in the old seaplane hangars. And the downtown and harbour areas which had been spared the freeway juggernaut began to attract pedestrians, keeping the streets alive 24 hours a day. 'Vancouverism' – creating high-density neighbourhoods for people who live close to their work and their play – has been a tremendous success. A heritage-preservation movement sprang up in the 1980s, helping the surviving historic neighbourhoods, from rich Shaughnessy to poor Strathcona, to retain their character. In Gastown, rocker Bryan Adams restored the old Oppenheimer Brothers warehouse as a recording studio.

In the 1970s, Asians began to immigrate in unprecedented numbers and transformed both rich and poor areas. Vietnamese fleeing the Communist takeover of their country were followed, once Britain had set a timetable for giving up Hong Kong, by large numbers of wealthy Chinese, who settled on the west side of Vancouver and in Richmond. South Asians gravitated to the streets of South Vancouver and to new suburbs such as Surrey.

The world's fair, Expo '86, which reused the CPR's old rail yards on False Creek, completed the transition while celebrating the city's centennial. Since redeveloped into condos, along with the adjoining Yaletown warehouse area, that part of the downtown peninsula now houses about 40,000 people. Downtown is young, hip and vibrant – almost inconceivably so compared with the quiet, laid-back provincialism of the post-war years.

But only a Pollyanna could see the new Vancouver in completely rosy terms. As a seaport – aka drugport – Vancouver has always had its mean streets, but they began to get meaner in 1980 when the deinstitutionalisation of mental patients and the exit of provincial and federal governments from public housing construction coincided with the gentrification of the downtown and its neighbourhoods. As a result, Vancouver has homeless, drug, gang and property-crime problems that are as 'world class' as its cultural achievements. The outer suburbs and towns in the Fraser Valley are unfortunately like anywhere else, with a mix of congested roads, big box stores, strip malls and large, ugly houses. It's much more of a have and have not society than a generation ago. But is there a city anywhere, in North America, Australasia or Europe, that has done better?

Vancouver Today

Can Vancouver survive its own success?

British Columbia is in the midst of 'a golden decade', at least according to second-term premier, Gordon Campbell. Mr Campbell's provincial Liberal Party is actually on the right of the political spectrum and governs with the tacit support of the federal Conservatives. His rhetoric is reflected in booming construction and trade figures, but doesn't acknowledge Vancouver's large and growing homeless population (it is estimated that between 500 and 1,200 people sleep on the street each night), its drug and crime problems, or its fraying social welfare contract (a general strike was only narrowly averted in 2004 and about a quarter of the population live below Statistics Canada's low-income cut-offs). Despite Campbell's 'you've never had it so good' message, voters reduced his majority to 13 seats in the 2005 provincial election, the opposition National Democratic Party (NDP) clawing back 33 constituencies after their near wipe-out in 2001.

If those election results signify misgivings about where things are going, that's only to be expected. Canada's third largest city, with a population of 550,000 (2 million in the Greater Vancouver Regional District, the GVRD), Vancouver is expanding at a startling rate. The city is bracing itself for the 2010 Winter Olympics, watching house prices go up and up, and casting its mind back to 1986, when Vancouver last played host to the world.

BACK TO THE FUTURE

Vancouver, barely a century old at the time, came of age with Expo 86. Incurring a debt in excess of $300 million (believe it or not, a success, as far as world's fairs go) the 172-day event attracted more than 22 million people (the population of Canada in 1986 was just over 26 million). Expo 86 put Vancouver on the map.

With transportation as its theme, Expo was the catalyst for several splashy projects that still serve the city today, like SkyTrain, BC Place Stadium and the Plaza of Nations, which now hosts conventions and concerts on one side, and houses a casino and a radio station on the other. Following the addition of 2000's Millennium line and the forthcoming Richmond-Airport-Vancouver (RAV) line, SkyTrain continues to expand, with the original Expo route serving as one of the last reminders of a name that was once on everything from drink cans to the tailfins of aircraft. The IMAX and OMNIMAX theatres are still there, but the buildings in which they are housed have undergone some changes. Canada Place, having built additional cruise ship space, continues to act as the anchor of the upmarket Coal Harbour development overlooking Stanley Park. Meanwhile, the Telusphere (formerly known as Science World) has accepted corporate sponsorship from a major local telephone company. Some of the other Expo projects have fared less well: the McBarge branch of McDonald's, in its heyday the second busiest fast-food outlet in the world, now floats forlorn and rusting up Burrard Inlet in the waters north of Capitol Hill in Burnaby, and the iffy monorail which ran between pavilions now transports passengers to and from their cars at Alton Towers theme park in Staffordshire, England.

Expo also sparked a housing crisis which continues to this day, as a rash of profiteering skid row hotel owners evicted their long-time residents and crammed unsuspecting tourists into the recently vacated (and usually woefully unsuitable) 'housekeeping rooms'. Given the economic make-up of the Downtown Eastside (officially the poorest district in the whole of Canada) and the lack of voice traditionally given to its residents, more than a few suddenly homeless old-timers were driven into early graves that summer.

WINTER OLYMPICS, 12-28 FEBRUARY, 2010

Have lessons been learned? Even the bid for the Games was divisive, reinforcing the split between the right-leaning, moneyed West Side and left-leaning voters, many of whom live in East Vancouver, wary of the Olympics' high cost and corporate ties. Put to a city-wide plebiscite in February 2003, the bid was endorsed by 64 per cent of voters.

With those 16 days in 2010 firmly in view, politicians of every stripe are finally putting their minds to where taxpayers' money is going,

West vs East

Canada is a very large chunk of real estate. The cities of Vancouver and Toronto lie almost 4,800 kilometres (3,000 miles) apart – a greater distance than that separating London and Moscow. Naturally, the ideologies differ somewhat and each comes with its own stereotype. Vancouver is the flaky, laid-back beach bum, the Canadian California. Toronto is slick, superficial, and supremely arrogant – the self-proclaimed Centre of the Universe. (How many Torontonians does it take to change a light-bulb? Just one, while the world revolves around him.) Although the labels are flung back and forth like insults, each city's residents will proudly claim some truth to its characterisation. Toronto does indeed consider itself the only Canadian city that really matters. Vancouver, meanwhile, is proud of its more relaxed pace.

Most of Canada's business elite is headquartered in Toronto. 'Hogtown', as it is still known, definitely qualifies as the Canadian London. Vancouver may not have a proper British equivalent. The most useful comparison would be between Los Angeles and New York, competing metropolises that don't seem to speak the same language. While Toronto boasts of its status as the nation's financial nerve centre, Vancouver revels in its natural beauty, its mountain backdrop and ocean setting. Thanks in part to a tradition of public activism that kept freeways out of the city, Vancouver developed into a place where people can live downtown and walk or cycle to work. Bemused Torontonians see their West Coast counterparts arrive for business meetings in Lycra shorts, still carrying bicycle helmets, and shake their heads. Flaky Vancouver.

If there is resentment in the relationship, it generally flows in one direction – west to east. The vast distance from the West Coast to the Toronto power centre leaves Vancouverites (and Western Canadians generally) feeling like junior partners in Canada's confederation, always on the short end of the stick. It is easily possible for a political party to form a parliamentary majority without electing a single MP in the 3,000 sparsely populated miles that stretch out west from Ontario to the Pacific Ocean. Consequently, Canadian politicians tend to focus their attention on central Canada, while the West fumes helplessly.

Canadian media is similarly Toronto-based, lending a strong bias to news and TV coverage. For years, Vancouver TV viewers had more opportunities to see the Maple Leafs, Toronto's pro-hockey team, than their own hometown Canucks. True rivalries, however, require reciprocity. Toronto may observe its irresponsible coastal cousin with a roll of the eyes. But for serious rivalry Toronto looks southward, measuring itself anxiously against the Big Apple. Many Vancouverites, too, roll their eyes when asked about West vs East. Long-time residents will tell you the whole rivalry issue is hackneyed, petty and pointless. After all, they insist, you need only look around to see where any busy Torontonian would rather live, given a choice in the matter. And sitting with a coffee at a café table looking out over English Bay, many Torontonians might find themselves agreeing.

taking an interest in urban renewal that is a career first for some. The flagship project here is Vancouver's $85 million Olympic Village, planned as a permanent sustainable urban development on reclaimed toxic land in south-east False Creek. It will have a mix of offices and affordable social housing (1,000 of 1,500 units), all powered from renewable energy sources emitting next to no greenhouse gases.

'People speculate wildly on condomania, although they know that one day this bubble is going to burst.'

For the construction industry, the Olympics are manna from heaven. Venue construction began in 2005, with the bulk of projects slated for completion by 2009, at which time the first tickets will go on sale. Speed skating events will take place inside a new $68 million facility in Richmond. To complement the existing World Cup level alpine skiing facilities 100 kilometres (59 miles) north in Whistler, building has begun on a $102 million nordic sports venue (to be used for cross-country skiing, ski jumping and biathlon), and a $55 million sliding sports centre on neighbouring Blackcomb Mountain for bobsleigh, luge and the ominously named skeleton. The twisting Sea-to-Sky Highway linking Vancouver and Whistler is getting a $600 million upgrade, which will supposedly knock almost an hour from the 2 hour 15 minute journey. Snowboarding and freestyle skiing are planned for Cypress Bowl, visible from the city at night like a small constellation set into the North Shore mountains. The Pacific Coliseum will host short track speed skating and the crowd-pleasing figure skating events, with curling getting a new home adjacent to the current Nat Bailey minor league baseball stadium in East Vancouver. Ice hockey, slated for GM Place Stadium and UBC, is likely to be one of the hottest tickets of the games. The opening and closing ceremonies are being held under cover, inside BC Place Stadium.

BOOM TOWN

In Vancouver's anticipation of the Olympics it's the success of Expo 86 rather than its failures that haunts the city. Over the last two decades tourism and immigration have grown fast. Between 1981 and 2001, the city's population expanded by a third. The influx of immigrants has fuelled a housing boom that is transforming the city. A third of the undeveloped Expo land was purchased, re-parcelled and later re-sold at a profit by Hong Kong billionaire Li Ka-Shing's investment firm, Concord Pacific. Despite its

The **Telusphere** (**Science World**).
See p19.

sometimes glacial pace, the redevelopment of the False Creek site has nonetheless been extremely successful, literally paving the way for trendy Yaletown, once thick with offices and mini-storage facilities, now commanding some of the highest rents and priciest amenities in the city. Building sites have flourished so much one could be forgiven for thinking the crane is BC's provincial bird (it is in fact the cheeky Steller's jay, as voted by the people in 1987). Glass and chrome condo towers now grow like weeds around the city and on most of the western part of the old Expo site. Property prices have risen just as fast – up by 50 per cent over the last five years – leading Yale economist Robert Schiller to dub this 'the most bubbly city in the world'. People here are conditioned to the threat of upheaval – the city lies on the San Andreas Fault, after all – but even as they speculate wildly on condomania, they know that one day this bubble is going to burst.

The buying frenzy and immigration are closely related. In the run-up to the handover of Hong Kong back to mainland China in 1997, Canada agreed to honour immigration applications from anyone holding a British or Commonwealth passport. The Canadian Consulate estimates about 30,000 Hong Kong citizens emigrated to Canada every year between 1991 and 1996, many choosing

The Seawall in Stanley Park.

Vancouver (or neighbouring Richmond) because of the city's firmly rooted Chinese community, its historic trade ties with Hong Kong and the physical similarities between the two ports. Huge financial incentives for wealthy investors also made Vancouver especially attractive to the richest of the rich. These new immigrants from Hong Kong (and later, Taiwan) were unlike the traditional settlers of the past: many husbands spent years as 'astronauts', buying homes for their families in Vancouver, then continuing to work in Asia, often for several years, leaving their offspring with money, fast cars, a big house and often no supervision. To say the city suffered a growth spurt is an understatement – from teachers to translators, skills in Mandarin and Cantonese have become increasingly lucrative. In 1981 only 13.9 per cent of the Lower Mainland's population were of non-European origin. By 2001 that figure had soared to 36.9 percent. Statistics Canada estimates that by 2017, fully half of the people living in the GVRD will be of Asian descent.

Despite crime rates too high for comfort (especially in the suburbs), immigration in Vancouver has been relatively painless. The Chinese community has prospered and China is now the Port of Vancouver's biggest trading partner (and more federal investment is promised to enhance BC's status as the Pacific gateway). The BC hate crimes unit consists of just two officers and their only high profile case last year turned out to be a hoax.

Nevertheless, some bemoan that prosperity comes with too high a price. Vancouver is justifiably proud to be counted one of the most liveable cities in the world, an index which owes more to environmental factors than to economic upswings. Hemmed in by mountains and the ocean, Vancouver has sprawled less than other cities; new housing has been concentrated in the vibrant downtown area. But the tension between such rapid expansion and the urge to conserve something as nebulous as the quality of life is a constant concern both for municipal authorities and the citizens they represent. Even only middle-aged locals hardly recognise the sleepy provincial town in which they grew up.

NO FUN CITY

On occasion, that paternalist municipal instinct has translated into stultifying red tape. Liquor licences are notoriously difficult to acquire and bylaws are so restrictive it can take years for a restaurant to get the go-ahead to put a few tables on the sidewalk. In 2000 Vancouver was dubbed 'No fun city' by a disgruntled organiser of the 'Symphony of Fire' fireworks display

after a tobacco company was barred from sponsoring the event. Whatever the rights and wrongs of that affair, the label seemed to fit. The city police contributed to the image by advising the public to stay home on New Year's Eve for their own safety. Stung by the negative publicity, the authorities have made a real effort to improve their game over the last few years. A bylaw prohibiting singing and dancing in restaurants was repealed. Bars and nightclubs have been granted extended hours (up to 3am on Granville Street's downtown entertainment strip). And arts funding has been increased. The new Vancouver International Film Centre is one beneficiary. Countless local and ethnic festivals have also sprung up.

> **'The jogging caffeine fiend and the health-conscious pothead are two venerable Vancouver stereotypes.'**

At the same time, it's worth remembering that, population-wise, Vancouver is half the size of Toronto and about the same size as Leeds. Neighbouring Seattle has approximately 1.5 million more citizens with which to support local businesses, sports teams, entertainment and art venues. So a certain provincialism is probably inevitable. The city punches above its weight in some areas (the Museum of Anthropology for example) but by no means in all. Culture remains a hard sell against the attractions of the great outdoors, and sometimes Vancouver can feel like a mid-sized city preening itself before a world-class mirror.

VANSTERDAM

The jogging caffeine fiend is one Vancouver stereotype. Another is the health-conscious pot smoker, who may disdain meat and tobacco, but leavens his yoga and cycling regimen with a little recreational weed (*see p79* **Potted history**). Known around the world as a producer of top quality marijuana – with an estimated 8,000 illegal home-based grow-ops operating at any given time – the city's reputation as 'Vansterdam' is also attributable to a relatively relaxed attitude towards the drug, allowing for more open smoking and grudging legislative acknowledgment of the herb's medicinal qualities, often to the dismay of authorities in the United States. However, don't expect to go into a pot café and buy anything other than smoking accessories – retail sale is still illegal. The best sources are found by word of mouth.

To be sure, law enforcement has had its hands full dealing with a different drug

The **Museum of Anthropology**. *See p23.*

undertook to confront the drug problem in a fresh way. The Four Pillars approach lays equal stress on treatment, prevention, harm reduction and enforcement. For Owen, set to retire, it was an impressively bold decision (albeit late in his mandate), and it found a vigorous advocate in his successor, the charismatic newcomer Larry Campbell (not to be confused with BC's premier, Gordon Campbell). The tell-it-like-it-is ex-coroner, legendary here as the inspiration for the TV detective drama *Da Vinci's Inquest* (and its spin-off, *City Hall*), swept the city off its feet, reflecting the essential dichotomy of Vancouver voters – who tend to be politically conservative but socially liberal. Campbell's progressive stance on drug policy has earned him legions of fans, critics and likely some enemies, especially south of the border. Most recently, Mayor Campbell was rewarded with a plum appointment to Canada's Senate.

Is the Four Pillars policy working? Currently, the City of Vancouver estimates that 9,000 residents are addicted to injection drugs, and 12,000 are addicted to alcohol, but some efforts have clearly been successful. Between 1997 and 2002 the number of methadone recipients doubled. With the highest levels of civic government accepting that abstinence is not always achievable for some addicts, the focus has turned to safety and cleanliness through clinics, front-line street nurses, and North America's first supervised safe injection site, called Insite, which opened in the fall of 2003. Here users can obtain needles and condoms, as well as information, counselling, first aid and referrals, all without judgement, in surroundings that look like they could be featured in an IKEA catalogue.

Vancouver still has its rough edges – for evidence all one need do is look at the intersection of mean streets and human misery that is the junction between Main and Hastings streets. But change is coming, albeit only gradually. Many see the real hope of the Downtown Eastside in the new Woodward's development, planned for a heritage site in Gastown under the beacon of its famous red neon 'W'. Founded in 1903, the Woodward's department store served as a neighbourhood anchor until its closure in 1993. Years of civic to-ing and fro-ing with zoning committees and bureaucrats left the site vacant and cemented the neighbourhood's decline, but the tide may turn yet again. After decades of wrangling (and an acrimonious two-month occupation by anti-poverty and housing activists in the fall of 2002), a design was approved that retains parts of the heritage façade, acknowledges the site's status as an emotional touchstone and aims to create an inclusive, welcoming space for all.

problem, the epidemic of crack and heroin addiction in the Downtown Eastside. As the housing crisis has played out, provincial government cuts have reduced services, and turned poor and mentally ill people out on the street. Even hardened Londoners are shocked by the numbers of homeless to be seen panhandling or scavenging food and returnable cans from dumpsters ('binning'), or even shooting up in the street. The city's most fragile citizens – their life expectancy is on average a full ten years less than those in surrounding neighbourhoods – tumble easily into drug and alcohol abuse. (It's important to remember that services for the homeless do still exist – including free meals – and future budgets are based on rates of usage.) The situation became especially grim when narcotic prices dropped in the summer of 1999 and the number of heroin and cocaine offences showed a marked jump; most of the time an overworked police force could do little more than sweep the problem along to the next location.

Finally, inspired by ideas in Switzerland, Germany and Australia, the City of Vancouver under the direction of then-Mayor Philip Owen

Rain city

You've heard it rains in Vancouver. Well, it's true. There are days when you can hardly see for the incessant deluge, as if the ocean itself has lifted up and stretched out a soaking arm over the city. And when it starts, it seems as though the tap will never be turned off. In January 2004, an entire month's worth – 100 millimetres (four inches) – poured down in just 48 hours. Vancouver's longest downpour began on 6 January 1953 and ended 29 days later. (Victoria beat that in 1986 with 33 days in a row.) On average, Vancouver's rainfall reaches 1,117mm (44.3 inches) over 164 wet days annually. That's almost half the year; in the middle of winter, it can feel more.

But look on the wet side. Vancouver boasts some of the most spectacular public gardens in North America. The whole region brims with a lush, diverse horticulture and the damp air keeps Vancouver's annual pollution index low.

Just as heat inspires a way of life in southern locales, rain shapes the culture on the Pacific Northwest. Easterners are known to observe that Vancouver's temperate climate (it rarely gets too cold or too hot because of the moderating influence of the sea) fosters a moderate people. Locals are neither wildly ambitious nor sluggishly laid-back. With the rising awareness of seasonal affective disorder (SAD), there was a noticeable upswing in complaints of depression-like symptoms during darker months, but the outbreak seems to have abated like just another waning fad. Rather than seek solace in light-emitting boxes, people prefer to appreciate the mildness that comes with rain instead of the deep snow and freezing temperatures of the rest of the country. Summer brings weeks on end of unbroken sunshine, but not the sweltering muggy torpor that engulfs other North American cities.

But when it rains? Well, another facet to Vancouver is the preponderance of coffee shops. At any given time, a hefty percentage of the local population can be found sheltering, a huge mug of steaming java in hand. And if there's a torrential downpour just the other side of that steamed-up window? Well then, there's no hurry to find something more constructive to do, is there?

Not that Vancouverites hide from the rain. Oh, no. They don high-tech, breathable, waterproof fabrics and, yes, enjoy the rain. Our favourite rainy day excursion? At **Dr Sun Yat-Sen Classical Chinese Garden** (*see p77*), covered walkways and pavilions are rimmed with hand-made drip tiles. In a downpour, collected roof water flows from the drip tiles like a crystal bead curtain. Ming Dynasty scholars recommended listening to the symphony of water hitting pebbled courtyard, smooth rocks and pond water.

It rains in other places, it's true. But the rain here is too ubiquitous to be simply avoided or endured. It must be embraced, relished even… Hopefully it won't be sunny the whole time you're in Vancouver.

Ron Terada
Entering the City of Vancouver (2002).

West Coast Art

BC's forests are a timbered choir, their mysterious song heard by artists from Emily Carr to Jeff Wall.

'There was an anti-logging protest going on outside the art gallery . . .' Douglas Coupland, *Eleanor Rigby*.

Douglas fir, shore pine, sitka spruce, yew, amabilis fir, western hemlock, arbutus, red and yellow cedar – you could make the case that Vancouver's evolution owes a lot to its trees. In fact, if these trees didn't cover the west coast in a dense cover of prickly green, there is a good chance that Vancouver wouldn't exist at all. They darken the mountains, lap up the never-ending rain, filter the air of pollutants and provide shelter, clothes, fuel and even the material for the north-west coast aboriginal peoples' vibrant cultural tradition. For the Kwakw'aka'wakw and the Salish, the forest equalled the sea for mystery and bounty, and yet it was a mundane thing too, a place of endless resources. And it is this paradox that persists today in local culture.

When the first Europeans arrived they found themselves surrounded by sky-scraping trees and impenetrable undergrowth, thick with sword ferns, huckleberries and salal. Timber was by far the biggest industry in town for a few generations, but has since been replaced by tourism: people coming to play among the trees they previously cut down. Everybody loves the trees – for some, they smell like money when logged; for others, they have the beauty of a Gothic cathedral and need to be treated with the same reverence. If a tree falls in a forest near Vancouver, everybody hears.

One of the earliest European artists to depict the forest was GM de L'Aubiniere who, along with her husband, was commissioned to paint 14 pictures to accompany an illuminated address for Queen Victoria in 1877. One such picture called, unsurprisingly, *Wood Scene*, shows a gentle, pastoral landscape, with a small pond and a few trees. It could be the suburbs of Paris. What kind of trees is she trying to paint? That might be a cedar at the water's edge, an alder over there, but really this could be anywhere. Yet there is also a feeling of claustrophobia, even mild threat. So perhaps she caught a whiff of the forest's essence in the density of trees and foliage, but for the most part this is an artist failing to see the newness of the landscape and the extraordinary, individual qualities of the trees. She looked into the forest and painted a self-portrait.

A generation later, Emily Carr, the founding mother of British Columbian art, fared a little better. She was, in fact, merely competent when it came to painting trees. Occasionally she gets it right, and the landscapes come with a whiff of tart cedar air, but most of the time we get thick slabs of undifferentiated green magma where we might expect the feathery fronds of a hemlock. It's all Carr – she replaces the cool, claustrophobic calm of the forest with the heavy broodiness that is a more accurate reflection of her mood than the forest itself. *Scorned as Timber, Beloved of the Sky* (1935) is probably her most popular image, and it is easy to see why: the tree stands out, proud yet forlorn, amid a devastated forest. The sky radiates around it as if heaven felt its pain and loneliness. It announces so much of what has become synonymous with west coast culture: at once a romantic identification with the landscape and an image of land stripped to exploit its resources. But it is also a great painting, full of pathos and brilliant touches.

But Carr is equally, and justifiably, famous for her paintings of the totem poles and villages of Haida Gwaii and Kwakw'aka'wakw – or, as they were then called, the Kwakiutl. There is no better record of a culture in rapid decline and transition than say, *Totem Poles, Kitseukla* (1912) or *Kwakiutl House* (1912). These are superb paintings, which blend anthropological research with the post-Impressionism that Carr discovered on her trip to France just two years earlier. With paintings like these, Carr established a tradition of art in Vancouver.

In 1926, FH Varley arrived from Sheffield, England, via Ontario, to take the position of Head of the Vancouver Art School (which then became Emily Carr College of Art and Design). He fell in love with the geography, producing paintings that carried on Carr's tradition. In 1932, he painted *Dhârâna*, a picture of his mistress on a wooden porch, her spine aligned with a thick post, transforming her into a kind of totem pole. A curtain of blue mountains fill the background and nearer, on the left, a cluster of faint totem poles tower with precarious thinness. Varley incorrectly understood the title to mean a mental union with the landscape (it more accurately describes a state of meditation). But this is an important point in the history of west coast culture: his figure, his mistress, has been transformed into a piece of wood, a totem, and the painting enacts a total union between human soul and tree. Later that same year, he wrote a letter to a friend in Sheffield, describing the landscape and concluding, 'we have yet to understand its nature'.

The lyrical landscape tradition inaugurated by Carr, Varley and others, was taken up with great energy by the next generation: Toni Onley, Gordon Smith and – the best of the bunch – Jack Shadbolt, to name a few. These artists developed it through the middle of the twentieth century and into the 1970s, and Shadbolt produced some of his best work well into the '80s. The tradition still persists today. But perhaps the west coast's true genius, a one-time student of Varley's, is EJ Hughes. He strips his palette of all the sodden, romantic muck of Carr. He's pragmatic, accurate, witty, direct where she is gooey and solipsistic. Hughes picks out the different trees, the rocky beaches, the blue-black sea, the strange, perfectly formed blankets of clouds that are carved by the mountains of the Olympic range

In Context

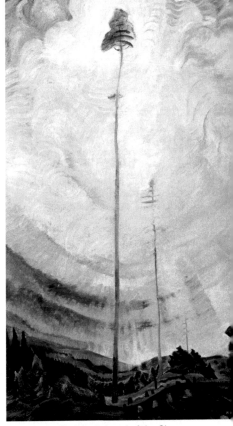

Scorned as Timber, Beloved of the Sky.

Off the Wall

Jeff Wall (born 1946) is arguably the most successful artist in Vancouver's short cultural history, a photographer whose fame has recently outstripped even that of Vancouver's previous favourite daughter Emily Carr. In September 1999, *ARTnews* magazine named him one of the world's ten best living artists, and in 2005 he had a major retrospective in Basel, Switzerland, which then travelled to Tate Modern, London. A smaller retrospective will open at New York's Museum of Modern Art in 2006, and then travel to major museums in Chicago and San Francisco. The world, in other words, is clamouring for his immense, backlit photographs.

But it wasn't always that way. Wall began by making what he called 'third-rate' conceptual art while also studying art history at the University of British Columbia. After pursuing graduate studies at the Courtauld, London, Wall returned to Vancouver to work at the Pacific Cinémathèque, where it was his job to inspect the quality of the prints before they were screened. The occasion deepened his appreciation of film as art, prompting him to write scripts and start a film project with fellow Vancouverite artists Ian Wallace and Rodney Graham. The film career failed to take off, so he started teaching art history at Simon Fraser University. Yet cinema remains a deep and lasting influence on his work.

He had the epiphany that launched his career while on holiday in Europe. Sitting on a bus in France, Wall noticed some illuminated advertisements. At the time, he was returning from a trip to Madrid's Prado, where the work of the old masters had left a deep, abiding impression. He put the two insights together – old master scope and ambition with the techniques of modern marketing – and he had his own language: backlit transparencies on a pictorial scale. Soon after, he started to make photographs that referenced the work of 19th-century masters like Delacroix (*The Destroyed Room*) and Manet (*The Storyteller*, among others), and described his own practice, after Charles Baudelaire, as 'the painting of modern life'.

Wall makes photographs that he calls either 'cinematographic' or 'documentary', though there is often some crossover between the categories. He sets up, like a filmmaker, the situations depicted in cinematographic photographs, and then shoots dozens or even hundreds of takes. Then he reduces these to one version, or uses digital montages of separate elements to create the final picture. The documentary photographs, on the other hand, are photographs of existing things, places or people with little or no intervention from the artist himself. Either way, Wall likes to call his photographs 'prose poems'.

In the early '90s, Wall started to use computer montage to create some of his pictures, photographing different elements both outside and in his studio before combining all the constituents with Adobe Photoshop to create the final picture. *A Sudden Gust of Wind (after Hokusai)* is such a picture, photographed partly in a cranberry farm near Vancouver and partly in his studio. The elements were then combined into a picture that was based on a well known woodblock print by the great 19th-century Japanese artist Katsushika Hokusai, one of his series of 36 views of Mount Fuji.

Dead Troops Talk (A Vision after an Ambush of a Red Army Patrol Near Moqor, Afghanistan, Winter 1986) is an elaborate tableau of a group of Russian soldiers waking up after being killed by the mujaheddin in an ambush. The entire picture was created in his studio, but meticulously researched so that the land, the soldiers and their wounds all have an extraordinary naturalistic intensity to them despite the artificiality of the set-up.

Don't imagine from this though that only Wall's 'cinematographic' work conveys such visceral and imaginative force, for his documentary work is equally powerful: he has an amazing knack for introducing a hint of the uncanny into the everyday world just by observing it in a certain way. Thus *Peas and Sauce*, a picture of an abandoned aluminium dish cradling a few peas and some slimy gravy, is a good example of this kind of picture, a seemingly slight combination of organic and artificial materials that reflects his interest in little spots of strange, overlooked beauty. *Dawn* is a photograph of an immense rock – probably a stubborn leftover from the last ice age – that stands unremarked on the nondescript corner of an East Vancouver intersection. The picture is both a simple, muted study of a nonedescript place and a poignantly beautiful revelation of a landscape that Wall's sympathetic eye made available to everyone.

Ian Wallace
Clayoquot Protest (9 August 1993)

and Vancouver Island. Hughes paintings are notable for the way the sky, stones and trees are picked out in almost preternatural detail. He shows the coast as a working place, speckled by boats and ferries, humdrum activities against a backdrop as homely and pastoral as it is sublime. His style has something of the naivety of Henri Rousseau, yet in that clarity, the careful description of individual trees – you can distinguish a fir from a cedar in a Hughes painting – is a desire to see this landscape unencumbered by the conflicting emotions of avarice and empathy.

In the late 1960s and early 1970s, a new generation of artists emerged, a group that includes Jeff Wall, Ian Wallace, Ken Lum, Rodney Graham and – a little younger – Stan Douglas and Roy Arden. These artists built upon Vancouver's traditional relationship with the landscape mostly by resisting any romantic attachment to it. And Ian Wallace, perhaps Vancouver's most influential artist and teacher over the last few decades, was the catalyst in this regard. His work *Clayoquot Protest* (9 August 1993) is a group of nine panels that form a superb evocation of how the forest has created a culture of deep ambivalence. A group of people have gathered to protest the logging of an important first-growth forest. Wallace documented the groups of people with a series of photographs, then applied them to canvas with prints of wood grains. The patterns of the wood are both decorative and utilitarian, a perfect emblem of why there is such a battle over these trees: for the protestors, the trees are beautiful things that need to be protected; for the loggers, they represent a pay cheque.

Stan Douglas takes up similar ideas with *Nu.tka*. Shot in Nootka Sound, on the west coast of Vancouver Island, the piece shows two videos projected on top of each other, and the ghostly double picture is accompanied by voice-overs meant to evoke two early explorers of the region, Englishman James Colnett and Spaniard Jose Esteban Martinez. At the time, fur was the target (all those sea otters), but what we see is the landscape: forests and water. The two men squabble over the rights to the land, while rarely discussing anything specific about the place and its inhabitants. Rodney Graham, who grew up partly in logging camps, represented Canada at the Venice Biennale in 1997, where he showed *Vexation Island*, a looped film about a buccaneer lost on a desert island who repeatedly awakes to shake a tree only to get knocked out by a falling coconut, ad infinitum. It conveys the ambivalence about trees inherent to the west coast: at once an object of desire, a resource and a potential danger.

'Trees with branches rooted in air.'

Jeff Wall (*see p28* **Off the Wall**), comes to the local landscape a bit more obliquely. But one photograph seems to be partly a direct response to Carr's *Scorned as Timber, Beloved of the Sky*. *Pine on a Corner* also features a towering tree, this time a pine that is not native to the coast (it's a lodgepole pine, a few hundred kilometres away from its native land). With this picture, Wall questions the romantic attachment to the landscape that is so common among the painters in a so-called west coast tradition. The picture is at once more mundane and more penetratingly strange than Carr's. In another picture, *Park Drive*, a road zips through the centre of a Stanley Park forest, a strange alien presence in an otherwise primeval landscape. The forest has become everything the road is not: a great hindrance, a strange curtain that blinds the drivers from the outside world.

In all these cases, the landscape sits in the background like a mute, defenceless witness to human madness, and this idea is played out superbly in *The Inert Landscapes of Gyorgy Ferenc*, a short story by Nanaimo-born writer Tamas Dobozy. The protagonist of the story describes the life of his father, a landscape painter celebrated in his native Hungary who brought his whole family to Canada to escape the Soviets. Upon arrival, however, he struggles with the new surroundings. 'My father was a landscape painter in a nation that would not be reproduced', the story opens, but it would not be reproduced only because his father considered the Canadian landscape a soulless, utilitarian place. The father was stuck in a romantic tradition, as described in the story by a fictional Hungarian critic: 'in his work . . . one senses the inextricability of geography and the soul'. Now, that's codswallop, and anyone who tells you different is probably trying to sell you a reproduction of an Emily Carr painting.

Ron Terada, a member of a younger generation of Vancouver artists, really tears into that idea with his piece *Entering the City of Vancouver*. The sculpture – or is it a picture? – addresses the landscape tradition of the city, from Emily Carr to Jeff Wall to Stan Douglas. A huge highway sign announces the geographical change, which is otherwise an invisible fiction: it's just a border. Terada replaces the oozing, romantic green of Carr with the utilitarian green of a highway sign. The sign itself is tree-like – a single looming field of green propped up by wood. But there is no inextricable link between geography and soul here, just a big, utilitarian sign that marks an artificial border.

With Ron Terada's sign, we have come full circle from GM de L'Aubiniere's *Wood Scene*. The former is a naïve attempt at the depiction of a landscape that outwits the artist, the second is a great big sign erected by the artist in an attempt to outwit the landscape. And yet the landscape, and the trees that it hosts, remains essential to the experience of Vancouver. Malcom Lowry lived – rather grumpily and drunkenly – along the Burrard Inlet for many years, where he finished his greatest book, *Under the Volcano*. In his poem 'Happiness', he lists, along with the 'blue mountains', gulls and eagles, the 'Trees with branches rooted in air' as a source of happiness. It's an image that brings to mind Carr's *Scorned as Timber* and Wall's *Pine on a Corner*. While Terada's sign parodies categorising art by region, it is, paradoxically, successful because it emerges from a tradition that begins in the omnipresence of trees.

Perhaps Varley is still right when he wrote, 'we have yet to understand its nature' about the west coast forest and landscape. But this will hasten things along. If you want to understand Vancouver's culture, by all means visit the Vancouver Art Gallery. Eat a cinnamon bun

and a turkey sausage, try some sockeye sashimi, shop in Chinatown, watch a hockey game, go for a swim at Kitsilano Beach, dance in the Commodore, have a gelato at sunset in English Bay, yes, do all that. But above all grab a book like *Plants of Coastal British Columbia* and go to Stanley Park. Crush some scaly red cedar leaves in your hands, open your palms and inhale the fragrance, then caress the rough, fibrous bark of a Douglas fir. Don't make it a religious experience, but a practical one: learn the names of every tree you meet and get to know them. Let's face it – if they weren't here, you'd have gone to Disneyland.

'X' marks the spot

If London has Martin Amis and New York Don DeLillo, then Douglas Coupland is Vancouver's brilliant and sardonic literary guide.

Coupland is, of course, best known for his debut novel *Generation X*, a witty glossary of pre-millennial disaffection. For coining such terms as 'McJob' and 'knee-jerk irony' he was designated 'the voice of a generation' by a grateful media. The 1991 book, pegged as the new *Catcher in the Rye*, would be the first of many – 18 so far – to affirm the North Vancouver writer's keen ability to catch the zeitgeist and document social trends.

Despite his disclaimers ('I speak for myself, not for a generation') Coupland litters his novels with brand names, up-to-the-second cultural references and, often, rich local detail. *Life after God* (1994) sifts the material effects of North American consumer society for a scrap of existential insight – and finds it deep in the forests of Vancouver Island. Set down the road in Seattle, his 1995 novel *Microserfs* – about the alienation of life on the information superhighway – was another demographic-defining novel, and one of the first reactions to the technology boom. *Girlfriend in a Coma* (1998), a tender, end-of-the-world-romance, begins with a typical Couplandesque setting: 'Karen and I deflowered each other atop Grouse Mountain among the cedars beside a ski slope.' *Hey Nostradamus!* (2003), about a Columbine-type massacre, is set in a fictional high school in North Vancouver.

Not surprising then that this observant multi-tasker – as renowned for his non fiction, artworks and other projects as for his fiction – would be commissioned to create a book dedicated to his home town.

Published in 2000, the picture book *City of Glass* 'is just the sort of whacked-out guide you wish was available for every great city in the world,' claimed the *Globe and Mail*. In lieu of landmarks, Coupland shows what the city feels like to somebody who lives here. 'I spent my 20s scouring the globe thinking there had to be a better city out there,' he writes, 'until it dawned on me that Vancouver is the best one going.'

From BC Ferries to YVR, dim sum to real estate, Coupland's lexicon of the city is uniquely personal and full of insight. 'If you're a Vancouverite, you find the city's lack of historical luggage liberating – it dazzles with a sense of limitless possibility,' he writes. 'We're at our best when experimenting with new ideas, and at our worst when we ape the conventions of elsewhere. Vancouver is, literally, one of the world's youngest cities. Some day we'll be old and creaky, but not now – right now is for being young.'

Two years later, Coupland would be welcomed as the tour guide for the country in the *Souvenir of Canada*, an art installation and two-volume book (and eventually a film) – all in loving tribute to stubbie beer bottles and bilingual cereal boxes.

Coupland's original plan was to be an artist, not a writer. He graduated from Vancouver's Emily Carr Institute of Art and Design in 1984, then studied in Italy, Japan and Hawaii before working as a designer at a Tokyo magazine. He returned to Vancouver in 1987 and was given a show of his sculptures at Vancouver Art Gallery. Since then, his paintings, collages and multi-media work have shown throughout Canada and the world. In 2004, he created and starred in the play *September 10*, and the following year saw the production of his screenplay *Everything's Gone Green*.

Nevertheless, he's still an astonishingly prolific writer. The forthcoming *jPod* will be 'a sequel, of sorts', to *Microserfs*. He loves writing, he says, so that's what he does: 'Since 1991 we've been through massive cultural, social, technological changes, and the only thing that protects me or you or anyone, the only thing that can protect you in all this is figuring out what it is that you like to do, and then sticking with it. Because once you start to do what people expect you to do, or what your parents think you should do, or whoever in your life thinks you should do, you're sunk.'

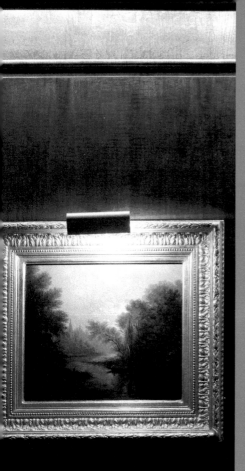

Where to Stay

Where to Stay 34

Features

The best Hotels 35
Magnum Opus 46
Howard Hughes slept here 48

Sutton Place Hotel. *See p37*.

Where to Stay

Rooms with views.

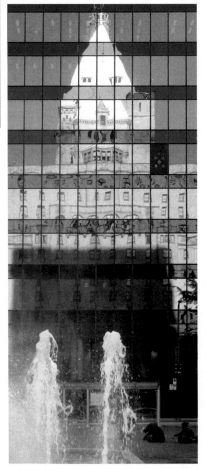

Fairmont Hotel Vancouver. *See p35.*

With more than 24,000 rooms available in Greater Vancouver, over 13,000 of them downtown, you're unlikely to find yourself having to sleep on the beach. And with the city's abundant coastline and gleaming skyscrapers, chances are you'll get a million-dollar view at a much lower rate.

Most visitors will want to stay in the downtown core. How you narrow it down from there doesn't really matter; a 10-minute cab ride will get you from one side of town to the other. Though less obvious during the day, the city's neighbourhoods are clearly defined at night. The West End, though quiet and leafy, perks up later on, the cafés and restaurants on Denman Street buzzing with locals. Conversely, Robson Street, though busy with shoppers in the day, closes down come nightfall. Yaletown is the trendy place to hang at night, with Vancouver's most upscale bars and a clutch of its favourite restaurants, but only one hotel, the self-consciously stylish Opus. Nearby Granville Street is known locally as the entertainment district and is home to cinemas, theatres and bars; it's also noisy and a bit seedy.

If you'd rather not stay in the hub, then the West Side is probably the best bet. Kitsilano's B&Bs offer easy access to the beach and there's no shortage of neighbourhood bars and great places to eat. For up-to-date information check with the Bed & Breakfast Association (www.wcbbia.com). Unless you plan to spend most of your trip on the mountains, the North Shore is probably too far to be convenient.

As the city spruces up in preparation for the 2010 Winter Olympics expect hotels to be renovating and refurbishing. Construction also continues apace and, due for completion early 2008, the 60 storeys of the Shangri-la building on the corner of West Georgia and Thurlow will make it the tallest structure in the city, housing condos, shops and restaurants, with 15 floors reserved for what will be Vancouver's top hotel.

RATES, GRADINGS AND SEASONS

For our purposes, hotels offering rooms under $100 are defined as budget; under $200 as moderate. When you get into the expensive and luxury categories, depending on the time of year and style of room you're after, the sky is the limit. The distinction between expensive and luxury is made on the range of services offered and the quality of the finishing touches.

Many hotels offer better rates via their websites and it's often possible to get a discount at the top hotels if their occupancy levels are lower than expected. High season in Vancouver is May to October. Tourism Vancouver's website (www.tourismvancouver.com) has good information on the city's accommodation.

Downtown

Luxury

Fairmont Hotel Vancouver
900 W Georgia Street, at Burrard Street, V6C 2W6 (604 684 3131/toll free 1-800 257 7544/fax 604 662 1929/www.fairmont.com/hotelvancouver). All city-centre buses. **Rates** $219-$489 single/double; $529-$1,500 suite. **Credit** AmEx, DC, MC, V. **Map** p249 K3 ❶

Originally a Canadian National Railway hotel (recognisable by its stone exterior and oxidised copper roof), the Hotel Vancouver is a city landmark in the heart of downtown. It has changed a lot over the years and, as a result, the rooms vary greatly in size and shape. However, all have been refurbished recently with trendy colour schemes and comfy beds. Best to avoid the lower floors where some of the rooms have been converted from meeting spaces and can be vast and impersonal. For an extra $100 or so, the Fairmont Gold floors provide a private lounge with complimentary snacks, drinks all day and a hearty breakfast. Alternatively, Griffins restaurant serves its own copious buffet breakfast with an Asian option featuring eggs, smoked fish and steamed rice. In the open yet cosy lobby bar they serve free hors d'oeuvres every night from 5-7pm, followed by live jazz until 11pm – sometimes later. The hotel's shops include Louis Vuitton, Gucci and the more local Snowflake. **Photo** *left*.
Bar. Business centre. Concierge. Disabled-adapted rooms. Gym. Internet (high speed). Parking ($27/ day). Pool (indoor). Restaurant. Room service (6.30am-1am). Spa. TV.

Fairmont Waterfront Hotel
900 Canada Place Way, at Hornby Street, V6C 3L5 (604 691 1991/toll free 1-800 257 7544/fax 604 691 1999/www.fairmont.com/waterfront). All city-centre buses/SkyTrain & SeaBus Waterfront. **Rates** $299-$499 single/double; $479-$2,199 suite. **Credit** AmEx, DC, MC, V. **Map** p249 L2 ❷

The Fairmont Waterfront, opened in 1991, has since become synonymous with Vancouver's skyline. The glass structure has accommodated everyone from the Queen to Bill Clinton. City or harbour views (or both in a corner room) grace the immaculate, spacious and bright accommodation. The outdoor pool area is positively grand, as is the herb garden alongside it. There's also a fully equipped gym with eucalyptus steam baths in each changing room.
Bar. Business centre. Concierge. Disabled-adapted rooms. Gym. Internet (high speed). Parking ($27/ night). Pool (outdoor). Restaurant. Room service (24hr). Spa. TV.

❶ Green numbers given in this chapter correspond to the location of each hotel as marked on the street maps. *See pp246-253.*

Four Seasons Hotel
791 W Georgia Street, at Howe Street, V6C 2T4 (604 689 9333/toll free 1-800 819 5053/fax 604 684 4555/www.fourseasons.com/vancouver). All city-centre buses. **Rates** $350-$1,000 single/double; $450-$1,120 suite. **Credit** AmEx, DC, MC, V. **Map** p249 K3 ❸

The lobby is vast and impersonal and the adjoining Garden Terrace café feels like a botanical garden. The Four Seasons' main restaurant, Chartwells, however, is one of the city's best. Awarded the prestigious 5 Diamond Award for more than 20 consecutive years, the hotel lost a diamond recently. Could this suggest things are slipping a bit? That said, the pool and spa are lovely, and you can pass directly into the adjoining Holt Renfrew department store and the Pacific Centre shopping mall.
Bar. Business centre. Concierge. Disabled-adapted rooms. Gym. Internet (high speed). Parking ($26.75/ night). Pool (indoor-outdoor). Restaurants (2). Room service (24hr). Spa. TV.

The best Hotels

For spa treatments
The **Fairmont Hotel Vancouver**'s new Absolute Spa (*see left*) is designed exclusively for men, with video games to distract you from your pedicure. Women should head to the **Century Plaza** (*see p37*).

For the view
The **Pan Pacific**: uninterrupted harbour, port, mountain and city views, cruise ships docking and seaplanes buzzing (*see p37*).

For style seekers
The **Opus Hotel**, where your cash brings a bit of flash and your inner self gets its own colour scheme (*see p46* **Magnum Opus**).

For hanging with the stars
The **Sutton Place Hotel**, where everyone from Judi Dench to Catherine Zeta-Jones, Elton John to Arnie have laid their weary heads (*see p37*).

For elegance
The **Wedgewood**, where opulent surroundings conspire with top-notch service to make this one of Canada's best hotels (*see p37*).

For a slice of local heritage
Barclay House, where crystal chandeliers, clawfoot tubs and complimentary sherry take you back to a more civilised age (*see p43*).

Hotel Le Soleil

567 Hornby Street, at W Pender Street, V6C 2E8 (604 632 3000/toll free 1-877 632 3030/fax 604 632 3001/www.lesoleilhotel.com). All city-centre buses. **Rates** $200-$800 suite. **Credit** AmEx, DC, MC, V. **Map** p249 K3 ④

With furniture custom designed in the 'Biedermeier' style, you might feel like you've walked into the 19th century. The beds are particularly luxurious, with feather pillows, down duvets, 100% Egyptian combed cotton sheets and silk brocade bedspreads. And the bathrooms are a dream worthy of Cleopatra – extensively tiled in the finest marble. Not sure if Cleo would have appreciated the Aveda Body Care products, but today's guests sure do. The two penthouse suites are extraordinary, with high ceilings and huge plasma televisions.

Bar. Concierge. Disabled-adapted rooms. Internet (dataport, web TV). Parking ($22/night). Restaurant. Room service (6.30am-10pm). TV.

Pan Pacific

300-999 Canada Place, at Burrard Street, V6C 3B5 (604 662 8111/toll free 1-800 663 1515/fax 604 685 8690/http://vancouver.panpacific.com). All city-centre buses/SkyTrain & SeaBus Waterfront. **Rates** $199-$590 single/double; $540-$3,500 suite. **Credit** AmEx, DC, MC, V. **Map** p249 L2 ⑤

Located above the famous white sails of the Trade and Convention Centre that have come to symbolise Vancouver, this rounded glass building has spectacular views of the North Shore mountains, Burrard Inlet, Stanley Park and the city all the way to the US border. The balcony suites are particularly impressive; you feel like you're on a cruise ship about to set sail for Alaska. The Five Sails restaurant is famous for its local seafood and fish dishes, as well as Alberta beef and foie gras from Quebec. The Pan Pacific has one of two American Automobile Association (AAA) 5 Diamonds in the city, the Michelin stars of the hotel world.

Bar. Business centre. Concierge. Disabled-adapted rooms. Gym. Internet (high speed). Parking ($20/24hrs). Pool (outdoor). Restaurants (2). Room service (24hr). Spa. TV.

Sutton Place Hotel

845 Burrard Street, between Robson Street & Smithe Street, V6Z 2K6 (604 682 5511/toll free 1-800 961 7555/fax 604 682 5513/www.vancouver.suttonplace. com). Bus 2, 5, 22. **Rates** $239-$450 single/double; $300-$700 suite. **Credit** AmEx, D, DC, MC, V. **Map** p249 K3 ⑥

Since opening in 1986, the Sutton Place has established itself as the haven for visiting movie stars shooting in Hollywood North. This is an AAA Five Diamond hotel, with fine attention to detail and possibly the most attentive staff in the city. A recent $5 million refurbishment means all the rooms are up-to-date, with new bedding, flatscreen TVs and DVD players, and London's Gilchrist & Soames toiletries in the bathroom. Wi-Fi is promised in all rooms by the end of 2006 – until then it's cable in the rooms and Wi-Fi in the public areas. A beautiful pool and

jacuzzi with an outside terrace, a state-of-the-art gym and the new, idyllic Vida Wellness Spa all make for a very luxurious stay. **Photo** *p38.*

Bar. Business centre. Concierge. Disabled-adapted rooms. Gym. Internet (high speed, wireless coming soon). Parking ($21.75/night). Pool (indoor). Restaurant. Room service (24hr). Spa. TV.

Wedgewood

845 Hornby Street, at Robson Street, V6Z 1V1 (604 689 7777/toll free 1-800 663 0666/fax 604 608 5348/www.wedgewoodhotel.com). All city-centre buses. **Rates** $225-$900 single/double. **Credit** AmEx, DC, MC, V. **Map** p249 K3 ⑦

This friendly, privately owned hotel is quite small with only 89 rooms and always has the most beautiful fresh-cut flowers in the lobby and rooms. The rooms are ornate and spacious; some have fireplaces. The award-wining restaurant and bar Bacchus is a favourite even with locals. Check out their intoxicating Martini list or the traditional afternoon tea.

Bar. Business centre. Concierge. Disabled-adapted rooms. Gym. Internet (dataport). Parking ($19/night). Restaurant. Room service (24hr). Spa. TV.

Expensive

Century Plaza Hotel and Spa

1015 Burrard Street, at Nelson Street, V6Z 1Y5 (604 687 0575/toll free 1-800 663 1818/fax 604 687 0578/www.century-plaza.com). Bus 2, 22. **Rates** $200-$400 single/double; $350-$550 suite. **Credit** AmEx, DC, MC, V. **Map** p248 J3 ⑧

Although the Century Plaza has one of the best spas and hair salons in the city, it is not a luxury hotel. It is, however, a great place to stay downtown and was completely renovated in 2004. Regular studios and suites have large kitchenettes, while the business suites make more of the work/living space. Check the website for deals where a spa treatment or night out is thrown in for less than the room-only rate. A comedic bonus for guests: Yuk Yuk's comedy club (*see p171*) is on the ground floor.

Bars (2). Concierge. Disabled-adapted rooms. Internet (dataport on request, high speed on request). Parking ($10/day). Pool (indoor). Restaurants (2). Room service (6am-8pm). Spa. TV.

Crowne Plaza Hotel Georgia

801 W Georgia Street, at Howe Street, V6C 1P7 (604 682 5566/toll free 1-800 663 1111/fax 604 642 5579/www.hotelgeorgia.bc.ca). All city-centre buses. **Rates** $179-$399 single/double. **Credit** AmEx, DC, MC, V. **Map** p249 K3 ⑨

A fully restored Georgian-style heritage building (1927) across from the Vancouver Art Gallery and Pacific Centre shopping mall. Although it is large and pleasant, it doesn't offer the same level of design and services as a luxury hotel. But its coffee shop, Sen5es, is a destination in itself for the creations of one of the world's leading pastry chefs, Thomas Haas, particularly his fabulous Stilton cheesecake. The blue and gold rooms with their dark wood furniture are fine, but don't really stand up to the exte-

Sutton Place Hotel. *See p37.*

rior. In its heyday, Elvis, Louis Armstrong and Nat King Cole stayed here; now, it's home to the Vancouver International Film Festival and so is particularly lively from late September to mid October. *Bar. Business centre. Disabled-adapted rooms. Gym. Internet (dataport, high speed). Parking ($22/day). Restaurant. Room service (24hr). TV.*

Metropolitan
645 Howe Street, between W Georgia Street & Dunsmuir Street, V6C 2Y9 (604 687 1122/toll free 1-800 667 2300/fax 604 602 7846/www.metro politan.com). All city-centre buses. **Rates** $195-$459 single/double; $389-$1,089 suite. **Credit** AmEx, MC, V. **Map** p249 K3 ⑩
Rooms feature Italian linen and duvets on oversized beds and great big soaker tubs – so if you're looking for more bed than space, this is a good place to stay. They have a skylighted lap pool and one of the city's finest Pacific Northwest restaurants: Diva at the Met (*see p92*). They are serious about their feng shui too, so if you want your bed to align with your Yan Nian or Tien Yi directions it's an ideal temporary domicile. And just to ensure the gods of luck stay on your side, rub the Chinese lion's head in the lobby on your way out to guarantee a lovely day. *Bar. Business centre. Concierge. Disabled-adapted rooms. Gym. Internet (high speed). Parking ($25/ night). Pool (indoor). Restaurant. Room service (24hr). TV.*

Sheraton Wall Centre
1088 Burrard Street, at Helmcken Street, V6Z 2R9 (604 331 1000/toll free 1-800 663 9255/fax 604 331 1001/www.sheratonwallcentre.com). Bus 2, 22. **Rates** $189-$399 single/double; $289-$639 suite. **Credit** AmEx, DC, MC, V. **Map** p248 J4 ⑪
Made up of two tall glass skyscrapers, the Wall Centre dominates the Vancouver cityscape. Light tubes at the pinnacle of each tower are 11m (36ft) high and lit by a single 250 watt metal halide bulb – a technology developed and patented at the University of British Columbia but now used around the world. With floor to ceiling windows, rooms on any of the 40-plus floors offer almost uninterrupted views of the ocean and mountains. The grand courtyard features waterfalls and a Roman-style, hand-laid stone driveway. Rooms can be small but each has a well-stocked refreshment centre. **Photo** *right. Bars (2). Business centre. Concierge. Disabled-adapted rooms. Gym. Internet (high speed). Parking ($22.80/night). Pool (indoor). Restaurant. Room service (24hr). Spa. TV.*

Westin Grand
433 Robson Street, at Hamilton Street, V6B 6L9 (604 602 1999/toll free 1-888 680 9393/fax 604 647 2502/www.westingrandvancouver.com). Bus 15. **Rates** $199-$429 suite. **Credit** AmEx, D, DC, MC, V. **Map** p249 L4 ⑫
Located on the edge of Downtown and Yaletown, this fully serviced boutique apartment hotel is chic, central and reasonably priced. All the suites have Westin's signature 'Heavenly Beds', as well as deep soaker tubs in the spacious and grand bathrooms. An efficient office space can be created with the room's functional desk, two line phone, dataport and high speed wireless internet access. It may be a high end chain in a pretty impressive building, but there isn't much soul here. *Bar. Business centre. Concierge. Disabled-adapted rooms. Gym. Internet (dataport, high speed). Parking ($18/night). Pool (outdoor). Restaurant. Room service (24hr). Spa (opening soon). TV.*

Moderate

Days Inn Downtown
921 W Pender Street, at Hornby Street, V6C 1M2 (604 681 4335/toll free 1-877 681 4335/fax 604 681 7808/www.daysinnvancouver.com). All city-centre buses. **Rates** $155-$219 single/double. **Credit** AmEx, D, MC, V. **Map** p249 K2 ⑬
Recently refurbished with a European-meets-West Coast design, this medium-range chain hotel does have some personality – albeit a bit on the busy bright side. Both rooms and one-bedroom suites are mostly suitable for two people but some can accommodate four. A complimentary shuttle service (7am-7pm) services the cruise ship terminals and Pacific Central (if you're catching a train or bus out of town). The Bull & Bear and Smiley O'Neal's bars are good for sports enthusiasts, and the many TVs ensure you won't miss what's going on.

Bars (2). Internet (high speed). Parking ($10/day). Restaurant. Room service (11am-10.30pm). TV.

Howard Johnson

1176 Granville Street, at Davie Street, V6Z 1L8 (604 688 8701/toll free 1-888 654 6336/fax 604 688 8335/www.hojovancouver.com). Bus 4, 6, 7, 10, 16, 17, 50. **Rates** $79-$219 single/double; $199-$419 suite. **Credit** AmEx, D, DC, MC, V. **Map** p248 J4 🔞

How things have changed. Howard Johnson used to have a reputation as a family-friendly chain with very little charm, but you could always count on a good ole Canadian pancake breakfast. But this recently refurbished Ho-Jo is stylish and central. With 100 rooms over five floors, you have the choice of rooms from twin, double or queen right up to one-bedroom suites with sofabeds. The prices are beyond reasonable too, especially given the location. It's true Granville Street can be noisy and a bit dodgy, but the hotel is just beyond the concentration of bars and restaurants. Pancakes are still available at the Wildfire restaurant.

Bar. Concierge. Internet (wireless). Parking ($14/24hrs). Restaurant. Room service (7am-11pm). TV.

Rosedale on Robson

838 Hamilton Street, at Robson Street, V6B 6A2 (604 689 8033/toll free 1-800 661 8870/fax 604 689 4426/www.rosedaleonrobson.com). Bus 5. **Rates** $150 -$550 suite. **Credit** AmEx, MC, V. **Map** p249 K4 🔞

Offering one and two bedroom suites, the Rosedale is proudly independent. Although its glass and light green exterior – as well as the interior colour scheme – scream 1990s, it remains a very convenient, well-equipped, child-friendly place to stay, with a lovely indoor swimming pool that is big enough to do a few laps and a communal terrace that can be used year round. A useful service for visitors that is provided is the information about what's going on every day in the city. On the ground floor is Rosie's, a popular New York-style deli.

Concierge. Disabled-adapted rooms. Gym. Internet (high speed). Parking ($8/day). Pool (indoor). Restaurant. Room service (7am-11pm). TV.

St Regis

602 Dunsmuir Street, at Seymour Street, V6B 1Y6 (604 681 1135/toll free 1-800 770 7929/fax 604 683 1126/www.stregishotel.com). All city-centre buses. **Rates** $79-$159 single/double; $99-$259 suite. **Credit** AmEx, MC, V. **Map** p249 K3 🔞

This used to be quite a dive but it has been completely refurbished and is now a decent, well-priced place to stay, particularly for this generally pricey area. The attached Starbucks coffee shop has brightened the busy corner it stands on, but hasn't done much for the building's 1920s architecture or heritage status. The hotel has 72 rooms over six storeys that vary in size and rate quite substantially, so check what you're getting. If you're on a budget you can get quite a good deal with breakfast and gym membership included. Located across from live music venue the Railway Club (*see p164*).

Bar. Business centre. Disabled-adapted rooms. Internet (dataport in some rooms). Parking ($4/day). Restaurant. TV.

Budget

Bosman's Hotel

1060 Howe Street, between Nelson Street & Helmcken Street, V6Z IP5 (604 682 3171/toll free 1-800 267 6267/fax 604 684 4010/www.bosmans hotel.com). Bus 4, 6, 7, 10, 16, 17, 50. **Rates** $99-$129 single/double. **Credit** AmEx, DC, MC, V. **Map** p248 J4 🔞

Bosman's is great value for its downtown location and lovely old heated outdoor swimming pool. You

Sheraton Wall Centre.

can overlook the slightly tacky decor in the lobby and rooms because they serve their purpose well and because the hotel is just so convenient. Recently refurbished, it's clean and the Side Bar Lounge and Grill has cheap food and you can play darts.
Bar. Concierge. Internet (pay terminal). Parking (free). Pool (outdoor). Restaurant. TV.

Kingston Hotel Bed & Breakfast

757 Richards Street, between Georgia Street & Robson Street, V6B 3A6 (604 684 9024/toll free 1-888 713 3304/fax 604 684 9917/www.kingston hotelvancouver.com). All city-centre buses. **Rates** $58-$155 single/double. **Credit** AmEx, MC, V. **Map** p249 K3 ⑱

Partly refurbished in 2004 with a new lobby and garden patio, the Kingston offers well-maintained single, double and twin bed rooms. Don't expect any extras, but you can count on a safe and central environment that is clean and a good price. Only nine rooms have private bathrooms and TVs, the remaining 46 have sinks but you must share the shower and toilets located on each of the four floors. They play old movies in the communal lounge almost every evening and it is one of the few hotels that offers complimentary breakfast.
Internet (dataport). Parking ($18/night). TV (in some rooms).

YMCA Hotel

955 Burrard Street, at Barclay Street, V6Z 1Y2 (604 681 0221/fax 604 681 1630/www.vanymca. org). Bus 2, 22. **Rates** $42-$60 single/double. **Credit** AmEx, DC, MC, V. **Map** p248 J3⑲

The YMCA is the most central bargain in town; located between the Sutton Place and Wall Centre, you'll feel like you're almost staying in the lap of luxury without breaking the bank. The accommodation is glorified single or twin dorm rooms, which are functional and are cleaned every day. The washrooms are separated by gender but they are shared. No rooms with private baths or any kitchens, but the café on the ground floor is decent enough. They rent by the night or week, or by the month on application. As a guest at the hotel you can also use the rudimentary but fully-equipped YMCA fitness facility, including a swimming pool.
Gym. Internet (pay terminal). Parking ($7.25/24hrs). Pool (indoor). Restaurant. TV (in some rooms).

YWCA

733 Beatty Street, at Robson Street, V6B 2M4 (604 895 5830/toll free 1-800 663 1424/fax 604 681 2550/www.ywcahotel.org). Bus 15. **Rates** $50-$150 single/double. **Credit** AmEx, MC, V. **Map** p249 L4 ⑳

Surprisingly immaculate and modern, the Y offers a good range of rooms: ranging from a single bed with desk, to double doubles (two beds for four people), to quints (five single beds). Rates are very reasonable considering the area and the fact that part of the proceeds goes towards helping families, women and children in need. Unlike a hostel, here the rooms are not shared; it isn't a dormitory, so you

only share with people you're travelling with. There's a fitness centre that includes a swimming pool, steam room, gym and aerobics studios.
Disabled-adapted rooms. Internet (pay terminal). Parking ($8/night). TV.

West End

Luxury

Westin Bayshore

1601 Bayshore Drive, at Cardero Street, V6G 2V4 (604 682 3377/fax 604 687 3102/www.westin.com/ bayshore). Bus 5 then 5min walk. **Rates** $229-$579 single/double; $449-$1,000 suite. **Credit** AmEx, D, DC, MC, V. **Map** p248 J2 ㉑

A classic Vancouver luxury hotel since 1930, the Bayshore had the first high-end hotel restaurant in town, Trader Vic's. It feels like a holiday resort in the midst of the city, with its West Coast modernist architecture and heated outdoor pool looking out to sea. Howard Hughes (*see p48* **Howard Hughes slept here**), Prince Charles and Tina Turner have all stayed. The hotel now features the 'Heavenly Bed', made up of a bespoke pillow-top mattress, down duvet, crisp sheets (thread count 180,250) and five plush pillows. They also have a free shuttle service, a hair salon, boat rentals and golfing packages.
Bar. Business centre. Concierge. Disabled-adapted rooms. Gym. Internet (dataport, or wireless on request). Parking ($23/night). Pools (1 indoor, 1 outdoor). Restaurant. Room service (24hr). TV.

Expensive

Listel Vancouver

1300 Robson Street, at Jervis Street, V6E 1C5 (604 684 8461/toll free 1-800 663 5491/fax 604 684 7092/www.listelvancouver.com). Bus 5. **Rates** $129-$600 single/double. **Credit** AmEx, D, DC, MC, V. **Map** p248 J2 ㉒

Their relationship with one of the city's leading commercial galleries, Buschlen-Mowatt (*see p150*), provides the Listel with an impressive collection of contemporary art in the lobby, at the lifts and in the rooms. Different configurations, colour schemes, bedding, furniture, style and artwork make each room unique. The lifts and hallways are a bit gloomy but there are free canapés in the sculpture gallery and O'Douls is a lively bar and restaurant with live jazz most nights. Aveda and local Deserving Thyme products are featured in the large bathrooms.
Bar. Concierge. Disabled-adapted rooms. Gym. Internet (wireless). Parking ($19/night). Restaurant. Room service (7am-11pm). TV.

Pacific Palisades Hotel

1277 Robson Street, between Bute Street & Jervis Street, V6E 1C4 (604 688 0461/toll free 1-800 663 1815/fax 604 688 4374/www.pacificpalisades hotel.com). Bus 5. **Rates** $125-$390 suite. **Credit** AmEx, D, DC, MC, V. **Map** p248 J2 ㉓

If you're hoping for a Hollywood encounter in Los

Angeles' damper northern suburb, then the Pacific is the place to stay. It's popular with film and TV stars on location, as the hotel offers fully serviced luxury suites with long-term rental rates, as well as film and television production offices. The lobby feels like a Park Avenue apartment (with a bit of South Beach thrown in), giving it more of a homey feel for those naturally accustomed to living in Park Avenue apartments. It is a bright and friendly place, offering evening receptions with complimentary wine for guests to mingle should they so desire. Both child and pet friendly, the latter even get a welcoming 'four paws program' and a designated animal corner with, of course, a photographer available upon request. Check their website for specials, as they can be half the rate card price.

Bar. Business centre. Concierge. Disabled-adapted rooms. Gym. Internet (high speed). Parking ($22/night). Pool (indoor). Restaurant. Room service (24hr). Spa. TV.

Moderate

Blue Horizon

1225 Robson Street, at Bute Street, V6E 1C3 (604 688 1411/toll free 1-800 663 1333/fax 604 688 4461/www.bluehorizonhotel.com). Bus 5. **Rates** $109-$299 single/double. **Credit** AmEx, DC, MC, V. **Map** p248 J2 ㉔

Free high speed internet access, whirlpool, lap pool, sauna and treadmills – all at an affordable price and, what's more, in the centre of town. Awarded the Green Hotel award in recognition of its environmentally friendly practices, Blue Horizon is a pleasingly conscientious place to stay. The spacious rooms have private balconies and the higher floors get the benefit of Vancouver's spectacular scenery. An outdoor café overlooks Robson Street in the summer, and there are two popular eateries open year round: Inlets Bistro (West Coast cuisine) and Shenanigan's sports bar and nightclub.

Bar. Gym. Internet (high speed). Parking ($10/day). Pool (indoor). Restaurants (2). TV.

Coast Plaza

1763 Comox Street, at Denman Street, V6G 1P6 (604 688 7711/toll free 1-800 716 6199/fax 604 688 5934/www.coasthotels.com). Bus 6. **Rates** $129-$419 single/double; $399-$799 suite. **Credit** AmEx, DC, MC, V. **Map** p248 H2 ㉕

One of the most popular hotels in the city because of its good value and location – fitness centre and pool membership are included in the room rate and Delilah's (*see p96*), a restaurant famous for Martinis and elaborate menus, is practically next door. Pet friendly rooms, large suites for extended stays, private balconies with big views – even a 400 seat cinema for private hire. Not for those with a fear of heights: this hotel has 35 floors.

Bar. Business centre. Concierge. Gym. Internet (high speed). Parking ($10/night). Pool (indoor). Restaurants (2). Room service (24hr). TV.

Empire Landmark Hotel

1400 Robson Street, at Broughton Street, V6G 1B9 (604 687 0511/toll free 1-800 830 6144/fax 604 687 2801/www.empirelandmarkhotel.com). Bus 5. **Rates** $79-$199 single/double; $299-$700 suite. **Credit** AmEx, DC, MC, V. **Map** p248 J2 ㉖

The tallest hotel in Vancouver boasts the revolving bar and restaurant Cloud 9 at its apex on the 42nd floor. There's a bit of a convention centre feel but the rooms are spacious – if garish. In contrast, the fitness room is fantastic, complete with a whirlpool and cedar wood sauna. A stark yet functional lobby includes a car rental and sightseeing tour desk, a visitor information kiosk and a business centre conveniently located near the entrance. Discounts gives guests 5-40% off at a wide range of shops in the area.

Bar. Business centre. Disabled-adapted rooms. Gym. Internet (dataport). Parking ($10/night). Restaurants (2). TV.

Riviera Suites Hotel

1431 Robson Street, between Broughton Street & Nicola Street, V6G 1C1 (604 685 1301/toll free 1-888 699 5222/fax 604 685 1335/www.riviera onrobson.com). Bus 5. **Rates** $78-$188 suite. **Credit** AmEx, MC, V. **Map** p248 J2 ㉗

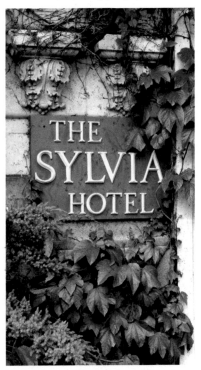

What it says on the sign. *See p43.*

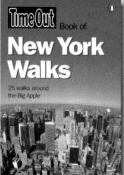

The hallways of this moderately priced hotel do indeed feel like a slice of the south of France transplanted to the rather wetter environs of the West End of Vancouver. Although the rooms are basic, the separate bedrooms and fully equipped kitchenettes make this a perfect place for a family or a group. All the rooms feature a view and the ones on higher floors have balconies. The storage space provided is generous and there are laundry facilities and vending machines on site.
Concierge. Parking (free). TV.

Sunset Inn & Suites

1111 Burnaby Street, at Thurlow Street, V6E 1P4 (604 688 2474/toll free 1-800 786 1997/fax 604 669 3340/www.sunsetinn.com). Bus 6. **Rates** $159-$269 single/double/suite. **Credit** AmEx, DC, MC, V. **Map** p248 H4 ㉘

A cheery place offering a choice of studio, standard or deluxe rooms, to be rented by the night, week or month. The rooms are spacious and clean, and include fully equipped kitchens, private balconies, and partial views of the beaches or mountains. The front-desk staff are very friendly and helpful, and the website includes a daily weather forecast and other useful links for the visitor to Vancouver.
Gym. Internet (wireless). Parking (free). TV.

Sylvia Hotel

1154 Gilford Street, at Beach Avenue, V6G 2P6 (604 681 9321/fax 604 682 3551/www.sylvia hotel.com). Bus 6. **Rates** $70-$310 single/double; $280-$400 suite. **Credit** AmEx, DC, MC, V. **Map** p248 G2 ㉙

You can't get much closer to the beach or Stanley Park than the Sylvia. Opened in 1913, this hotel started out as an apartment block, but was converted into a hotel in 1936 to help provide accommodation for merchant marine crews during the Depression. In 1954, the hotel opened the first cocktail bar in Vancouver, one that remains a local favourite today. Eight floors high, it was once the tallest building in western Canada and is now listed and a city landmark, with Virginia vines growing up the light brick exterior. The rooms range from small singles to two bed, two bath suites. **Photo** *p41.*
Bar. Parking ($7/night). Restaurant. Room service (7am-11pm). TV.

Budget

Buchan

1906 Haro Street, at Gilford Street, V6G 1H7 (604 685 5354/toll free 1-800 668 6654/fax 604 685 5367/www.buchanhotel.com). Bus 5. **Rates** $45-$135 single/double. **Credit** AmEx, DC, MC, V. **Map** p248 H2 ㉚

Built in 1926, the Buchan is a small hotel with a big, old house feel. It is ideally located for those wanting easy access to Stanley Park and, though far from luxurious, the price is right and the rooms are clean. No breakfast, but free coffee is provided.
TV.

Bed & breakfasts

Barclay House

1351 Barclay Street, between Jervis Street & Broughton Street, V6E 1H6 (604 605 1351/fax 604 605 1382/www.barclayhouse.com). Bus 5. **Rates** $125-$245 single/double. **Credit** MC, V. **Map** p248 J3 ㉛

The winner of many best bed and breakfast awards and accolades, Barclay House, with its vintage chandeliers and crisp white linen, is the most sophisticated B&B you'll find in Vancouver. The restored heritage building offers a gourmet three course hot breakfast, including organic coffee and speciality teas. The spacious rooms boast en suite bathrooms complete with either clawfoot tub or power shower and gorgeous, luxuriously thick terry cloth robes. Nice touches include a selection of newspapers and magazines, free evening sherry, Judith Jackson Spa products in the bathrooms, and cookies and bottled water delivered to your room every day. **Photos** *p44.*
Concierge. Internet (wireless). Parking (free). TV.

English Bay Inn

1968 Comox Street, between Gilford Street & Chilco Street, V6G 1R4 (604 683 8002/toll free 1-866 683 8002/fax 604 683 8089/www.english bayinn.com). Bus 6. **Rates** $130-$225 single/double; $180-$295 suite. **Credit** AmEx, DC, MC, V. **Map** p248 G2 ㉜

The Inn is a charming Tudor-style house that looks like its been transplanted from leafy Surrey to the even leafier West End. Should you wake up one morning and think you're on the wrong continent a glance outside at the surrounding, resolutely north American, residential high-rises will soon set your perceptions right. The main floor has a communal living room with chintzy sofas, antiques and a big fireplace, plus an adjacent dining room with Chippendale furniture. The four rooms and two suites are available for virtual tours on their website. The Secluded Getaway is particularly nice.
Concierge. Internet (shared terminal). Parking (free). TV (in some rooms).

'O Canada' House

1114 Barclay Street, at Thurlow Street, V6E 1H1 (604 688 0555/toll free 1-877 688 1114/fax 604 488 0556/www.ocanadahouse.com). Bus 5. **Rates** $135-$265 suite. **Credit** MC, V. **Map** p248 J3 ㉝

In a house built in 1897, this B&B maintains its late Victorian style and feel. Its name comes from the Canadian National Anthem, *O Canada*, written by the original owner of the house, Mr Ewing Buchan. If it's available, try to book the cottage, with French doors that open on to a private terrace. Breakfast ranges from simple toast and coffee to waffles and maple syrup and eggs Benedict. The back garden and the front porch are tranquil places to rest between bouts of sightseeing – or to enjoy your nightly complimentary sherry. Please note that children under 12 and pets are not allowed.
Concierge. Internet (wireless). Parking (free). TV.

Vancouver's most sophisticated B&B: **Barclay House**. *See p43.*

Gastown

Budget

Dominion
*210 Abbott Street, at Water Street, V6B 2K8
(604 681 6666/toll free 1-877 681 1666/www.
dominionhotel.ca). Bus 4, 7.* **Rates** $49-$69
single/double; $79-$99 queen. **Credit** AmEx,
MC, V. **Map** p249 M3
You could call the Dominion Vancouver's 'funkiest'
hotel. That, at least, suggests its originality. But
don't think 'funkiness' equates to luxury: it doesn't.
Above the Lamplighter Pub, the Dominion looks off-
putting from the outside and has some bedrooms
that are not quite up to scratch. But, it also has seven
rooms, each decorated by a different local artist
including the Wonderlust Room, billed as the alternative honeymoon suite, the butterfly-filled Red
Feast for the Senses, and an *Alice in Wonderland*-
inspired room designed with the unlikely themes of
isolation, solitude and madness in mind. The building dates from 1899 and is famous for being one of
the first places in town to serve 'intoxicating refreshment' to women. **Photo** *right.*
Bar. Concierge. Restaurant. TV.

Yaletown

Luxury

Opus Hotel
*322 Davie Street, at Hamilton Street, V6B 5Z6
(604 642 6787/toll free 1-866 642 6787/fax 604
642 6780/www.opushotel.com). Bus 15.* **Rates** $189-
$300 single/double; $369-$2,000 suite. **Credit** AmEx,
MC, V. **Map** p249 K5
For review, *see p46* **Magnum Opus**. **Photos** *p46.*
*Bars (2). Business centre. Concierge. Disabled-
adapted rooms. Gym. Internet (high speed). Parking
($25/night). Restaurant. Room service (24hr). TV.*

West Side

Expensive

Granville Island Hotel
*1253 Johnston Street, Granville Island, V6H 3R9
(604 683 7373/toll free 1-800 663 1840/fax 604
683 3061/www.granvilleislandhotel.com). Bus 50
then 5min walk.* **Rates** $150-$230 single/double;
$199-$300 suite. **Credit** AmEx, D, MC, V.
Map p251 J5

Far enough from the main public market area to avoid the crowds but close enough to walk to in minutes, this hotel boasts a spectacular view, quite different from any other establishment in a city well endowed with spectacular outlooks. A low-rise, contemporary West Coast building studded with windows, the rooms are tastefully done, some overlooking the water with classic wooden shutters, some with local style, post-and-beam architecture, while yet others are more elaborate, with marble floors and Persian rugs. Six suites with floor to ceiling windows allow you to watch the Aquabus ferries, kayaks and houseboats do their thing on the water below. The Dockside bar and restaurant are great but can get quite loud at weekends.
Bar. Concierge. Disabled-adapted rooms. Internet (high speed). Parking ($7/night). Restaurant. Room service (7am-10pm). TV.

Bed & breakfasts

Escape to the Point B&B

1318 Cypress Street, at Whyte Avenue, V6J 3L2 (604 250 5300/fax 604 732 8827/www.escapeto thepoint.com). Bus 2, 22. **Rates** $95-$160 single/double. **Credit** V (for reservations only). **Map** p251 G5 ③⑦

Kits Point is a quintessentially West Coast residential area. Escape's exterior is Tudor in style but well mixed with local architectural elements. Inside, there's a bright and comfortable living room if you should feel like being social or playing with the house dog, Logan. If the weather's good you can laze about on the deck-chairs in the back garden or walk over to the best outdoor pool in town. Breakfast can be taken in the dining room or in your room, where it is beautifully presented on a wooden tray. All three guest rooms are gems, at least in name: Amber, Tiger Eye (the loft) and Topaz.
Parking (free street-side). Room service (breakfast). TV.

Mickey's Kits Beach Chalet

2142 W 1st Avenue, between Yew Street & Arbutus Street, V6K 1E8 (604 739 3342/toll free 1-888 739 3342/fax 604 739 3342/www.mickeysbandb.com). Bus 2, 22. **Rates** $80-$145 single/double/suite. **Credit** AmEx, MC, V. **Map** p251 F5 ③⑧

Location, location, location. That's the key to Mickey's. It's close to Vancouver's liveliest beach, Kits, and only a five minute bus or cab ride to downtown. Three different rooms accommodate everyone from a single traveller to a family or small group. The York Room has a kingsize bed (but could also be made up of two single beds), the south-facing Arbutus Room is perfect for sunlight (if it's not raining) and the Yew Room has a kingsize bed and pull-out sofa in a separate living area with a wood burning fireplace. All the rooms have phones and wireless internet access. Mickey's takes pride in catering to their guests' needs, especially dietary – just let them know when you make your booking.
Internet (wireless). Parking (free). TV.

Hycroft

1248 W 15th Avenue, between Birch Street & Alder Street, V6H 1R8 (604 307 2300/fax 604 733 2963/www.hycroft.com). Bus 10, 17. **Rates** $100-$350 suite. **Credit** AmEx, MC, V. **Map** p251 J7 ③⑨

This high end B&B is a fully restored 1929 house, on the edge of Shaughnessy and all its beautiful big old houses – perfect for a walk or jog around. There's a choice of a one or two bedroom suite, both with kitchen and en suite bathroom. Fireplaces and heated slate flooring are nice features, plus there's a private entrance for guests, so you don't feel like you're walking in through someone else's living room.
Internet (high speed). Parking (free). TV.

North Shore

Moderate

Lonsdale Quay Hotel

123 Carrie Cates Court, at Rogers Avenue, Lonsdale Quay, V7M 3K7 (604 986 6111/fax 604 986 8782/www.lonsdalequayhotel.com). SeaBus Lonsdale Quay. **Rates** $115-$250 single/double; $225-$350 suite. **Credit** AmEx, MC, V. **Map** p253 Z5 ④⓪

Dominion. *See p44.*

Magnum Opus

Ever wondered if you are a Billy, a Mike, a DeDe, a Susan or a Bob & Carol? Well the **Opus Hotel** has, and has created profiles of these five personality types with rooms to match. Within their 96 rooms, they offer seven different configurations and five different colour schemes depending on your tastes and lifestyle: wall colours include (lime) green, (hot) red, (demure) taupe, (electric) blue and (butter) yellow and rooms range from standard to deluxe courtyard to executive suite to penthouse. If you're a Billy, then you're an artful and eclectic creative type and they'd recommend you stay in the green room, eat at Brix or Banana Leaf, have coffee at Soma, dance the night away at Sonar, shop for furniture at Koolhaus and

sunbathe at Wreck Beach. But if you're a DeDe, you're a fussy LA drama queen. You'd probably stay in the taupe room, eat at Feenie's or Tojo's, party at Ginger, go to the Spa at the Century Plaza and shop at Leonie's. For a day trip, you'd go Rollerblading or you might pop into the Yaletown Cosmetic Surgery Clinic for a quick botox fix. Get the picture? The website (www.opushotel.com) tells all in much greater detail, if you feel like indulging yourself in your demographic!

Located in the trendy, ex-warehouse district of Yaletown, the Opus Hotel is the hippest place to stay in Vancouver – it was even voted one of the World's Best Places to Stay by readers of *Condé Nast Traveler*. Michael Stipe and Cher are among their rock star guestlist

The Lonsdale Quay Hotel is part of the Lonsdale Quay market development, which is being built within close proximity to the North Shore mountains. Lovely big rooms or suites boast great city and harbour views and downtown is just a SeaBus ride away. The hotel is child friendly and there are even two suites that come with kids' rooms – including a TV, VCR and single bunk bed with slide.
Bar. Concierge. Disabled-adapted rooms. Gym. Internet (high speed). Parking ($7/night). Restaurant. Room service (24hr). TV.

Budget

Horseshoe Bay Motel

6588 Royal Avenue, at Bruce Street, West Vancouver, V7W 2B6 (604 921 7454/ toll free 1-877 717 3377/fax 604 921 7464). Bus 250, 257. **Rates** $89-$119 single/double. **Credit** AmEx, MC, V.
If you're setting off from Vancouver to the wide open spaces of BC, this is an option. From Horseshoe Bay you catch the ferry to Nanaimo, Bowen Island and

(note the dent in the floor of the lift from the latter's personal StairMaster).

The rooms feel like a stylish urban *pied à terre*, with velvet sofas to hang out on while watching a ginormous flatscreen TV. Indeed, they have had guests say it's like getting the keys to a friend's place for the weekend and losing yourself in their space. They even leave a few books, CDs and DVDs around to further the home-away-from-home feeling. All the rooms include movies, Sony Playstation, and top of the line stereo systems.

If you feel like staying in, you can request an Opus Bath Experience – which is when an attendant comes to your room, draws your bath and creates a calming environment with the right lighting and essential oils, as well as

serving a glass of wine, champagne or all-natural, non-alcoholic drink, as you prefer. The package includes l'Occitane products, Loofah sponge, mineral water and use of a bath caddy and ultra soft facecloths. Bliss for under $50.

Daniel Craig, the general manager (and no relation to the new James Bond), is an inspired and friendly soul, and the architect of the hotel's clever marketing. He it was who managed to get the hotel featured in the Academy Awards goodie bags two years in a row, offering presenters and winners a three-night stay. The freebies are, sad to say, non-transferable; only ten-12 celebs out of a possible 125 redeemed theirs last year.

For listings, *see p44*.

the Sunshine Coast. It is also the last stopping place before Squamish on the road to Whistler. You can catch a glimpse of the water and ferry activity from the motel, but you might have to stand on your tippy toes. Rooms are fine but basic, with en suite bathrooms and TVs. The staff are a bit indifferent and the hotel doesn't offer any services, but if you're catching an early ferry or you get in late it'll do. You can grab a coffee on the nearby pier or a full breakfast at the Boathouse Restaurant at the marina. *TV.*

Hostels

Hostelling International – Vancouver Central

1025 Granville Street, at Helmcken Street, Downtown, V6Z 1L4 (604 685 5335/toll free 1-888 203 8333/fax 604 685 5351/www.hihostels. ca/vancouvercentral). Bus 4, 6, 7, 10, 16, 17, 50. **Rates** $25-$32 dorm; $62-$76 private. **Credit** MC, V. **Map** p249 K4 ④

The most central and newest of the three HIs, this is

a fun place to stay, with new comfy beds, free linen and clean private bathrooms. No surprise it has won HI's Cool Atmosphere, Ideal for City Beat and Out of This World hostel awards. Like, totally.
Bar. Internet (pay terminal). Restaurant.

Hostelling International – Vancouver Downtown

1114 Burnaby Street, at Thurlow Street, West End, V6E 1P1 (604 684 4565/toll free 1-888 203 4302/ fax 604 684 4540/www.hihostels.ca/vancouver downtown). Bus 2, 22. **Rates** $25-$32 dorm; $62-$76 private. **Credit** MC, V. **Map** p248 H4 ⓰
Despite the 'downtown' in its name, this HI is in the West End. Bike rentals and daily tours/activities around the city are offered, as well as a shuttle service to the train station. A smoke free and family friendly place, it also caters well to the backpacker. Friendly, experienced staff will point you in the right direction for local grocery stores.
Internet (wireless & kiosk). Parking (free, limited).

Hostelling International – Vancouver Jericho Beach

1515 Discovery Street, West Side, V6R 4K5 (604 224 3208/toll free 1-888 203 4303/fax 604 224 4852/www.hihostels.ca/vancouverjerichobeach). Bus 4 then 5min walk. **Rates** $18.50-$22.50 dorm; $58.50-$67.50 private. **Credit** MC, V.

Only open May-Sept, this HI is the most interesting in terms of architecture (ex barracks) and location (on the beach), although it is far from the centre of town. To compensate for the distance, they offer a free shuttle service to and from downtown. Shared and private rooms, a great licenced café, a big communal kitchen and loads of sporting equipment to use at the nearby beach makes for a flexible stay.
Internet (pay terminal). Parking ($5/24hrs).

Samesun Backpacker Lodge

1018 Granville Street, at Nelson Street, Downtown, V6Z 1L5 (604 682 8226/toll free 1-877 562 2783/ www.samesun.com). Bus 4, 6, 7, 10, 16, 17, 50. **Rates** $24-$27 dorm; $43-$53 private. **Credit** MC, V. **Map** p249 K4 ⓱
As they aim to 'maximise your mingling' the Samesun is ideal for lone backpackers or travellers looking to meet young, like-minded people on shoestring budgets. It's raucous and noisy but also clean, fun and very, very central. They provide good value food and drinks, host live bands and sell cheap Vancouver Canucks hockey game tickets and Big Kahuna ski packages through the front desk. The social director will tell you all about the best bars and clubs in town, and may even join you. Not one for those who value peace and quiet.
Bar. Internet (pay terminal).

Howard Hughes slept here

In 1972, Vancouver was abuzz with news that the elusive billionaire Howard Hughes was coming to town. He checked into the Westin Bayshore (*see p40*) (then called the Western International) and stayed for six months – less a day. One day longer and he would have had to declare his assets to the government.

His people called to reserve a number of rooms and, when told that the hotel was full, responded that Hughes would buy the place – just as he had done with the Desert Inn in Las Vegas in 1966. The top four floors were quickly made available for him and his entourage of Mormons, English boxer bodyguards and a personal chef. The lifts were shut off to these floors and surveillance cameras installed.

From hang-gliders flying by to snap a photo, to cub reporters sneaking up the stairs attempting a scoop for the local paper, everyone was trying to get a glimpse of the reclusive Mr Hughes, who had not been photographed or seen in public for 15 years. But no one ever saw him – not that was reported anyway. It is rumoured that he went to an ice hockey game but that could be a typically Canadian urban myth...

Why Vancouver? Some say it was for his own security, others that he was involved with the CIA, or maybe for tax reasons, or to buy a local airline, or, well the list goes on. But a reliable source at the hotel insists it was for perhaps the most obvious of reasons: to see a woman: local actress/singer Yvonne de Carlo (Lily in TV's *The Munsters*).

When Hughes and his entourage finally left the hotel, staff found that plywood partitions had been erected, aluminium foil stuck on the windows and a very big mess had been left behind. The entire space (24 rooms) had to be completely refurbished. Today the Hughes Suite is No. 2090 and it goes for up to $1,000/night, depending on how many adjoining rooms you take.

Presumably because of de Carlo, Hughes's infamous visit wasn't his first, although it would prove to be his last. From Vancouver, he went to Nicaragua, then London, then Mexico for four years. He died during the flight back to Houston in April 1976.

Hughes had one further connection to British Columbia: his Spruce Goose plane (featured in the movie *The Aviator*) was made of timber from the Queen Charlotte Islands.

Sightseeing

Introduction   50
Downtown   53
Stanley Park   60
The West Side   67
East Vancouver   76
North Shore   81

Features

The best Sights   51
The space man   54
Dogville   59
On your bike   62
Where the wild things are   65
Walk on the West Side   70
Skinny dipping   72
Blooming marvellous   74
Potted history   79
The shore thing   82
Downhill racers   84

Maps

Stanley Park   63

Vancouver Art Gallery. *See p56.*

Introduction

The lie of the land.

There is nothing half so much worth doing as simply messing about in boats.

A combination of happenstance, civic activism and clever urban planning, Vancouver's vibrant downtown – a thriving mix of office towers, shopping districts and innovative, high-density apartment developments that has brought a stream of residents into the city centre over the last decade – is now an international benchmark. 'The Vancouver Model', as it is called, is being replicated around the world, in communities ranging from nearby Portland, Oregon to far-off Dubai, whose sultan has built a full-scale replica of False Creek.

Downtown Vancouver is a large peninsula, bordered on three sides – north, west and south – by water, and capped by the vast green expanse of Stanley Park. To the east lie the more troubled but vibrant communities of East Vancouver. Gastown, the city's main tourist district, was historically the city centre but lost its importance as power moved west, to the business canyons of Howe Street and across

the Cambie Street bridge to City Hall. Gastown is undergoing a second revival at the moment, as the planners and developers responsible for the Vancouver Model search out innovative ways to revive the area, still suffering from its proximity to Hastings and Main streets (the notorious Downtown Eastside). Connecting the suits and ties of the central business district and the densely packed neighbourhood of the West End lies the glittering retail strip of Robson Street. Among downtown's man-made highlights are the Vancouver Public Library, the Vancouver Art Gallery and the shiny new towers of Coal Harbour and Yaletown.

Downtown morphs into East Vancouver at Main Street, which includes the second largest Chinatown in North America, after San Francisco, and the lively Commercial Drive district. Over the Lions Gate and Second Narrows Bridges, the North Shore has the mountains, hiking and more great beaches.

The city's museums are mostly located on the West Side, which is to say in the Kitsilano/Point Grey area south-west of the Burrard Bridge. This neighbourhood is celebrated for its long strip of sandy beaches (running all the way west to the Pacific Spirit Regional Park) and for some spectacular parks and gardens. It's also on the West Side that you'll find Granville Island, with its maze of artist's studios, artisan stores and indoor market.

Everywhere across the city you'll find good food, quirky shopping and varied (if not always very distinguished) architecture. But most of Vancouver's pleasures derive from its setting in the midst of a temperate rainforest, the vistas of mountains that appear at the end of busy downtown streets, the sparkling waters of English Bay, and the many everyday epiphanies that come from the mix of city and nature so closely entwined.

Getting around

A small and compact city by North American standards, Vancouver is easy to negotiate on foot, at least until you venture over Burrard Inlet to the North Shore. TransLink oversees an efficient public transport system; the bus service is as good as the sometimes congested roads allow, and as a rule the bus drivers tend to be remarkably sympathetic, offering travel advice and turning a blind eye if you don't have the exact change ($2.25 buys you 90 minutes' travel anywhere in zone 1).

Two SkyTrain lines are primarily aimed at commuters from sprawling East Vancouver and Surrey, though tourists may find them a safe and reliable means to access Science World, Commercial Drive, or Canada's second largest shopping mall, Metropolis at Metrotown. The Waterfront transport nexus close to the sails of Canada Place is also the terminal for the SeaBus to North Vancouver.

Mostly, though, visitors base themselves in downtown and rarely stray far beyond Kitsilano beach on the West Side, Chinatown to the east, Van Dusen gardens to the south and Stanley Park to the north – all within a 20 minute bus ride of Robson Square.

Streets run in gridlike blocks and street numbers climb 100 per block as you head south from Canada Place pier or west from Carrall Street (in downtown) or Ontario Street (the West Side). Note that suite or room numbers precede the building number in addresses. (East of Main Street the street numbers climb again and take on the prefix East.) It sounds confusing but it seems to work. And remember, if you lose your bearings in Vancouver, look for the mountains – always due north.

Tours

It's possible to tour Vancouver by coach, by trolley car, by horse-drawn carriage, by boat and by seaplane. For details see the Getting Around section of the Directory. The most distinctive bus tour is with the **Vancouver Trolley Company** (604 801 5515, www. vancouvertrolley.com) which offers a hop on, hop off service featuring 23 stops around the downtown area for $30 (children are half price).

Gray Line of Vancouver (604 879 3363, www.grayline.ca) has a three and a half hour city tour departing daily at 9.15am for $55. Hotel pick-up is complimentary.

Between mid June and September the Park Board has a **free shuttle bus** with 14 stops around Stanley Park. Not to be confused with the **Stanley Park Express Bus** (604 681 5115, www.stanleypark.com) which operates between downtown and the park, mid March to the end of October, and which is free to customers who buy tickets for the aquarium or the horse-drawn carriage.

The best Sights

The Beaches
Take your pick: downtown boasts four, the North Shore has a bundle, and then there's the long sandy strand of the West Side. *See p69 and p82* **The shore thing**.

Granville Island
A community hub, this covered market and warren of shops and artist's studios brings the waterfront to life. *See p67*.

Grouse Mountain
Not many cities can boast their own mountain, but North Vancouver is gradually encroaching on the snow line. Tackle the Grouse Grind – or take the cable car, as you like. *See p85*.

Museum of Anthropology
A superbly designed showcase for Northwest coast art and carving. *See p74*.

Stanley Park
If you visited Vancouver and skipped the park, you wouldn't have been here at all. *See p60*.

Van Dusen Gardens
Around the world in 55 acres of ravishing flowerbeds, water features, rockeries and shrubs. *See p74* **Blooming marvellous**.

One destination...
a dozen discoveries.

Come and discover the best of Vancouver's attractions. There's an experience for every taste. Every lifestyle. Everyone.

01 IMAX THEATRE AT CANADA PLAC
02 VANCOUVER LOOKOUT
03 BURNABY VILLAGE MUSEUM
04 SCIENCE WORLD
05 GROUSE MOUNTAIN
06 VANCOUVER AQUARIUM
07 CAPILANO SUSPENSION BRIDGE
08 HELL'S GATE AIRTRAM
09 DR. SUN YAT-SEN GARDEN
10 MINTER GARDENS
11 HARBOUR CRUISES
12 STORYEUM

1.888.433.3735

VISIT OUR WEBSITE FOR GROUP TOUR, TRAVEL
CONTACT AND ADDITIONAL INFORMATION

www.vancouverattractions.com

VANCOUVER ATTRACTIONS

come for the fun of it!

Downtown

Art, architecture, and water, water everywhere...

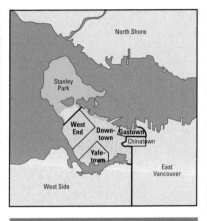

Downtown

Small is beautiful. The ocean placed a natural cap on Vancouver's urban sprawl. When the population started booming, builders found the only way to go was up – with the result that the downtown core of this 21st-century city remains eminently walkable. And that's definitely the best way to appreciate it.

When planning your sightseeing, you could easily organise it as a series of walks radiating out from the centre of town, usually considered to be the Vancouver Art Gallery. You don't have to stray far to cover the bases: shopping, great restaurants, beaches and nature are cheek-by-jowl and you can taste them all in a day (although you'll need longer to really savour them). Walk 15 minutes in any direction and you'll begin to appreciate what makes Vancouver the most liveable city in the world.

The city's premier cultural institute, the **Vancouver Art Gallery** (VAG), stands at the very heart of downtown on Robson Square. The building started life as Vancouver's courthouse when the Francis Rattenbury-designed building opened in 1911. Arthur Erickson renovated the interior of the gallery in 1983 (he also designed the radical new Law Courts Building, which stands across the way at 800 Smithe Street, *see p54* **The space man**). The gallery is bursting at the seams in its current configuration and the next few years will see big changes as it ponders how best to expand. The Gallery Café's patio is a wonderful oasis for a glass of chilled white wine on a sunny summer day (*see p89*), and the gallery's main steps on Robson have become a favourite spot for Vancouverites to eat, drink, chat, protest and people watch.

A block north-west of Robson Square, **Christ Church Cathedral** (W Georgia Street & Burrard Street, 604 682 8441) is a mere stripling by European standards. Completed in 1895, it is the oldest surviving church in Vancouver. The sandstone Gothic revival architecture certainly supplies a contrast with the glass and cement pyramids that surround it. Be sure to check out the results of the 2004 $8.6 million restoration, which refurbished the 1895 Douglas fir floor and ceiling, once hidden behind white acoustic panels. For a different kind of cathedral, try the nearby HSBC building, at 885 W Georgia Street, long considered to be one of the city's finest examples of high-capitalist architecture (circa 1987), and home to the Pendulum Gallery, with its 27 metre (80 foot) aluminium pendulum.

From Hornby to Bute, Robson Street is the city's main see-and-be-seen promenade, an orgiastic display of high-end chain shopping, exclusive boutiques and the people who frequent them. Once fondly known as 'Robsonstrasse' for the preponderance of European merchants who lined its modest pavements, the area has vastly changed. Weekend evenings see bumper-to-bumper traffic as young men from the suburbs crawl along in tricked-out vehicles in a pre-clubbing ritual. At Thurlow, there are, famously, two Starbucks sitting diagonally opposite each other. Both do roaring business and attract completely different crowds. From Bute to Denman, Robson's cavalcade of retail slows down considerably – but if you persevere down the hill, you will find yourself in the Asian student district, with its bars and restaurants.

North of Robson and west of Canada Place, **Coal Harbour** is Vancouver's newest downtown residential district, a shining spread of office towers and apartment blocks with stunning views – along with the Yaletown district ten years its senior, it is one of the reasons Vancouver has been nicknamed 'the City of Glass'. Coal Harbour offers a charming seawall walk between the dazzling high-rises and Burrard Inlet. Floatplanes still work the harbour and the marinas are full of oversized

The space man

It's easily mistaken for a swimming pool – the glass roof, the waterfall, the seasonal ice rink under the street – but the Robson Square Law Courts in downtown Vancouver perfectly illustrate the sly genius of architect **Arthur Erickson** (born 1924). Designed in 1973, the building is conceptually and materially a departure from traditional Halls of Justice. Transparent materials literally expose the workings of the law to the surrounding city.

The Vancouver Art Gallery (*see p56; pictured*), which faces the courts and was designed by Erickson, is set in a heritage building that was the city's original court. The resulting town square invites a series of dialogues between past and future, between the laws and the people, and between art and society. Not bad for a little glass and cement.

From his first major project in 1963 – the winning design for the hilltop campus of Simon Fraser University on Burnaby Mountain – to the Native longhouse-inspired Museum of Anthropology designed in 1971, the Waterfall Building at 1540 W 2nd Street (1996) and the Scotiabank Dance Centre (2003), Erickson reaffirms his artistry with every structure. Time and again he returns the role of architect to the definition it found in ancient Greece: he is a craftsman whose unique mastery of materials releases their magic, creating a community open to anyone eager to share the space. His next project – a triangular glass skyscraper that will appear to twist 45 degrees as it rises 167 metres (548 feet) – is likely to begin construction on its downtown site in 2006.

Some have called Erickson a 'concrete poet', others see him as a philosopher, but above all else he is really an iconoclast. The quintessential Canadian modernist (admittedly inspired by Frank Lloyd Wright), he is contemptuous enough of the 'imagineered' excesses of post-modern architecture to have labelled Disney 'the great Satan'.

Despite decades of success, Arthur Erickson's story is surprisingly dramatic, careening from rags to riches and back again more than once. Financial mismanagement left him famously bankrupt and literally homeless in the 1990s, but through his own hard work (and the benevolence of a couple of wealthy friends) he was both able to buy back his custom-built, self-designed house and regain his career momentum. Still, walking in the shoes of the homeless left an indelible mark on Erickson, who has always felt that it is 'only by moving through a space [that] we come to understand it, to feel it'. Mindful of the often dreadful impact architecture has had on the lives of the urban poor, Erickson turned his talents to the Downtown Eastside's Portland Hotel, designing a place that combines social housing and a wide array of services and community outreach. For Erickson, it's ultimately less about aesthetics and more about being 'interested in what buildings can do'. And for the city of Vancouver, that means a legacy of buildings that are honest about who they serve, what they do and how they interrelate to the people, the city and the natural beauty all around them.

luxury boats. The Seawall starts at the foot of Burrard and continues into the West End and Stanley Park. Along the way there are several fair-to-middling places to eat – Vancouver is still trying to solve the good food/good view conundrum. Of these, Lift is the most ambitious, architecturally speaking at least (*see p96*).

Jutting out into Burrard Inlet at the foot of Burrard and Howe Streets, **Canada Place** (999 Canada Place, 604 647 7390) is probably downtown's most photographed spot. A cruise ship terminal, IMAX movie theatre, convention centre, and restaurant and hotel complex, the sail-like structure is a legacy of the city's first large-scale international event, Expo 86 (*see p19*). Deliberately and perhaps unfortunately designed as a riposte to Sydney's famed Opera House, its cruise-ship lines are not original, but they are distinctive, and the site has become a civic landmark. Views across the inlet from the exterior promenade are particularly fine.

While in the vicinity, take a moment to notice the beauty of the venerable Marine Building, on the cusp of the harbour at the corner of Burrard and W Hastings. Inspired by New York's Chrysler Building, the circa-1920 Marine, a legacy of Vancouver's increasing early-20th century prosperity, was the tallest 'skyscraper' in the city until 1939. An art deco treasure, the building is festooned with many materials and designs, while the walls and polished brass doors are decorated with depictions of sea snails, skate, crabs, turtles, carp, scallops, seaweed and sea horses, and the exterior is studded with flora and fauna, tinted in sea-green and touched with gold.

Heading east, a couple of minutes' walk brings you to the **Waterfront Station** (601 Cordova Street). The downtown transit hub, this handsome red-stone building between Granville and Seymour was built by the Canadian Pacific Railway in 1914 as the terminus of its transcontinental passenger trains. The beaux-arts interiors were restored to their original glory in the late 1970s, but it is perhaps most historically important now as the site of Vancouver's first ever Starbucks.

On your way to Gastown you may pass by the **Harbour Centre** (555 W Hastings Street, 604 689 7304), an undistinguished mall, capped by a large observation tower and the Top of Vancouver Revolving Restaurant (604 669 2220). The lookout tower offers those willing to shell out for admission panoramic views of the city, accessed by an external glass lift. At 177 metres (581 feet) this is currently the tallest building in BC.

The downtown area borders False Creek north of Yaletown. It's the one district given over to typical North American freeway-style

Get high. The **Harbour Centre.**

development, with the Georgia Viaduct looming over various leftovers from Expo 86. Save for a family day out at Science World (1455 Quebec Street, *see p143*), tourists are unlikely to venture here, unless it's to take in a game at the sports nexus of the city: **GM Place** and its neighbour, BC Place. The 20,000-seater GM Place on Expo Boulevard is the brash upstart of the two, built in 1995 as home to the vastly popular Vancouver Canucks hockey team, a '70s-era franchise that has never quite captured the Stanley Cup but still has the hearts of most citizens in a vice-like grasp. Large music concerts are frequently hosted here (*see p162*). BC Place, another legacy/relic of Expo 86, is famous for its vast air-supported dome and white elephant status. A 60,000-seater, it's home to the BC Lions football team, but has never found its role in the city. Occasionally it becomes a cavernous host to various trade fairs – and it will host the opening and closing ceremonies for the Winter Olympics, 2010. Stadium tours depart Gate H every Friday, mid-June through September at 11am and 1pm, and at Gate A there's the **BC Sports Hall of Fame and Museum**.

Heading west up Robson Street from BC Place you'll find one of the more controversial buildings in Vancouver, the **Vancouver**

Public Library (350 W Georgia Street, 604 331 3603). Debuting in 1995 at a cost of over $100 million, the Moshe Safdie-designed structure's fans and many users are delighted by its handsome lines and ease of use. Detractors wonder why a modern building in Vancouver resembles Rome's Coliseum.

BC Sports Hall of Fame and Museum

Gate A, BC Place Stadium, 777 Pacific Boulevard South, at Expo Boulevard (604 687 5520/www.bc sportshalloffame.com). Bus 15/SkyTrain Stadium. **Open** 10am-5pm daily. **Admission** $8; $6 concessions; $15 family. **Credit** MC, V. **Map** p249 L4.

Unless you have a keen interest in BC sports heroes (few of whom made much impression on the international scene) this modest exhibit in the inner corridors of BC Place stadium isn't likely to detain you for very long. Most of the galleries feature shirts, trophies and faded photographs in glass cabinets. An interactive room with a ball pit and table hockey will amuse the children for a while, and a couple of internal windows reveal the football field far below. A gallery dedicated to Canadian hero Terry Fox (who lost a leg to cancer but made it his mission to run coast to coast) is the highlight.

Harbour Centre Lookout Tower

555 W Hastings Street, at Seymour Street (604 689 0421/www.vancouverlookout.com). All city-centre buses. **Open** 16 Oct-30 Apr 9am-9pm daily. *1 May-15 Oct* 8.30am-10.30pm daily. **Admission** $10; $4-$9 concessions; free under-4s. **Credit** AmEx, MC, V. **Map** p249 L3.

In a city of great vistas, the Lookout Tower offers a bird's-eye view. On a clear day you can see for miles in every direction, although the thickets of new condos to the south and west obscure some of Vancouver's most cherished landmarks. For sure this is the best vantage point to admire the older architecture and the docks of the Downtown Eastside. A meal at the revolving restaurant one floor up saves you the admission fee; the cost is mediocre food at high prices.

Vancouver Art Gallery

750 Hornby Street, at Robson Street (604 662 4700/www.vanartgallery.bc.ca). All city-centre buses. **Open** 10am-5.30pm Mon-Wed, Sat; 10am-9pm Thur, Fri. **Admission** $15; $6-$11 concessions; free under-4s. **Credit** AmEx, MC, V. **Map** p249 K3.

The VAG is known for its collection of works by Emily Carr, Canada's most celebrated female artist, whose work is on the third floor (*see pp26-32*). But if you find Carr an overrated, provincial, 1920s modernist, as some observers do, it's still worth going, as the gallery also has rotating exhibitions that range from crowd-pleasing blockbusters and old masters to cleverly curated showings of challenging contemporary work, and it is building a reputation for its first-rate photography collection. **Photo** *p54*.

The West End

One of North America's most densely populated neighbourhoods, the West End is a major reason Vancouver's downtown is so liveable. Leafy, residential, full of reasonably priced rental units, it's home to the city's vibrant gay community, plus many Asian students, service industry workers (who appreciate the convenience and cheap rents) and people who just love the hustle and bustle.

Still, away from the main roads it's easy to find quiet areas that reward a slow saunter past little corner stores, street corners patrolled by friendly tabby cats and children's playgrounds. The West End was first developed in the late 19th century by the Canadian Pacific Railway, which built grand residences for its officials in the area. At Barclay and Nelson, you'll find some vestiges of the old, genteel West End at Barclay Heritage Square, which preserves nine Victorian-era houses, including the Roedde House Museum, an 1893 family house in Queen Anne Revival style that offers guided tours (1415 Barclay Street, 604 684 7040, www. roeddehouse.org). West of Denman Street, the leafy byways are reminiscent of New York's Upper West Side and the neighbourhood melts into Stanley Park.

At the foot of Robson, turn south along Denman Street and proceed to Davie Street and English Bay, passing dozens of little shops and restaurants, cafés, gelato joints and the odd condom or gourmet dogfood store. Many a summer evening ends with a stroll to English Bay to watch the sun come down.

From English Bay you can join the Seawall, either heading west to Stanley Park, or east around False Creek, where it threads its way through residential developments and increasingly offers fine dining choices. Of these, the newest and perhaps the best is Nu, beneath the Granville Street Bridge (*see p92*).

Parallel to Robson, Davie Street has a funkier, more residential feel. Heading east from Denman you'll pass by Gabriola, the old Rogers Mansion at Davie and Nicola, built entirely from Gabriola Island stone by the head of BC Sugar in 1900. It's now home to the Macaroni Grill restaurant (the indignity!). It's also occasionally taken over by film crews. You're now on your way up the road to Davie Village (between Bute and Hornby), the home of Vancouver's gay community, featuring shops, restaurants and, of course, nightclubs. Highlights include Little Sister's Book & Art Emporium, a gay and lesbian bookstore famous for a long-running battle with Canada Customs and a real community centre, and the PumpJack Pub (for both, *see p156*).

The would-be iconic **Canada Place**. *See p55*.

Gastown

Three blocks east of Canada Place, past the Seabus terminal at Waterfront Station, the historic district of **Gastown** begins. The birthplace of frontier-era Vancouver, this area was once the very heart of the city. It burned to the ground in the fire of 1886, was rebuilt in the years immediately following, but fell on hard times during the middle of the last century.

Gastown is now going through another metamorphosis, as intelligently planned redevelopment turns it from what was once a revived tourist area with a smattering of souvenir shops, dubious restaurants and decaying long-stay hotels for men and women of no fixed income, into a living, working part of the city that still has many delights for the discerning visitor. Even the choice of restaurants is improving.

Walk east along Water Street to observe the many finely restored circa-1890s buildings and warehouses, most now operating as retail businesses and office spaces for funky design firms and the like. Most of the retail along Water is still very mass-market tourist-orientated, offering up multiple combinations of Cowichan sweaters, smoked salmon and maple syrup. There's highly recommended innovative tapas-style Japanese food on offer at Guu With Otomokae at 105-375 Water Street (*see p101* **Izakaya time**). At Water and Cambie, the **Steam Clock** is an ingenious device that takes advantage of the old steam heating system that runs beneath Gastown's streets. Lest you think it's a part of Vancouver's deep heritage, be aware that the clock dates from the mid-'70s and, while charming, is not a part of Gastown's deep history. Further down at Water and Abbott, you'll find the Dominion Hotel (*see p44*), an 1899 building that is in the process of being rehabilitated. The pub on the ground floor, the Lamplighter, has become a favourite hangout for the twentysomething indie music scenesters (*see p163*).

Storyeum (*see p143*) is an innovative attempt at telling BC's history through theatre and multimedia presentations. Byrnes Block, at 2 Water Street, stands on the site of the original Deighton House, a saloon owned by 'Gassy' Jack Deighton, the hard-living barkeeper who gave his name and rather seamy reputation to the area. There's a statue of Jack watching over Maple Tree Square, the cobbled streets of which cap Water Street.

Just up Carrall Street you'll find one of the area's best bistros, the Irish Heather (*see p117*), a refreshingly shamrock-and-leprechaun-free Celtic establishment with a charming back room and a whiskey bar that looks over Gaolers Mews, the site of Vancouver's first jail.

Off Water, on Cordova and other nearby streets, there are plenty of unique shops, full of curios and designer clothes and free of tourist tat – see Small Medium Large (334 W Cordova Street, 604 696 5211) for a selection of Vancouver's best furniture design, for instance – but be aware that if you wander much further south-east than Cambie and Cordova, you'll be in the drug-infested no-man's-land that separates Gastown from Chinatown, where it would really be wise not to venture. A couple of

blocks further east the **Vancouver Police Centennial Museum** offers some revealing scraps of the city's history in a cramped space.

Vancouver Police Centennial Museum

2nd floor, 238-240 E Cordova Street, at Main Street (604 665 3346/www.city.vancouver.bc.ca/police/ museum). Bus 4, 7. **Open** 9am-5pm Mon-Sat. **Admission** $7; $5 concessions; free under-6s. **Credit** MC, V. **Map** p249 N3.

The most noteworthy items in the museum, at least for the ghoulishly inclined celebrity hound, are the autopsy pictures of Errol Flynn, who died in the city in 1959 in the arms of his 19-year-old assistant. It's the way he would have wanted to go. There is also a collection of unusual weapons confiscated over the years and records of dastardly crimes committed by nefarious citizens. The museum shop offers a host of very specialised mementoes for sale. Not a large attraction, but guaranteed to fill a rainy afternoon.

Yaletown

This former warehouse district east of Granville and south of Smithe had run into hard times by the early 1990s. It stood empty and decaying, a notorious site for prostitution and drug

The Seawall in **David Lam Park**. See p59.

Dogville

If Mahatma Gandhi was right that 'the greatness of a nation and its moral progress can be judged by the way its animals are treated', then Vancouver is either the most progressive or most decadent place on earth. On the other hand, if Jerry Seinfeld was right when he observed that in the struggle for supremacy between man and dog, it's the dogs who are on top (who picks up whose poo?) then Vancouver is some sort of canine apotheosis. City Hall estimates that there are 50,000 resident dogs.

Like most rumours and stereotypes about the city, the kernel of truth can be found in Kitsilano. At the intersection of 4th Avenue and Yew **Three Dog Bakery** and **Urban Puppy** fight it out for the doggy dollar. At the bakery patrons queue for 'Beagle Bagels', cat-shaped cookies, and an Oreo-like carob cookie that sells for $9.95 per 369 grammes. Then there are the accessories, like tiny vests from 'Puppia Tokyo' retailing for $69.95 or 'leave-on pet conditioner' for that just washed and wriggle-dried look.

Across the street, the Urban Puppy offers much the same inventory, minus the pastries and with the addition of actual puppies. For $100, you can carry your four-legged pal in a Sherpa Bag, 'the leader in style, safety and comfort for the pet on-the-go'.

Perhaps for obvious reasons, the Vancouver dog obsession tends to flourish where the money is: in affluent West Vancouver, owners can check their friends in to Love Your Dog Daycare ('Your dog can spend the day in our playroom socialising, playing games, cavorting in our outdoor splash pool, having quiet time and lots of cuddles') and Spa ('Put your four paws up and experience the works'). In the West End, pooches are as spoiled as they are omnipresent, and it's here that you find the **Love Thy Dog** deli (985 Denman Street). To ensure no dog has to eat alone, the low round tables are designed to accommodate man and mutt. And, yes, they will do doggie bags.

The human resistance hasn't looked this pitiful since Dr Zaius caged Charlton Heston.

trafficking, as well – since the creatures of the night love a little background grit – as being home to some of the city's best nightclubs. Then the city planners got to work in the first wave of Vancouver's massively successful urban revitalisation movement, and **Yaletown** exploded. The empty warehouses became the perfect spaces for high-tech companies and new media upstarts. Artists and would-be artists alike loved the retro-fitted lofts and the empty ground-floor spaces filled up with cutting-edge boutiques and ambitious, go-for-broke restaurateur dream projects. Today the area has weathered the dot-com bust, run most of the nightclubs out to the Granville main drag, become a centre of fine dining and high-end shopping in the city, and gone from a sterile attempt at civic planning to a model of success

being copied by cities from Oregon to China. The expensive and rather trendy supermarket Urban Fare, at 177 Davie (*see p131*) has become a neighbourhood hub, but you'll find that the restaurants and stores are centred on Hamilton and Mainland streets. The area doesn't have an entirely lived-in feel yet, but David Lam Park is a green focus point for residents in the summer, and an appropriately modern contrast to the city's older and more staid recreational parks and gardens. Dress well and head off for an afternoon of shopping – the retail emphasis is definitely on clothes, which befits Yaletown's traditional role as the city's garment district – then drop by George (1137 Hamilton, *see p117*) for a cocktail and a nibble before doing the Vancouver thing and heading on to one of the area's restaurants as the evening's capper.

Stanley Park

Nature on your doorstep.

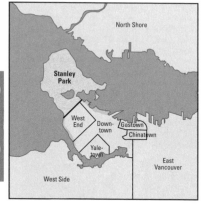

Stanley Park has been called the soul of the city and the envy of the world. At 400 hectares (988 acres) it's slightly bigger than New York's Central Park, making it the largest urban park in North America. Yet its greatest virtue is that it's almost an island, wrapped with a seawall that offers nine kilometres (5.5 miles) of spectacular waterfront views. At its heart are natural landscapes that belie the fact that almost all of the trees are second growth.

Yes, Stanley Park was logged, beginning in the 1860s. But treacherous currents along its north shore stymied plans to turn much of the area over to other forms of industry. So in 1886 Vancouver's city council was able, as its first act, to call on the federal government to transfer the peninsula to the city as a public park. Of course, some city fathers may have been trying to enhance the value of their own large, adjoining real estate holdings. But whatever their reasons, the park was created in September 1888 and dedicated the following year by Governor General Sir Frederick Arthur Stanley (who is also commemorated by ice hockey's Stanley Cup).

But Stanley Park's history is not entirely one of beauty. In 1888, smallpox wiped out the Squamish village of Khawaykhway, at the site now known as Lumberman's Arch, and the buildings were razed. Squatters lived in the park until the 1920s and even today it is populated by homeless people, with one estimate putting the summer population at 200.

It's also been the site of grisly murders. In 2001, it saw the homophobic beating to death of a man near Second Beach, where gays engage in 'trail hopping' in the woods at night. In 1953, two long-dead children were found under a woman's fur coat, next to the axe used to kill them. The tragedy has become part of the city's lore. It's also central, along with the park's homeless population, to Timothy Taylor's acclaimed 2001 novel, *Stanley Park*.

Mostly though, the park is an oasis of calm and beauty that Vancouverites and visitors are grateful to drink from. The presence of the West End's dense apartments next to an expansive rainforest provides a stunning contrast. For those wondering what the contrast might have been like if the park had never been logged, the astonishing fact is that the old forest would have been taller than many of those blocks. To see what we mean, take a look at the tree growing on the terrace atop the 17-storey, 60-metre (200-foot) Eugenia Place building at 1919 Beach Avenue, English Bay. That's the

height of the original forest. Truly, this is an age of pygmies.

Stanley Park can be divided into three sections. The more developed eastern portion, from Pipeline Road to Coal Harbour, includes the Vancouver Aquarium, the totem poles, and a children's playground, waterpark, petting zoo and miniature railway. The central portion west of Pipeline Road and north of Second Beach is a largely undeveloped tract of forest and walking trails. A smaller triangle adjoining the West End and English Bay features a public pool, pitch-and-putt golf, lawn bowling, the Fish House restaurant and a picnic area.

East from Coal Harbour

You can get to the park by bus (numbers 5, 6, 19, C21); by the Stanley Park Express Bus, which picks up from major hotels and which is free if you purchase a ticket to the aquarium or for the horse-drawn carriage; or on foot, along the Coal Harbour Seawall from the Seaplane Terminal. The latter, an easy one kilometre (half mile) stroll, affords beautiful views of the North Shore, and passes some of the city's most attractive waterfront bars and restaurants (try Lift or Carderos – *see p96*).

Most visitors to the park combine trees with ocean views by heading round the perimeter on the Seawall (or, for those confined to cars and buses, along Stanley Park Drive). Bicycles, joggers and skaters are directed anticlockwise around the park. Although the outer edge of the Seawall is reserved for pedestrians only, most walkers choose to travel in the same direction as their wheeled brethren. The circuit (about ten kilometres or six miles) takes some 45 minutes on a bike, 90 minutes of slow jogging or two to three hours of brisk walking.

As you enter the park, either from Coal Harbour or along West Georgia Street, on your left above Stanley Park Drive are statues of Lord Stanley, Queen Victoria and Robbie Burns, and the first of a handful of children's playgrounds. Below the road is the 1911 Tudor-style Vancouver Rowing Club, which fostered a strong BC rowing tradition that persists today.

A few hundred metres on, there's a rudimentary information booth at the junction of Stanley Park Drive and a spur road that leads to **Vancouver Aquarium**. Stanley Park Horse-Drawn Tours (604 681 5115, www.stanleyparktours.com) begin just east of the booth, offering hour-long carriage rides from mid March to the end of October ($20.55; $13.05-$18.65 concessions).

The essential Britishness of the park's heritage continues as you proceed east along the Seawall, past the entrance to the Royal Vancouver Yacht Club and then Deadman's Island, a native graveyard that was annexed

Sightseeing

Stanley Park.

and named the HMCS *Discovery* by the Royal Canadian Navy in 1942. To the north, Brockton Oval still features cricket and rugby matches.

Views of the city and the port – the third-largest in North America – along this stretch are stunning. In the foreground, float planes drop to the water behind the fuel barges. At dusk, the city's glass towers reflect the setting sun. If you're in the park on a late summer's evening, listen for the Nine O'Clock Gun, installed in 1894 to help ships set their chronometers, and still fired nightly.

As you swing around the Seawall at its easternmost tip, Brockton Point, there's a modest 1915 lighthouse. However, the real attraction near here is a stand of totem poles. Mostly replicas, the eight totems include one made by Haida icon Bill Reid.

Further west is Lumberman's Arch, formed by an imposing first-growth tree that, after World War II, replaced an intriguing classical-style pavilion of raw logs built in 1912 to honour Prince Arthur, the Duke of Connaught, then Canada's Governor General. The grassy

On your bike

Vancouver is a bicycle-friendly city, thanks to the temperate climate, the efforts of some city councillors and planners, and a culture that tends to value the environment.

For visitors, though, cycling is mainly for Stanley Park. In summer the Seawall throngs with bikers and bladers, who are now blessedly separated from the pedestrian traffic (look for the lane demarcations on the path; wheels get the inside track and generally overtake on the left). If you are planning to spend a day in the park, a bicycle is a very attractive travel option. There are many rental shops on Denman and Davie streets (*see below*), and several more throughout the downtown core offering a wide selection, including tandem bikes, chariots for toddlers and often inline skates. Daily rentals vary between $20 and $25 and weekly rentals between $75 and $100.

Of course, in Vancouver most people have mountain bikes, even though they never go off road. Put it down to the same cultural predisposition that gives the city so many SUVs. Mind you, if you really want to use a mountain bike for its intended purpose, you are in the right place. The North Shore is world-renowned for its extensive network of bike trails. But for most of us, cycling remains a mainly urban pursuit. The regional transport authority, TransLink (www.translink.bc.ca), publishes a route map available at most bike stores, and its website details bike access rules on buses, Seabus and SkyTrain.

Preferred destinations? The Seawall connects Stanley Park in an almost unbroken manner to a waterfront ride all the way to West Point Grey's Pacific Spirit Park, where there are lovely, mostly level forest trails. If you don't want to go that far, the route from the park along English Bay and around False Creek is a pleasant way to double the length

of a trip around the park. If you ride around to Granville Island, the charming Aquabus passenger ferry will take you and your bike back to the foot of Hornby Street downtown for a 50-cent premium on the $2.50 fare.

The Cambie Bridge has a wide bike-friendly eastern sidewalk. And while the Granville and Burrard bridges are a little narrow for comfort, the City of Vancouver is planning to dedicate two automobile lanes on the Burrard Bridge exclusively to bike traffic (a trial goes into effect in 2006). And speaking of bridges, a ride out to the centre of the Lions Gate Bridge is a detour worth considering.

For a cyclist in Vancouver, though, it's not so much a matter of where, as where not. In that regard, respect pedestrians and hikers who choose a bike-free place to walk. And watch out for drivers on their cell phones.

Bayshore Bike Rental

745 Denman Street, between Robson Street & Alberni Street, West End (604 688 2453). Bus 5. **Open** 9am-dusk daily. **Rates** $5.60/hr; $14.80/4hrs; $19.80/8hrs. **Credit** MC, V.

Denman Bike Shop

710 Denman Street, at Alberni Street, West End (604 602 9899). Bus 5. **Open** 9am-5pm daily. **Rates** $3.50/hr; $9/half day. **No credit cards.**

Spokes Bicycle Rentals

1798 W Georgia Street, at Denman Street, West End (604 688 5141/www.vancouver bikerental.com). Bus 5. **Open** 9am-dusk daily. **Rates** $3.75-$5.60/hr; $11.75-$16.82/half day. **Credit** AmEx, MC, V.

Stanley Park Cycle Rentals

768 Denman Street, at Robson Street, West End (604 688 0087). Bus 5. **Open** 10am-6pm daily. **Rates** $3.50-$5/hr. **Credit** MC, V.

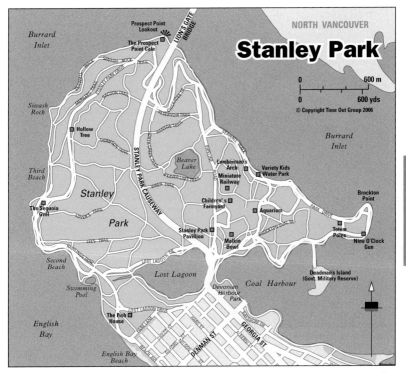

field adjoining the children's water park nearby has long been a popular picnic area. In fact, the field sits on a native 'midden' of discarded shells, a remarkable indication of its past use.

To the left is the spur road that leads up to the Aquarium and back towards Coal Harbour. This section of the park once included a modest display of animals, including a rather sad polar bear exhibit. That spectacle helped galvanise opposition to the zoo, which has been almost completely eliminated from the park. The Vancouver Aquarium, too, has its share of critics, and the last of its popular orcas was shipped off to Sea World San Diego in 2001. Tension persists over whether the remaining beluga whales provide a vital educational tool or a cruel example of imprisonment – a three-year-old born and bred in the aquarium died of causes unknown in summer 2005.

Just west of the aquarium is a 1920 monument honouring the Japanese-Canadian soldiers who served in World War I. An avenue of Kwanzen cherry trees, which bloom in March, leads to a beautiful column on a pedestal that represents a lotus flower.

Beyond the monument is the Children's Farmyard and Miniature Railway (see p144). At Hallowe'en and Christmas the railway hosts stylish, popular seasonal displays of art and theatre. Nearby, towards the park's entrance, is Malkin Bowl, built in 1933. The modest facility hosts community theatre productions in the summer, as well as the occasional concert.

Vancouver Aquarium

*Stanley Park (604 659 3474/www.vanaqua.org).
Bus 19 then 10min walk.* **Open** 10am-5.30pm daily.
Giftshop 10am-6pm daily. *Café* 10am-5pm daily.
Admission $17.50; $9.95-$12.95 concessions; free under-3s. **Credit** AmEx, MC, V. **Map** p63.
Despite public qualms over the display of captive marine mammals no one seems to care much for the feelings of fish. So while the orcas have died or been moved, and the belugas still attract controversy, the extensive displays of West Coast marine life are the core attraction. Tides and temperature make BC's coast one of the richest marine environments in the world. If you're not prepared to go scuba diving, the aquarium is the best way to see it. The displays effectively re-create a wide range of underwater BC tableaux, featuring sharks, salmon, sea otters, sea lions, seals (which you may also see in the harbour),

Lions Gate Bridge.

and more spiny, colourful rockfish than you can name. But don't forget the belugas. They are still a popular spectacle (less circus-like than it once was) and the Amazon Gallery is intriguing. Children are fascinated. So are adults, although they're less inclined to squeal. What's more, the restaurant by the beluga pool offers the best concession-style food in the park. If you're looking for the province's most popular tourist attraction, this might be it.

The central park

Tour buses flock to the northern apex of the park, Prospect Point, a high bluff with great views of First Narrows, the Coast Mountains, and Lions Gate Bridge (see p84).

If you travel west along the Seawall from Prospect Point, you pass the site of the wreck of the SS *Beaver*, which gave its name to the lake in the centre of the park. The *Beaver* was the first steamboat in the Pacific, in 1835, and came to its end near First Narrows in 1888. Its remnants are still visible during very low tides.

Alternatively, the shuttle bus takes Stanley Park Drive past the oft-photographed Hollow Tree, down to Ferguson Point, where the Sequoia Grill offers fine sunset views (see p99). At the point where the road turns from

Ferguson Point down to the relatively quiet Third Beach (which has its own modest concession stand), a cairn marks the grave of Pauline Johnson, who died in 1913. Johnson was a poet, the scion of an English mother and Mohawk father, and beloved by a Canadian and British public entranced by her exoticism. Lost Lagoon, into which she used to paddle in her canoe when it reached as far as English Bay, takes its name from one of her poems: 'O! Lure of Lost Lagoon'.

The Seawall offers a close look at a volcanic outcropping known as Siwash Rock. In *Legends of Vancouver*, Johnson recorded a story told to her by Squamish Chief Joe Capilano about its origins. As was the tradition, a young man was washing himself clean by swimming in the sea while his wife was in labour. Four supernatural men, paddling a canoe, ordered him out of their path but he would not give way. In awe at his courage, the gods turned the young man to stone so that he might live forever as a symbol of his commitment to his family.

The north-west sector of the park also offers remnants of the original forest. Most are huge stumps, and you can often see the small cuts in the sides where loggers located their springboards, to avoid cutting into the rot at the base of the tree. A few remnants are first-growth giants. Still, even the second growth forest is relatively mature, and if you're weary of the Seawall's hubbub it's easy to remove yourself into the total quiet of the forest. The canopy, consisting mainly of Douglas fir, western red cedar, spruce and alder, shelters a wide range of plants, from huckleberry and salal to the ubiquitous sword ferns.

The Siwash Rock Trail, which runs high above the Seawall from Prospect Point down to Third Beach, is one recommended route. Another is the Ravine Trail to Beaver Lake, a ten-minute walk that begins along the Seawall at the stone bridge just past Lumberman's Arch. But don't worry about which trail to take: the important thing is to plunge into the forest on foot, even if only for a few minutes. For those wanting guidance, the Lost Lagoon Nature House (604 257 8544, www.stanley parkecology.ca) in the south-east corner of the lagoon offers information, interactive displays and a range of historical and nature walks.

English Bay

As you come round towards English Bay, you enter one of the Seawall's busiest stretches, as predominantly local visitors stream into the park from the West End. The Seawall passes the summer-only, outdoor Second Beach Pool (another concession stand offers the usual drinks, hot dogs, ices, and fish and chips). Second Beach itself is a narrow stretch of sand at high tide, and usually crowded in the summer, but with the *de rigueur* spectacular view. And if you're looking for First Beach, there isn't one, though English Bay and (further south) Sunset Beach Park could claim the title.

If you want a place to stop and replenish, the Fish House on Stanley Park Drive, overlooking the charming pitch and putt golf course, is the park's best restaurant, with a pleasant deck and bar (*see p97*). From here it's just a ten-minute stroll to the West End and the shops and restaurants of busy Denman Street.

To return to the park's Georgia Street entrance walk, cycle or drive past Lost Lagoon. If you're walking or riding this way,

the obvious route is through the willows on the north shore, but there is also a rhododendron garden that stretches from the Lagoon to the pitch and putt. The lagoon has since been 'naturalised' but once every 20 years or so it gets cold enough for Vancouverites to flock out onto the lake in their ice skates.

Stanley Park
West End (www.city.vancouver.bc.ca/parks/ parks/stanley). Bus 6, 5, 19, C21.
The Stanley Park Shuttle bus service is free, with 14 stops around the perimeter of the park, from mid June-mid Sept only. Buses run every 12-15mins, 10am-6.30pm daily. The Stanley Park Express Bus (604 681 5115/www.stanleypark.com) is free with purchase of tickets to the aquarium or horse-drawn carriage, 1 May-31 Oct only.

Where the wild things are

Vancouver has a lot of animals, and we're not talking about drunken fans of the Vancouver Canucks. Most ubiquitous in Stanley Park are the eastern grey squirrels, which joined the noisy, native, brown Douglas squirrels around 1914 as a gift from New York's Central Park. Grey squirrels often come begging for nuts.

If you are keen to see a racoon, your odds are good at Prospect Point and along the north side of Lost Lagoon, where any number of well-meaning people violate park bylaws by feeding them. Racoons live throughout the city, plundering rubbish bins and eviscerating the odd housecat. You may also see a skunk. They're commonly seen at night in the West End, mainly because of the park, but can also be found, or smelled, throughout the city.

Deer and coyote both inhabit the park, but since they have become widespread through being unobtrusive you're unlikely to see one, though deer can sometimes be spotted swimming to the park from the North Shore.

Black bears have been pushed north by urban settlement, but when foraging is poor in the mountains they often make their way down into North and West Vancouver scavenging for rubbish. Although there's a chance you might glimpse one on a North Shore mountain hike, it's small. You're more likely to see one on the fringe of a dump, or from a chairlift in late spring or summer.

Cougars, occasionally a threat to people in isolated parts of the province, are also sometimes present on the North Shore. In the late 1980s, one confused animal somehow ended up in the Pacific Coliseum in Vancouver's Hastings Park.

Bald eagles offer far easier wildlife spotting opportunities. In the city, they're often seen being harassed by a small murder of crows. In December and January it's worth the hour's drive north towards Squamish to the Brackendale Eagle Reserve (*see p215*), where they congregate in thousands to feast on salmon that have spawned and died. Another birder's paradise, particularly from October to December, is the Reifel Migratory Bird Sanctuary (5191 Robertson Road, 604 946 6980, www.reifelbirdsanctuary.com) 30 minutes south of the city centre in Ladner.

One of Stanley Park's common spectacles is the great blue heron, a dozen of which roost in the trees near the Park Board office in the south-eastern corner of the park. They're big – a metre tall with a two-metre wingspan (three feet by six feet) – and can often be seen at close range making an ungainly landing along the shoreline. Further bird life can be spotted by looking out across the ocean, where you're guaranteed coal-black cormorants perched along the rocks.

Around Lost Lagoon, along with the mallards, wood ducks and non-native mute swans, is a small resident population of Canada Geese. In fact, their numbers got so out of control a decade ago, after they began over-wintering in the park, that they often stopped rush-hour traffic with their processional marches across Georgia Street and the Stanley Park Causeway.

And then there are the flocks of brazen, scavenging seagulls. If you're eating a hot dog anywhere in Stanley Park, watch your back, and guard your wiener.

Sightseeing

VanDusen Gardens.
See p74 **Blooming marvellous.**

The West Side

Museums, long sandy beaches and Granville Island Market.

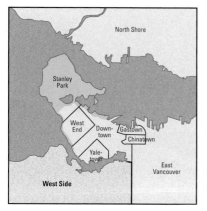

Visitors who base themselves in the West End are puzzled to look south across English Bay to what locals call 'the West Side'. (Even more confusingly, West Vancouver is a satellite on the North Shore). For many, the short journey across Burrard or Granville bridges is a psychological block to further exploration, although the small passenger ferries running from the Aquatic Centre or from David Lam Park to Granville Island and Vanier Park make getting there simple and fun.

A pretty residential area that includes laid-back Kitsilano, affluent Point Grey and the elite Shaughnessy, the West Side makes the most of its long, sandy beaches and spectacular views of the city's gleaming glass towers, set off by Stanley Park to the left and the mountains behind. Strict planning controls and residents keen to preserve the neighbourhood have kept out the big box stores that blight so many North American suburbs, and there is a 12-metre (40-foot) height restriction on new building projects.

The obvious tourist attractions are Granville Island, the beaches, the museums in Vanier Park and the world class Museum of Anthropology at the University of British Columbia (UBC). This area also includes some of the finest public gardens in North America. But if you want to get a real taste of the life on the West Side, throw away your tour schedule and simply take a quiet stroll…

Sightseeing

Granville Island

A lot of history is packed onto this small parcel of land under the Granville Street Bridge, *pictured p73*. Coming from downtown, take one of the ferries that run across False Creek to the island year round. You could try driving, but to blend in you'll have to find a free spot to leave your car. Vancouverites will circle Granville Island for 20 minutes rather than pay to park.

Granville Island dock.

Granville Public Market. *See p69.*

Granville Island isn't really an island, and False Creek is so-called because it isn't a stream, it's a long, narrow inlet extending from English Bay. That's the result of a lot of very deliberate engineering and digging. In 1915, crews started dredging 760,000 cubic metres of mud out of the marshy coastline to create Vancouver's harbour. They dumped most of that mud in one place, creating what was called Industrial Island when it opened in 1916. Its name was apt; tenants were businesses such as Vulcan Ironworks, Wallace Shipyards, coal companies, rope makers and sawmills. The island was a rail terminal and shipping nexus, and the buildings that housed many of those businesses are still here.

By the early 1970s its industry was fading, and a series of fires destroyed the remaining businesses. Starting in 1973, the city worked to transform Granville Island into a mixed-use commercial and social centre. That renaissance was completed in 1979 with the opening of the Granville Public Market with its emphasis on local BC produce (*see p128* **Granville Island**, *pictured p68*). The market opens at 9am. Arrive before 10.30am to avoid the crowds.

There are a couple of mini-museums here, though they're not what you might expect. Conveniently, they're at the same address, the Granville Island Museum (1502 Duranleau Street, 604 683 1939). One features model trains, another displays model boats and a third focuses on sport fishing. Less esoteric, perhaps, the Emily Carr College of Art and Design (1399 Johnston Street, 604 844 3800) is one of the finest art schools on the continent; its gallery and café are open to the public, as are many of the artist studios along Railspur Alley. This is also a lively fringe theatre spot, with licensed buskers and occasional outdoor shows.

There is no shortage of snack stops amid Granville Island's warren of boutiques, galleries and craft stores. Bridges Restaurant (1696 Duranleau Street, 604 687 4400, www.bridges restaurant.com) is a local landmark for its bright yellow exterior and patio overlooking the marina, but there's an equally fine view looking east towards Science World from Dockside Restaurant and Brewery in the Granville Island Hotel (1253 Johnson Street, 604 685 7070, www.docksidebrewing.com). And if you have children don't miss Sutcliffe Park, behind the Kids Market, with its water park slides, duck pond and lush green space (*see p145* **Water babies**). The more active can rent a kayak to explore False Creek and English Bay (Ecomarine Kayak, 1668 Duranleau Street, 604 689 7575, www.ecomarine.com). Before you sign up for whale watching, be aware that this involves a drive to Steveston or further.

Kitsilano

Running west from Burrard Street as far as Alma, and south from the Burrard Inlet to 16th Avenue, Kitsilano (or 'Kits') was named by the Canadian Pacific Railway in 1904 for Chief Khahtsahlanough of the coastal Salish First Nations. It's doubtful the natives appreciated the honour. Three years earlier the government had displaced them – including August Jack, Khahtsahlanough's grandson – from their settlement at Sun'ahk, in the vicinity of what is now Vanier Park.

A popular destination for day-trippers who would row across English Bay to partake of the long, attractive beach – still the area's prime attraction – Kits was developed more slowly than downtown. It became home both to workers in the False Creek sawmills and to the upper middle classes (who gravitated west to Point Grey and south to Shaughnessy).

In the 1960s and early '70s Kits became a hippie hangout, Vancouver's very own Haight-Ashbury. The neighbourhood's main thoroughfare, 4th Avenue retains some of the groovalicious attitude of those days, although it has become quite gentrified with an influx of maternity and baby stores vying with sports and yoga boutiques. For a taste of its former

Get your kit off on **Kitsilano Beach**.

ragged glory, head to Sophie's Cosmic Café (*see p104*) at 4th and Arbutus Street, its walls bedecked in yard sale treasures. Across the street, browse at Zulu Records (1972 W 4th Avenue, 604 738 3232, *see p134*) a genuine indie haunt, or further west, sample 24-hour vegetarian fare at the popular Naam (*see p108*). Vancouver's coolest video rental store is another neighbourhood fixture: Videomatica (1855 W 4th Avenue, 604 734 0411, www.video matica.bc.ca) stocks the sort of stuff, interalia, Blockbuster wouldn't touch.

Walk on the West Side

Start: Granville Island.
Finish: Cornwall Avenue at Point Grey Road.
Length: 3 kilometres (2 miles) approximately.
Time: 60-90 minutes – longer if you visit the museums.

This scenic coastal walk (or easy cycle) affords romantic views, great beaches, and – if you have the cultural stamina to go with your cardio-vascular fortitude – takes in three of the city's more notable museums. Kicking off on the south side of Granville Island (*see p67*) you will have to resist the lure of the upmarket furniture and antiques stores further along South Granville Street and instead bear west (right) down Island Park Walk beside the marina.

The government dock here is an excellent place to buy seafood and open-air chippie Go Fish (*see p104*) is one of the city's best kept secrets. Alternatively you might also take a short diversion up Anderson Road to 1540 W 2nd Avenue, to see the Waterfall Building, an innovative mixed-use building of glass, cement, steel and water from Vancouver's own Arthur Erickson (*see p54* **The space man**). The courtyard is open to the public and there are galleries among the ground floor offices. Cutting down Mariner Walk will bring you back to Island Park Walk and the Seawall.

Sticking to the Seawall, and what is officially known as the False Creek Urban Heritage Trail, you will pass underneath the Burrard Bridge, opened in 1932 (in 2006 the City plans to dedicate two of its six traffic lanes to cyclists on a trial basis). You are now on the eastern edge of **Vanier Park**. It's pronounced VAN-yay, and named for Georges Vanier, Canada's Governor-General from 1959 through 1967, the time during which Canada became less a British colony and more of a sovereign nation. His bilingualism and commitment to the country's youth made him a popular figure, and it's probably the main reason so many schools and parks across Canada are named after him. If you're going through Vanier Park anytime between the beginning of June and the end of September, look for the white tents or listen for the Elizabethan cadences of the Bard on the Beach Shakespeare festival (*see p138*), one of Western Canada's largest celebrations of William of Avon. Any time of year, further west, look for Ray Bethell flying his kites: three of them – each red, white and blue. His mix of simultaneous precision control and improvisational aerobatics is inspiring and almost impossible not to smile at.

The white building that looks like a flying saucer to your left houses the **MacMillan Space Centre** (*see p142*) – with plenty of rainy day activities for young families, including a planetarium – and the Vancouver Museum which is currently undergoing a major refit. Apparently architect Gerald Hamilton intended the dome to evoke a coastal Salish hat. The entrance, with its popular giant crab fountain, is on the south side. The Gordon MacMillan Southam Observatory (www.hrmacmillanspacecentre. com/observatory) is tucked around the corner, and open from sunset to midnight Friday & Saturday when the skies are clear.

On the headland Kits Point, looking out over English Bay, there's the **Vancouver Maritime Museum** (*see p142*) with a yellow bathyscaph in its backyard. Inside the A-frame building you'll find the *St Roch*, an arctic patrol vessel with plenty of history of its own (the first vessel to navigate the Nortwest Passage in both directions). The dock to the right of the museum is a ferry stop in summer months, offering rides back to the Aquatic Centre and Granville Island; 'Dog beach' to the left, allows canines to run off-leash.

On the south face of the Maritime Museum look for the bald eagles who like to perch singly or in tandem on the tall (30.5 metres, 100 feet) Mungo Martin totem pole – a replica of a pole presented to Queen Elizabeth II in 1958. Continue your walk around the headland towards Kitsilano Beach. If it's raining, look for a boulder inscribed with some rainy day philosophy. If the sun is shining, the beach will likely be clogged with volleyball games, and the path

West Broadway (five blocks south) is the other main shopping street, but it's not really worth taking the trouble to walk along until you get as far west as Macdonald Street. Between there and Alma there's a sprinkling of good second-hand bookstores, the cavernous

Kidsbooks at 3083 W Broadway (604 738 5335, www.kidsbooks.bc.ca), independent shoe and clothing outlets, and numerous restaurants including many unpretentious Greek tavernas and a couple of good Mediterranean delis (this is the city's Greek enclave). Back east a couple

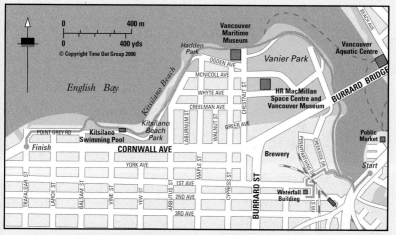

heaving with cyclists, in-line skaters, and pushchairs. The water here is allegedly the warmest in the bay, but the Kits body-beautiful brigade generally prefer to lounge against the logs provided for this purpose.

Walking south adjacent to the beach you'll get to the newly rebuilt Kits Beach restaurant, the Watermark. A handsome glass-fronted structure that opened in the summer of 2005, it boasts a restaurant upstairs with great vistas to the north and west, and a cheaper concessions bar underneath, selling fish and chips, sushi and snacks (*see p109*). Alternatively it's a only a five-minute walk to Yew Street, climbing the hill away from the water towards 4th Avenue, with its own cluster of cafés, pubs and restaurants.

If you've a mind to keep going along the Seawall, the path takes you past the open-air Kitsilano Pool – the longest in the country, at 137 meters (450 feet). It's open from mid May through to Labor Day (the first Monday in September), and the water is chlorinated saltwater. If you don't feel like swimming, instead admire the breeze-driven *Wind Swimmer* whirligig sculpture – known as 'Ann on a Fan' – at the eastern end of the pool, or the yoga practitioners or performers who may have taken over the stage of the Kitsilano

Showboat, an amphitheatre up against the pool. Fifty years ago, this was the venue for one of the first rock 'n' roll hops in the country – it drew thousands of teenagers and made headline news.

Sticking to the beaches, you could continue along the relatively wild Trafalgar, followed by Jericho, Locarno, Spanish Banks, Point Grey and Towers – each a little bit less manicured than the last – all the way up to the University of British Columbia campus, the Museum of Anthropology and the infamous Wreck Beach (*see p72* **Skinny dipping**) – about eight kilometres (five miles) in all.

However, for our purposes: climb the stairs on the left and turn right on to Point Grey Road. A leafy, generous curve, this quiet section of Point Grey Road boasts the beautifully refurbished homes of the local wealthy elite. Though those on the north side of the street are actually best viewed from the Seawall below, a stroll along this stretch gives a feel for how exclusive the neighbourhood (which includes the Kitsilano Yacht Club) really is. This is where scientist and environmentalist David Suzuki lives. Where Point Grey Road intersects with Cornwall Avenue, take a number 2 or 22 bus back over the Burrard Bridge to Downtown.

of blocks three highly rated eateries – Lumière (2551 W Broadway, 604 739 8185, www.lumiere.ca, *see p104*), Feenie's (2563 W Broadway, 604 739 7115, www.feenies.com, *see p103*) and Mistral (2585 W Broadway, 604 733 0046, *see p105*) sit along one strip, making for a veritable gastronomic grand prix.

From Alma Street walk a block south (stopping off for a cinnamon bun at Grounds For Coffee) and you'll soon hit the beginnings of a more upscale neighbourhood shopping street along West 10th Avenue. Or for a breath of ocean air, turn north and walk the few blocks down to Jericho beach and its views over Burrard Inlet and across to the North Shore.

Incidentally, the tree-themed street names running north-south between 4th and W Broadway were originally supposed to run alphabetically, from Alder to Yew, but the Canadian Pacific Railway surveyor Lauchlan Alexander Hamilton was out of town when his draughtsmen drew up the plans for the streets, beginning at Ash and proceeding randomly through Heather, Willow, Laurel and so forth.

If you decide to visit Kitsilano, it is only a ten-minute taxi ride from downtown across Burrard Bridge, or, even better, you can take the passenger ferry from the Aquatic Centre (1050 Beach Avenue, at the south end of Thurlow Street) to Vanier Park (False Creek Ferries, www.granvilleislandferries.bc.ca, daily Apr-Oct, weekends only in winter, $2.50-$5). Bus routes 2, 4, 7, 16, 17 and 22 run between Kitsilano and downtown.

Skinny dipping

If there is a single place in Vancouver to experience the west coast lifestyle, Wreck Beach is probably it. Canada's only and thus infamous nudist beach affords a panoramic view of the ocean and distant San Juan Islands, half a mile of sandy shore on which to bare your bunnies to the temperate air, a backdrop of coniferous forest containing Vancouver's only remaining old growth, and the occasional eagle to remind you that you're at the edge of wilderness. It also features more dreadlocks than you can shake a stick at, a carnival atmosphere at weekends, and tuneful, partially clothed hawkers who sell everything from Chinese steamed rolls ('Get your hands on my nice hot buns!') to pot cookies made by Wreck's most famous regular, British Columbia marijuana poster girl, Watermelon.

The beach is divided by tradition into three areas: at the bottom of the access stairs, turn right to reach the quieter family section, left towards the driftwood towers and the sound of bongo drums for party central (and your best access to comestible substances); head all the way past the vendor stations to the far left to find the gay area. Wandering hawkers and semi-permanent kiosks sell everything from tie-dyed T-shirts to tarot readings to daiquiris. Consumed discreetly, almost anything goes, though you're likely to get told off if you ask anyone for crack or crystal meth: 'We don't do that shit down here.' Since 2003, Mary's Wave Massage has offered dollar-a-minute de-stressing by a tanned and friendly blonde in a hula skirt (every day except Wednesdays, Fridays and rainy days). Stormin' Norman's Spirit Grill (in business since 1981) sells tasty dress-your-own veggie, beef and wild game burgers for $6, and, at a premium, a few handy supplies like rolling papers and sunscreen.

While the most spectacular views at Wreck may involve the clientele rather than the scenery, beach etiquette requires you not to gawk. Yes, everybody casts a discreet glance now and again, and that well-oiled South Asian Fabio parading his prodigious goods up and down the strand probably wants to be looked at – but don't ogle. Overt sexual activity is also unacceptable. Visit www.wreckbeach.org for more notes on etiquette. Not everyone goes starkers: the word is clothing-optional, so dress for your own comfort.

Getting there

Located at the far west end of the University of British Columbia, Wreck Beach is separated from the campus by a steep but well maintained stairway officially known as Trail 6. There's parking (cheap at weekends, pricey mid-week) beside the Place Vanier residences off Northwest Marine Drive; or take the convenient 99 bus to its terminus at University Bus Loop, follow University Boulevard downhill to Marine Drive, cross Marine Drive, and take the roadside trail to the right. A minute's walk will find you at the head of the stairway, where it's a good idea to buy water from the vendor whose sign announces 'Best Prices at Wreck Beach': it's true, and once you're settled on the sand in your skivvies, you won't want to ascend those multitudinous stairs till it's time to leave.

Granville Street Bridge. *See p67.*

University of British Columbia (UBC)

Apart from the Museum of Anthropology, don't miss the Botanical and Nitobe gardens (*see p74* **Blooming marvellous**), the Chan Centre for the Performing Arts, and the surrounding National Endowment Lands.

Museum of Anthropology

6393 NW Marine Drive, at West Mall (604 822 5087/ www.moa.ubc.ca). Bus 4, 17, 44 then 10min walk. **Open** *Sept-May* 11am-9pm Tue; 11am-5pm Wed-Sun. *May-Sept* 10am-9pm Tue; 10am-5pm Wed-Sun. **Admission** $9; $7 seniors and students; free under-6s. Free 5-9pm Tue year round. **Credit** MC, V.

Canada's largest teaching museum, and arguably Vancouver's only truly world-class cultural institution, the Museum of Anthropology began life in the 1920s in the basement of the UBC library. Designed by Arthur Erickson in 1976, the current building is an ingenious amalgam of concrete and glass, modelled to reflect traditional wooden west coast post-and-beam structures. Look through the soaring glass walls of the Great Hall and you'll see some of them in the re-creation of two Haida longhouses in the museum's grounds. These windows allow the Great Hall's range of aboriginal sculptures, totem poles, feast dishes and masks to be admired in natural light. You are also encouraged to touch some exhibits, notably Bill Reid's cedar bear and sea wolf.

Reid (1920-1998) is considered the museum's most important artist, and his history is indivisible from

Blooming marvellous

The West End has Stanley Park, but the West Side boasts the highest concentration of spectacular public gardens in Canada. With its relatively mild winters and temperate climate, the lower mainland is fertile ground for a wider range of plants than eastern provinces can support. The **VanDusen Gardens**, on the edge of Shaughnessy at 37th Avenue and Oak Street, is rated one of the best botanical gardens in the world. Although this former golf course hasn't the geological interest of Vancouver Island's

gaudy Butchart Gardens, VanDusen's 55 acres are a horticultural delight; re-creating an astonishing array of eco-systems from the Far East, Africa, South America, Europe and Australasia. The Rhododendron Walk and Sino-Himalayan Garden are standouts. But there are many gems – including gardens devoted (separately) to roses, herbs and heathers. And there's an Elizabethan hedge maze tucked away in the western corner. The features are set among hillocks, pocket lakes and winding paths, all with a northward view of the city and mountains. A dazzling Christmas Festival of Lights, woven through the garden, draws families through December. The site includes a large garden shop and the Shaughnessy Restaurant for fine, casual dining (reservations are recommended: 604 261 0011).

East of VanDusen Gardens, at the summit of Queen Elizabeth Park (itself the city's highest point), a spacious geodesic dome houses the **Bloedel Floral Conservatory**. Step from the (usually) cool park air into the climate-controlled conservatory to experience it. Born in Victoria, on Vancouver Island, in 1920, to a European-Canadian father and Haida mother, he initially knew nothing of his First Nations ancestry. It was later, when studying jewellery-making at Ryerson in Toronto that he became fascinated with the art of the north-west coast. Reid devoted himself to exploring the visual vocabulary of the Haida, working with the last practitioners among the older generation, notably the wood carver Mungo Martin (1881-1962). Reid worked with the UBC Department of Anthropology on totem pole salvage and restoration, and gradually became a near permanent fixture there. His own work ranges from the most intricate jewellery to the monumental – like the huge jade canoe *Spirit of the Haida Gwaii* sculpture in the international departures hall of Vancouver airport and the arching bronze *Lord of the Under Sea* out-side the aquarium in Stanley Park. *Raven and the First Men*, a large yellow cedar sculpture depicting a Haida creation myth, gets pride of place in the museum, in its own artfully lit rotunda. By his death in 1998, Reid was credited with resurrecting a Native Canadian art form that had almost been obliterated.

In addition to works by Reid and Martin, the museum showcases beautiful carvings from First Nations communities of the Pacific Northwest. Even before you get inside you pass two imposing figures by Musqueam and Nuu-chah-nulth artists, and the magnificent wooden doors are by four Gitxsan wood workers, dating from 1976. Collections from Africa, Asia, Central America and further afield sometimes sit strangely with the local artefacts, but the museum's visible storage is another treasure trove, allowing the public to browse through 13,000 objects.

an environment that runs from tropical rainforest with trickling water to bone-dry desert with exotic palms. More than 100 birds – including Charlie the (charismatic) Cockatoo – fly free. Myriad blooms add to the colour. Below the dome lies the park's well-loved Quarry Garden – the site looks over the downtown peninsula – and there is a rose garden on the park's southern slope.

The **UBC Botanical Garden**, on the University of British Columbia campus, is a somewhat hidden (and sizeable) jewel. The garden sprawls over 110 wildly distinctive acres with, at one extremity, an Asian garden with rare rhododendrons and, at another, an alpine rockery growing rare vines and dwarf conifers. Other features include the Physic Garden, with plants from England's Chelsea Physic Garden, and the Food Garden, with elaborately espaliered fruit trees. The site can be walked briskly in 90 minutes. An extensive trail system includes the Walk in the Woods through an undisturbed second-growth forest.

Also at UBC, a five minute stroll from the Museum of Anthropology, is the smaller **Nitobe Memorial Garden**. An exquisite Japanese garden named for scholar-statesman Dr Inazo Nitobe, this tranquil haven is an authentic expression of Japanese garden artistry and philosophy. Cherry trees bloom in spring, irises in summer (by the arched wooden bridge); in autumn, leaves create a spectacular effect. The site includes a traditional teahouse, with occasional openings for a formal tea ceremony.

All the gardens are wheelchair accessible, although most paths are unpaved.

Bloedel Floral Conservatory

Off Cambie Street and W 33rd Avenue (604 257 8570/www.city.vancouver.bc.ca/ parks/parks/bloedel). Bus 15. **Open** *9am-8pm Mon-Fri; 10am-9pm Sat, Sun.* **Admission** *$4.25; $2-$3.20 concessions; free under-6s.* **Credit** *AmEx, MC, V.*

Nitobe Memorial Garden

1903 West Mall, off NW Marine Drive (604 822 6038/www.nitobe.org). Bus 4, 17, 44 then 10min walk. **Open** *Mid Mar-Thanksgiving 10am-6pm daily. Thanksgiving-mid Mar 10am-2.30pm Mon-Fri.* **Admission** *Mid Mar-Thanksgiving $4; $2.50-$3 concessions; free under-6s; $8 double-entry with UBC Botanical Garden. Thanksgiving-mid Mar free.* **Credit** *MC, V.*

The UBC Botanical Garden

6804 SW Marine Drive, at W 16th Avenue (604 822 9666/www.ubcbotanical garden.org). Bus 4, 17, 44 then 15min walk. **Open** *Mid Mar-Thanksgiving 10am-6pm daily. Thanksgiving-mid Mar 10am-sunset daily.* **Admission** *Mid Mar-Thanksgiving $6; $3-$4 concessions; free under-6s; $8 double-entry with Nitobe Memorial Garden. Thanksgiving-mid Mar free.* **Credit** *MC, V.*

VanDusen Botanical Garden

5251 Oak Street, at W 37th Avenue (604 878 9274/www.vandusengarden.org). Bus 17. **Open** *10am-sunset daily.* **Admission** *Apr-Sept $7.75; $4-$5.50 concessions; free under-6s; $18 family. Oct-Mar $5.50; $2.25-$3.75 concessions; free under-6s; $12 family.* **Credit** *AmEx, MC, V.*

Sightseeing

East Vancouver

Get off the tourist track to find Vancouver's bohemian East Side.

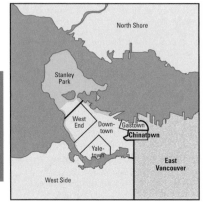

In case you're wondering, Vancouver's cross-streets are designated east or west according to their relationship with Main Street. Main is one of the oldest thoroughfares in the city, dating from 1888, and initially connecting mill workers' homes in Mount Pleasant with the factories and city wharf on Burrard Inlet. While the West Side attracts wealthier citizens, **East Vancouver** has always been a diverse area where a succession of immigrants have lived before moving on to other parts of the city. Its mixed neighbourhoods – including Commercial Drive, Main Street to the Punjabi Market,

Strathcona and, closest to downtown, Chinatown (which, in fact, bears West Side addresses, but East Side attributes) – are places to experience daily life on Canada's west coast. It's not about tourist attractions; here's where people shop, eat and hang out, paint their homes purple and show folk art on front lawns.

Chinatown

Vancouver's **Chinatown**, the third largest in North America (after New York and San Francisco), is a busy marketplace crammed with restaurants, tea houses, grocers, exotic interior-design stores, and souvenir and pop-culture shops. Chinese music echoes in the street and pigs barbecued orange glisten from hooks in shop windows. Chinatown is bounded by Pender, Union, Gore and Carrall Streets, with the historic core found along Pender and Keefer. Avoid Hastings Street, where Canada's worst skid row thrives.

Vancouver's Chinese haven't had it easy and you can still see traces of a dark past. In the 1880s, low-paid Chinese labourers settled in a ghetto in the Pender Street area. There were two race riots and a hefty immigration tax made it near impossible to bring family over. Opium was the preferred vice; as many as eight opium factories operated in Vancouver in 1889. But by the turn of the century a merchant class had emerged, and various clans began to construct the area's impressive, southern China-

Dr Sun Yat-Sen Classical Chinese Garden. *See p77.*

style architecture. Typically these buildings contained a storefront with closet-sized rooms to house the poor on the first and second floors. Stricter by-law enforcement in the 1970s reduced the number of residences in these heritage buildings, but their use remains relatively unchanged.

The **Chinese Cultural Centre** (50 E Pender Street, 604 658 8865, www.cccvan. com) offers a free brochure describing all of Chinatown's heritage buildings, including its oldest, the 1889 Wing Sang Building (51 E Pender Street). Most visitors though, head straight for the world's narrowest commercial building, the **Sam Kee Company**.

Across the street **Dr Sun Yat-Sen Classical Chinese Garden** is a major Vancouver attraction. The first of its kind created outside China, the garden is a near-exact replica of a Ming-Dynasty scholar's retreat. The adjacent Dr Sun Yat-Sen Park, where admission is free, provides a hint of the enchantment next door. At the end of the park, the **Chinese Cultural Centre Museum and Archives** (555 Columbia Street, 604 658 8880) displays the history of Chinese-Canadians in Vancouver.

Afterwards, walk up Keefer and slip into Ten Ren Tea & Ginseng Co (550 Main Street, 604 684 1566), an oasis of calm with a bewildering number of infusions and free tastings. Then hit the streets to explore Chinatown's shops (where ginseng can go for $10 to $400 an ounce) and, on Friday nights in summer, the **Chinatown Night Market** (see p133).

Since the 1980s, the suburb of Richmond has become a major base for Vancouver's quarter-million Chinese population, and while the general consensus may give it the culinary honours, there's still plenty of gustatory satisfaction to be had in Chinatown. Floata Seafood Restaurant (400-180 Keefer Street, 604 602 0368), Canada's largest eatery, serves up dim sum, dinner for two, or elaborate 12-course banquets for 1,000 people. Maxim's Bakery Restaurant (257 Keefer Street, 604 687 0949) is the place for hot buns or sit-down dishes, Hon's Wun-Tun House (see p102) is a perennial award-winner for best Chinese restaurant meal under $10 and Park Lok (544 Main Street, 604 688 1581) attracts regulars for its palate-blowing Peking duck.

Dr Sun Yat-Sen Classical Chinese Garden

578 Carrall Street, at Keefer Street (604 662 3207/ www.vancouverchinesegarden.com). Bus 10, 16, 20. **Open** *15 June-31 Aug* 9.30am-7pm daily. *Sept, May-14 June* 10am-6pm daily. *Oct* 10am-4.30pm daily. *Nov-Apr* 10am-4.30pm Tue-Sun. **Admission** $8.75/ $7 concessions. **Credit** MC, V. **Map** p249 M4.
Constructed in 1986 using traditional methods – no

nails or power tools – this magnificent garden features rare rockery and architectural materials, horticulture similar to Chinese gardens and jade-green waterways. Exquisite courtyards and pavilions are connected by a maze of covered walkways and bridges. Simultaneously gaudy and serene, the retreat abounds with Buddhist, Confucian and Taoist symbolism. A guided tour sheds light on why pavilion rooftops arch to the sky, tiled walkways zig-zag, and the pine leans over the water. **Photo** *p76.*

Sam Kee Company

8 W Pender Street, at Carrall Street. Bus 10, 16, 20. **Map** p249 M3.
A private accounting business operates here but visitors can view it through large exterior windows. Chang Toy, who dominated early trade in Chinatown, originally owned a nine-metre (30-ft) lot on this site, but most of it was appropriated in 1912 to widen Pender Street. Indignant that he wasn't paid for the rest, Chang went ahead and built his 1.8m (six ft) office anyway, maintaining the original size below the street. Glass block windows to his basement rooms are embedded in the sidewalk.

Strathcona

Vancouver's oldest neighbourhood, **Strathcona** occupies a spit of land just east of Main Street and Chinatown. Age is no barrier to cool, however, as it's now the hippest parish in the city. Stroll or cycle through the quiet, tree-lined streets and take in the plethora of arty 19th- and early 20th-century homes: there's not much else to do here other than snack at the down-homey Union Food Market (810 Union Street, 604 255 5025) or Benny Foods Ltd (598 Union Street, 604 254 2746). But you never know who you'll run into. During the autumn Culture Crawl, artists open their studios for a three-day procession of gawkers and in the spring, Strathcona Artist at Home is a performance arts festival with homes as venues. And to think Strathcona (bounded by Pender and Prior Streets, Campbell and Jackson Avenues), was up for demolition. Luckily, residents mobilised in opposition, but not before 15 blocks had already been razed. Those public housing projects surrounding the area? Brought to you by the 1950s.

Main Street

Once known as Antique Row, **Main Street** has adopted a newer, fresher character. Indeed, Main has made a comeback and it's now one of the most happening areas in the city.

The street has three areas of interest: Broadway and Main's galleries, shops and cafés; Vancouver's indie fashion district squeezed in from 19th to 21st Avenues; and Antique Row between 20th and 30th Avenues.

Chopping Block.

CDs (3561 Main Street, 604 324 1229), which houses several thousand vinyl LPs, from 78s to Arcade Fire. Vancouver's famed Antique Row begins just south of here. Many stores feature traditional antiques and 20th-century nostalgia, ranging from art deco accessories to 1950s and '60s kitschy retro items.

Time for drinks, live music and food? Cottage Bistro (4468 Main Street, 604 876 6138), Purple Crab (3916 Main Street, 604 484 2436) and Café Montmartre (4362 Main Street, 604 879 8111) will cater to your needs.

Savvy, youthful enterprise characterises Main Street, especially around Broadway, where queues form outside Foundation (2301 Main Street, 604 708 0881, see p112), a tofu-meets-electronica experience, and Budgies (44 Kingsway, 604 874 5408), a closet-sized cheap burrito joint with more bad velvet paintings than a grandmother's house in Vegas.

At Main and 8th Avenue, Lark (152 E 8th Avenue, 604 879 5275) offers imaginative, locally made clothes, while across the street, Wink (151 E 8th Avenue, 604 676 8994) serves a healthy deli spread to tunes by Thievery Corporation. If you see anyone getting a hair-do next door at Chopping Block (155 E 8th Avenue, 778 371 2467), they're probably famous; the clientele is a who's who of the art scene. Elaborate stained glass, chandeliers and antiques crowd the internationally renowned Architectural Antiques at Main and 8th (2403 Main Street, 604 872 3131).

Two small galleries catering to emerging artists, Dadabase (183 E Broadway, 604 709 9934, www.dadabase.ca) and Blanket Gallery (4-2414 Main Street, 604 709 6100, www.blanket gallery.com), are worth a look. Slickity Jim's Chat & Chew (2513 Main Street, 604 873 6760) is a legendary all-day breakfast spot; if you're not hungry, pop in for a look at the wild paraphernalia on its red walls. Two blocks east of Main, on 8th, Vancouver's first artist-run centre, Western Front (303 E 8th Avenue, 604 876 9343), features an art gallery, performance hall and multi-media studios.

Further up Main, indulge in a fashion-as-art aesthetic in several clothing stores offering fresh local designs (see p127 **Streetlife**). Music lovers should check out Neptoon Records &

Punjabi Market

It can take hours to explore this vibrant, little version of India, a four-block area at Main Street and 49th Avenue, where exotic Indian groceries, Bollywood-loaded video stores, over-the-top jewellery shops and sari emporiums stuffed with dazzling embroidered silk cater to Vancouver's approximately 125,000 Indian immigrants. Hungry? Try the all-you-can-eat buffets offered for a mere $7.50 at both All India Sweets and Restaurant (6507 Main Street, 604 327 0891) and Himalaya Restaurant (6587 Main Street, 604 324 6514). The two eateries compete in presenting excellent curries, the most colours at a dessert counter and the cheesiest pop music videos. On the corner at Delhi Pan Centre (209-6692 Main Street, 604 327 0358), you can stock up on areca nut and betel.

Commercial Drive

Cafés, delis, unique shops and its cosmopolitan, constituency make '**The Drive**' a diverse street experience. The faintly shabby, funky enclave was originally called 'Little Italy', but it's now Vancouver's most bohemian neighbourhood.

Still, a visitor may be more impressed with the variety of ethnic shops and restaurants the 15-block street supports, including Jamaican, Ethiopian and Moroccan cafés, Thai fast food, Spanish tapas bars, Portuguese coffee shops, sushi joints, organic and Chinese grocers, Italian tailors, French bakeries and the requisite hipster clothing shops. You can do a virtual tour at www.thedrive.ca and the area is easily accessed from the SkyTrain stop at Broadway and Commercial Drive.

The action doesn't really get going until five blocks north of the SkyTrain, but you'll pass Café Deux Soleils first (2096 Commercial Drive, see p119), which serves fortifying breakfasts, afternoon pints, live music and slam poetry. There's something like a culinary Expo between 5th and 6th Avenues, each shop crammed with a different nationality of food. Bibliophile (2012 Commercial Drive, 604 254

5520) and Audiopile (2016 Commercial Drive, 604 253 7453) should appease book and record collectors, while foodies must slip into the sensory heaven that is First Ravioli Store (1900 Commercial Drive, 604 255 8844), an Italian deli with hand-rolled pastas and imported treats galore. Speaking of celestial experiences, Fratelli's (1795 Commercial Drive, 604 255 8926) serves up angelic cream puffs.

Most arrive at the Drive to stock up on giant cans of olive oil and organic groceries, and then to caffeinate. Coffee is a serious undertaking here. You'll pass JJ Bean, Prado, Calabria and the Continental Café before crossing 1st Avenue, then Roma's, Joe's, Turks and at least a dozen others, each with their own faithful clients.

Gelato is another indulgence; Dolce Amore (1590 Commercial Drive, 604 258 0006) and Gelato Time (1110 Commercial Drive, 604 251 4426) draw a steady stream of ice-cream fanatics, but nothing like the mayhem that accosts La Casa Gelato (several industrial-wasteland blocks west of the Drive, at 1033 Venables Street, 604 251 3211) every summer when ice-cream fiends descend from all over the globe to sample some 209 flavours, including garlic, lavender, basil and hot chilli.

Highlife Records (1317 Commercial Drive, 604 251 6964), respected for its discerning collection of world and pop music, and the adjacent Magpie, with the most diverse range of magazines in the city, are worthy perusals, as is Beckwoman's (1314 Commercial Drive, 604 254 8056), a brimming hippie's paradise of crystals, moonstones and trinkets.

House-browsers should hike east on any of the streets north of 1st Avenue to view the large, colourful, early-20th century homes of Vancouver's first suburb. At Victoria Park (between Kitchener and Grant Streets), try to figure out who's winning at *bocce*, played daily by the elderly denizens of Little Italy. Back on the Drive, Grandview Park (at Napier Street) hosts mini-lawn sales, music jams, hyperactive kids and events, such as the Parade of the Lost Souls (Saturday before Hallowe'en, to 'honour the dead, wake the living and overcome our fears') and July's Bare-Breast Fest.

In the evenings, the Drive comes alive with nightly live entertainment in Rime (*see p166*), Latin Quarter (1305 Commercial Drive, 604 251 1144), Bukowski's (*see p119*) and the aforementioned Café Deux Soleils. Havana (1212 Commercial Drive, 604 253 9119), a popular Cuban restaurant, theatre and art gallery, and Waazubee Café (1622 Commercial Drive, 604 253 5299) offer evening revellers more good vibes sans bands.

Potted history

Vancouver's marijuana scene is widely regarded as one of the most enticing in the world. In fact, *High Times* has selected it over Amsterdam as the best place on the planet for smokers of the pungent weed. The city's relaxed attitude about toking (while not legal, police allow it) has helped turn BC into a major North American producer of some of the drug's strongest strains, with potencies ten times the levels of the Woodstock-era grass. No wonder *High Times* raved: 'It's a stoner's paradise.'

Marijuana is estimated to be a $6 billion-a-year export here, just behind timber and tourism as the leading business in BC. The best place to hang out if you're interested in exposure to local pot culture is the 300 block of West Hastings (between Carrall and Abbott Streets). BC Marijuana Party Book Shop (307 W Hastings Street, 604 682 1172) offers a bewildering array of pot paraphernalia and the Museum of Psychoactive Substances, an elaborate collection of narcotics-related artefacts. Next door, the New Amsterdam Café (301 W Hastings Street, 604 682 8955)

welcomes marijuana smoking in a laid-back café-like setting. But visitors should remember that, unlike in Amsterdam, you can't simply walk into a shop and buy some pot. It's also worth noting that this area edges the worst part of town.

And finally, to repeat: the possession of marijuana has not been decriminalised and prosecutions do still occur. And lighting up any variety of weed is not much approved here, so don't expect to toke everywhere.

Sightseeing

North Shore

Hiking, biking and beaches.

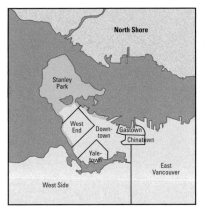

Vancouver's most desirable suburban districts, West and North Vancouver, sprawl along the Burrard Inlet foreshore between Deep Cove and Horseshoe Bay, and up the mountain slopes to just above the Upper Levels Highway. While the **North Shore** is primarily residential, with a total population of 171,000, there are parks and other spaces worth seeking out. Access is via the Lions Gate Bridge (First Narrows) or Ironworkers' Memorial Bridge on Highway 1 (Second Narrows). Coast Mountain buses (604 953 3333, www.translink.bc.ca) pick up on Georgia Street in downtown for travel to North and West Vancouver.

A third entry point, particularly to North Van, is the passenger-only SeaBus from Vancouver's Waterfront Station to Lonsdale Quay. The crossing takes 12 minutes. From the quayside terminal, buses run to most North Shore destinations, including the major parks. All trips from Vancouver and around the North Shore cost $3.25 ($2 for children and seniors).

North Vancouver

The **Capilano River Regional Park**, off Capilano Road and Capilano Park Road in North Vancouver, illustrates the best of the original mountain habitat. In this deep, granite gorge, water tumbles down precipices and eddies around coves and pools. Traverse the wooden suspension bridge and a right turn will take you into a cluster of centuries-old Douglas

firs. The largest is said to be 2.4 metres (eight feet) in diameter and 60 metres (200 feet) tall. Above the gorge you can see the 90 metre (295 foot) Cleveland Dam spillway.

This Greater Vancouver Regional District (GVRD) park is not to be confused with privately run **Capilano Suspension Bridge & Park**, a touristy and pricey destination on a wilderness theme on Capilano Road.

Venturing over the suspension bridge at **Lynn Canyon Park** (off Lynn Valley Road and Peters Road) costs you nothing. Near the park entrance, the bridge over Lynn Creek (don't let 'creek' fool you – these streams become raging torrents) swings above a steep-sided canyon with a 27 metre (90 foot) waterfall. The 250 hectare (617 acre) district-run wilderness also has trails and an ecology centre suitable for kids (3663 Park Road, 604 981 3103, www.dnv.org/ecology/). In summer an unofficial swimming hole is hugely popular.

A potentially demanding wilderness with 75 kilometres (47 miles) of trails, **Lynn Headwaters Regional Park** (604 224 5739, www.gvrd.bc.ca/parks) is entered off Lynn Valley Road. Confine yourself to an amble around Rice Lake near the entrance, or download a map from the website and spend the day climbing the steep paths to Lynn Lake or several peaks. Beware of changeable weather and wandering bears.

The public is also permitted into the vast source of Greater Vancouver's drinking water, the **Lower Seymour Conservation Reserve** (604 990 0483, www.gvrd.bc.ca/water/LSCR.htm). From June to September the GVRD hosts free bus and walking tours exploring the ecology of the Seymour Watershed (604 432 6410 to reserve).

At the east end of North Van reposes the pretty village of **Deep Cove** (*see p84* **Downhill racers**) on a long fjord known as Indian Arm. This is a base for canoeing, kayaking, motor-boating, fishing, mountain biking and hiking (www.deepcovebc.com).

Capilano Suspension Bridge & Park
3735 Capilano Road (604 985 7474/www.capbridge. com). SeaBus Lonsdale Quay then bus 246. **Open** 8.30am-8pm daily. **Admission** $24.95; $6.25-$12.50 concessions; free under-6s. **Credit** AmEx, MC, V. **Map** p253 X3.
In existence since 1889, the big attraction is a 137m (450ft) swaying plank bridge that crosses the

Capilano River, 70m (230 ft) above the canyon floor. If you're scared of heights, stay away: it doesn't take many people crossing to make the bridge sway. Once over, forest interpretative tours, totem poles, and native carvers at work can easily fill half a day. A recent addition is the Treetops Adventure, a cable bridge (mercifully relatively stable) that walks you through a series of trees 33m (100ft) above the forest floor. The woodsy, if kitsch site includes a restaurant, takeout café and souvenir shop. **Photo** *p83*.

West Vancouver

West Vancouver (or 'West Van', as it is commonly called) is a 20-minute bus ride from downtown to the mega-shopping complex of **Park Royal** (*see p122*) at its entrance, and another 20 minutes out to **Horseshoe Bay**.

Originally settled by aboriginals, West Van's lovely contours caught the attention of a Welsh deserter from the British Navy in the 1870s. 'Navy Jack' then went on to earn a living ferrying Vancouverites across Burrard Inlet by rowboat for picnicking and camping, before a ferry-boat service began in the early 1900s.

Immigrant Brits in particular took a fancy to this Cornwall-away-from-home, and built 'villages' along the waterfront with names like Caulfeild (after gentleman-scholar pioneer Francis William Caulfeild), West Bay, Dundarave and Ambleside.

In 1938, the Guinness family, recognising the potential of the view from the forested West Van hillside, built the Lion's Gate bridge over the First Narrows. Today the 1,500 hectares (3,700 acres) for which the family paid $80,000 would sell for millions. Indeed, there are not many homes on the West Van mountainside (still sometimes called 'the British properties') that would sell for under a million, and those on the waterfront are up in the stratosphere.

This privileged community is not known for its open arms. A few years ago a series of concrete plinths installed along Marine Drive to mark the entry points to secluded beaches mysteriously disappeared. The one and only hotel was demolished in 2005, although there's a motel in Horseshoe Bay (*see p46*) and a handful of B&Bs.

The shore thing

West Van's beaches are an unpredictable blend of stone, sand, scattered logs and driftwood on a rocky foreshore. Most are poorly marked at best and the most remote are difficult to access. Neighbourhood signage can be unwelcoming. On the plus side, West Van has a superb Blue Bus system (604 953 3333, www.translink.bc.ca) that runs from downtown Vancouver along Marine Drive, and the driver will let you off at any of the following.

The first four are coves above which the rainforest meets country garden, and expensive houses cling to the hillside.

Whyte Bay, Whytecliff Park

At the extreme end of Marine Drive, west of Horseshoe Bay, Whytecliff Park sprawls over five hectares (12.5 acres) of bluff and forest. Whyte Bay beach looks out on big-rock Whyte Island, reachable at low tide. A drawback is that the beach is a training ground for scuba divers, so expect lots of rubber suits and oxygen tanks. There's a good takeout nearby.

Eagle Harbour

On Eagle Harbour Road, just before Fisherman's Cove, and a walkable distance from Marine Drive, reposes Eagle Harbour and its small yacht club. This idyllic inlet is

ideal for languorous swimming and the sandy beach is suitable for kids. Picnic tables and washrooms are available.

Sandy Cove

West Van's original 'secret hideaway', Sandy Cove is reachable by a short stairwell that begins on the north side of Marine Drive at Rose Crescent and runs under the road. Expect families on a hot day; teens at night.

Caulfeild Park Beach

This gorgeous beach on wide Caulfeild Bay is accessible by steps and woodsy paths from a small parking lot where Dogwood Road meets Pilot House Road, just west of Piccadilly South and Marine Drive. There's also a path from the latter junction.

Dundarave and Ambleside

The most public beaches, they can get Coney Island-ish in summer. Dundarave, at 25th Street, kicks up a good surf when the wind is up; there's a protected bay, pier, park and facilities. The Beach House restaurant (*see p112*) is upscale. Ambleside Beach, at 13th Street, is vast, with full amenities. Despite exposure to winds, sand-castle building is big when conditions are right. Both beaches are close to eateries and shops.

Capilano Suspension Bridge & Park. *See p81.*

At the north-western extremity of West Vancouver snuggles **Horseshoe Bay**. Once a popular boating and picnicking destination, today it largely serves as the launching pad for BC Ferries trips to Howe Sound (particularly Bowen Island), the Sunshine Coast and Vancouver Island (*see p195*).

The loveliest part of the North Shore is unquestionably the waterfront between Horseshoe Bay and Dundarave (*see p82* **The shore thing**). Despite over use, 75 hectare (185 acre) **Lighthouse Park** remains a gorgeous reserve of old growth, with ten kilometres (six miles) of forest and shoreline trails. To its east nestles the community of Caulfeild, with the well-loved St Francis-in-the-Wood church (4773 Piccadilly South, 604 922 3531) and cottagey houses that recall West Vancouver in its British heyday. From below the church follow Pilot House Road along the foreshore called Caulfeild Park and you'll see what all the fuss is about.

Lions Gate Bridge

Named for 'the Lions', two hump-like peaks above the North Shore, the Lions Gate Bridge was built over the First Narrows during the 'Dirty 30s'. It was the brainchild of local capitalist 'AJT' Taylor. Taylor persuaded the Guinness (beer) family that a bridge would foster development of an expanse of properties it owned in West Van. The Guinness syndicate coughed up $6 million.

A decade of planning, involving everybody who was anybody in Canada at the time, was bitter and fractious; the engineering immensely complicated. Yet thanks largely to Taylor, this sublime suspension bridge – three spans and a viaduct totalling 1,823 metres (5,980 feet) – opened in 1938. It was an immediate success, and fed the post-war growth of the North Shore.

In 1955 the province bought the bridge, neglected it, then talked of replacing it with a soulless tunnel. Heritage advocates, and all but the most commuting-obsessed residents of the North Shore, were outraged. Ultimately, the government took the cheaper route, and rebuilt. In 2002, over 56 nights during which the bridge was closed from 8pm to 6am, workers cut free the decks and replaced them with 54 20 metre (66 foot) long segments. The 112 ton sections were hoisted from barges and slipped into place.

Today, the Lions Gate Bridge is a beloved icon and National Heritage site – even if its three lanes (the centre one reversible) come to a crawl at rush hour. As for 'AJT' Taylor, such were the politics of the day that he watched the opening ceremonies from the sidelines. His story is said to be sealed in one of the stone lions that guard the bridge's southern entrance.

Downhill racers

The North Shore is blessed with some of the most demanding mountain biking terrain in the world, but then the sport was practically invented here. Precipitous rain-soaked mountainsides, bisected with unforgiving torrents of runoff and strewn with fallen, rotting coniferous trees, provide more than enough thrills and spills.

For more than two decades **Cove Bikes** at Deep Cove (4310 Gallant Avenue, 604 929 1918, www.covebike.com) has been building bikes to cope with the crazy conditions and (some might say) their crazier owners. The store also serves as a hub for the mountain biking community. (There's a second store in East Van: 1389 Main Street, 604 929 2222.)

As legend has it, in the earliest days co-founder and now sole owner Chaz Romalis, worked and lived in the shop, sharing his energy bars with rats. Times have changed: custom-built in a factory near Vancouver, state-of-the-art Cove Bikes are sold around the world. You can still buy the Hummer model launched in the 1990s ('the classic,

epic ride'), along with the likes of the G-Spot, Peeler, Hooker, Handjob, Hustler and Playmate – the latter 'for those who love grinding'. Choose a frame for the terrain you prefer (downhill, cross-country, adventure, etc), then pick the parts that suit you. The basic price is about $1,500 but the top of the range runs to $5,000 – though you can rent a bike from $35 for 24 hours.

Treks & trails

Six peaks straddle the North Shore: Black, Strachan, Hollyburn, Grouse, Fromme and Seymour. Pioneer hikers have blazed trails up, across and over their steep-sided slopes. The Grouse Grind on **Grouse Mountain** boasts it's the most hiked trail in the world. Over 100,000 people stagger up every year.

Cypress Provincial Park (wlapwww.gov. bc.ca/bcparks/), off the Upper Levels Highway in West Vancouver, embraces **Hollyburn**, **Black** and **Strachan**. Trails up Black and Strachan (1,220 and 1,450 metres – 4,000 and 4,750 feet – respectively), including moderately difficult Black Mountain Loop Trail, deliver great outlooks. **Hollyburn Mountain** (1,326 metres, 4,350 feet) remains a paradise of rustic log cabins and tiny lakes. The Howe Crest Sound Trail, for the fittest only, traverses to Porteau Provincial Park up Howe Sound.

Mount Seymour Provincial Park (1,455 metres, 4,774 feet), is accessed via the Mount Seymour Road off Mount Seymour Parkway (North Vancouver). From the parking lot, relatively easy trails go to Goldie, Mystery and Flower lakes and Dinky and Dog peaks. A longer, well-tramped route climbs to First and Second Pump peaks, from which (on a fine day) you can see to Vancouver Island. A full ten hour (round-trip) hike continues on to Elsay Lake.

Veteran hikers may consider the Baden-Powell Trail, running 48 kilometres (30 miles) across all six mountains, between Deep Cove and Horseshoe Bay (www.trailsbc.ca).

While much of the terrain has been logged, some old growth with lush undergrowth remains; wild berries and flowers proliferate. Residents include deer, black bear, coyote, raven, jays, woodpeckers, grouse and owl. Caution: dress appropriately, tell someone where you're going, carry a good map, and stay on the trail. Every year hikers get lost and despite the efforts of the volunteer North Shore Rescue Society (604 983 7441), a few will perish.

Grouse Mountain

6400 Nancy Greene Way, North Vancouver (604 984 0661/snow report 604 986 6262/www.grouse mountain.com). Bus 232, 236, 247. **Open** *Skyride* 9am-10pm daily. *Office* 8am-8pm daily. *Grouse Grind* May-Oct 6.30am-6pm daily weather permitting, daylight hours.* **Admission** $29.95; $10.95-$27.95 concessions. **Credit** AmEx, DC, MC, V. **Map** p253 Y1. Built largely of big wooden steps, the Grouse Grind gains about 1,000m (2,800ft) in 2.9km (1.8 miles), with a gradient steeper than 50 degrees in parts. Yet, strangely, some people like it like that, and there's plenty here to warn off the rest. Signs caution that the 'extremely difficult and strenuous climb' is open May-Oct, but closes due to weather, erosion, 'or

Grouse Mountain the hard and easy way.

search and rescue'. Still confident? You can buy a Summit Seeker card (at Guest Services) and 'swipe in' to the timer at the bottom and the top. Inside the lodge, a computer spews out results. It will also let you know what you've achieved over the season – for example, six Grinds equals Kilimanjaro, eight equals K2. And it will help prepare you for the popular Grouse Grind Mountain Run held every September. Just don't expect to beat the record times (24.22 minutes for men, 32.54 minutes for women).

If you don't fancy the Grind, there's always Skyride, a giant gondola that whisks you straight to the summit in a mere ten minutes. Access to the refuge for endangered wildlife – with orphaned grizzly bears and wolves – is included in the price of your lift ticket, as are lumberjack and falconry shows in summer. In winter, there is an ice-skating rink, with skates for hire, ski and snowshoe rentals. But the main draw is the patio with its panoramic views of the city, ocean and mountains. Here Grouse Grinders down well-deserved pints of beer and eat the most deserved nachos in the city.

London's
weekly
listings
bible

OUT EVERY TUESDAY

Eat, Drink, Shop

Restaurants & Cafés   88
Bars   113
Shops & Services   121

Features

The best Restaurants   89
Caffeine fix   92
Izakaya time   101
Something fishy   102
Know your noodles   106
Cheap eats   108
Korea moves   111
The best Bars   113
Nu man   114
Microbreweries   116
Napa of the north   118
Streetlife   127
Granville Island   128
Shop with the chefs   131

Richard Kidd. *See p126.*

Restaurants & Cafés

Small plates go a long way.

The art of coffee at **Caffè Artigiano**.

Vancouverites love their food. They really do. If you're wondering what people do in the evenings, take a peek in to the city's heaving restaurants. All 4,000 of them.

Small plate menus are all the rage in the city: bigger than traditional tapas, they are perfect for sharing – something everyone likes to do here. Seafood is a staple: fresh, usually local and often wild, fish is always a good bet when ordering. Look out for black cod (sablefish), spot prawns and wild sockeye salmon.

Unsurprisingly, given the city's ethnic make-up, some of the best eating can be found at Japanese and Chinese joints. Sushi is ubiquitous and staggeringly cheap, but much of the most interesting Japanese dining is at *izakayas* (*see p101* **Izakaya time**). For great Chinese cooking (*see p106* **Know your noodles**), you need to look beyond Chinatown to East Vancouver and, if you're really dedicated, get in a car and drive to the suburb of Richmond.

Weekend brunch is almost a religion so expect to queue. Reservations are also advised

for dinner, and considered essential at the weekend. Many places serve quite late, but eating early (around 7pm) is commonplace.

Though some of the best places in town are quite swish, this is the West Coast and, as far as dressing for dinner is concerned, pretty much anything goes. Children are welcomed.

Tipping is generally 12-15 per cent, but arguments rage as to whether this should be before or after tax is added to the bill. If you plump for before, the easiest thing to do is simply match the tax.

Downtown

Cafés

Caffè Artigiano

763 Hornby Street, between W Georgia Street & Robson Street (604 696 9222/www.caffeartigiano. com). All city-centre buses. **Open** 6.30am-9.30pm Mon-Sat; 6.30am-7pm Sun. **Credit** MC, V. **Map** p249 K3 ①

Co-owner Sammy Piccolo's signature *insieme* (a blend of espresso, curry, bittersweet chocolate, egg yolks and raw sugar) has earned him the title of Canadian Barista Champion – twice – and second place at the 2004 World Latte Art competition. If you're just looking for a plain old shot of espresso, Caffè Artigiano pulls the best coffee in town. Panini and pastries don't match the beverages. **Photo** *p88.*
Other locations: 1101 W Pender Street; 740 W Hastings Street; 2154 W 41st Avenue; J5-925 Main Street, Park Royal, West Vancouver.

Gallery Café
750 Hornby Street, between Robson Street & W Georgia Street (604 688 2233/www.vanartgallery. bc.ca). All city-centre buses. **Open** 10am-5.30pm Mon-Wed, Fri-Sun; 10am-9pm Thur. **Main courses** $5-$11. **Credit** MC, V. **Map** p249 K3 ❷
Tucked inside the Vancouver Art Gallery, this upscale cafeteria boasts one of the prettiest terraces in the city. Slide your tray onto a wrought-iron table, surrounded by Romanesque stone columns and shaded by leafy greenery. Elegant lunch mains range from Thai noodles and wild-mushroom pasta to Cobb salads and prosciutto panini.

Belgian

Chambar
562 Beatty Street, between Dunsmuir Street & W Pender Street (604 879 7119/www.chambar.com). Bus 10, 16, 20. **Open** 5.30-11pm Mon-Sat. **Main courses** $9-$15. **Set menu** $45. **Credit** AmEx, MC, V. **Map** p249 L4 ❸
The name is a spin on *chambard*, the French expression for the raucousness that explodes when a teacher leaves the classroom. And, given the craziness that erupted on this Moroccan-infused hot spot's opening, it seems fitting. Vancouverites went mad for the sleek, modern dining room and 25 varieties of Belgian beer. Chef-owner Nico Schuermans lives up to the hype with a menu that includes braised lamb shanks dusted with cinnamon, figs and honey, big bowls of spicy Congolese moules frites and a delicately sinful rosewater crème brûlée.

Diners

Elbow Room
560 Davie Street, between Richards Street & Seymour Street (604 685 3628/www.theelbowroom cafe.com). Bus 4, 6, 7, 10, 16, 17, 50. **Open** 8am-4pm daily. **Main courses** $3-$12. **Credit** AmEx, MC, V. **Map** p249 K4 ❹
Prepare to be offended. Owner Patrick Savoie, a flamingly gay Quebecois, specialises in (well

❶ Purple numbers given in this chapter correspond to the location of each restaurant and café as marked on the street maps. *See pp246-253.*

rehearsed) verbal abuse that he and his staff hurl with every cup of coffee. Celebrities appreciate the theatrics: framed photos of Hollywood customers line the walls. A bizarrely unique brunch spot.

Templeton
1087 Granville Street, at Helmcken Street (604 685 4612/www.thetempleton.com). Bus 4, 6, 7, 10, 16, 17, 50. **Open** 9am-11pm Mon-Wed; 9am-1am Thur-Sun. **Main courses** $6-$12.95. **Credit** MC, V. **Map** p248 J4 ❺
For hearty comfort food with a health-conscious twist, head to the Templeton, an authentic '30s diner nestled among the nightclubs and sex shops on the seedy side of Granville Street. Their burgers are made with organic beef, the prices are cheap, portions huge and the service is friendly. **Photo** *p104.*

French

Bacchus
845 Hornby Street, between Robson Street & Smithe Street, (604 608 5319/www.wedgewoodhotel.com/hotel/ bacchus.html). All city-centre buses. **Open** 6.30am-10pm Mon-Fri; 7am-1am Sat; 7am-10pm Sun. **Main courses** $29-$38. **Credit** AmEx, MC, V. **Map** p249 K3 ❻

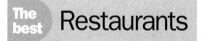

The best Restaurants

For al fresco
Sequoia Grill at the Teahouse (*see p99*).

For breakfast/brunch
Brioche Urban Baking (*see p100*).

For casual dining
Go Fish (*see p104*).

For Chinese
Ho Yuen Kee (*see p106* Know your noodles).

For fusion
Bin 941 (*see p92*).

For modern Japanese
Hapa (*see p101* Izakaya time).

For romance
Parkside (*see p97*).

For splurging
Lumière (*see p104*).

For traditional Japanese
Tojo's (*see p105*).

For vegetarian
Foundation (*see p112*).

For West Coast
West Restaurant (*see p109*).

Eat, Drink, Shop

The best London bars & restaurants, just a click away.

Subscribe today and enjoy over 3,400 constantly updated reviews from *Time Out*'s acclaimed *London Eating & Drinking, Cheap Eats, Bars Pubs & Clubs* Guides and *Time Out London weekly*.

Located in the Wedgewood Hotel, Bacchus is one of the city's most popular spots for power lunches. But when the sun goes down and the Murano-glass chandeliers are dimmed, this sumptuous room with its velvet banquettes, cosy booths, rich dark woods and Persian carpets is transformed into a most romantic place for dinner. The executive chef Lee Parsons, who trained with Raymond Blanc, uses local seasonal ingredients in his lusty French cuisine – Queen Charlotte halibut with a fricassée of artichokes and fennel, or braised Fraser Valley duck with fondant potatoes and red-wine cherry sauce. As you would naturally expect in a restaurant of this calibre, the service is impeccable.

Cassis Bistro

420 W Pender Street, at Homer Street (604 605 0420/www.cassisvancouver.com). Bus 10, 16, 20. **Open** 11.30am-2.30pm, 5.30pm-midnight Mon-Wed; 11.30am-2.30pm, 5.30pm-1am Thur, Fri; 5.30pm-1am Sat; 5.30pm-midnight Sun. **Main courses** $6-$17. **Credit** MC, V. **Map** p249 L3 **❼**

Veer off the beaten path on to this grubby stretch of West Pender to find robust French country cooking in a stylish bohemian heritage building with soaring ceilings and polished wood floors. Bistro favourites include slow-simmered daube de boeuf, house-made sausages and lusty bowls of bouillabaisse jazzed up with Pernod, fennel and orange peel. Portions are small, but so are the prices, with most mains ringing in under $12. A ho-hum wine list will set you back more than the meal.

Fusion

Wild Rice

117 W Pender Street, at Abbott Street (604 642 2882/www.wildricevancouver.com). Bus 10, 16, 20. **Open** 11.30am-midnight Mon-Thur; 11.30am-1am Fri; 5pm-1am Sat; 5pm-midnight Sun. **Main courses** $14-$19. **Credit** MC, V. **Map** p249 M3 **❽**

Strikingly lit minimalist decor, low-slung lounge tables and artful presentation combine with experimental small plates – Indian candied salmon, crispy wontons and Kung Po chicken with spicy twice-cooked peanuts – to push Chinese food beyond the same old, same old. The kitchen's inconsistent execution, alas, sometimes turn the dishes into squishy pieces of bruised fruit that taste like they've travelled too many bumpy miles.

Italian

Don Francesco Ristorante

860 Burrard Street, between Robson Street & Smithe Street (604 685 7770/www.donfrancesco.ca). Bus 2, 5, 22. **Open** 11.30am-4pm, 5-11.30pm Mon-Fri; 5-11.30pm Sat, Sun. **Main courses** $21-$45. **Credit** AmEx, MC, V. **Map** p249 K3 **❾**

Don Francesco's is a swanky celebrity hotspot, largely because of its location, right across the street from the Sutton Place hotel and its many guests working in Hollywood North (*see p37*). The owner,

a passionate opera singer who performs on Saturday nights, caters to his fat-conscious clientele with numerous seafood options and wild game. For those not watching their diets, there are lots of pastas too.

Il Giardino

1382 Hornby Street, at Pacific Boulevard (604 669 2422/www.umberto.com). Bus 2, 22. **Open** 11.30am-3.30pm, 6pm-midnight Mon-Fri; 6pm-midnight Sat. **Main courses** $24-$48. **Credit** AmEx, MC, V. **Map** p248 J4 **❿**

The owner is known simply as 'Umberto' – a one-name wonder who put Tuscan cooking on the map in Canada. At one time he had 17 restaurants, but currently presides over four (two in Vancouver, two in Whistler), plus a cookery school/hotel/vineyard 45 minutes south of Florence. Il Giardino, the time-honoured yellow house that opened in 1973 and eventually expanded into a bigger room next door, was his first on the West Coast. Umberto's hearty grilled meats and simple pastas, still referred to as 'new' Italian, have never impressed us much, but continue to draw a well-heeled business crowd.

Japanese

Okada Sushi

2nd Floor, 101-888 Nelson Street, at Hornby Street (604 899 3266/www.okadasushi.com). All city-centre buses. **Open** 11.30am-2.15pm, 5-10.15pm Mon-Fri; 5-10.15pm Sat. **Main courses** $6.50-$21.95. **Credit** AmEx, MC, V. **Map** p248 J4 **⓫**

Okada is a calm, very traditional Japanese restaurant. The sushi and sashimi are excellent and complemented by robata, lobster and crab from the live tanks, and a selection of chazuke (rice bowls mixed with green tea). You won't get any surprises, but what they do, they do well and, considering the maki rolls are (unlike in many places locally) more fish than rice, prices are competitive.

Seafood

C Restaurant

2-1600 Howe Street, at Seabreeze Walk (604 681 1164/www.crestaurant.com). Bus 4, 7, 10, 16, 17, 50. **Open** 5.30-11pm daily. **Main courses** $28-$49.50. **Credit** AmEx, MC, V. **Map** p248 H5 **⓬**

Executive chef Rob Clark gets high marks from environmentalists for his sourcing of sustainable products. Yet anyone who says C offers the best seafood dining in the country – and there have been many who have made this claim – must really disdain the taste of fish. Wonderful fresh ingredients (Pacific sardines, Nova Scotia lobster and Kagan Bay scallops) are completely drowned out with the heavy-handed use of smoke, dark veal stock reduction and foie gras. Chef de cuisine Robert Belcham (who now runs the day-to-day operations) has a lighter touch, but not enough control over the menu. Service, however, doesn't get smoother than this: the staff trains with choreographers from Ballet British Columbia and voice coaches.

Eat, Drink, Shop

Steaks

Gotham Steakhouse & Cocktail Bar

615 Seymour Street, at Dunsmuir Street (604 605 8282/www.gothamsteakhouse.com). All city-centre buses. **Open** 5-11pm daily. **Main courses** $25.95-$48.95. **Credit** AmEx, MC, V. **Map** p249 K3 ⑬

Holy cow, Batman! The portions are almost as substantial as the prices, which start at $30 for shish kebab and edge towards $50 for Porterhouse. That's without any potato or veg, which must be ordered separately. Your bill subsidises the handsome room, appointed with high ceilings, dark wood and bold art-deco paintings. If you must go to see and be seen, eat on the lounge side, which has an unadvertised smaller menu with more reasonable prices.

West Coast

Bin 941

941 Davie Street, between Hornby Street & Burrard Street (604 683 1246/www.bin941.com). Bus 2, 6, 22. **Open** 5pm-2am daily. **Main courses** $14-$15. **Credit** MC, V. **Map** p248 J4 ⑭

There have been many imitators, but this is the original – a funky hole in the wall, where the music throbs, the tables are tight and the flavours rock 'n' roll. Executive chef and owner Gord Martin, a former heavy-metal singer, catalysed Vancouver's craze for small plates (larger than traditional tapas). The prices have gone up in recent years, but are still great value. Drinks are limited to a selective list of wine and beer. Desserts are so-so.

Diva at the Met

645 Howe Street, between Dunsmuir Street & W Georgia Street (604 602 7788/www.metropolitan.com/diva). All city-centre buses. **Open** 6.30am-10pm Mon-Fri; 7am-10pm Sat, Sun. **Main courses** $24-$42. **Credit** AmEx, MC, V. **Map** p249 K3 ⑮

Ten years ago, when Diva at the Met opened its doors at the Metropolitan Hotel with chef Michael Noble in charge, the restaurant ranked as one of the city's premier dining destinations. And although many local critics and guidebooks still highly recommend the room, its inflated reputation is undeserved. After burning through several young chefs, Ray Henry (Noble's former sous chef) was appointed executive chef in 2004. But with a style that relies on odd flavour combinations and sauces so sweet they're overwhelming, he still has a long way to go before returning Diva to its glory days.

Nu

1661 Granville Street, on the north shore of False Creek (604 646 4668/www.whatisnu.com). Bus 4, 7, 10, 16, 17, 50. **Open** 11am-1am Mon-Fri; 10.30am-1am Sat; 10.30am-midnight Sun. **Main courses** $18-$20. **Credit** AmEx, MC, V. **Map** p248 H5 ⑯

Robert Clark redeems himself with Nu (French for naked), which describes the clean approach to the cuisine in contrast to C Restaurant's heavy-handedness (*see p91*). The gourmet finger foods are all

underpriced, and fun to eat too. Crispy fried oysters are skewered with plastic shots of Granville Island lager (pop it in your mouth and squeeze). Chicken wings are stuffed with goat's cheese. The custom-designed bar, featuring two suspended booze racks that spin like roulette wheels, offers exciting cocktails and an exclusive wine list. The design theme is retro cruise ship, appropriately enough, since the circular restaurant is surrounded by a yacht club. Pull up a swivel stool and pretend you've sailed off on the *Love Boat*. **Photo** *p93*.

West End

Cafés

Café Crepe

874 Granville Street, at Smithe Street (604 806 0845). All cross-city buses. **Open** 8am-11pm Mon-Thur, Sun; 8am-1am Fri, Sat. **Main courses** $4-$10. **Credit** MC, V. **Map** p249 K3 ⑰

With its glossy red-wine walls, oversized art nouveau poster art and throbbing techno music, this French franchise is pure Parisian. The menu offers five types of stuffed savoury crêpes that, with various add-ons, make a satisfying, light dinner. Baguettes are also available, but not nearly as good as the crêpes, which also come in about two dozen dessert varieties. Gobble them down with cheap red wine or kick-ass espresso.

Other locations: throughout the city.

Delaney's Coffee House

1105 Denman Street, at Nelson Street (604 662 3344). Bus 6. **Open** 6am-11pm Mon-Fri; 6.30am-11pm Sat, Sun. **Credit** V. **Map** p248 H2 ⑱

Caffeine fix

● Average cups of coffee consumed by Vancouverites per day: 2.6.
● Percentage of British Columbians who drink coffee daily: 61.
● Most popular size of coffee: 16 fl oz.
● Number of litres of coffee 61 percent of Vancouverites drinking one 16 fl oz cup of coffee every day would consume in one year: 227,588,997.
● Average cost of a 16 fl oz cup of coffee: $1.71.
● Best excuse for being late for work in Vancouver, according to a poll conducted by the *Georgia Straight*: 'Long line at Starbucks.'

Sources: Stats Canada, The Coffee Association of Canada, Starbucks Coffee Company

Nu. See p92.

The Belgian chocolate brownies are divine, the coffee comes from JJ Bean, the wooden tables are always crowded and the atmosphere is friendly – very friendly. Located in the heart of the gay village, this is a hot daytime pick-up spot. It's also handy for takeout coffee to drink while walking the Seawall. **Other locations**: 3089 Edgemont Boulevard, North Vancouver (604 985 3385); 2424 Marine Drive, West Vancouver (604 921 4466).

Mondo Gelato

1094 Denman Street, at Comox Street (604 647 6638/www.mondogelato.com). Bus 6. **Open** 10am-midnight daily. **No credit cards. Map** p248 H2 ⑲
Diehard fans swear by Mondo Gelato, a local company that recently expanded to Beijing. Proximity to the beach and limitless free samples guarantee long queues in summer, but a mind-boggling array of fresh flavours make it worth the wait. Pistachio, biscotti, chocolate, mango and Nutella are all perennial favourites. Or try black sesame seed.

Aboriginal

Liliget Feast House

1724 Davie Street, between Bidwell Street and Denman Street (604 681 7044/www.liliget.com). Bus 6. **Open** 5-10pm daily. **Main courses** $12-$29. **Credit** AmEx, MC, V. **Map** p248 G2 ⑳
Descend the stairs to discover a tranquil little room, designed after a Northwest Coastal longhouse, with twinkling lights, pebbled floors, wooden walkways, sunken tables, cedar poles and a heady cloud of

smoke wafting in from the alderwood grill. Liliget is touted as the country's only First Nations fine dining restaurant. 'Fine' might seem a stretch if you have yet to acquire a taste for steamed herring roe on kelp with oolican (smelt oil), but the food is authentic. The platter for two provides a wide sampling of bannock bread, oysters, mussels, venison strips, duck breast, elk, buffalo, berry sauces, sweet potatoes, vegetables and rice. Wash it down with wines from BC's aboriginal-owned Nk'Mip Cellars.

Diners

Fatburger

1101 Denman Street, at Nelson Street (604 689 8858/www.fatburger.com). Bus 6. **Open** 10.30am-11pm daily. **Main courses** $7-$12. **Credit** MC, V. **Map** p248 H2 ㉑
The first Canadian franchise of the US chain had locals lined up for the grand opening of this retro-style diner with its neon lighting, open grill and faux-vintage jukebox. The single-patty fatburger is actually kind of lean. It's served on a soft white bun, with two types of fries (fat or skinny), and can be topped with egg, cheese, bacon or chilli. Shakes are made with hand-scooped vanilla ice-cream.

Hamburger Mary's

1202 Davie Street, at Bute Street (604 687 1293/www.hamburgermarys.ca). Bus 6. **Open** 8am-3am Mon-Thur; 8am-4am Fri, Sat; 8am-2am Sun. **Main courses** $7-$15. **Credit** AmEx, MC, V. **Map** p248 H3 ㉒

Lift Bar and Grill. See p96.

A West End landmark since 1979, this diner hopped on the '50s bandwagon before it became trendy everywhere else. With its neon lights beckoning until 4am on Friday and Saturday, a Hamburger Mary's chilli-cheese burger after a long night at the bar has been a rite of passage for most Vancouverites. The burgers are standard, but come in a large variety of flavours, including wild game, and are served with hand-chipped fries. The all-day breakfast is also popular, as is people watching on the sidewalk patio. Service can be slow.

French

Le Crocodile
100-909 Burrard Street, at Smithe Street (604 669 4298/www.lecrocodilerestaurant.com). Bus 1, 2, 5, 22, 98. **Open** 11.30am-2pm, 5.30-10pm Mon-Sat. **Main courses** $24-$40. **Credit** AmEx, MC, V. **Map** p248 J3 ㉓
Since opening Le Crocodile in 1983, chef Michel Jacob has set the standards for French cuisine in Vancouver and trained many of the city's finest chefs (including Canada's most renowned, the Lumière's Rob Feenie). His signature menu items – classic onion tarts, garlic-sautéed frogs' legs, gin-and-tomato soup – hail from the Alsace region in France and have proved consistently pleasing to pampered downtown palettes. Service in this upscale bistro with formally dressed waiters, half-curtained windows and creamy yellow walls is appropriately sniffy, but rarely off-putting.

Saveur
850 Thurlow Street, between Robson Street & Smithe Street (604 688 1633/www.saveurrestaurant. com). Bus 5. **Open** 11.30am-2pm, 6-10pm Mon-Fri; 6-10pm Sat. **Main courses** $13-$38. **Credit** AmEx, MC, V. **Map** p248 J3 ㉔
This underrated gem (formerly Piccolo Mondo) offers classic French cuisine, with a few nods to Italy, and not a whiff of pretension. Chef Stephane Meyer and his wife Nathalie learned their craft in several Michelin starred restaurants in Europe, before eventually bringing disciplined artistry and impeccable service with them to the New World. The regularly changing *prix-fixe* menu and a discerning wine list spell great value. And, for a change, the solo diner is not hidden away in corners like an unwanted guest but given pride of place at a large communal table in the middle of the room.

Greek

Characters Taverna
1103 Davie Street, at Thurlow Street (604 685 9607/www.characterstaverna.com). Bus 6. **Open** 11.30am-6am daily. **Main courses** $9-$14. **Credit** MC, V. **Map** p248 J3 ㉕
The only thing to recommend about this run-of-the-mill Greek restaurant is the fact that it offers full kitchen service until 6am. When you're stumbling out of the clubs at 3am, a roast lamb dinner can be more enticing than a hot dog. At weekends, the place is packed with bar staff coming off shift.

Taki's Taverna

1106 Davie Street, at Thurlow Street (604 682 1336). Bus 6. **Open** 11am-10.30pm Mon-Sat; noon-10.30pm Sun. **Main courses** $8-$14. **Credit** AmEx, MC, V. **Map** p248 J3 ㉖
This homey Greek restaurant offers the usual taverna fare: chicken souvlaki, deep-fried calamari, roasted lemon potatoes, inexpensive prices and plastic tablecloths. Those wanting to combine chiromancy with food should come on Wednesday nights, when Anna is on hand to read palms.

Italian

Café Luxy

1235 Davie Street, between Bute Street & Jervis Street (604 669 5899/www.cafeluxy.com). **Open** 11am-10.30pm Mon-Fri; 9am-10.30pm Sat, Sun. **Main courses** $6-$16. **Credit** AmEx, MC, V. **Map** p248 H3 ㉗
A popular neighbourhood bistro with candlelight, wood panelling and mirror-lined walls. Luxy will satisfy any carbohydrate craving with dozens of cheap pasta dishes and several daily specials. Portions are generous, and come with garlic bread and side salad. Decent breakfasts.

Cin Cin Ristorante and Bar

1154 Robson Street (upstairs), between Thurlow Street & Bute Street (604 688 7338/www.cincin.net). Bus 5. **Open** 11.30am-11pm Mon-Fri; 5-11pm Sat, Sun. **Main courses** $18-$45.50. **Credit** AmEx, MC, V. **Map** p248 J3 ㉘
This popular Tuscan restaurant did not make its mark by being highly inventive. However, recently the kitchen has improved considerably under a new chef who has stretched the menu beyond the standard osso bucco, even if he does sometimes stray from Cin Cin's Italian roots with oddities like panko-crusted halibut. Prices are steep, but a wide range of pastas, risottos, and meats or pizzas from the wood-fired grill and oven should satisfy all tastes. The wine list is extensive, and comes with hefty mark-ups. Desserts are overrated.

Japanese

Gyoza King

1508 Robson Street, at Nicola Street (604 669 8278). Bus 5. **Open** 5.30pm-2am Mon-Fri; 11.30am-3.30pm, 6pm-2am Sat; 11.30am-3.30pm, 6pm-midnight Sun. **Main courses** $10-$20. **Credit** AmEx, MC, V. **Map** p248 J2 ㉙
Sick of sushi yet? Then Gyoza King is more than worth a try. Dumplings are the speciality at this dark hovel that attracts young Japanese visitors looking for cheap eats and some of the city's best chefs working after shift in their own restaurants. Gyoza are fatly stuffed with shrimp, pork and all sorts of vegetable combinations. The tapas-style menu also offers barbecued beef, deep-fried tofu, grilled fish, noodles, pork cutlets and any number of specials. Pop a cold beer and dive in.

Kintaro Ramen

788 Denman Street, at Robson Street (604 682 7568). Bus 5. **Open** noon-11pm Tue-Sun. **Main courses** $5-$15. **No credit cards.** **Map** p248 H2 ㉚
Looking for the perfect bowl of soup? Look no further. Pork-based broths are the signature here, except on Saturdays, when the chef also simmers up a seafood-based Forest Fire ramen with kelp instead of noodles. Ladled out in huge bowls, the soup is ordered according to grade (light, medium or rich), then layered with twelve spices, spring onions, corn and thin slices of barbecue pork (fatty or lean). Pull up a ringside seat at the steamy no-frills counter.

Zakkushi Charcoal Grill

823 Denman Street, between Robson Street & Haro Street (604 685 1136). Bus 5. **Open** noon-3pm, 5.30pm-midnight Mon-Thur, Sun; noon-3pm, 5.30pm-1am Fri, Sat. **Main courses** $8-$18. **Credit** AmEx, MC, V. **Map** p248 H2 ㉛
A loud and boisterous yakitori diner where skewers of charcoal-grilled meats (tsukune) take centre stage, as does the grill, with its glowing red-hot coals. The stick foods, which cost less than $2 each, range from conventional (chicken meatballs, chicken wings, pork, beef with ponzu, vegetable skewers) to courageous (chicken heart, chicken liver and beef tongue). Other small, cheap plates include bitter squash with eggs, barbecue rice balls in tea soup, chicken teriyaki bowls and noodles. The Japanese servers speak fluent English, but can sometimes be really slow.

Korean

Hal Mai Jang Moi Jib

1719 Robson Street, at Bidwell Street (604 642 0712). Bus 5. **Open** 10am-2am Mon-Thur, Sun; 10am-5am Fri, Sat. **Main courses** $6-$10. **Credit** AmEx, MC, V. **Map** p248 H2 ㉜
There are so many Korean restaurants on this side of Robson Street, the area has been dubbed Little Korea. Ask any of the homesick ESL students with their funky fashion sense and dyed orange hair, and they'll lead you straight to this loud little hole in the wall where the prices are cheap and the dishes are plentiful. Start with pork neckbone soup, followed by haemool pajun, a huge seafood pancake topped with crispy fried noodles.
Other locations: 395 Kingsway (604 872 0712).

Latin American

Lolita's South of the Border Cantina

1326 Davie Street, at Jervis Street (604 696 9996/ www.lolitasrestaurant.com). Bus 6. **Open** 5pm-2am daily. **Main courses** $6-$20. **Credit** MC, V. **Map** p248 H3 ㉝
Home-made corn tortillas, a friendly vibe, shaken Margaritas, funky bamboo furnishings and late-night kitchen service make Lolita's a cosy neighbourhood cantina. The menu isn't strictly Mexican (fish is served in a chilli tomato coconut broth), but

everything is made in-house and the prices are reasonable too. Go for slow-roasted pulled beef taquitos or pan-seared halibut tacos, and then wash them down afterwards with a sweet and nippy Loco Limonada (gold tequila and mango liqueur with muddled chilli and mango lemonade).

Samba Brazilian Steak House

1122 Alberni Street, between Thurlow Street and Bute Street (604 696 9888/www.thaihouse.com/ samba). Bus 2, 5, 22. **Open** 11.30am-3pm, 5.30-10.30pm daily. **Main courses** $23.95. **Credit** AmEx, MC, V. **Map** p248 J1 ❸

A meat lovers' paradise awaits those willing to brave the plastic palm trees and shiny disco balls in this garish basement. The all-you-can-eat rodizio, imported directly from Rio de Janeiro, works like this: sirloin, pork sausage, leg of lamb, quail, chicken hearts and all manners of meat are barbecued on a rotisserie, then impaled on giant swords and carved tableside by strolling passadores that you flag down as often as you like. A salad bar and seafood options will satisfy non-carnivores. Wear it all off on the dancefloor with live Latin bands that heat things up at weekends.

Seafood

Cardero's

1583 Coal Harbour Quay, at Cardero Street (604 669 7666/www.vancouverdine.com/cardero). Bus 5 then 5min walk. **Open** 11.30am-11pm Mon-Sat; 11.30am-10pm Sun. **Main courses** $10.95-$22.95. **Credit** AmEx, MC, V. **Map** p248 J2 ❸

For a city by the sea, Vancouver's restaurants are curiously lacking in simply grilled fish. You can find it here at this casual nautical-themed dining room in the middle of a yacht club, along with steaks, pizzas, burgers and Asian wok fries (be sure to try the crispy chilli-coriander squid). With its wonderful views of the inner harbour and mountains to accompany your meal, the heated patio is worth waiting for. Prices are right and service is friendly, especially in the fireside pub where they indicate your table is ready by sending a flag up a line.

Joe Fortes Seafood and Chop House

777 Thurlow Street, at Robson Street (604 669 1940/www.joefortes.ca). Bus 5. **Open** 11am-11pm daily. **Main courses** $20-$60. **Credit** AmEx, MC, V. **Map** p248 J3 ❸

More than 20 years later, Joe Fortes' heated rooftop garden is still a favourite cocktail-hour destination for Vancouver's high-flying brokers and the last of the city's smokers. For something decadently different, tuck in to an icy seafood tower on sunny Saturday afternoons. Surrounded by visiting rock stars and glammed-up American Robson Street shoppers, you'll feel like you just landed in LA. The restaurant's signature cedar-planked salmon, crab legs and steaks are pricey, but portions are generous and the kitchen dependable.

Lift Bar and Grill

333 Menchions Mews, at Bayshore Drive (604 689 5438/www.liftbarandgrill.com). Bus 5 then 5min walk. **Open** 11.30am-11pm Mon-Fri; 11am-11pm Sat, Sun. **Main courses** $9-$38. **Credit** AmEx, MC, V. **Map** p248 J1 ❸

Floating on a concrete pad at the far edge of Coal Harbour, this sleek waterfront restaurant with vanishing glass walls offers a million-dollar view of the mountains. Make that $8 million, which is what Lift cost to build. If only the owners had invested in a kitchen large enough to accommodate the well-heeled crowds this new hotspot attracts. Without reservations, you'll typically have to wait an hour for a table. Food service is none too swift either. Chef Keith Krentz strives to make his seafood inventive (fresh oysters on the half shell are garnished with spiced watermelon brunoise; mussels are simmered in a prosciutto, melon and basil white-wine broth). You'll do best to keep it simple with drinks and sushi next to the fire pit on the upper deck. **Photo** *p94*.

West Coast

Delilah's

1789 Comox Street, at Denman Street (604 687 3424/www.delilahs.ca). Bus 6. **Open** 5.30-10pm daily. **Main courses** $21-$25. **Credit** AmEx, MC, V. **Map** p248 H2 ❸

A West End institution for 20-plus years, Delilah's boasts of being the North American birthplace of the cocktail Martini. Whether she did actually beat New York to the punch is a question worth debating at the restaurant's friendly bar, where fruit-infused vodkas reign alongside the drag queen entertainers who frequently pop in. Hand-painted cherubs dancing on the ceiling and lush velvet banquettes lend high-camp glamour to the dining room. A three-tiered tapas menu runs the gamut from juniper-and-gin pickled salmon to house-cured elk carpaccio. Full-size mains are also available.

Earls On Top

1185 Robson Street, between Thurlow Street & Bute Street (604 669 0020/www.earls.ca). Bus 5. **Open** 11.30am-1am daily. **Main courses** $9-$19. **Credit** AmEx, MC, V. **Map** p248 J3 ❸

Earls is a surprising exception to the pedestrian standards of chain restaurants that dominate this busy shopping district. With more than 50 locations across Western Canada and the United States, this family-friendly organisation ensures quality by supplying fresh produce from its own Fraser Valley farms and cooking all dishes on-site from scratch. Spicy wok stir-frys, oven-roasted chickens, thin-crust pizzas and monthly specials make up a wide-ranging menu that offers something for everyone. The food is expected to get even better now that local celebrity chef Michael Noble (ex-Diva at the Met) has stepped in as director of culinary and product development. The overall great value even extends to the one-price wine list. **Other locations**: throughout the city.

Parkside

1906 Haro Street, at Gilford Street (604 683 6912/
www.parksiderestaurant.ca). Bus 5. **Open** 6-11pm
Mon-Thur, Sun; 6pm-midnight Fri, Sat. **Main courses**
$28. **Credit** MC, V. **Map** p248 H2 ④
Tucked away on a leafy residential street near
Stanley Park, Parkside combines the feel of a cosy
neighbourhood haunt with the elegance of a classical European kitchen. Chef/owner Andrey Durbach
has developed a cult following with his daily-chang-
ing three-course menus, hand-picked wine list and
heady selection of after-dinner cognac and eau de
vie. Cuisine leans towards the rich and meaty, with
strong French and Italian influences, but is balanced
with zesty touches from local produce.

Raincity Grill

1193 Denman Street, at Davie Street (604 685 7337/
www.raincitygrill.com). Bus 6. **Open** 5-10pm Mon-
Fri; 10.30am-2pm, 5-10pm Sat, Sun. **Main courses**
$19-$31. **Credit** AmEx, MC, V. **Map** p248 G2 ④
Raincity Grill was an original pioneer of Pacific
Northwest cuisine and remains one of the city's best.
Harry Kambolis (the owner of C and Nu) deserves
high praise for a long-standing commitment to local
small-lot farmers and sustainable fisheries that supply the seasonal menus. Chef Andrea Carlson lets
unfussy flavours speak louder than her ego, and has
expanded the kitchen's repertoire with home-baked
breads and pastries. Arrive between 5 and 6pm for
the early bird three-course tasting menu, or linger
as the sun sets over English Bay while trying to put
a dint in the list of 100 regional wines by the glass.
In spring and summer, the takeout window offers
sandwiches and salads for gourmet picnics.

Stanley Park

Cafés

Stanley Park Pavilion

610 Pipeline Road, opposite Malkin Bowl (604 602
3088/www.stanleyparkpavilion.com). Bus 19 then
10min walk. **Open** *Bar & Grill* autumn/winter 9am-
5pm daily; spring/summer 9am-9pm daily. *Tea*
House 2-5pm Sat, Sun. **Main courses** *Bar & Grill*
$7.95-$12.95. *Afternoon tea* $34.95. **Credit** AmEx,
MC, V. **Map** p63.
This quaint heritage building, circa 1911, is located
in the heart of Stanley Park, next to the rose gardens.
The casual self-service Veranda Bar and Grill, open
year-round, offers gourmet baguette sandwiches,
burgers, salads, home-baked cakes and ice-cream.
During the summer season (weekends only) the Rose
Garden Tea House serves up a traditional Victorian
afternoon tea with loose-leaf teas and three-tiered
trays of finger sandwiches, scones and fresh pastries. Reservations recommended.

Seafood

The Fish House in Stanley Park

8901 Stanley Park Drive, at Lagoon Drive (604 681
7275/www.fishhousestanleypark.com). Bus 6 then
5min walk. **Open** 11.30am-4pm, 5-10pm Mon-Sat;
11am-4pm, 5-10pm Sun. **Main courses** $19.95-
$29.95. **Credit** AmEx, MC, V. **Map** p63.
Chef Karen Barnaby is a celebrity in the city and a
really cool broad who tells it like it is. A stint at the
Rivoli Restaurant in Toronto and a jaunt around

Eat, Drink, Shop

Go Fish. *See p104.*

DINING OUT IN PARIS AND LONDON?

Mexico where she worked as a personal chef gives her serious bohemian street cred. And, oh yeah, she's a pretty darn good cook, who has carved out a speciality with creative low-carb dishes and numerous books. The Fish House is a little frilly for an oyster bar, but it does serve an exceptional afternoon tea.

West Coast

Sequoia Grill at the Teahouse
Ferguson Point, Stanley Park Drive (604 669 3281/ www.vancouverdine.com). Bus 19 then 5min walk. **Open** 11.30am-9.45pm Mon-Sat; 10.30am-9.45pm Sun. **Main courses** $9-$34. **Credit** AmEx, MC, V. **Map** p63.

This ain't your grandma's teahouse any more, but she'll still love the panoramic view of English Bay. When Brent Davies (Cardero's, Seasons, Sandbar) took over this Stanley Park landmark in 2004, he threw out the doilies, landscaped the patio and turned this formerly fussy tourist trap into a modern West Coast bistro. The menu might bore if you've been to this group's other restaurants. But on sultry summer nights, there's no better place to relax, sip a strawberry-basil Martini and watch the sun go down over the Georgia Strait.

Yaletown

Cafés

Cito Espresso
116 Davie Street, at Pacific Boulevard (604 633 2486/www.citoespresso.com). Bus 15. **Open** 7am-10pm Mon-Sat; 8am-10pm Sun. **Main courses** $6-$10. **Credit** MC, V. **Map** p249 K5 ⓐ

The beautiful people of Yaletown now have a beautiful café where they can flirt or, even better, just admire themselves in the mirrored walls. This tall, airy room with designer furniture and lots of blond wood and blonder people is as inviting as the pastries behind the marble counter. The custom-blend coffee is deliberately cheaper than Starbucks across the street. Breakfast is happening.

French

Elixir Bar and Restaurant
350 Davie Street, between Richards Street & Homer Street (604 642 0557/www.elixirvancouver.ca). Bus 15. **Open** 6.30am-2am Mon-Sat; 6.30am-midnight Sun. **Main courses** $7-$34. **Credit** AmEx, MC, V. **Map** p249 K5 ⓐ

This brassy brasserie – part bistro, part nightclub – pumps up the Moulin Rouge cabaret vibe with a dash of Baz Luhrmann's rococo kitsch. With a DJ spinning in the middle of the floor and gussied-up cougars prowling the bar, dinner can be a frenzied experience. Elixir's late-night *petit plats* menu features smaller versions of regular mains (steak frites, lobster ravioli, seasonal salads, etc) that are first-rate and available until 12.30am.

Italian

Cioppino's Mediterranean Grill & Enoteca
1133 & 1129 Hamilton Street, between Helmcken Street & Davie Street (604 688 7466/www.cioppinos yaletown.com). Bus 15. **Open** noon-3pm, 5.30-11pm Mon-Fri; 5.30-11pm Sat. **Main courses** $18.95-$45. **Credit** AmEx, MC, V. **Map** p249 K4 ⓐ

Cioppino's is the place where expense accounts go to die. Pino Posteraro's prices are on the steep side, but still comparable to other upscale Italian joints in the area and by far the best of the bunch. Indeed, the owner's deceptively simple pastas, pan-seared fish and hearty grilled meats make it one of the top fine-dining restaurants in the city and a favourite of visiting celebrities. Where else are they going to find 1959 Dom Perignon for $3,288 a pop?

Seafood

Blue Water Café & Raw Bar
1095 Hamilton Street, at Helmcken Street (604 688 8078/www.bluewatercafe.net). Bus 15. **Open** *Bar* 4pm-midnight daily. *Restaurant* 5pm-midnight daily. **Main courses** $22.50-$43.50. **Credit** AmEx, MC, V. **Map** p249 K4 ⓐ

Freshly shucked oysters, delicately flavoured sushi and simply prepared seafood in a swanky room liberally sprinkled with professional hockey players and Hollywood celebrities. What's not to like about Blue Water Café? Main courses can be pricey, but you'll find decent value and an unforgettable tasting experience at the semi-circular raw bar. The main bar offers 20 wines by the glass, a wide variety of chilled sakes and more than 60 single-malt whiskies. Feeling extravagant? Try a three-tiered tower of shellfish, sushi and a whole Dungeness crab.

Coast Restaurant
1257 Hamilton Street, between Drake Street & Davie Street (604 685 5010/www.coastrestaurant.ca). Bus 15. **Open** 4.30pm-midnight daily. **Main courses** $23-$40. **Credit** AmEx, MC, V. **Map** p249 K5 ⓐ

The best way to enjoy this high-energy restaurant is to sit at the large communal table on the main floor where the chef prepares the freshest catch of the day right in front of you. The room's clean contemporary design – lots of wood and light – is reflective of the menu, which features a huge variety of freshly grilled local fish and exotic flavours from around the world, including South Pacific John Dory and Cuban lobster tails. You won't be disappointed. **Photo** *p100*.

Thai

Simply Thai
1211 Hamilton Street, at Davie Street (604 642 0123/www.simplythairestaurant.com). Bus 15. **Open** 11.30am-3pm, 5-11pm Mon-Fri; 5-11pm Sat, Sun. **Main courses** $8.95-$25.95. **Credit** AmEx, MC, V. **Map** p249 K4 ⓐ

The best of the west. **Coast Restaurant**. *See p99.*

Simply Thai is simply the best Thai restaurant in the city. Mind you, there isn't a great deal of comptition in Vancouver. The chef/owner Siriwan Rerksuttisiridach (call her Grace) apprenticed with Penpan Sittitrai, a celebrated fruit and vegetable sculptor who trains chefs for the Thai royal family. She goes back every year for a refresher course. Arrive early for lunch and wrap your lips around some cho muang, purple flower-shaped dumplings stuffed with minced chicken, onions and secret spices. Grace only makes about five orders of these a day. There's an outstanding wine list.

West Coast

Brix Restaurant and Wine Bar

1138 Homer Street, between Helmcken Street & Davie Street (604 915 9463/www.brixvancouver. com). Bus 15. **Open** 5pm-2am Mon-Sat. **Main courses** $8-$34. **Credit** AmEx, MC, V. **Map** p249 K4 48

The city's most charming patio has raised the bar even further with a high glass-ceilinged enclosure for year-round dining. This brick-walled keyhole courtyard tempts you to slide back into a comfy cushioned chair and pretend you've traipsed back in time. Elaborate floral displays only add to the old-world ambience. The seasonal menu, however, is pure West Coast fusion with many small plates for sharing, late-night fondues and an exceptional selection of wines by the glass.

Hamilton Street Grill

1009 Hamilton Street, at Nelson Street (604 331 1511). Bus 15. **Open** 11.30am-2.30pm, 5pm-2am Mon-Fri; 5pm-2am Sat, Sun. **Main courses** $12-$36. **Credit** AmEx, MC, V. **Map** p249 K4 49

This unassuming steakhouse is full of delicious surprises. Owner Neil Wyles is a passionate chef who sources his products from the city's best suppliers. Don't miss the butcher's cut hanger steak if it is available, and BC's giant honey mussels, when in season. The home-made gingerbread pudding has a widespread following. And the not-so serious monthly wine tastings are a good deal.

Section (3)

1039 Mainland Street, at Nelson Street (604 684 2777/www.sectionthree.com). Bus 15. **Open** 11.30am-1am Mon-Wed; 11.30am-2am Thur-Sat; 5pm-midnight Sun. **Main courses** $8-$27. **Credit** AmEx, MC, V. **Map** p249 K4 50

Originally, and rather cheekily, called De Niro's Supper Club, in homage to the actor, this varied diner acquired a new name after the man himself threatened legal action against the restaurant, citing Section 3 of the British Columbia Privacy Act. Certain celebrities still dig the dark, punkish Goth vibe. Kelly Osbourne has been a regular diner. With DJs spinning at weekends and an inexpensive menu offering lots of pizza, pasta and small plates, it doubles as a lounge and a restaurant.

Gastown

Cafés

Brioche Urban Baking

401 W Cordova Street, at Homer Street (604 682 4037/www.brioche.ca). Bus 4, 7. **Open** 7am-7pm Mon-Fri; 9am-5pm Sat, Sun. **Main courses** $6-$10. **Credit** MC, V. **Map** p249 L3 51

The pastries are divine, but there's so much more to enjoy here. Start with robust, white bean and pancetta soup and a hunk of freshly baked Calabrian bread. For light snacks, grab a thick slice of Sicilian pizza, garlicky Caesar salad or Italian meatball sandwich. The pasta plates are massive and the desserts are made from scratch every morning. With dishes priced under $10 and a liquor licence to boot, Brioche bakes up one of the best deals in town.

Cook Studio Café

374 Powell Street, between Gore Avenue & Dunlevy Avenue (604 696 9096/www.foodandservice.net). **Bus** 4, 7. **Open** 8am-2pm Mon-Fri. **Main courses** $4.95-$7.95. **Credit** MC, V. **Map** p249 N3 🔢

Imagine the unemployed misfits in *Jamie's Kitchen* running a more casual daytime restaurant at a seedier location in town. This 45-seat deli and catering company gives 20 troubled youth professional training each year. Coffee, freshly baked muffins, cinnamon buns and takeout sandwiches are available when the doors open for breakfast. Lunch offers 20 or so simple dishes that are tasty and generous. Government training grants subsidise the prices, which are extremely modest.

Indian

Sapphire South Asian Fusion

216 Abbott Street, at Water Street (604 669 7785/www.sapphirecanada.com). Bus 4, 7. **Open** 11am-3pm, 5-10pm Tue-Sat; 11am-3pm Sun. **Main courses** $9-$16. **Credit** AmEx, MC, V. **Map** p249 M3 🔢

South Asia doesn't stop at the mainland but includes the food of the Resplendent Isle on its menu. Sri Lankan hoppers and lampries jostle for your palate with South Indian dosas and thali at this family-owned Gastown dining room where the service is exceptionally friendly – in a good way. Creative curries, noodles and rice bowls shake up the menu. The prices are reasonable and even cheaper at lunch.

Italian

Incendio

103 Columbia Street, at Alexander Street (604 688 8694). Bus 4, 7. **Open** 11.30am-3pm, 5-11pm Mon-Fri; 5-11pm Sat; 4.30-10pm Sun. **Main courses** $8-$13. **Credit** AmEx, MC, V. **Map** p249 M3 🔢

Good thin-crust pizza is hard to find in Vancouver but Incendio fills the void with the best skinny pizza pies in town, hand-flipped and baked hot in a brick oven. For something different, try the smoked-duck sausage or mango-basil butter sauce. The owners of Stella's Tap and Tapas Bar (*see p112*) also make pretty darn good pastas in this funky heritage-building room, where local artwork hangs on exposed brick walls. Service is swift.

Other locations: Incendio West, 2118 Burrard Street (604 736 2220).

Mexican

The Mouse and Bean Café

207 W Hastings Street, at Cambie Street (604 633 1781). Bus 10, 16, 20. **Open** noon-6pm Mon-Thur; noon-8pm Fri, Sat. **Main courses** $6-$15. **No credit cards**. **Map** p249 L3 🔢

Izakaya time

Vancouver being just a long hop from Tokyo, the city offers dining experiences rarely found outside Japan. Perhaps the most popular of the post-sushi wave of eateries from the east are *izakaya* restaurants.

Izakayas (the word translates roughly as 'sit and drink spot') evolved as student hangouts in Japan. Despite the name, izakayas are not pubs. They are unpretentious open-kitchen diners that serve small Japanese and Korean dishes alongside lots of beer and sake. A visit to an izakaya offers a fascinating glimpse of casual Japanese cooking, combined with an ambience that can take newcomers by surprise.

That surprise begins at the door when everyone starts yelling at you. Patrons are usually greeted by the entire staff with a hearty shout of 'Irashimase!' ('Welcome!'). Servers will politely take your order, then turn and bellow Japanese instructions to the cooks in the open kitchen. It can make you jump the first time.

Izakayas like the very popular **Hapa** (1479 Robson Street, 604 689 4272) and the Tokyo import **Shiru Bay: Chopstick Café** (1193 Hamilton Street, 604 408 9315) offer a more upscale atmosphere while maintaining prices that are very reasonable. And there's something undeniably cool about drinking sake out of bamboo. Others like **Guu** (838 Thurlow Street, 604 685 8817; Guu with Garlic, 1698 Robson Street, 604 685 8678; Guu With Otomokae, 105-375 Water Street, 604 685 8682) opt for a more casual feel.

E-Hwa (1578 Robson Street, 604 688 9555) bills itself as a 'Korean izakaya', a student-friendly hangout with Korean specialities replacing the Japanese.

Small dishes are the general rule here – grilled fish, sashimi, rice or noodles; deep-fried chicken is common. For those who crave sushi, Shiru Bay includes the sublime dragonball, made from shrimp, salmon roe, flying fish eggs and avocado. Hapa counters with nama harumaki, a tasty variation on the familiar California roll. Both establishments offer a succulent slice of mackerel seared at your table with a hand-held blowtorch; beware the flames, and the fumes!

This authentic Mexican restaurant, tucked inside the old Dominion Building, is worth seeking out. The Ascenzio family makes all their own rojas, salsa verdes and refried beans. The prices are so cheap, even the most expensive item (the plato mixteco with thinly sliced carne asada, black beans, rice, cactus salad and cheese enchilada) is hardly a splurge. Service is charming, but erratic. Breakfast is promised soon; the dining room still closes early.

Chinatown

Hon's Wun-Tun House
108-268 Keefer Street, between Main Street & Gore Avenue (604 688 0871). Bus 3. **Open** 11am-11pm Mon-Thur, Sun; 11am-midnight Fri, Sat. **Main courses** $6-$10. **Credit** AmEx, MC, V. **Map** p249 N4 🦈

What began as a cramped storefront with a fresh noodle factory at the back in the 1970s has now grown to a chain of five restaurants with retail outlets attached selling anything from noodles and barbecue meats to their signature line of potstickers and other cooked and frozen foods. Look for the well-priced, periodically changing chef's suggestions for interesting new twists on traditional favourites such as seafood in egg sauce over fried rice noodles. Portions are satisfying and the quality consistent.

Kam Gok Yuen
142 E Pender Street, between Main Street & Columbia Street (604 683 3822). Bus 3. **Open** 10.30am-8.30pm daily. **Main courses** $5-$10. **No credit cards. Map** p249 M4 🦈

A kitschy, cavernous room provides no-nonsense efficient service, though things get a touch chaotic when busy. The food is solid, comforting noodle-house fare and the barbecued repertoire from ducks to crispy-skin pork are across-the-board excellent. Wontons are classically prepared – chunky with shrimp and bound with just the right amount of fatty pork to add flavour – and come in a tasty broth scented with dried flounder and sprinkled with yellow chives. Curried beef brisket with rice and peppered beef over rice noodles are also good bets.

Kim Saigon Sandwich Bar
265 E Hastings Street, between Main Street & Gore Avenue, at the rear of Asia Market (604 688 6824). Bus 10, 16, 20. **Open** 9.30am-5.45pm daily. **Main courses** $2.50. **No credit cards. Map** p249 N3 🦈

To get here you have to trek through a desolate stretch of Downtown Eastside, but your reward is an unbeatable meal-in-a-bun that is an artful study in taste and texture for a pauper's price of $2.50. The bacon spice banh mi is a mini baguette first crisped in the toaster oven then smeared with liver pâté and stuffed with slices of Vietnamese ham and pork belly, pickled daikon and carrots, a stick of cucumber, sliced jalapeños, coriander sprigs and a moistening dash of Maggie sauce. Meatball, chicken and vegetarian versions are available.

New Town Bakery & Restaurant
158 E Pender Street, between Main Street & Columbia Street (604 681 1828). Bus 3. **Open** 6.30am-8.30pm daily. **Main courses** $4-$8. **No credit cards. Map** p249 M4 🦈

Complete with six stools at the counter and booths along one wall, New Town is, in spirit and decor, one of the very few true diners still thriving in trend-chasing Vancouver. Regulars come for familiar banter with the waitresses and rustic dim sum dispensed from stacks of giant steamers by the cashier's desk. Order a coconut cocktail bun with a cup of Hong Kong tea – brewed extra-strong and creamy with evaporated milk – or a meal-sized chicken deluxe big bun stuffed with chicken, ground pork, Spam and a salted duck egg yolk, then relax and feel the clock turn back to gentler times.

Phnom Penh
244 E Georgia Street, between Main Street & Gore Avenue (604 682 5777). Bus 3. **Open** 10am-10pm daily. **Main courses** $6-$14. **Credit** AmEx, MC, V. **Map** p249 N4 🦈

Expect constant queues at lunch at the best Cambodian-Vietnamese restaurant in town. Hot and sour soup with fish, prawns or chicken, is chunky

Something fishy

Fish has been an essential part of life in Vancouver for some 10,000 years and even today most restaurants in Vancouver cook with wild salmon. Five types are indigenous to the area: coho, spring (also known as king, chinook or tyee), chum (silver bright), sockeye (red, kokanee) and pink. Chum is most commonly found on local plates, owing to its delicious, moist flavour and relatively low cost.

Pink salmon is often mistaken by visitors to be the tastiest breed, but chefs refer to pink as 'dogfish' – fit only for your hound. Spring and sockeye are the higher-end breeds, as reflected by their price. Sockeye is famous for its red, lean flesh and deep flavour, whereas spring is flaky and fatty. Coho, in the middle, price-wise, has a softer texture than other stocks.

Smoked salmon – both cold smoked and cooked – is available in gift shops around the city (a good, central store is Salmon Village, 779 Thurlow Street, 604 685 3378, www.salmonvillage.com), but for a closer look at the different varieties, head to Granville Island. And for a West Coast treat, try Indian Candy – salmon cured with 60 per cent sugar and 40 per cent salt, and then hot smoked.

Burger and fries for gourmets. **Feenies**.

with tomatoes, bean sprouts and pineapples. Refreshing Vietnamese chicken salad tosses impossibly crisp cabbage with mint, Thai basil, coriander and nuoc cham. Marinated butter beef is carpaccio seared on a hot plate splashed with lime juice, fish sauce and fried garlic. There's also fried oyster cake, stewed pork hot pot, garlic frogs' legs... And a new dessert: black rice pudding steeped in rice wine lees.

West Side

Cafés

Arbutus Real Food Market

2200 Arbutus Street, at W 6th Avenue (604 736 5644). Bus 4, 7. **Open** 6am-6pm Mon-Fri; 8am-6pm Sat, Sun. **Main courses** $6-$8. **No credit cards**. **Map** p251 F6 ⑥
This is a genuine neighbourhood coffee shop, beloved by its regulars, where everything is baked on site. Standouts include the deep-dish fruit pies and the German chocolate cake with sticky coconut topping; soups and paninis are reliably tasty.

Pane From Heaven

1670 Cypress Street, at W 1st Avenue (604 736 5555). Bus 2, 22. **Open** 7am-7pm daily. **Main courses** $6-$7. **Credit** MC, V. **Map** p251 G5 ⑥
A useful spot for before or after the Vanier Park museums, just a block beyond Starbucks, and well worth crossing the road for. A cup of organic fair trade coffee with fondant-filled pain au chocolat goes down a treat; you won't find better in the city.

Canadian

Feenie's

2563 W Broadway, between Trafalgar Street & Larch Street (604 739 7115/www.feenies.com). Bus 9, 17. **Open** 11.30am-2.30pm, 5.30-11.30pm Mon-Fri; 10am-2pm, 5.30-11.30pm Sat, Sun. **Main courses** $19. **Set menu** $35. **Credit** AmEx, MC, V. **Map** p250 E6 ⑥
Can't afford the 11-course chef's menu at Lumière (*see p104*)? Vancouver's most celebrated chef created this casual Canadian bistro next door to give fans a taste of the chow he cooks at home. Rob Feenie's favourites might sound like ordinary staples, but they tickle the taste buds with inventive flair: shepherd's pie is layered with duck confit, mushroom duxelle, corn and truffled mashed potatoes; the infamous Feenie's weenie is a custom-cured cheese smokie, smothered in sauerkraut, sautéed onions and lardons. Unfortunately, the servers are so insufferably hip – and don't they know it – they hurt an otherwise fabulous food experience. **Photo** *above*.

Diners

Moderne Burger

2507 W Broadway, at Larch Street (604 739 0005/www.moderneburger.com). Bus 9, 17. **Open** noon-8.45pm Tue-Sat; noon-8pm Sun. **Main courses** $6.95-$9.45. **No credit cards**. **Map** p250 E6 ⑥
This tiny, turquoise diner is always packed, drawing people back time and again for its top-notch burgers. The menu is short and to the point: choose

from steak, turkey, wild salmon, veggie or lamb and customise from a succinct list of toppings. A platter, with hand-cut chips, makes for a serious plateful. Old-fashioned shakes, malts, floats and flavoured colas add to the retro feel.

Sophie's Cosmic Café
2095 W 4th Avenue, at Arbutus Street (604 732 6810/www.sophiescosmiccafe.com). Bus 4, 7. **Open** 8am-9.30pm daily. **Main courses** $6.95-$12.95. **Credit** MC, V. **Map** p251 F6 ⑥⑤
Since 18 years is almost a geological time scale in restaurant terms Sophie's, which has been providing comfort food to the locals since 1988, certainly qualifies as a Kitsilano institution. The interior is crammed with '50s memorabilia and knick-knacks, making it a fun space to enjoy a burger or a slice of key lime pie. The food is nothing to get excited about, although weekend brunch is incredibly popular; if you're not in by 9am, expect to wait. **Photo.**

White Spot
2518 W Broadway, between Larch Street & Trafalgar Street (604 731 2434/www.whitespot.ca). Bus 9, 17. **Open** 6.30am-11pm Mon-Thur, Sun; 6.30am-midnight Fri, Sat. **Main courses** $7.99-$19.49. **Credit** AmEx, MC, V. **Map** p250 E6 ⑥⑥
The staple casual family chain across British Columbia, White Spot serves up decent, good value meals geared towards the family market. The usual suspects – burgers, fish and chips, ribs – are complemented by Asian rice bowls, big salads and pastas. The kids' menu (a very reasonable $4.99) comes in a cardboard ship; the cocktail and beer menu needs no tarting up for weary parents.

Sophie's Cosmic Café.

Fish & chips

Go Fish
1505 W 1st Avenue, at Creekside Drive (604 730 5040). Bus 50. **Open** 11.30am-6.30pm Wed-Fri; noon-6.30pm Sat, Sun. **Main courses** $6-$15. **No credit cards. Map** p251 H5 ⑥⑦
Tucked away on the Seawall between Granville Island and Vanier Park, this little shack serves up some of the best fish and chips in town. Owner Gord Martin (of Bin 941, *see p92*) buys fish fresh from the boats at the end of the jetty and when it runs out, he shuts up shop for the day. Choose from cod, salmon or halibut in a crispy, tempura-like batter with chips and Asian-inspired slaw, sandwiches (salmon, ahi tuna or oyster) or tacos. Daily specials include soups, grilled fish on greens and the always delicious ceviche. The food is cooked to order and very popular, so expect to queue. **Photo** *p97*.

French

Bistro Pastis
2153 W 4th Avenue, between Arbutus Street & Yew Street (604 731 5020/www.bistropastis.com). Bus 4, 7. **Open** 11.30am-2pm, 5.30-10.30pm Tue-Fri; 11am-2pm, 5.30-10.30pm Sat, Sun. **Main courses** $19.50-$37. **Credit** AmEx, MC, V. **Map** p251 F6 ⑥⑧
Originally an upmarket dining room, Bistro Pastis was transformed into a more casual French bistro in 2003 (although you'd hardly guess it by the prices). Still, this romantic room with its crackling fireplace and hanging bread baskets is one of the best places in the city for coq au vin, braised veal cheeks and other traditional French fare. The deep cellar stores a wide selection of fine Gallic wines, many available by the glass. Weekend brunch offers yummy, runny omelettes and full-strength champagne without any of that dastardly fruit fizz.

Lumière
2551 W Broadway, between Larch Street & Trafalgar Street (604 739 8185/www.lumiere.ca). Bus 9, 17. **Open** 5.30-11pm Tue-Sun. **Prix fixe** $100. **Tasting menus** $120-$130. **Credit** AmEx, MC, V. **Map** p250 E6 ⑥⑨
If you can afford it, Lumière will provide one of the most memorable meals of your life. Since opening ten years ago, chef-owner Rob Feenie has developed an international following (and the prestigious stamp of approval as Canada's only freestanding Relais & Chateaux restaurant) with unfussy flavours that transcend the establishment's foundation of classic French cuisine on feather-light Asian wings. Sablefish marinated in sake-and-maple syrup and mascarpone-stuffed ravioli (sometimes available in the more accessibly priced tasting bar) will make you moan aloud. The only spots on this pearl are service, which can sometimes be obsequious, and the fact that Feenie is so busy making guest appearances around the world that these days he can rarely be found cooking in his own kitchen.

Mistral

2585 W Broadway, at Trafalgar Street (604 733 0046/www.mistralbistro.ca). Bus 9, 17. **Open** 5.30-10pm Mon; 11.30am-2pm, 5.30-10pm Tue-Sat. **Main courses** $12-$28. **Credit** AmEx, MC, V. **Map** p250 E6

Perched on the opposite end of the block from Lumière, Mistral opened in autumn 2005 and immediately upped the culinary ante of the area. Chef-owner Jean-Yves Benoit's CV includes a couple of three-Michelin starred restaurants in Europe (El Bulli, Arpege) and his own award-winning L'Emotion in West Van. An unpretentious room belies the seriousness of the cooking here. Cassoulet, boudin noir, daube de boeuf – all done to perfection and without a twist of fusion in sight. Flavours are true and deep, service is attentive and friendly.

Indian

Maurya

1643 W Broadway, between Fir Street & Pine Street (604 742 0622/www.mauryaindiancuisine.com). Bus 9, 17. **Open** 11.30am-2.30pm, 5-11pm Mon-Fri; 5-11pm Sat, Sun. **Main courses** $10.95-$18.95. **Credit** AmEx, MC, V. **Map** p251 G6 ⑦

A gorgeous dining room with soaring ceilings, majestic drapery, polished wood tables and sparkling tiled floors certainly helps Maurya stand out. But it's the mouth-watering Delhi dishes – that rely on reduced stocks simmered overnight rather than butter, cream and deep fryers for their rich flavours – that make a meal in this elegant restaurant a worthwhile occasion. The always-fresh and expansive buffet is a good option for lunch.

Vij's

1480 W 11th Avenue, at Granville Street (604 736 6664/www.vijs.ca). Bus 10, 98. **Open** 5.30-10pm daily. **Main courses** $18-$25. **Credit** AmEx, MC, V. **Map** p251 H7 ⑦

Jamie Oliver described his dinner at Vij's as the most memorable of his trip to Canada. But don't take his word for it. Just ask the mobs that line up outside the doors every night why they keep coming back for wine-marinated lamb 'popsicles' in fenugreek cream curry, savoury jackfruit on cornmeal chapatti and other fusion dishes. Get there early and relax in the lounge with complimentary nibbles and a glass of wine, beer or cider from the short but selective drinks list. And please don't bother bitching about how they don't take reservations.

Italian

Adesso

2201 W 1st Avenue, at Yew Street (604 738 6515/www.adessobistro.com). Bus 2, 22. **Open** 11.30am-2pm, 5.30-11.30pm Tue-Fri; 10am-2.30pm, 5.30-11.30pm Sat, Sun. **Main courses** $12-$32. **Credit** AmEx, MC, V. **Map** p251 F5 ⑦

Halfway between Kits beach and West 4th, Adesso occupies a spot that's seen many restaurants come

Federico's Supper Club. *See p111.*

and go. From the insalata Adesso, with garbanzo beans and anchovy dressing, through the spaghettini with prawns and scallops to the grain-fed veal chop, this is tasty cooking – although the kitchen can be inconsistent. Weekend brunch offers classy versions of classic dishes, while the deliciously thin and crispy pizzas are a steal at $12.

Japanese

Tojo's

2nd Floor, 777 W Broadway, at Willow Street (604 872 8050/www.tojos.com). Bus 9, 17, 99. **Open** 5-10pm Mon-Sat. **Main courses** $15.75-$28.95. *Omakase* (chef's menu) $50-$100. **Credit** AmEx, MC, V.

No other Vancouver Japanese chef better exemplifies the true spirit of Japanese cooking – a profound respect for locality and season – than Hidekazu Tojo. A signature roll, inspired by the northern lights in Whitehorse, wraps gossamer-thin cucumber sheets around prawn tempura, mango and avocado. Smoked sablefish is steamed in yuzu-scented broth with pine mushrooms and gobo in autumn and fresh bamboo shoot and asparagus in spring. The omakase (chef's choice menu) offers one of the most sophisticated and artistic tasting menus of local specialities in the region. It's expensive, but worth it.

Yuji's Tapas

2059 W 4th Avenue, between Arbutus Street & Maple Street (604 734 4990). Bus 4, 7. **Open** 5-11.30pm Tue-Thur; 5pm-12.30am Fri, Sat; 5-11pm Sun. **Main courses** $6.50-$18.50. **Credit** MC, V. **Map** p251 F6 74 ⑦

Know your noodles

Each day by 11am the noodle maker at **Legendary Noodle** (4191 Main Street, 604 879 8758, pictured) is hard at work. He slaps, stretches and twirls loaves of dough, first into ropes, then, as if by sleight of hand, into long strands of fresh noodles ready for the pot. Blanched until tender yet chewy, the noodles are topped with a creamy rich, deftly garlicky broth studded with chunks of lamb shanks and scented with chopped coriander. But for the clean air and the white-capped North Shore mountains, one might imagine this scene in a *hutong* in Beijing rather than midtown Vancouver. The dish, fresh lamb soup with noodles ($6.80, number 25 on the menu), was praised by the *New York Times*.

But this is unusual: big-city media attention is most often lavished on the large, well-established Hong Kong-style 'seafood' restaurants such as **Sun Sui Wah** (3888 Main Street, 604 872 8822), **Kirin** (102-1166 Alberni Street, 604 682 8833; 555 W 12th Avenue, 604 879 8038) and the **Imperial** (355 Burrard Street, 604 688 8191). It's true, they were the pioneers: arriving in the 1990s in the wake of well-heeled immigrants seeking to hedge their bets in advance of the former British colony's return to Chinese control, they raised the bar and bolstered Vancouver's reputation as a great place for Chinese food. Thankfully, along with affluence came discernment and variety. This diversity is what justifies the hype. Take note: the best restaurants are not in Chinatown, but you don't have to travel far to eat very well indeed. These spots are not about ambience and decor – the only guarantee is good food.

Noodle houses (often fully fledged restaurants in disguise) are always a good bet for a meal. Many have a separate chef's menu featuring what they think they do best, so be sure to ask for that. Sometimes these are only in Chinese, so ask them for a translation or recommendation.

Closest to downtown is **Congee Noodle House** (141 E Broadway, 604 879 8221). Congee – the rice porridge universally loved by the Chinese for its soul-soothing, cure-all properties – is frothily boiled to a silken turn and laden with quality ingredients such as fresh ling cod slices or tender boneless chicken and Chinese mushrooms. It makes a belly-warming snack after a strenuous bout of clubbing. Try congee with a portion of steamed-to-order rice rolls filled with succulent scallops and sea-sweet prawns.

In **Kwong Chow Congee Noodle House** (3163 Main Street, 604 876 8520), ostrich is available in eight permutations from chilli-spiked to stir-fried with snow peas. Adventurous diners are rewarded with retro-rustic Cantonese soul-food dishes such as

Eat, Drink, Shop

steamed pork patty with dried squid, and newly minted fusion fare like clams in lemongrass and fish sauce.

The friendly **Mui Garden Restaurant** (4265 Main Street, 604 872 8232) is a self-proclaimed Hong Kong-style coffee shop with a Pacific Rim twist. Chiu Chow rice noodle soups with house-made fish, cuttlefish and beef meatballs authentically seasoned with pickled brassica, fried garlic and nori vie for attention here with creamy, coconut-enriched Malaysian curried lamb, and an odd but satisfying German salt pork knuckle hot pot.

But the best in this genre is **Ho Yuen Kee** (6236 Fraser Street, 604 324 8855). A basic dish of sautéed beef with green kale (actually Chinese broccoli) is testament to the chef's competence: the beef tender, the vegetables toothsome, crunchy and scented with ginger. The cold 'hand-shredded' chicken, moistened with a creamy, galangal-spiced sesame dressing, is top-notch. Their signature dish – lobster or Dungeness crab steamed over lotus-wrapped sticky rice seeded with sweetcorn and tobikko – draws regulars from the West Side and Richmond. Even better though, are the golden garlic chilli crab or prawns. First deep-fried in a crust of corn starch and chilli paste, the crustacea are tossed in a mound of fragrant, wafer-thin garlic crisps that are wickedly addictive in their own right. Resistance is futile.

For something different try **Landmark Hot Pot House** (4023 Cambie Street, 604 872 2868), Vancouver's first, and still the best, Chinese hot pot restaurant, where do-it-yourself, fondue-style cooking – traditionally for the warming of body and soul on long wintry nights – is now an all season affair. Start with the duo soup base of satay and chicken broth and the seafood combination of heaped platters of meats, seafood, vegetables and cellophane noodles.

A bit farther afield, at the Northern/Shanghai-style **Green Village** (2461 Nanaimo Street, 604 258 9018) pork is the crowning theme: whole hocks are braised and draped in sweet soya glaze, and ground pork is shaped into 'lion's head' meatballs and served in hot pots with bok choy. An opulent boneless eight-treasures roast duck stuffed with glutinous rice, Chinese sausage and bacon, chestnuts, gingko nuts and mushrooms requires a day's advance notice.

For authentic Taiwanese food, try **Kalvin's Restaurant** (5225 Victoria Drive, 604 321 2888). While you may want to steer clear of the pig blood soup, you'll like the lamb, bean curd and vegetable hot pot, the classic smoked duck and the spare rib and bitter melon in black bean sauce. Consider calling 24 hours ahead for the fabulous wonton chicken (a large terrine of wonton soup made with a whole chicken) and the chopstick-tender, generously-portioned braised pork shank in brown sauce.

But the highest concentration of Chinese restaurants is in the suburb of Richmond just east of Vancouver International Airport. Here the choice becomes dizzying. Try **Sea Harbour Seafood Restaurant** (3711 No.3 Road, Richmond, 604 232 0816) for succulent hand-shredded salt-baked chicken and a rich rustic braised pork belly with pickled vegetables; and **Shanghai River Restaurant** (110-7831 Westminster Highway, Richmond, 604 233 8885) for juicy steamed Shanghai dumplings made in the see-through kitchen, the confit-like crisp-fried brined duck and the jellied pork. Or just look around and order what looks good at the next table – you really can't go wrong here. Reservations are recommended for both.

Eat, Drink, Shop

Cheap eats

On a tight budget? You can still feast for less than $25 a day. There's no better spot in Terminal City for a hearty, greasy breakfast than **Bon's Off Broadway** (2451 Nanaimo Street, 607 253 7242), just a ten minute walk from Commercial Drive. It's just $2.95 (tax included) for the two-egg all day special (open 7am weekdays; 8am weekends) so it's no surprise that queues build up quickly.

A quest for the best lunchtime value will send you rocketing back downtown to **Save-On-Meat** (43 W Hastings Street, 604 683 7761) where a classic lunch counter hides at the back of a sprawling butcher's shop. Beware: all of their burgers are double meat, and grown men have been known to quiver before the mammoth portions. The bacon cheeseburger plus fries for $5.50 is a must for larger appetites.

Come dinner time look for the neon seahorse that marks out the **Only Seafoods Café** (20 E Hastings Street, 604 681 6546), located in the same spot since 1912. Vancouver's redevelopment has meant that the café has found itself on the wrong side of the tracks in recent years, but that hasn't stopped it from continuing to prepare some of the best ocean fare in the Lower Mainland. Take a half crab for $8.50 or the dinner special – fish chowder followed by two fillets of salmon with fries, coleslaw and bread – for $10. Not a spot for a cheap, late-night romantic meal: they close at 8pm.

When you're ready for desert, head to **La Casa Gelato** (1033 Venables Street, 604 251 3211). Made from natural ingredients on-site, the ice-cream comes in over 200 flavours. Sampling spoons allow you to try before you buy, so before settling for the usual tiramisu or vanilla live a little: give the wasabi or garlic a try. It's $3.50 for a single scoop; $5.50 for a double.

Yuji's makes inventive sushi: mango, kiwi fruit, prosciutto, duck breast – there's even a BLT roll. Not that there isn't traditional sushi and sashimi available too. A modern, unpretentious room provides a pleasing backdrop to a menu that's light-hearted in tone but serious in execution. Beautifully presented dishes are good for sharing; it's easy to find yourself working your way through the menu.

Mexican

Las Margaritas

1999 W 4th Avenue, at Maple Street (604 734 7117/www.lasmargaritas.com). Bus 4, 7. **Open** 11.30am-10pm Mon-Thur, Sun; 11.30am-11pm Fri, Sat. **Main courses** $11.25-$19.45. **Credit** AmEx, MC, V. **Map** p251 F6 🕖

The food is more Southern California than Mexican and the frozen Margaritas are too sweet to be authentic, but the menu's all-encompassing variety of enchiladas, tacos, fajitas and every known Mexican beer will satisfy your inner gringo until the next wild and crazy booze cruise in Cancun. The long list of vegetarian options is a nice twist, but the grilled salmon burrito really makes us wonder just how far West Coast fusion can be stretched.

Thai

Khai Thai To Go

2184 Cornwall Avenue, at Yew Street (604 677 6767). Bus 2, 22. **Open** 5-10pm Mon-Thur; 11am-10pm Fri-Sun. **Main courses** $6.50-$8.95. **Credit** MC, V. **Map** p251 F5 🕖

Don't expect to be taken back to the beaches of Ko Pang Ngan – though a takeaway will survive the trip to Kits beach right across the road. Curries are adequate, the yam neua (beef salad) has all the requisite flavour including the roasted rice, and noodle dishes are decent. Soups are blandly disappointing.

Vegetarian

The Naam

2724 W 4th Avenue, between Stephens Street & Macdonald Street (604 738 7151/www.thenaam. com). Bus 2, 4, 7, 22. **Open** 24hrs daily. **Main courses** $4.50-$12.50. **Credit** AmEx, MC, V. **Map** p250 D6 🕖

The Naam has been serving up its vegetarian staples since 1968, when West 4th was still known as Rainbow Road. It has retained its funky, hippie feel and remains a very popular spot, particularly in the evenings when there is live music, and at weekends. The food is mostly good, though it can verge on the worthy. Salads are great and the blueberry milkshake is too good to be reserved for children alone.

West Coast

Bishop's

2183 W 4th Avenue, at Yew Street (604 738 2025/ www.bishopsonline.com). Bus 4, 7. **Open** 5.30-11pm Mon-Sat; 5.30-10pm Sun. **Main courses** $32-$38. **Credit** AmEx, MC, V. **Map** p251 F6 🕖

It took a chef from Wales to introduce Vancouver to a modern regional style of cooking now known, and widely emulated, as Pacific Northwest. Nearly 20 years ago, John Bishop committed himself to using nothing but the freshest seasonal bounty of the region's oceans, rivers, fields and forests. The kitchen is now totally organic. Bishop's continues to attract a loyal clientele of fashionable foodies, including Goldie Hawn, who come for the food and the restaurant's consummately charming but ever quirky host, who can sometimes be found trailing dirt to starched white linen tables to show off gargantuan beets and freshly foraged funghi.

Cru

1459 W Broadway, at Granville Street (604 677 4111/www.cru.ca). Bus 9, 10, 16, 17, 98, 99. **Open** 5-11pm daily. **Main courses** *small plates* $9-$16; *three-course prix fixe* $36. **Credit** AmEx, MC, V. **Map** p251 H6 **⑦**

Cru makes the most of its space: a long, thin room, warmed by chocolate tones, banquettes along one wall and three choice tables, with small sofas and silky cushions. The prix fixe menu at $36 is a steal, but the real fun is to be had with the small plates. Steamed local mussels and clams are fresh and plump, braised beef short rib is melt-in-the-mouth tender; bitter chocolate torte is the real deal. The wine list is helpful and updated weekly. You'll be pushed to eat as well anywhere else for the price.

Watermark

1305 Arbutus Street, at Whyte Avenue, on Kits Beach (604 738 5487/www.watermarkrestaurant.ca). Bus 2, 22. **Open** 11am-11pm daily. **Main courses** $11.95-$29.75. **Credit** AmEx, MC, V. **Map** p251 F4 **⑧**

Vancouver's restaurateurs still haven't worked out how to combine a beach location with good food.

Take Watermark: the gorgeous looks are deceiving. Locals spent three years fighting the restaurant's development for fear it might spoil their slice of paradise. Then the two-storey building turned out to be understatedly sleek and perfectly suited to the site. But behind the exterior the food can't compare to the architecture or the breathtaking view of English Bay. Almost everything on the menu was very mediocre when the restaurant opened in the summer of 2005. Still, the bar is a sleek spot for drinks, which are reasonably priced and include selections from some of British Columbia's best wineries.

West Restaurant

2881 Granville Street, at W 13th Avenue (604 738 8938/www.westrestaurant.com). Bus 10. **Open** 11.30am-11pm Mon-Fri; 5.30-11pm Sat, Sun. **Main courses** $29.50-$44.50. **Credit** AmEx, MC, V. **Map** p251 H7 **⑧**

West or Lumière? Local critics are torn each year when it comes to choosing the city's best restaurant. In 2005, West came out on top and deservedly so, not just for taste but also for consistency. This swanky dining room is the showpiece in owner Jack Evrensel's collection of restaurants that include Blue Water Café, Cin Cin and Araxi in Whistler, but the kudos goes to executive chef David Hawksworth, who spent more than a decade in the UK, working alongside Marco Pierre White at the Canteen and Raymond Blanc at Manoir aux Quat'Saisons, before returning home with a fanatical commitment to sourcing nothing but the very best local seasonal ingredients. His slow-cooked, sous vide meats are melt-in-your mouth divine. **Photo** *below.*

Eat, Drink, Shop

The best place to eat in Vancouver? **West Restaurant**.

Reef.

East Vancouver

Cafés

Continental Coffee

1806 Commercial Drive, at E 2nd Avenue (604 255 0712). Bus 20. **Open** 7am-7pm Mon-Fri; 8am-6pm Sat; 9am-4pm Sun. **Credit** MC, V. **Map** p252 Q6 ⑫
Three generations have percolated here, producing the best dark roast and organic coffee on the Drive and promoting fair trade. Jordan Allan and family also have their own roasting plant: try the famiglia.

Soma

2528 Main Street, between E Broadway & E 10th Avenue (604 873 1750). Bus 3, 9, 99. **Open** 6am-11pm daily. **Main courses** $5.50-$8. **Credit** MC, V. **Map** p252 N7 ⑬
This contemporary-minimalist café with skinny chairs attracts a young crowd. They don't seem to mind the slow service, happy to wait for baked goods or a slice of vegan cheesecake.

African/Middle East

Zanzibar Café Bar

1851 Commercial Drive, between E 2nd Avenue & E 3rd Avenue (604 215 2008). Bus 20. **Open** 9.30am-8pm Mon-Thur; 9.30am-9pm Fri-Sun. **Main courses** $6.55-$6.99. **No credit cards. Map** p252 Q6 ⑭

Authentic Moroccan food served by knowledgeable and friendly staff. Despite bargain prices, the mint tea comes in a silver teapot. Lamb tagine, fall-off-the-bone tender with prunes and apricots, is outstanding and running a close second is chicken almond bastela: a perfect balance of sweet cinnamon with caramelised onion in filo pastry. Breakfast starts at 9.30am with everything under $5.

The Americas

Reef

4172 Main Street, at E 26th Avenue (604 874 5375/www.thereefrestaurant.com). Bus 3, 25. **Open** 10am-11pm Mon-Thur, Sun; 10am-1am Fri, Sat. **Main courses** $8-$17. **Credit** AmEx, D, MC, V. **Map** p252 N9 ⑮
Always busy, this bright and breezy Main Street haunt serves up generous portions of Caribbean cooking. Food with bite includes jerk chicken, goat curry and, at brunch, a signature jerk salmon eggs benedict. Cocktails are unapologetically tropical and the rum list is fabulously extensive; home made ginger beer provides a safer option. **Photo** *above.*

Rinconcito Salvadoreno

2062 Commercial Drive, at E 4th Avenue (604 879 2600). Bus 20. **Open** 3-10pm Mon, Wed-Sun. **Main courses** $2.50-$12.50. **No credit cards. Map** p252 Q6 ⑯

A colourful and cheery room with good food at good prices. Papusas (handmade cornflour tortillas) are filled with beans, cheese and pork for $2.50 a pop. But despite the temptation at those prices to stuff, keep some room for the deep-fried, batterless, whole fresh fish. Fresh tropical juices are served on tap, and at weekends ask for a glass of horchata, made from seeds only found in El Salvador. Licenced.

Asian

Ch'i

1796 Nanaimo Street, at E 2nd Avenue (604 215 0078/www.chirestaurant.ca). Bus 7. **Open** 5pm-midnight Tue-Sun. **Main courses** $4-$20. **Credit** AmEx, MC, V. **Map** p252 S6 ⑰

Ch'i brings a touch of hip elegance to its East Van neighbourhood, with its tea-infused Martinis and Indo-Thai menu. Olives come cured in wasabi and ginger, sablefish with a curry-coconut polenta; the chilli chocolate molten cake is pure decadence. There's also a good list of wines by the glass and a lychee mojito that could turn a nun to drink.

Italian

Federico's Supper Club

1728 Commercial Drive, at E 1st Avenue (604 251 3473/www.federicossupperclub.com). Bus 20. **Open** 5.30pm-midnight Wed-Sun. **Main courses** $17.95-$39.95. **Credit** AmEx, MC, V. **Map** p252 Q6 ⑱

The velvet curtains, art deco flourishes, children crawling under tables and the Fuoco Family Band serenading the sweaty dancefloor with equal measures of Italian schmaltz and Vegas-style bombast, will make you feel like you landed on the set of *The Wedding Singer* with a couple of Tony Soprano's

mob thrown in. Dinner is served up New-Jersey banquet style on long candlelit tables. The hearty pastas and tender veal scaloppini are like something mamma would make in the old country. **Photo** *p105.*

Japanese

Toshi Sushi

181 E 16th Avenue, at Main Street (604 874 5173). Bus 3. **Open** 11.30am-10pm Mon-Thur, Sun; 11.30am-11pm Fri, Sat. **Main courses** $5.50-$9.50. **Credit** MC, V. **Map** p252 M8 ⑲

Toshi Saito presides over this compact, warm and efficient SoMa 30-seater where hour-long queues are routine. Good quality nigiri, makis and foot-long house roll are main draws for the hip regulars. Tasty yakimonos such as an impossibly tender ika shoga (grilled squid with ginger soy) and a succulent gin tara saikyo (black cod in miso) are also immaculately and artfully presented.

Seafood

The Cannery

2205 Commissioner Street, on the waterfront (604 254 9606/toll free 1-877 254 9606/www.cannery seafood.com). No buses. **Open** 11.30am-2.30pm, 5.30-9pm Mon-Thur; 11.30am-2.30pm, 5.30-9.30pm Fri; 5-9.30pm Sat; 5-9pm Sun. **Main courses** $23-$34.95. **Credit** AmEx, MC, V.

Recent port security measures haven't made it easy to access this establishment: check the detailed map on their website. Once safely ensconced, dip into house-made lobster infused olive oil while perusing a global seafood menu, sipping from a sophisticated wine list, and enjoying one of the best views – and sunsets – of the inner harbour.

Korea moves

Korean menus can present a challenge to western palates unprepared for certain parts of cow and swine. Never mind the searing, throat-ripping heat. But don't be put off: there are plenty more familiar tastes available.

First comes the ban-chan: complimentary plates of appetisers. One of these will always consist of kimchee, the spicy cabbage that is Korea's national dish (often served with a pair of scissors to cut it up).

Korean dumplings can usually be ordered fried or steamed, and should be familiar to anyone who loves Japanese gyoza or Chinese potstickers. Then look for favourites like beebimbop, a tasty rice dish that includes meat and vegetables and a fried egg – the hot sauce comes on the side, so you can control the level of heat. Korean seafood pancakes

are also good – something akin to a fried pizza – and, like the spare ribs, are always popular. Spicy soft tofu hot pot is a common choice, though it can be a strange textural experience for the uninitiated. Safety can be found in stir-fry dishes based around pork, beef, chicken, squid, octopus and the like. For those wanting new tastes, cow feet soup, pork spine stew, tripe and tongue, should provide adventure enough.

Most of Vancouver's Korean restaurants are concentrated downtown near the western stretch of Robson Street. **Hai Mai Jang Mo Jib** (*see p95*) is among the most popular, as are **Spice Alley** (1333 Robson Street, 604 685 4468) and **Norboo**'s (1536 Robson Street, 604 806 0369) usually has an expectant and hungry queue.

Vegetarian

Foundation

2301 Main Street, at E 7th Avenue (604 708 0881/ www.the-foundation.ca). Bus 3. **Open** 4.30pm-1am Mon-Fri; noon-1am Sat, Sun. **Main courses** $6.50-$9.50. **Credit** MC, V. **Map** p252 M6 ⓰

Bargain basement prices and an innovative vegan-friendly menu has made the Foundation a popular and lively spot for residents of East Vancouver. Alongside the expected houmous and nachos are more adventurous choices including black beans with bananas and pasta with mango, jalapeño and coconut sauce. The only downside is the service, which can sometimes be slow and surly.

West Coast

Aurora Bistro

2420 Main Street, between E 8th Avenue & E Broadway (604 873 9944/www.aurorabistro.ca). Bus 3, 9, 99. **Open** 5.30-11pm Tue-Sat; 10am-2pm, 5.30-10pm Sun. **Main courses** $18-$25. **Credit** AmEx, MC, V. **Map** p252 N7 ⓱

With its funky DIY design and inventive modern cuisine, Aurora has raised the bar on Main Street. Chef-owner Jeff Van Geest is committed to promoting the best local produce including a wine list sourced only from vineyards in British Columbia. Attention to detail is evident in pairings such as Hazelmere Farm beet salad with Okanagan goat's cheese and root beer braised bison short ribs, while brunch includes black truffle scrambled eggs. Seafood is all approved as ocean-friendly.

Stella's Tap and Tapas Bar

1191 Commercial Drive, at William Street (604 254 2437/www.stellasbeer.com). Bus 20. **Open** 11am-11.30pm daily. **Main courses** $5-$12. **Credit** AmEx, MC, V.

Great moules – with a bucket of fries on the side naturally – are best washed down with one of the several Belgian beers that are available on tap. Try the L'Orange, which comes, as the name suggests, with fresh squeezed orange and, surprisingly, coconut milk. The beer list also features bottled choices from Unibroue, the award winning Belgian-style brewery in Quebec. Beer spills into dessert in a delectable chocolate cake made with Bellevue Kriek.

North Shore/ West Vancouver

Cafés

Bean Around the World – Dundarave

1522 Marine Drive, at 15th Street, West Vancouver (604 925 9600). Bus 250. **Open** 5.30am-9pm daily. **Main courses** $4.95-$7.95 **Credit** MC, V. **Map** p253 Y4 ⓲

All the baking at Bean Around the World – Dundarave is done in-house, with fresh daily muffins and many healthy options like their vegan loaf. There's even a wheat-grass press. Select from many organic and fair trade coffees, then hit the back deck for a leisurely cup of java.

French

La Régalade

103-2232 Marine Drive, at 22nd Street, North Shore (604 921 2228/www.laregalade.com). Bus 250. **Open** 11.30am-2pm, 5.30-10pm Tue-Fri; 5.30-10pm Sat. **Main courses** $14.55-$24.95. **Credit** MC, V.

Even though Brigitte and Alain Rayé doubled the seating in renovations, this French bistro is still the toughest place on the North Shore at which to get a table. Generous portions of veal cheeks or beef bourguignon are served in cocottes, and the stellar wine list showcases French and BC varieties.

Seafood

Salmon House on the Hill

2229 Folkestone Way, off Skilift Way, North Shore (604 926 3212/www.salmonhouse.com). No bus. **Open** 11.30am-2.30pm, 5-9.30pm Mon-Sat; 11am-2.30pm, 5-9pm Sun. **Main courses** $23-$31. **Credit** AmEx, MC, V.

This North Shore landmark boasts a view that stretches from Vancouver Island to Mount Baker on a clear day – when it's raining you get a good view of the window. A seasonal 'uniquely BC' menu sits alongside main menu offerings such as smoked sockeye salmon and seafood mixed grill. The cedar-walled dining room features a fine collection of First Nations art and the wine list focuses on BC.

West Coast

Beach House at Dundarave Pier

150 25th Street, at Bellevue Avenue, West Vancouver (604 922 1414/www.atthebeach house.com). Bus 250. **Open** 11.30am-9pm Mon-Sat; 10.30am-3pm, 5-9pm Sun. **Main courses** $16-$36. **Credit** AmEx, MC, V.

Just a few steps from the beach, this waterfront locale is the perfect spot to dig into a tower of Dungeness crab and hand-peeled shrimp. Come in the summer for the spectacular views of Point Grey, Lions Gate Bridge and Stanley Park.

Moustache Café

1265 Marine Drive, between Hamilton Avenue & Hanes Avenue, North Shore (604 987 8461/ www.moustachecafe.com). Bus 239. **Open** 11.30am-10pm Mon-Fri; 5-10pm Sat, Sun. **Main courses** $15-$28. **Credit** MC, V. **Map** p253 Y4 ⓳

Chef/owner Geoff Lundholm's pride and passion shows in two small and cosy rooms snuggled into this heritage home. The show-stopper is the venison confit ravioli: marinated, braised, chopped and stuffed, it's a two-day labour of love.

Bars

Come in out of the rain.

Vancouver's reputation as the rainiest spot on earth is, mercifully, only applicable eight months of the year. June's clear skies and glorious, dry heat carry through to the long Indian summers of September. Thus, many of the city's bars function as either a respite from the damp gloom of winter, or a sun-dappled terrace from which to inhale the sea air and bask in its inimitable beauty.

A series of neighbourhoods – homogeneous, mainstream Kitsilano; bohemian, multi-ethnic Commercial Drive; set-designed, antiseptic Yaletown – offer something to accommodate all tastes, be it the modest tippler in search of quiet, a boisterous gang out for a night of ear-splitting music and drunken bliss, or blasé hipsters who will only sip Negronis in the company of other blasé hipsters.

Sadly (or not, if hordes of bevvied-up 19-year-olds is your thing), most downtown bars are clustered around a brash, trashy six-block strip of **Granville Street**. Those willing to wander are rewarded with more diversity in venues and crowds. Renascent neighbourhoods (**Gastown, South Main**) hold appeal for many reasons, not the least of which is dynamic nightlife.

A common complaint is the paucity of seaside bars. But times are changing, and nowhere more so than in Yaletown, where Martini bars and charming *boites* on the boardwalk flourish by the water's edge.

Downtown

Aqua 1066

1066 W Hastings Street, between Thurlow Street & Burrard Street (604 683 5843/www.aqua1066.com). Bus 22. **Open** phone for details. **Admission** free-$15. **Credit** AmEx, MC, V. **Map** p249 K2 ❶
The business district of downtown is virtually abandoned after 6pm but here they have to beat away underdressed, overtanned suburbanites. Water's the theme, so with wonky aquatic decor, low ceilings and sweaty bodies pressing in on all sides, asphyxiation must be part of the draw. Amid the thump of music, trays float past, bearing drinks pink and blue.

Atlantic Trap & Grill

612 Davie Street, at Seymour Street (604 806 6393/www.trapandgrill.com). Bus 4, 6, 7, 10, 16, 17, 50. **Open** noon-midnight Mon, Sun; noon-1am Tue-Sat. **Admission** free. **Credit** MC, V. **Map** p248 J4 ❷
If the bought-in-bulk Limerick green paint and 'Newfie parkin only, b'ye!' sign on the wall don't

The best **Bars**

For alfresco drinking
Nu (*see p115*).

For cocktails
Nu (*see p115*).

For romance
Bacchus Piano Lounge (*see below*).

For singles
SkyBar (*see p115*).

allude enough to the rollicking, Celtic revelry the Trap is famous for, the myriad photos of drunken patrons will. Newly arrived, homesick Maritimers from Canada's Atlantic coast, local media and dotcommers bang elbows at this stopover between the hordes of drunken bridge-and-tunnellers on the Granville strip (two blocks west), and the yuppie-chic of Yaletown (two blocks east).

Bacchus Piano Lounge

The Wedgewood Hotel, 845 Hornby Street, at Robson Street (604 689 7777/www.wedgewoodhotel.com). All city-centre buses. **Open** 6.30am-midnight Mon-Wed, Sun; 6.30am-1am Thur-Sat. **Credit** AmEx, MC, V. **Map** p249 K3 ❸
Strange name, really. There are no toga'd revellers and there is nothing particularly Bacchanalian about the silent nods asking for another round. The room exudes upscale warmth and crisp elegance, and the service sets the standard for the entire city.

Bin 941

941 Davie Street, between Burrard Street & Hornby Street (604 683 1246/www.bin941.com). Bus 2, 6, 22. **Open** 5pm-1.30am Mon-Sat; 5pm-midnight Sun. **Admission** free. **Credit** MC, V. **Map** p248 J4 ❹
Bin 941 is Vancouver's most electric space. Manager Ed Perrow acts as host, furniture mover and party facilitator, stoking up the riotous energy of the cramped bar that feeds in to the rest of the room. The no-reservation policy means pop stars must wait like the rest of us.

❶ Pink numbers given in this chapter correspond to the location of each bar as marked on the street maps. *See pp246-253.*

Eat, Drink, Shop

The Cambie Bar & Grill

300 Cambie Street, at W Cordova Street (604 688 9158/www.cambiehostels.com). Bus 3, 4, 7. **Open** 9am-1am Mon-Thur; 9am-2am Fri, Sat; 11am-midnight Sun. **Admission** free. **Credit** MC, V. **Map** p249 L3 ⑤

The room, down-at-heel and decorated as if by explosion, is one step up from squalor. So obviously it's immensely appealing to slumming university students. Grizzled bikers, sundry reprobates and off-duty longshoremen can all also be found downing their drinks here. Pool tables, a big patio, cheap food and cheaper beer further explain its allure.

Gerard (Sutton Place Hotel)

845 Burrard Street, at Smithe Street (604 682 5511). Bus 2, 5, 22. **Open** 11am-1am Mon-Sat; 4.30pm-midnight Sun. **Admission** free. **Credit** AmEx, MC, V. **Map** p249 K3 ⑥

This is the cosy spot where the celebrity-obsessed wait in hope for a glimpse of Al Pacino or other visiting Hollywood stars, shooting films in Tinseltown north. The piano tinkles in the background, bag-laden shoppers fresh from Robson Street's boutiques gulp Cosmopolitans and chew their way through bowls of complimentary almonds, while bankers clang Manhattans in a toast to a closed deal.

Ginger 62 Cocktail Den & Kitchen

1219 Granville Street, at Davie Street (604 688 5494). Bus 4, 6, 7, 10, 16, 17, 50. **Open** 8pm-1am Wed, Thur, Sun; 7pm-3am Fri, Sat. **Admission** free-$10. **Credit** MC, V. **Map** p248 J4 ⑦

The name is a homage to famous Gingers (Rogers, Fred Astair's dancing partner, and Grant – actress Tina Louise – the one from *Gilligan's Island*), while the bar attracts cool men in black and women in spaghetti straps (the savviest of whom arrive early to claim a sofa from which to hold court). The calm amber lighting seems to make everyone beautiful. Inventive Martinis, Asian-fusion tapas, and some of the city's sharpest DJs make for a memorable night.

Honey Lounge

455 Abbott Street, at W Pender Street (604 685 7777). Bus 10, 16, 20, N20, N35. **Open** noon-10pm Mon-Thur; noon-2am Fri; 4pm-1am Sat; closed Sun. **Admission** free-$7. **Credit** AmEx, MC, V. **Map** p249 M3 ⑧

A beacon between Gastown and Yaletown, lurid Honey Lounge – gold patina'd walls, Marrakech-kitsch banquettes, aubergine tiled bar – welcomes all. They come in search of different grails: some to dance, some to preen, some to queen, but most to get their drinks in and their rocks off.

Nu man

When **Jay Jones** – Vancouver's best and highest profile bartender – moved from West to open Nu (*see p92*) in the summer of 2005, there were seismic shifts as his Westside clientele followed him over the Granville Street Bridge. From humble roots

as a barback at the Cactus Club, Jones soon climbed to the top of the city's highly competitive restaurant food chain when he created West's wine list and invented cocktail after award-winning cocktail.

His influence helped West win *Vancouver Magazine*'s restaurant-of-the-year awards in 2003 and 2005. TV interviews, invitations to global cocktail competitions and spreads in women's glossies soon followed. His shock of raven hair, brooding flamenco-dancer scowl and roadmap of tattoos make him ideal for photo spreads, but the image belies a modest, understated and generous spirit. As a host he never discriminates between the solitary wallflower at his bar and the visiting Hollywood starlet and her entourage.

In Nu Jones may well have found the home he has long sought. Together with chef, Rob Clark, Jones's goal of pairing the finest of indigenous ingredients (Rob Clark's obsession with the sea rivals Jones's fixation on the bottle) with the most painstaking and satisfying drinks reaches fruition. Jones is pioneer and proselytiser of the decidedly West Coast-casual trend of dining at the bar – a trend which, due in no small part to Jones's passion, is here to stay.

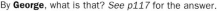

By **George**, what is that? *See p117* for the answer.

Lucy Mae Brown

Downstairs, 862 Richards Street, at Smithe Street (604 899 9199/www.lucymaebrown.ca). All city-centre buses. **Open** 5.30pm-2am daily. **Admission** free. **Credit** AmEx, MC, V. **Map** p248 K4 ❾
Epicurean snobs prefer to keep the restaurant upstairs a secret. With similar stealth, the restaurant's lounge bar, called the Opium Den in a nod to the area's past, attracts ethereal women and Zara'd men. They come from 10pm onwards, lean against the bar, drink mojitos and feel as if they've arrived.

Morrissey Irish House

1227 Granville Street, at Davie Street (604 682 0909). Bus 4, 6, 7, 10, 16, 17, 50. **Open** 8am-2am Mon-Thur, Sun; 8am-3am Fri, Sat. **Admission** free. **Credit** AmEx, MC, V. **Map** p248 J4 ❿
Not to be confused with the local chapter of The Smiths fan club, this is the modern-day blueprint for a sleek, stylish Irish bar. There are better-lit caverns, but here the dimness serves its purpose, allowing the visual warmth of the fireplace to set the mood during the bleaker, winter months.

900 West Lounge

Hotel Vancouver, 900 W Georgia Street, between Burrard Street & Hornby Street (604 669 9378). All city-centre buses. **Open** 11.30am-midnight Mon-Thur, Sun; 11.30am-1am Fri, Sat. **Admission** free. **Credit** AmEx, MC, V. **Map** p249 K3 ⓫
900 wears its status as the city's poshest hotel bar with aristocratic insouciance. The attitude is shared by its clientele: bankers, you-only-live-once tourists and elegant singles, seemingly waiting for their shipping magnate to come in to port. The room's abuzz from cocktail hour (complimentary hors d'oeuvres between 5pm and 6pm), with the silky sounds of a jazz trio and the smell of money filling the air.

Nu

1661 Granville Street, on the north shore of False Creek (604 646 4668/www.whatisnu.com). Bus 4, 7, 10, 16, 17, 50. **Open** 11am-1am Mon-Fri; 10.30am-1am Sat; 10.30am-midnight Sun. **Admission** free. **Credit** AmEx, MC, V. **Map** p248 H5 ⓬
Late arriving (due June, opened Labor Day 2005), but worth the wait. The best new patio in the city, the most ambitious drinks bar menu this side of San Francisco, and a sweeping, see-it-to-believe-it floating bar worth a visit on its own. (*See p114* **Nu man.**)

The Roxy

932 Granville Street, between Smithe Street & Nelson Street (604 331 7999/www.roxyvan.com). All city-centre buses. **Open** changes nightly; phone or check website for details. **Admission** free-$10. **Credit** AmEx, MC, V. **Map** p249 K4 ⓭
The Granville strip on a weekend is not for the claustrophobic, and the Roxy's velvet rope bulges. The 1980s never ended at Vancouver's busiest bar, but with ironic sentiment so in vogue this behemoth is more popular than ever. Drinking in Herculean quantities is the order of the day, thus ensuring city's best flair bartenders fade into a blur.

SkyBar

670 Smithe Street, at Granville Street (604 697 9199/www.skybarvancouver.com). All city-centre buses. **Open** phone for details. **Admission** free-$15. **Credit** AmEx, MC, V. **Map** p249 K4 ⓮

Three spectacular floors (the first a 'radiant fiber optic martini bar', the second a nightclub, the third a rooftop patio) exude the tropical warmth and detached cool of South Beach or Sunset Strip. The VIP room attracts the siliconed and the tanned, all with the hope of a celebrity spotting. Queues start early, snaking well around the corner.

Wild Rice

117 W Pender Street, at Beatty Street (604 642 2882/www.wildricevancouver.com). Bus 10, 16, 20, N20, N35. **Open** *11.30am-midnight Mon-Thur; 11.30am-1am Fri; 5pm-1am Sat; 5pm-midnight Sun.* **Admission** *free.* **Credit** MC, V. **Map** p249 L3 ⓯
Wild Rice is anything but. Rather it suits the blasé set to a tee, with its appearance-enhancing under-lit bar and Gotan Project soundtrack. Owner Andrew Wong works the bar with apparent fringe-theatre solemnity. Don't be fooled, though, his enthusiasm for Asian-fusion food-wine pairings is infectious.

Yaletown

Bar None

1222 Hamilton Street, at Davie Street (604 689 7000/www.barnonenightclub.com). Bus 15. **Open** *9pm-2am Mon, Tue, Thur; private bookings Wed, Sun; 9pm-4am Fri, Sat.* **Admission** *free-$12.* **Credit** MC, V. **Map** p249 K4 ⓰
The elegant, snaking post-and-beam room of Bar None, Yaletown's most enduring it-spot, was converted from a warehouse in 1992 and ever since then the place has been luring transfixed punters, as the queues testify. But persevere and you'll soon hear why its reputation as a turntabler's destination has not diminished in the nearly two decades since it opened its doors. Soul, funk and vinyl in Monday's 'Soul Stream' compete with Zak Santiago's Saturday Miami beats, as hipper-than-thou patrons bump along, trying not to spill their drinks.

Microbreweries

Eat, Drink, Shop

There are those who argue that the pre-eminence of Vancouver microbreweries – in quality, if not in quantity – is the result of a collective thumbing of the nose at the dominant national breweries of the east: Labatt and Molson. Such Canadian 'brand' beers might be better than their American counterparts, but westerners merely see this as the tallest among midgets. 'Make mine a Labatt Blue,' is seldom heard on the left coast. 'Two Granville Island Winter Lagers, thanks,' rolls off the tongue and down the throat so much better.

The aforementioned **Granville Island Brewery** (GI for those in the know) has been the standard bearer of quality and innovation since the release, in 1984, of the legendary – and still wildly popular – Island Lager, brewed in the traditional Bavarian style. An embarrassment of riches were to follow from the little-brewery-that-could: Gastown Amber Ale, English Bay Pale Ale, Maple Cream Ale, Cypress Honey Lager, named in honour of nearby city landmarks. 2004 saw the release of Robson Street Hefeweizen, intended for 'sizzling, sunny days'. An acquired taste, this rewarding brew is unfiltered, so as to create subtle fruit flavours and a murky appearance. Slice of lemon optional. Purists and proud locals drink nothing but GI – not hard to do, it's available all over town – and the loyalty is deserved. Granville Island remains the mark of the best in West Coast taste.

If only for the view of the snow-capped mountains across Burrard Inlet, the

Steamworks Brewpub (375 Water Street, 604 689 2739) would be destination enough. But inventive, unique beers such as a charming, pale golden honey wheat ale only improve the view. (Fun fact: the beers are brewed by steam heat, provided by the Vancouver Central Heat Company, the same company that supplies the steam for Gastown's landmark steam clock.) The **Yaletown Brewing Company** pub (1111 Mainland Street, 604 681 2739) is found in a vast, dilapidated warehouse. Its range of beers is ambitious, if occasionally off the mark. Of the seven or so disparate offerings some sing (an almondy, autumnal nut brown ale, a fruity pale ale), while others sadly sink (the Double Dome Stout is about as subtle as a punch in the face).

At the **Dockside Restaurant and Brewery** on Granville Island (1253 Johnston Street, 604 685 7070) the Pilsner, Dortmunder, Hefeweizen, Kölsch-style and Altbier beers suggest the German roots of the owners. A prettier locale to enjoy hearty beer-food pairings in the city is hard to find. Taxis are available for those bold or mad enough to try everything. In North Vancouver, **Sailor Hägar's Brewpub** (86 Semisch Street, 604 984 7669) concentrates on making some of the Lower Mainland's best beer, with quiet Scandinavian pride and purity of flavour. The drinks on offer range from a full-bodied Honey Pilsner to a more delicate, clovery Scandinavian Amber Lager, to a brawny Grizzly Nut Brown Ale.

George

*1137 Hamilton Street, at Helmcken Street, Yaletown
(604 628 5555). Bus 15.* **Open** 4pm-2am Mon-Sat.
Admission free. **Credit** AmEx, MC, V.
Map p249 K4
This is where the Pretty Young Things come to be
seen in the city's best incarnation of a smart London
bar. The room is dominated by a sculpted-glass sea
anemone, aglow in the dim light. Southern hemisphere cocktails are the draw, reinvented with poise
for advanced-course tipplers. **Photo** *p115.*

Opus Bar

*350 Davie Street, at Hamilton Street (604 642 0557/
www.opushotel.com). Bus 15.* **Open** 11.30am-1am
Mon-Thur, Sun; 11.30am-3am Fri, Sat. **Admission**
free. **Credit** AmEx, MC, V. **Map** p249 K5
For 15 minutes Opus Bar was popular with those
who are always looking for the Next Big Thing.
They've moved on but the eponymous boutique
hotel's smallish lounge – furnished in Philippe
Starck/Louis XIV-garage sale style – attracts beautiful people with longer attention spans. They come
in droves to sip Cosmopolitans while pretending not
to notice one another. Arrive early (or very late) or
risk appearing suburban while standing in line.

Soho

*1144 Homer Street, between Helmcken Street &
Davie Street (604 688 1180/www.sohocafe.ca).
Bus 15.* **Open** 11am-2am Mon-Fri; noon-3am Sat;
noon-midnight Sun. **Admission** free. **Credit**
MC, V. **Map** p249 K4
The oldest (est. 1991) bar in Yaletown, the room and
its patrons seem blissfully oblivious to the surrounding chic. True to the neighbourhood's rough-
and-tumble past, the room – exposed fir beams and
creaky planks – is as cosy and inviting as any in the
city come winter. It casts its gaslight glow on bil-
liards (six tables) and whispering couples, while doubling as the home bar of the Yaletown Football Club.

Subeez

*891 Homer Street, at Nelson Street (604 687 6107).
Bus 15.* **Open** 11.30am-1am Mon-Fri; 11am-1am Sat;
11am-midnight Sun. **Admission** free. **Credit** MC, V.
Map p249 K4
Subeez is a welcoming and unpretentious venue
that's become one of downtown's most reliable spots
for a solid, predictable, loud night out: a few rounds,
a casual flirt, a possible rejection. The room appears
to have been designed by someone infatuated with
all things metal (and imposing art installations). The
packed weekends are best. On other evenings the
crowd is dwarfed by the vastness of the space.

Gastown

Alibi Room

*157 Alexander Street, between Main Street &
Columbia Street (604 623 3383/www.alibiroom.com).
Bus 3, 4, 7.* **Open** 5pm-midnight Mon-Thur; 4.30pm-
2am Friday; 10am-2am Sat, Sun. **Admission** free.
Credit AmEx, MC, V. **Map** p249 M3

Smiling eyes at **The Irish Heather**.

While the glacial, pretentious service from aspiring
actors can be annoying the gorgeous room makes
up for it: narrow communal tables, vaulted ceilings
and a slimbar. Hordes of local mediacrities, artists
and film types call this their home from home. The
weekends downstairs are lively for DJ scratches and,
of course, much posing. So come along and preen.

The Irish Heather

*217 Carrall Street, at Water Street (604 688 9779).
Bus 50.* **Open** noon-midnight daily. **Admission**
free. **Credit** MC, V. **Map** p249 M3
While the Emerald Isle's diaspora is the reason for
so many Irish pubs around the world, most pander
to the tired clichés of leprechauns and shamrock. Not
so here, where owners Sean and Erin Heather's
dream has become Gastown's darling. Exposed
brick in the front room, a charming glassed-in back
patio, and the best poured pint of the dark stuff in
the city make this the first (and often only) stop for
recently arrived Irish nationals, beer and whiskey
purists, and loyal-as-a-dog regulars.

West Side

Bimini's Tap House

*2010 W 4th Avenue, at Maple Street (604 732
9232/www.biminis.ca). Bus 4, 7.* **Open** 11am-
midnight Mon-Thur, Sun; 11am-1am Fri, Sat.
Admission free-$5. **Credit** AmEx, MC, V.
Map p251 F6

The front room suggests a frat house – a beaten sofa here, a pool table and slot machine there – yet venture upstairs and you'll find yourself in the West Side's top singles bar. The ground floor (with a more restrained mezzanine looking over it) is packed tube-train tight on weekend nights.

The Cellar Jazz

3611 W Broadway, at Dunbar Street (604 738 1959/www.cellarjazz.com). Bus 7, 9, 17, 99, N9, N17. **Open** 8pm-midnight Mon-Wed; 7pm-midnight Thur-Sun. **Admission** free-$20. **Credit** AmEx, MC, V. **Map** p250 B6 **㉔**

Kitsilano's legendary live jazz joint basks like a diamond in the dirt of its more workaday neighbours. Owner Chris Weeds is a working saxophonist himself and he's created the kind of venue musicians dream of. It's intimate (only 67 seats), and a strict noise policy puts the music first, so don't expect to gab. Do expect the best jazz in the city, nightly.

Hell's Kitchen

2041 W 4th Avenue, between Arbutus Street & Maple Street (604 736 4355/www.hells-kitchen.ca). Bus 4, 7. **Open** 11.30am-1am Mon-Thur; 11.30am-2am Fri; 10am-2am Sat, Sun. **Admission** free. **Credit** AmEx, MC, V. **Map** p251 F5 **㉕**

Home to trust-fund regulars and neighbourhood newbies, the east slope of lower Kitsilano owes much of its nightlife appeal to the Kitchen's boozy swagger. The colour scheme might best be described as postmodern abattoir, from faux *Inferno*, dark brick walls to the curved, salacious bar, and winsome staff. There's an impressive menu on offer too, though it's provided for a crowd that is more in search of sauce and, ultimately, each other.

Tatlows Broiler Bar

2741 W 4th Avenue, between Stephens Street & Macdonald Street (604 739 8668). Bus 2, 4, 7, 22. **Open** 11am-2am Mon-Fri; 9.30am-2am Sat, Sun. **Admission** free. **Credit** AmEx, MC, V. **Map** p250 D6 **㉖**

When asked to describe the wood and dark leather decor so endemic to bars south of downtown one patron summed it up – with admirable succinctness and a well-tuned ear for a properly rhymed phrase – thus: burnt umber lumber. Tatlows attracts a loyal, cheerful crowd, especially during the long grey days and dank nights of Kitsilano's winters, when the fireplace beckons passers-by in. Weathered sofas act as the perfect *mise-en-scène* for star-crossed lovers, while the goings-on at the long, maple bar fill the room with a raucous energy.

Napa of the north

The top ten wine picks from British Columbia's best wineries.

BC has a colourful history of wine production that dates from the 1800s. Wonder why you've never heard of it? The short answer: not all monks make good wine. Missionaries had limited success with European grapes, and while American hybrids like Concord performed well, the resulting wine did not. Only in the early 1980s did a handful of small-scale winemakers introduce the more temperamental Vinifera vines, starting a continuing trend of quality over quantity in BC wine production.

In the past ten years, the Okanagan has attracted winemakers from all over the world, including tenth-generation French vintner Olivier Combret (*see* **Domaine Combret**) who chose the region as one of two microclimates in the world that would support his style of cultivation without pesticides and herbicides (the other is in China). In recent years, many small producers have opted to grow and harvest their own grapes (rather than buying grapes from other producers) so they can have more control over the end product. Most of the wineries below sell out quickly, but

good restaurants and bars will carry a selection from most. It's also worth trying the boutique wine shops around town or ordering online. Of course, if you have the time, nothing beats visiting the winery yourself, *see p210* **Grape expectations**.

Black Hills Estate Winery

30880 Black Sage Road, RR #1, Site 52, Comp 22, Oliver (250 498 0666/ http://blackhillswinery.com). **Open** by appointment only. **Credit** MC, V.

Senka Tennant takes the classic approach of the French *vigneron*, overseeing every aspect of the winemaking process at this exquisite estate winery that produces just two types of wine. **Best bottle**: the Bordeaux-style 2001 Nota Bene blend.

Blue Mountain Vineyard and Cellars

RR #1, Site 3, Comp 4, Okanagan Falls (250 497 8244/http://bluemountainwinery.com). **Open** by appointment only. **Credit** MC, V.

This estate is probably best known for wine made in the *méthode traditionelle*. **Best bottle**: Brut sparkling.

Urban Well

1516 Yew Street, at Cornwall Avenue (604 737 7770/www.urbanwell.com). Bus 2, 22. **Open** 2pm-2am Mon, Fri, Sat; 3pm-2am Tue-Thur; 3pm-midnight Sun. **Admission** free. **Credit** AmEx, MC, V. **Map** p251 F5 **㉗**

Many different people come here to draw water (and other liquids) from the well. The sidewalk patio is popular for people-watching on summer afternoons (Kitsilano beach is only a stone's throw away), while the varied menu draws in diners. Later on, the evenings are taken over by a twenty-something bar crowd. Comedy improv nights are also popular, if only for the chance to catch a glimpse of Robin Williams, whose impromptu sets are becoming the stuff of legend. Mr Williams has made three films in Vancouver in the last couple of years and he has adopted the Urban Well as a home away from home.

East Vancouver

Bukowski's

1447 Commercial Drive, at Grant Street (604 253 2777). Bus 20. **Open** 3pm-1am Mon-Fri; noon-1am Sat; 11am-midnight Sun. **Admission** free. **Credit** MC, V.

While the name conjures up louche drunkards and hangdog writers crying in their beer, the reality is actually quite the opposite: a packed room with a feel-good vibe, pretty ochre walls and a mural of clouds and sky on the ceiling. A seat on the shady, vine-covered patio is a much coveted place to while away a sunny summer afternoon.

Café Deux Soleils

2096 Commercial Drive, at E 5th Avenue (604 254 1195). Bus 20. **Open** 8am-11pm (later if busy) daily. **Admission** free-$8. **Credit** V. **Map** p252 Q6 **㉘**

The bric-a-brac design – including a painted plywood visage of a sun smiling down beatifically on the crowd – indicates the Two Suns' hippy stance. The place is crowded for its series of unplugged live acts, but the brunches, among the best on the Drive, are served sans music.

Five Point

3124 Main Street, at E 15th Avenue (604 876 5810). Bus 3. **Open** 11.30am-1am Mon-Fri; 10am-1am Sat; 10am-midnight Sun. **Admission** free. **Credit** MC, V. **Map** p252 N8 **㉙**

The burgeoning neighbourhood of South Main – fancified as 'SoMa' by status-conscious locals – is as lacking in bars as Prohibition-era Utah. So it's no

Burrowing Owl Estate Winery

100 Burrowing Owl Place, off Black Sage Road, Oliver (toll free 1-877 498 0620/ www.burrowingowlwine.ca). **Open** *Easter-1 July, Thanksgiving-Halloween* 10am-5pm daily. *1 July-Thanksgiving* 10am-6pm daily. **Credit** MC, V.

Some of the most solid red wines to be produced in BC. **Best bottles**: Merlot, Syrah and Pinot Noir.

Domaine Combret

32057 #13 Road, Oliver (250 498 6966/ 1-866 837 7647/http://combretwine.com). **Open** *May-Oct* 9am-6.30pm daily. *Nov-Apr* by appointment only. **Credit** MC, V.

Like his wines, winemaker Olivier Combret is very French. **Best bottles**: try the 2001 Magali, named for Combret's daughter, or the Burgundy-style 2000 Pinot Noir.

Joie Farm Cooking School

2825 Naramata Road, Site 5, Comp 4, Naramata (toll free 1-866 422 5643/www. joie.ca). **Open** *Wine Sales* by appointment only. *Retreat* year-round. **Rates** Weekend

Epicurean Retreats $560 single; $830 couple. **Credit** MC, V.

Joie Farm is owned by a young pair of chef-sommeliers new to the business. Nevertheless, their first year's small-scale production in 2004 arrived to so much acclaim that they replaced orchard trees with grape vines to bump up future production. **Best bottle**: Pinot Noir Rosé.

▶

surprise that this stylish room in a refurbished heritage house has drawn thirsty locals since it opened. The dim lighting suits the gaggles of single girls and their would-be lotharios, waiting at the bar. For those not prowling for partners, the patio is a fine place to spend an afternoon in the shade of the elms.

Havana
1212 Commercial Drive, between Charles Street & William Street (604 253 9119/www.havana-art.com). Bus 20. **Open** 11am-11pm Mon-Thur; 11am-midnight Fri; 10am-midnight Sat; 10am-11pm Sun. **Admission** free. **Credit** MC, V.
Feeling depressed by another grey and rainy February day in Vancouver? Escape to Havana. Winter gloom is as foreign here as grey skies in Cuba. Brunches – on its wide, noisy patio, or bustling, friendly dining room – are among the city's best secret, but night time is best for dining at the bar: the music is loud, the mojitos suggest sunburns and the heady campesino food can't be beaten.

The Reef
4172 Main Street, at E 26th Avenue (604 874 5375/www.thereefrestaurant.com). Bus 3, 25. **Open** 11am-midnight Mon-Wed, Sun; 11am-1am Thur-Sat. **Admission** free. **Credit** AmEx, DC, MC, V. **Map** p252 N9 ③⓪

All right, the Reef may claim to be a restaurant, but this Main Street institution is really not primarily an eaterie. Outside, the lime-green sign beckons to the Caribbean bar oasis awaiting within. The decor may look like it's been combed from a beach, jumbled with the contents of a shanty hut and had some additional input from a skimboarder's garage, while the wooden floors may creak beneath the weight of the massed weekend crowds, but Eastsiders still flock here for fab jerk chicken and superb late-night DJs.

Whip
209 E 6th Avenue, at Main Street (604 874 4687). Bus 3. **Open** 11.30am-midnight Mon-Fri; 10am-midnight Sat, Sun. **Admission** free. **Credit** MC, V. **Map** p252 M6 ③①
The South Main artsy set consciously avoid the yuppie narcissism of Yaletown – a stone's throw away across False Creek – and instead opt to don their thoughtful eyewear and monochrome clothes to visit the Whip, SoMa's bar-cum-art gallery. When you arrive, ask for the manager, Nice Guy Steve, who will lead you past the austere, my-favourite-colour-is-black bar and atrium, to the more relaxing atmosphere of the mezzanine. This is the ideal place to settle back into the groove of a long DJ set while relaxing with friends at a giant communal table.

▶ **Napa of the north (continued)**

La Frenz
740 Naramata Road, Penticton (250 492 6690/www.lafrenzwinery.com). **Open** *May-Oct* 10am-5pm daily. *Nov-Apr* by appointment only. **Credit** MC, V.
Husband and wife team Niva and Jeff Martin set up shop on the Naramata Bench having produced wine here and in their native Australia for 20 years. **Best bottles**: the Semillon and the ever-crisp Viognier.

Laughing Stock
1548 Naramata Road, Penticton (250 493 8466/www.laughingstock.ca). **Open** by appointment only. **Credit** MC, V.
Another husband-and-wife team, this time of ex-stockbrokers, pursued their dream of having a winery despite derision from some quarters, and the early indicators are anything but laughable. **Best bottles**: the 2003 Portfolio, a Bordeaux-style blend of Merlot, Cabernet Sauvignon and Cabernet Franc.

Poplar Grove Winery
1060 Poplar Grove Road, Penticton (250 492 4575/www.poplargrove.ca). **Open** *May, June* 11am-5pm Sat, Sun. *July-Sept* 11am-5pm daily. *Oct-Apr* appointment only. **Credit** MC, V.

Poplar Grove is positioned on the beautiful Naramata Bench. The winery produces some exceptionally fine wines that can occasionally be hard to find: if you don't have time to visit the vineyard, look for them in restaurants or order online. **Best bottles**: the 2002 Pinot Gris has been called the best in the country, and the red vintages have sold out in a mere eight days.

Venturi-Schulze Vineyards
4235 Trans Canada Highway, Cobble Hill, Vancouver Island (250 743 5630/www.venturischulze.com). **Open** by appointment only. **Credit** MC, V.
The winemaker cultivates his own grapes without the use of pesticides or herbicides. Also noteworthy is the balsamic vinegar. **Best bottle**: Sole semi-sparkling.

Wild Goose
2145 Sun Valley Way, Okanagan Falls (250 497 8919/www.wildgoosewinery.com). **Open** *Apr-Oct* 10am-5pm daily. *Nov-Mar* by appointment only. **Credit** MC, V.
No wild goose chase here – just clean, crisp, award-winning wines. **Best bottle**: the 2000 Pinot Gris was named best in Canada.

Shops & Services

More bang for your buck.

It may be a small city, but when it comes to retail therapy Vancouver is big. **Robson Street** is the main shopping strip, with flagship stores for all the international chains beginning at Granville Street and going west for five blocks. Interspersing these are those independent shops that can afford the city's priciest real estate. **Burrard Street** from Robson to Georgia holds a sprinkling of international designer boutiques, culminating at the Fairmont Vancouver Hotel on West Georgia Street, which houses Gucci and Louis Vuitton. Other designer boutiques (like Chanel) have shrewdly congregated close to the cruise ship terminal on **West Hastings Street**. The fashion and restaurant district of **Yaletown** is pretty sleepy before noon, but in summer the cobblestone loading bays become drinks patios, and fashion markets pop up in the parks. **Gastown** has seen a renaissance of late, with most of the new, gallery-style shops located on Abbott and Water Streets. Mind the plentiful tourist traps, however: we guarantee that moose head sweatshirt will seem like a mistake when you get home. In East Vancouver, young, local designers have begun to congregate on **South Main Street**, also called SoMa (*see p127* **Streetlife**), often next door to the vintage clothing shops from where a lot of them get their inspiration. Over on the West Side, **Kitsilano** (dubbed 'Kitsafornia' for its beachy, New Age culture) is bisected by W 4th Avenue, where children's boutiques and organic groceries run dense among the surf shops between Burrard and Balsam. **Granville Island** is a tourist destination in itself, while **South Granville** is the city's most upscale shopping district, often doubling as New York's Fifth Avenue in film shoots.

PRICES

Though the Canadian dollar (or 'looney') has strengthened of late, prices remain attractive, especially to Brits. CDs in particular are a very good buy: pay in dollars what you would in pounds. Books, however, are expensive and, like everything else, they are taxed. Expect to add 7 per cent goods and services tax (GST) and another 7 per cent provincial sales tax (PST) to most marked prices. But keep your receipts. As a visitor, you can claim back the GST on any purchase over $50 via the visitor refund scheme (*see p234*).

One-stop shopping

Department stores

Holt Renfrew

Pacific Centre, 633 Granville Street, at W Georgia Street, Downtown (604 681 3121/www.holtrenfrew. com). All city-centre buses. **Open** 10am-7pm Mon-Wed; 10am-9pm Thur, Fri; 9.30am-6pm Sat; 11am-6pm Sun. **Credit** AmEx, DC, MC, V. **Map** p249 K3.
Canada's designer department store chain manages to feel intimate, though new premises within the same mall pegged for 2007 may make the shopping experience swisher. Organised by designer, there are shops for Hermès, Tiffany, Gucci and more, and a fine shoe-and-handbag department. Sharpen your elbows for the end-of-summer 'Last Chance' sales.

Hudson's Bay Company

674 Granville Street, at W Georgia Street, Downtown (604 681 6211/www.hbc.com). All city-centre buses/SkyTrain Granville. **Open** 9.30am-9pm Mon-Fri; 8am-9pm Sat; 9.30am-7pm Sun. **Credit** AmEx, MC, V. **Map** p249 K3.
Canada's first, and most famous department store began as a trading outpost for furriers in Eastern Canada. While there is still a fur department, most sales now take place on the ground-floor cosmetics and fragrance areas. It's worth venturing up to the Canadian by Design floor for a rare example of a Canadian retailer supporting its own, while the HB Signature house brand offers collectible classics like the striped wool 'Bay blanket'.

Sears

701 Granville Street, at Robson Street, Downtown (604 685 7112/www.sears.ca). All city-centre buses. **Open** 9.30am-9pm Mon-Fri; 8am-7pm Sat; 11am-6pm Sun. **Credit** AmEx, MC, V. **Map** p249 K3.
Mass-market, inexpensive US wares.

Malls

Metropolis at Metrotown Centre

4700 Kingsway, at McKay Avenue, Burnaby (604 630 3340/www.metropolisatmetrotown.com). Bus 19/SkyTrain Metrotown. **Open** 10am-9pm Mon-Fri; 10am-7pm Sat; 11am-6pm Sun. **Credit** varies.
This is the country's second largest mall. It's in the suburbs but children will love the trip by SkyTrain (allow 30 minutes from Downtown). A Silvercity movie theatre and/or the Jellybean Daycare can keep them amused while parents cruise the complex of close to 500 stores, including chains like Old Navy and Town Shoes, as well as independent stores.

We kid you not, **Richard Kidd** is a tourist attraction in its own right. *See p126.*

Park Royal

Taylor Way and Marine Drive, West Vancouver
(604 216 7272/604 925 9576/www.shopparkroyal.
com/www.thevillageatparkroyal.com). Bus 239, 246,
250, 251, 252, 253, 254, 255, 257, 258. **Open**
10am-9pm Mon-Fri; 10am-6pm Sat; 11am-6pm Sun.
Credit varies.
Park Royal was the first mall in Canada. It now comprises three shopping centres: **Park Royal North**, **Park Royal South**, and **The Village at Park Royal**. In good weather, the Village is the place to go: completed in 2005, its wide, outdoor walkways, waterfalls and high-end independent shops are the cutting edge of mall retailing in North America. As you might expect in Canada's wealthiest postal code, wares are appropriately exclusive. Catering to the health-and-wealth set are Whole Foods Market (stop for lunch) and Total Home Environment (T.H.E.) Store, where even the cotton swabs are organic and the beeswax Buddha candles are practically edible. Old Navy (casual sportswear), Oliver Barrett (edgy streetwear) and Lotuswear (yoga) are best for fashion, Kiss & Make-up sells cult beauty products, and Caffe Artigiano wins international awards for its artistic lattes. The North and South malls, which are starting to show their age (built in the 1960s), hold few surprises, but lots of reliable shops for walking shoes and large discounters of clothing and linens (rich folks love a bargain too).

Discount stores

Winners

798 Granville Street, at Robson Street, Downtown
(604 683 1058/www.winners.ca). All city-centre
buses. **Open** 9.30am-9pm Mon-Sat; 11am-6pm Sun.
Credit AmEx, MC, V. **Map** p249 K3.

Men's designer dress shirts, Samsonite and Benetton luggage, and high-end cooking pots are sharply reduced at this first downtown location of the Canadian discount chain (located on the first floor of the building). Walk the store's perimeter for the random designer labels that show up from time to time. New stock arrives Thursdays.

Antiques & retro

Metropolitan Home

217 W Hastings Street, at Cambie Street,
Downtown (604 681 2313). Bus 10, 16, 20, 135.
Open 10.30am-5.30pm Mon-Sat; noon-5pm Sun.
Credit MC, V. **Map** p249 L3.

Mid 20th century modern is the theme; it's one of the few antique and retro shops to have kept a retail presence, rather than choosing to cater exclusively to Vancouver's film industry.

Shaughnessy Antique Gallery Inc

3025 Granville Street, between W 14th Avenue
and W 15th Avenues, West Side (604 739 8413/
toll free 1-866 689 9778). Bus 10, 98. **Open**
10.30am-5.30pm Mon-Sat; noon-5pm Sun. **Credit**
MC, V. **Map** p251 H7.

The variety is the draw, whether you're interested in 1960s stainless steel desks or Victorian teacups.

Beauty products

BeautyBar

2142 W 4th Avenue, at Arbutus Street, West Side
(604 733 9000). Bus 4, 7. **Open** 10am-7pm Mon,
Tue, Sat, Sun; 10am-8pm Wed-Fri. **Credit** MC, V.
Map p251 F6.

Belly jelly for pregnant women, beard lube for not-so-macho men and fabulous make-up and skin care.

BeautyMark

103-1120 Hamilton Street, between Helmcken Street & Davie Street, Yaletown (604 642 2294/www.beautymark.ca). Bus 15. **Open** 10am-7pm Mon-Sat; noon-5pm Sun. **Credit** AmEx, DC, MC, V. **Map** p249 K4.

If you've got an event, book here for an eyebrow shaping and make-up application, but be prepared to leave with a load of new cosmetics and jewellery that you just couldn't do without.

Other locations: 991 Denman Street (604 688 7407).

Books & magazines

Book Warehouse

2388 W 4th Avenue, at Balsam Street, West Side (604 734 5711/www.bookwarehouse.ca). Bus 4, 7. **Open** 9am-11pm Mon-Sat; 9.30am-10pm Sun. **Credit** MC, V. **Map** p251 E6.

An across-the-board 10% discount on new titles is one reason to come here, but the bargain bins hold treasures too. Don't miss the local authors' section, and the comprehensive Vancouver aisle.

Other locations: 632 W Broadway (604 872 5711); 4444 W 10th Avenue (604 221 5744); 1051 Davie Street (604 685 5711); 550 Granville Street (604 683 5711); 1068 Homer Street (604 681 5711).

Chapters/Indigo

2505 Granville Street, at W Broadway, West Side (604 731 7822/www.chapters.indigo.ca). Bus 9, 10, 16, 17, 98, 99. **Open** 9am-10pm Mon-Sat; 11am-10pm Sun. **Credit** AmEx, MC, V. **Map** p251 H6.

Popular fiction, CDs, magazines, coffee bars, comfy chairs – it's the perfect place to wait out a downpour.

Other locations: 788 Robson Street, Downtown (604 682 4066).

Mayfair News

1535 W Broadway, at Granville Street, West Side (604 738 8951). Bus 9, 10, 16, 17, 98, 99. **Open** 8am-10.30pm daily. **Credit** MC, V. **Map** p251 H6.

If you're looking to catch up on your favourite magazine, or the latest political scandal from home, or you're just addicted to magazines, this is a fantastic place. Besides the abundance of periodical titles on scores of subjects and in several languages (26 Italian magazines alone), they offer at least 120 different daily newspapers in ten languages.

Comics

Comic Shop

2089 W 4th Avenue, at Arbutus Street, West Side (604 738 8122). Bus 4, 7. **Open** 11am-6pm Mon, Tue, Thur; 11am-7pm Wed; 11am-8pm Fri; 10am-6pm Sat; noon-5pm Sun. **Credit** AmEx, MC, V. **Map** p251 F6.

With three floors of merchandise, it's easy to get distracted, but thankfully there's enough on offer here to please the whole family. Send your truculent teenagers to the basement to look at the games, the children can pick through the kiddie books on the main floor, which gives you time to sift properly through the reams of comics upstairs.

Golden Age Collectibles

830 Granville Street, at Robson Street, Downtown (604 683 2819/www.gacvan.com). All city-centre buses. **Open** 10am-9pm Mon-Sat; 10am-6pm Sun. **Credit** AmEx, MC, V. **Map** p249 K3.

Golden Age Collectibles lives up to its name. If you're searching for early issues of *Batman*, a 1970s *Star Wars* figure or a rare *Magic: The Gathering* card, this is the place to come.

Used books

Macleod's Books

455 W Pender Street, at Richards Street, Downtown (604 681 7654). All city-centre buses. **Open** 10am-6pm Mon-Sat; noon-5pm Sun. **Credit** MC, V. **Map** p249 L3.

It may seem like you've stepped into complete chaos but ask for help and you'll soon discover a sense of order. Specialising in Canadian history, Macleod's stocks a wide selection of tomes on First Nations, BC and Vancouver history, including that often overlooked bunch, Canadian cowboys. No trashy reads, but they do carry a good variety of modern and classic novels at reasonable prices.

Tanglewood
2932 W Broadway, between Carnarvon Street & MacKenzie Street, West Side (604 731 8870). Bus 2, 9, 17, 22. **Open** 11am-8pm Mon-Wed; 11am-9pm Thur, Fri; 11am-6pm Sat; noon-6pm Sun. **Credit** MC, V. **Map** p250 D6.
The best in a good street for second-hand bookstores. A fast turnover means you might find the latest bestseller in the window, but the dusty first edition of your favourite book might be here too. **Other locations**: 1553 W Broadway (604 736 8876).

Dry-cleaner

Kerrisdale Cleaners
2313 W 41st Avenue, between Vine Street & Balsam Street, Kerrisdale (604 261 2912). Bus 16, 41, 43. **Open** 8am-6.30pm Mon-Fri; 8am-6pm Sat; closed Sun. **Credit** MC, V.
Call for hotel pick-ups and deliveries for your most precious garments, evening gowns and formal suits. **Other locations**: 2383 W 4th Avenue, West Side (604 738 0626).

Electronics & computers

Future Shop
798 Granville Street, at Robson Street, Downtown (604 683 2502/www.futureshop.ca). All city-centre buses. **Open** 10am-9pm Mon-Sat; 11am-6pm Sun. **Credit** AmEx, MC, V. **Map** p249 K3.
The DVDs are competitively priced and if you're a gadget-geek, you'll be in heaven. **Other locations**: 1740 W Broadway (604 739 3000).

MAC Station
2-1109 Homer Street, at Helmcken Street, Yaletown (604 806 6227/www.macstation.com). Bus 15, 17. **Open** 10am-6pm Mon, Tue, Thur, Fri; 10am-9pm Wed; 10am-5pm Sat; 11am-5pm Sun. **Credit** AmEx, MC, V. **Map** p249 K4.
When your iBook implodes, head here, pronto.

Fashion

Athletic/Yoga

Lululemon Athletica
2113 W 4th Avenue, at Arbutus Street, West Side (604 732 6111/www.lululemon.com). Bus 4, 7. **Open** 10am-6pm Mon-Wed, Sat, Sun; 10am-7pm Thur, Fri. **Credit** AmEx, MC, V. **Map** p251 F6.
If there is one store that sums up the pioneering spirit, raging entrepreneurialism, health-obsession,

body-perfectionism and anti-establishmentarianism of Vancouver, this is it. And the rest of the world is catching on too. The Lululemon 'athleisure' empire now expands to California, Asia and beyond, with its colourful, comfortable, men's and womenswear. **Other locations**: 148 Robson Street, Downtown, (604 681 3118); Suite 189, 650 W 41st Avenue, West Side (no phone number); Unit B-1, 940 Main Street, West Vancouver (604 921 6125).

TNA
2899 Granville Street, at W 13th Avenue, West Side (604 714 5937/www.tna.ca). Bus 10, 98. **Open** 10am-7pm Mon-Wed; 10am-8pm Thur, Fri; 11am-6pm Sat, Sun. **Credit** AmEx, MC, V. **Map** p251 H7.
The cheeky name of this sportswear store targeted at teenaged girls and their mummies reflects the LA-style clothing. And you'll need tiny cheeks to fit into the body conscious garments that come in high-quality fabrics and forward styles. **Photos** *p135*.

Boutiques

Aritzia
1110 Robson Street, at Thurlow Street, Downtown (604 684 3251/www.aritzia.com). Bus 5. **Open** 10am-10pm Mon-Wed; 10am-11pm Thur, Fri; 10am-9pm Sat; 11am-8pm Sun. **Credit** AmEx, MC, V. **Map** p248 J3.
The city's most service-conscious, design-forward and trend-setting store for young women. It's a rite of passage for local girls to work here before going on to become bankers, lawyers or journalists.

Atomic Model
1036 Mainland Street, between Nelson Street & Helmcken Street, Yaletown (604 688 9989/www.atomicmodel.com). Bus 15, 17. **Open** 11am-7pm Mon-Sat; noon-6pm Sun. **Credit** AmEx, MC, V. **Map** p249 K4.
Yes, Atomic Model is where the models shop, for top LA and New York labels that are hot today and then forgotten tomorrow. Don't forget your pink lap dog and massive sunglasses: they are completely necessary shopping accoutrements. **Photo** *p126*.

Babe Belangere
1092 Hamilton Street, at Helmcken Street, Yaletown (604 806 4010). Bus 15, 17. **Open** 11am-7pm Mon-Wed; 10.30am-8pm Thur, Fri; 10.30am-6pm Sat; noon-5pm Sun. **Credit** AmEx, MC, V. **Map** p249 K4.
Finally, a store where women over 30 are able to find dresses nice enough for New Year's Eve, yet understated enough for a beach date. The local newscasters are often seen scouring the rails for something that won't fade into insignificance under studio light.

Betsey Johnson
1033 Alberni Street, between Burrard Street & Thurlow Street, Downtown (604 488 0314/www.betseyjohnson.com). Bus 2, 5, 22. **Open** 11am-7pm Mon-Sat; 11am-6pm Sun. **Credit** AmEx, MC, V. **Map** p249 K3.

Mutually assured desire. **Atomic Model.** *See p125.*

New Yorker Betsey Johnson is well known for her wild and wacky designs. Now she brings her unique brand of flirty, feminine clothing to this city in one of her very few international shops.

Club Monaco

1290 Robson Street, at Jervis Street, Downtown (604 687 8618/www.clubmonaco.com). Bus 5. **Open** 10am-9pm Mon-Wed; 10am-9.30pm Thur-Sat; 11am-7pm Sun. **Credit** AmEx, MC, V. **Map** p248 J2.
Have $150, need cool, new outfit? Both men and women head here, where everything fits right, the fabrics and colours are on-trend, and there are no logos. Wilder colours are to be found in the upstairs discount outlet, where European visitors have been known to abandon their entire former wardrobes on the fitting room floors in a sudden fit of enthusiasm for the New World and its endless possibilities. **Other locations:** Pacific Centre, 701 W Georgia Street, Downtown (604 687 5550); Eaton Center Metrotown, 1179-4700 Kingsway, Burnaby (604 437 6000); Oakridge Centre, 650 W 41st Avenue, West Side (604 266 8864).

Richard Kidd

65 Water Street, between Abbott Street & Carrall Street, Gastown (604 677 1880/www.richard kidd.net). Bus 50. **Open** 10am-6pm Mon-Sat; noon-5pm Sun. **Credit** AmEx, MC, V. **Map** p249 M3.
A tourist attraction in its own right, this massive, modern store (patterned after the likes of Colette in Paris) is a glassed-in space between two heritage buildings on the waterfront. It's the only place in the city (nay, the planet) where you'll find hand-knitted cashmere Cowichan sweaters with sterling silver zippers and feather pulls for children, tagged at $2,500 (hence the store's nickname, Rich Kidd). Cult jeans for big people are artfully rumpled and hung on whitewashed deer antlers. If you only have time to visit one fashion emporium while you're in town, then this it. **Photos** *pp122-123.*

Children

Crocodile

2156 W 4th Avenue, between Yew Street and Arbutus Street, West Side (604 742 2762/www. crocodilebaby.com). Bus 4, 7. **Open** 10am-6pm Mon-Sat; 11am-5pm Sun. **Credit** MC, V. **Map** p251 F6.
Big-ticket baby items, like Mountain Buggy strollers for trail running, high-end crib linens and Swedish wooden highchairs. You'll find plenty of competition along this stretch of W 4th.

Designer

Bacci's/Bacci's at Home

2788 Granville Street, at W 12th Avenue, West Side (604 733 4933/www.baccis.ca). Bus 10, 98. **Open** 9.30am-5.30pm Mon-Sat. **Credit** AmEx, MC, V. **Map** p251 H7.
European designer clothing and posh housewares: what more could the discerning shopper want? Oh, you want designer shoes and Keihl's skincare, as well? Well, it so happens you're in luck. **Photo** *p130.*

Hill's of Kerrisdale

2125 W 41st Avenue, at Arbutus Street, Kerrisdale (604 266 9177/www.hillsofkerrisdale.com). Bus 16, 41, 43. **Open** 9.30am-6pm Mon-Wed; 9.30am-9pm Thur, Fri; 9.30am-6pm Sat; 11am-5pm Sun. **Credit** AmEx, MC, V.
A family-owned institution that was once a dry-goods shop, the younger generations of the Hill clan have taken this clothing store on to new levels of hipness. One son developed the young women's department into one of the country's top national chains (Aritzia), a daughter created a successful string of boutiques out of the jewellery counter (Blue Ruby) while yet another son created an outcrop of the young men's department (Ray Rickburn). But out here in the suburbs is where it all began.

Leone

Sinclair Centre, 757 W Hastings Street, between Granville Street & Howe Street, Downtown (604 683 1133/www.leone.ca). All city-centre buses/SkyTrain Waterfront. **Open** *9.30am-6pm Mon-Fri; 9.30am-5.30pm Sat; noon-5pm Sun.* **Credit** *AmEx, DC, MC, V.* **Map** *p249 L3.*

If it is Italian and designer, this is one of the best places in Vancouver to find it. But you'd better know you'll be competing with movie stylists on a label hunt for leading ladies like Uma Thurman. The heritage building houses an Italian café and January's indoor sidewalk sale sees Dolce & Gabbana coats going for a song. Well, an aria anyway.

Streetlife

Barefoot Contessa

There's nowhere better than the intersection of Main Street and 21st Avenue to experience the current batch of emerging designers in Vancouver. Grab a coffee and a gingerbread man at Liberty Bakery (3699 Main Street, 604 709 9999) and start wandering: from top to bottom, it's all pointedly local. Eugene Choo (3683 Main Street, 604 873 8874, www.eugenechoo.com) is South Main's flagship fashion store, where a brother/sister team turned their eye for vintage into a local label mecca for him and her. Behind the white sheers at PowderKeg (3628 Main Street, 604 709 9060, www.powderkeg.ca) lies a hair salon and modern make-up emporium that fulfils the neighbourhood's 'purposely undone' aesthetic. Smoking Lily (3634 Main Street, 604 873 5459, www.smokinglily.com) was born when a pair of wacky chicks from

Vancouver Island started silk screening underwear with prime ministers' faces, T-shirts with skulls and squid, and skirts with bugs. And what do you know? It caught on big time. Umeboshi (3638 Main Street, www.umeboshishoes.com) is the area's first shoe store, stocking limited editions and lesser-known labels with a utilitarian edge. Think cool gumboot, not diamante stiletto. Basics-with-a-twist describes the high-quality dress shop, Narcissist Design Co (3659 Main Street, 604 877 1555, www.narcissist.com). Front & Co (3772 Main Street, 604 879 8431) takes up most of the block with its expanding range of men's and women's clothing and housewares. If it glitters, shimmers, flounces or flips, you'll find it at Barefoot Contessa (3715 Main Street, 604 879 1137, www.thebarefootcontessa.com).

Eat, Drink, Shop

Granville Island

While it's not strictly an island, the best way to get to this artists' enclave under the Granville Street Bridge is by water taxi. The tiny, rainbow-striped Aquabuses stop all over False Creek, including Yaletown and English Bay, and cost about the same as city buses. Granville Island is known for its corrugated steel warehouses, most of which are no longer for industrial use, but are more likely to house sculptors, art schools, glass blowers, jewellery makers, or – this being one of the city's top tourist destinations – cars. The Net Loft complex (1666 Johnston Street) has a fantastic Japanese stationery store called Paper-Ya (604 684 2531, www.paper-ya.com) as well as the Postcard Place (604 684 6909), and Barbara-Jo's Books to Cooks, for cookery books (604 684 6788, www.bookstocooks.com). Opus Framing and Art Supplies (1360 Johnson Street, 604 736 7028, 1-800 663 6953, www.opusframing.com) is a good place to buy a sketch-book, should you feel inspired by the scenery, or to pick up photography tips from the art students who work there. Whether or not you are in the market for a live lobster it's fun to poke around the tanks at the Lobster Man (1807 Mast Tower Road, 604 687 4531, www.lobsterman.com, pictured), where staff in hip waders and wellies trade in sea urchins, snails, crab and oysters from the local waters. The Charles H Scott Gallery (1399 Johnston Street, 604 844 3811) is one of the best for modern art and photography and its shop, Read, has fine art-and-architecture tomes. Also visit the Crafthouse (1386 Cartwright Street, 604 687 7270, www.cabc.net) for a selection of work by BC artisans. The Granville Island Market (1689 Johnston Street, 604 666 5784, www.granvilleisland.com) is the area's hub: go early and pick tomatoes with local chefs. The market's gems include Oyama Sausage Company (604 327 7407, www.oyamasausage.com, pictured), purveyors of delicious game charcuterie, like duck prosciutto; South China Seas Trading Company (604 681 5402, www.southchinaseas.ca), for Asian wares and cookery books; the Granville Island Tea Company (604 683 7491, www.granvilletea.com), where teas are brewed at the best temperature and the chai is home-ground.

Luxe International

1011 Alberni Street, at Burrard Street, Downtown (604 685 7910/www.luxe-international.ca). Bus 2, 5, 22. **Open** 10am-7pm Mon-Sat; 11am-7pm Sun. **Credit** AmEx, DC, MC, V. **Map** p249 K3.
Wealthy Hong Kong residents fly their personal shoppers here for Fendi handbags and the like.

Discount

Allison

1628 W 4th Avenue, between Fir Street & Pine Street, West Side (604 736 6262). Bus 4, 7. **Open** Phone for details. **Credit** MC, V. **Map** p251 G6.

In a world of increasing homogeneity and less and less time, Allison comes as a pleasant surprise. Not only are you never sure to find it open (not that the owner is lazy, rather that she's frequently away on buying trips around the world), but you have to buzz to be let in. Society ladies shop here for half-price skirt suits (DKNY and such) and the kind of comfortable-yet-elegant label clothing that every mature woman wants but is damned if she can find.

Lingerie

Diane's Lingerie
2950 Granville Street, between W 13th Avenue & W 14th Avenue, West Side (604 738 5121/www. dianeslingerie.com). Bus 10, 98. **Open** 10am-6pm Mon-Wed, Sat; 10am-8pm Thur, Fri; noon-5pm Sun. **Credit** AmEx, MC, V. **Map** p251 H7.
Where local lasses go for wedding trousseaus. Look out for Vancouver label Patricia Fieldwalker, one of the world's best lingerie designers, but easier to find in the United Arab Emirates than here.

Menswear

Brooklyn
418 Davie Street, at Homer Street, Yaletown (604 683 2929/www.brooklynclothing.com). Bus 15. **Open** 11am-9pm daily. **Credit** AmEx, MC, V. **Map** p249 K4.
Hot jeans and deconstructed sweats for the guy who is over Levi's but not interested in skinny black suits.

Mark James
2941 W Broadway, at Bayswater Street, West Side (604 734 2381/www.markjamesclothing.com). Bus 9, 17. **Open** 10am-6pm Mon-Thur, Sat; 10am-7pm Fri; 11.30am-5.30pm Sun. **Credit** AmEx, MC, V. **Map** p250 D6.
Suits from better labels like Paul Smith, plus a jeans shop and even a restaurant, should the shopping go long and late. Twice yearly clearance sales see sharp bargains for the sharply dressed man.

Ray Rickburn
2100 W 4th Avenue, at Arbutus Street, West Side (604 738 9177/www.rayrickburn.com). Bus 4, 7. **Open** 10am-7pm Mon-Wed, Sat; 10am-9pm Thur, Fri; 11am-6pm Sun. **Credit** AmEx, MC, V. **Map** p251 F6.
You've probably seen all these labels elsewhere, but rarely all in the same place, making this store perfect for hip guys who like to shop, but not that much.

Streetwear/Clubwear

Anti-Social
2425 Main Street, at Broadway, East Vancouver (604 708 5678/www.antisocialshop.com). Bus 3, 9, 99. **Open** 11am-6pm Mon-Sat; noon-5pm Sun. **Credit** MC, V. **Map** p252 M7.
Set up like an art gallery (or a posh skate kid's dream bedroom, take your pick) it's a shrine to West Coast skateboarding culture.

Dadabase
183 E Broadway, at Main Street, East Vancouver (604 709 9934/www.dadabase.ca). Bus 3, 9, 99. **Open** noon-8pm daily. **Credit** AmEx, MC, V. **Map** p252 M7.
Part art gallery, part techno hub, part fashion store specialising in reworked military clothing, it's all cool at this tiny shop that hosts regular parties.

Headquarter
1232 Burrard Street, between Davie Street and Burnaby Street, Downtown (604 688 0406/ www.headquarterstore.com). Bus 2, 6, 22. **Open** 11am-8pm Mon-Sat; noon-7pm Sun. **Credit** AmEx, MC, V. **Map** p248 J4.
Weird Japanese collectable toys provide wacky eye candy amid the club gear and streetwear.

Tailor

Stitch International
Pacific Centre, 777 Dunsmuir Street, at Howe Street, Downtown (604 689 2429). All city-centre buses. **Open** 10am-7pm Mon-Wed; 10am-9pm Thur, Fri; 9.30am-6pm Sat; 11am-6pm Sun. **No credit cards.** **Map** p249 K3.
A walk-in spot with five locations where they'll fix a hanging hem while you wait.

Vintage & second-hand

True Value Vintage
710 Robson Street, at Granville Street, Downtown (604 685 5403). All city-centre buses. **Open** 11am-8pm Mon-Wed, Sun; 11am-9pm Thur-Sat. **Credit** MC, V. **Map** p249 K3.
This store is so well organised and edited that you don't need to get your hands dirty, an attribute much appreciated, naturally, by TV stylists and design teams for major design labels like Gap. Londoners and New Yorkers often leave the shop all agog at our untapped vintage market.

Value Village
1820 E Hastings Street, between Salisbury Drive & Victoria Drive, East Vancouver (604 254 4282/ www.valuevillage.ca). Bus 10, 16. **Open** 9am-9pm daily. **Credit** AmEx, MC, V.
Value Village is a large repository for second-hand goods from across British Columbia. Ever wondered where vintage stores get their goods from? We'll let you in on a secret. Their buyers start here, so you might as well go straight to the source.
Other locations: 6415 Victoria Drive, East Vancouver (604 327 4434).

Handbags & leather goods

Ocean Drive Leather
2-1026 Mainland Street, between Nelson Street & Helmcken Street, Yaletown (604 647 2244/www. oceandriveleather.com). Bus 15. **Open** 11am-6pm Mon-Sat; noon-5pm Sun. **Credit** AmEx, DC, MC, V. **Map** p249 K4.

Both Fergie and Eddie Murphy have had leather trousers custom made here, which is certainly saying something – although quite what, we're not sure. Fabulous jackets in sumptuous skins off the rack.

Roots
1001 Robson Street, at Burrard Street, Downtown (604 683 4305/www.roots.ca). Bus 2, 5, 22. **Open** 9.30am-10pm Mon-Sat; 11am-8pm Sun. **Credit** AmEx, DC, MC, V. **Map** p249 K3.
The smart execs at Roots hired some of the country's top magazine fashion directors to collaborate on their bag collections, creating a far more fashion-forward look than we've ever seen before.
Other locations: throughout the city.

Hats

Edie's Hats
11-1666 Johnston Street, at Duranleau Street, Granville Island (604 683 4280/www.ediehats.com). Bus 50. **Open** 10am-7pm Mon-Fri; 9.30am-7pm Sat, Sun. **Credit** AmEx, MC, V. **Map** p248 H5.
Although the signature Vancouver headgear is definitely the knitted toque you can buy all manner of fancy and casual toppers from this local milliner.

Jewellery

Birks
698 W Hastings Street, at Granville Street, Downtown (604 669 3333/www.birks.com). All city-centre buses. **Open** 10am-6pm Mon-Fri; 10am-5.30pm Sat; noon-5pm Sun. **Credit** AmEx, MC, V. **Map** p249 L3.

Canada's answer to Tiffany, this is where to get a proper engagement ring. Excellent contemporary designs, but some of the most covetable pieces are to be found among the antique jewellery.
Other locations: see website for details.

Blue Ruby
1089 Robson Street, at Thurlow Street, Downtown (604 899 2583/www.blueruby.com). Bus 2, 5, 22. **Open** 10am-10pm Mon-Sat; 11am-8pm Sun. **Credit** AmEx, MC, V. **Map** p248 J3.
Jewellery is the ultimate travel souvenir: if it's interesting, everyone asks, and you get to say, 'Oh, this? I bought it in Vancouver.' Here's where to go to get that conversation started for sure.
Other locations: see website for details.

Flowers

Hilary Miles
1-1854 W 1st Avenue, between Burrard Street & Cypress Street, West Side (604 737 2782/www.hilarymiles.com). Bus 2, 22. **Open** 9am-5.30pm Mon-Fri; 10am-5pm Sat. **Credit** AmEx, MC, V. **Map** p251 G5.
Even the tiniest little posy from here will be the height of glamour and sophistication, guaranteed.

Food & drink

Cupcakes
1116 Denman Street, between Pendrell Street & Comox Street, West End (604 974 1300). Bus 6. **Open** 10am-10pm Mon-Thur, Sun; 10am-11pm Fri, Sat. **Credit** MC, V. **Map** p248 H2.

Good enough to kiss. **Bacci's/Bacci's at Home**. *See p126.*

Shop with the chefs

A culinary triumvirate has recently taken shape on the little strip of W 2nd Avenue at the south foot of Burrard Bridge. All three shops attract chefs and food stylists as well as serious amateurs looking to brush up their cooking skills. Many of the top restaurants in the city shop at **Les Amis Du Fromage** (1752 W 2nd Avenue, 604 732 4218, www.buy cheese.com) for their cheese courses. Takeaway meals, wine-and-cheese pairing classes, lots of French and local choices, all run by a mother-daughter team who really know their fromage – all 400 varieties of it. A short way down the street, **Patisserie Lebeau**

(1728 W 2nd Avenue, 604 731 3528) is famous for its waffles and chicken sandwiches (the bread is made in imported French ovens), plus standout coffee in a city known for its love of the bean. In typical French fashion, when they sell out, they sell out: hard luck if you arrive too late. The newest arrival is a flagship for **Barbara-Jo's Books to Cooks** (1740 W 2nd Avenue, 604 688 6755, www.bookstocooks.com), a city institution, where cult culinary magazines and delicious coffee-table food books are a backdrop to cooking demos by visiting celebrity chefs and local culinary heroes.

Forget doughnuts, cupcakes are the quintessential North American treat: brightly coloured, full of air and sugar and yet somehow deeply satisfying. This store itself is so pink and cute, it begs you to buy a dozen and have yourself a tea party.

Gourmet Warehouse
1340 E Hastings Street, at Clark Drive, East Vancouver (604 253 3022/www.gourmet warehouse.ca). Bus 10, 16, 135. **Open** 9am-5pm daily. **Credit** MC, V.
This out-of-the-way warehouse stocks cool culinary gifts, like edible gold flakes for decorating chocolate desserts, and is next to the city's first cookery school.

Meinhardt Fine Foods
3002 Granville Street, at W 14th Avenue, West Side (604 732 4405/www.meinhardt.com). Bus 10, 98. **Open** 8am-9pm Mon-Sat; 9am-9pm Sun. **Credit** AmEx, MC, V. **Map** p251 H7.
Like a French market with its flowers spilling on to the street, the takeout deli is a repository of well heeled bachelors on their way home from work. There's an adjoining patisserie and lunch spot, Picnic.

T&T Supermarket
179 Keefer Place, at Abbott Street, Chinatown (604 899 8836/www.tnt-supermarket.com). Bus 10, 16/SkyTrain Stadium. **Open** 9am-9pm daily. **Credit** MC, V. **Map** p249 M4.
On the edge of Chinatown sits this gleaming, teeming supermarket full of everything Asian. Try the black sesame soy drink, the salty but satisfying dried shrimp and seaweed crackers, or the delectable dried guava – all great hiking snacks.

Urban Fare
177 Davie Street, at Pacific Boulevard, Yaletown (604 975 7550/www.urbanfare.com). Bus 15. **Open** 6am-midnight daily. **Credit** AmEx, MC, V. **Map** p249 K5.
It's easy to lose track of time here while marvelling at how those with enormous incomes can spend so much on mere groceries. That the baking section of this futuristic supermarket is negligible is but one indication that its clients don't cook. But why should you, when there are fancy pre-packaged meals, $15 crackers, gourmet water and Poilane bread flown in weekly from France at $100 a loaf?

Wines & spirits

See p230 **Directory**.

BC Liquor Stores Specialty Shops
1120 Alberni Street, West End (604 660 4572/www.bcliquorstores.com). Bus 5. **Open** 9.30am-11pm Mon-Sat; 11am-6pm Sun. **Credit** AmEx, MC, V. **Map** p249 K3.
When the government runs the liquor stores, it's no surprise they close on Sunday and holidays – precisely when people tend to want libations. These two speciality stores, however, have longer hours, large selections and staff that actually know something about wines and spirits.
Other locations: 5555 Cambie Street (604 660 9463).

Marquis Wine Cellars
1034 Davie Street, between Burrard Street & Thurlow Street, Downtown (604 684 0445/www.marquis-wines.com). Bus 6. **Open** 11am-8pm daily. **Credit** AmEx, MC, V. **Map** p248 J4.
Located squarely downtown, this long-standing private wine store also sells Riedel crystal and inexpensive pine crates for shipping gifts. Informal tastings occur on weekends.

Taylorwood Wines
1185 Mainland Street, at Davie Street, Yaletown (604 408 9463/www.taylorwoodwines.com). Bus 15. **Open** 10am-9pm Mon-Sat; noon-7pm Sun. **Credit** AmEx, MC, V. **Map** p249 K4.
Young professionals in Yaletown meet up at this BC wine specialist for complementary wine tasting happy hours on Wednesday and Sunday afternoons. Cheers to that we say.

Eat, Drink, Shop

Gifts & specialist

Bang On

961 Robson Street, at Burrard Street, Downtown (604 602 0371/www.bang-on.ca). Bus 5. **Open** 10am-10pm daily. **Credit** AmEx, MC, V. **Map** p249 K3.

This custom T-shirt maker started by a local vintage dealer is a shrine to wacky 1980s music and TV memorabilia, like keyboard guitars, old-skool Michael Jackson before, well, everything, and, of course, rainbow shoelaces. It's done so well, it's franchising throughout the US and Mexico.

Buddha Supply Centre

4185 Main Street, at E 26th Avenue, East Vancouver (604 873 8169). Bus 3, 25. **Open** 9am-6pm Mon-Sat; 11.30am-5pm Sun. **No credit cards**. **Map** p252 M9.

For the Buddhist or the budding one, this tiny shop provides all your temple needs. Along with the exquisite porcelain and brass statues are incense and candles. Most diverting are the huge array of paper goods for burning as offerings; everything from Gameboys to shirts and dollar bills.

Puff The Out of Sight Smoke Shop

712 Robson Street, at Granville Street, Downtown (604 684 7833). All city-centre buses. **Open** 11am-7pm Mon-Thur; 11am-8pm Fri, Sat; noon-6pm Sun. **Credit** MC, V. **Map** p249 K3.

While stores selling marijuana come and go, this shop vending smoking paraphernalia, like pipes and bongs, lives on. That's awesome, dude.

Rubber Rainbow Condom Co

953 Denman Street, between Barclay Street & Haro Street, West End (604 683 3423). Bus 5. **Open** 11am-9pm Mon-Sat; noon-9pm Sun. **Credit** MC, V. **Map** p248 H2.

With the warm and friendly salespeople, buying a condom here is a happy, no-pressure experience. From basic to exotic, there is surely a shape and colour to tickle everyone's fancy, and for those easily irritated by latex they even carry wonderful lambskin versions (at $69.95 per dozen!).

Vancouver Art Gallery Shop

750 Hornby Street, between W Georgia Street & Robson Street, Downtown (604 662 4706/www.van artgallery.bc.ca). All city-centre buses. **Open** 10am-6pm Mon-Wed, Sat, Sun; 10am-9pm Thur, Fri. **Credit** AmEx, MC, V. **Map** p249 K3.

The buyers here are always on to the hottest local jewellery designer or great art book. Start here for your best Vancouver souvenirs.

Hairdressers

Axis

1111 W Georgia Street, at Thurlow Street, Downtown (604 685 0200). Bus 5. **Open** 8am-9.30pm Mon, Tue, Thur, Fri; 10am-7pm Wed, Sat; 11am-6pm Sun. **Credit** MC, V. **Map** p249 K3.

It doubles as a hairdressing school and alumni have gone on from here to cut the gleaming locks and flowing tresses of the likes of famous model Gisele Bundchen, and Leonardo DiCaprio in New York. **Other locations**: 757 W Hastings Street (604 608 0860).

JDs Barbershop

235 Abbott Street, between Cordova Street & Water Street, Gastown (604 331 8441/www.jdsbarber shop.com). Bus 4, 7. **Open** 10am-7pm Tue-Sat. **Credit** MC, V. **Map** p249 M3.

Hot shaves and inexpensive trims are the speciality of this hip young barber who also has a following among the female fashion set.

Housewares

Caban

2912 Granville Street, between W 13th Avenue & W 14th Avenue, West Side (604 742 1522/www.caban. com). Bus 10, 98. **Open** 10am-7pm Mon-Wed, Sat, Sun; 10am-9pm Thur, Fri. **Credit** AmEx, MC, V. **Map** p251 H7.

Some of the world's best-designed clothing, furniture and home wares, all from little-known, and mostly inexpensive brands, mixed with cool food products (and a demonstration kitchen) and a carefully edited selection of CDs and books. Started by the lifestyle gurus at Canadian Club Monaco clothing label (now owned by Ralph Lauren), this shop epitomises West Coast chic. **Photos** *p133*.

The Cross

1198 Homer Street, at Davie Street, Yaletown (604 689 2900/www.thecrossdesign.com). Bus 15. **Open** 10am-6pm Mon-Sat; 11am-5pm Sun. **Credit** AmEx, MC, V. **Map** p249 K4.

Cowhides, chandeliers and accessories for fitting out your ski chalet, modern loft or heritage home.

Inform Interiors

97 Water Street, at Abbott Street, Gastown (604 682 3868/www.informinteriors.com). Bus 4, 7, 50. Moving across the street early 2006. **Open** 10am-6pm Mon-Fri; 10am-5.30pm Sat; noon-5pm Sun. **Credit** AmEx, MC, V. **Map** p249 M3.

Big ticket designer furniture and inventive home accessories are as fun to browse as to buy. The owner is a designer too, with his Ribbon Chair in the permanent collection at New York's MOMA.

Markets

Chinatown Night Market

Keefer Street, between Gore Street & Columbia Street, Chinatown (604 682 8998). Bus 3/SkyTrain Main. **Open** 6.30-11pm Fri-Sun. Closed Oct-June. **No credit cards**. **Map** p249 N4.

Like a scene from Blade Runner this frenetic street market is fun to wander for the smells, sights and neon signs that remind you Vancouver is indeed on the Pacific Rim. Go early and visit the very first Ming Wo Cookware location at 23 E Pender Street

(604 683 7268), where every university student in Vancouver equipped their kitchen, and several interesting stores of Chinese antiques and modern furniture surrounding it. Chinese herbalists will prescribe all manner of inedible things for what ails you, while apothecaries and teashops abound.

Punjabi Village

Fraser and Main Streets, above 49th Avenue.
Since pashmina shawls, Indian jewellery, and beaded slippers and tunics have hit the mainstream, many of the best shops have closed to become internet businesses (claiming clients like Nicole Kidman). But try Frontier Cloth House (6695 Main Street, 604 325 4424) and Rokko Sarees and Fabric (6201 Fraser Street, 604 327 3033) for fashion finds.

Trout Lake Farmers Market

3350 Victoria Drive, at E 15th Avenue, East Vancouver (604 879 3276/www.eatlocal.org). Bus 20/SkyTrain Broadway then 10min walk. **Open** 9am-2pm Sat. Closed Oct-Apr. **No credit cards**. **Map** p252 R8.
In the parking lot of a park, this is the best of the summer farmers' markets. What starts as plants in May and June, blooms into an Eden of produce, preserves and baked goods by the height of summer.

Music

Vancouver is renowned for having some of the cheapest new CD prices in the world. Even greater savings can be realised by checking out

second-hand stores such as Charlie's Music City (819 Granville Street, 604 688 2500) or vinyl specialists Neptoon Records & CDs (3561 Main Street, 604 324 1229). Those looking for a mom-and-pop experience might want to investigate Red Cat Records (4307 Main Street, 604 708 9422). Furthermore, the city offers many boutique shops for your more esoteric needs. Beat Street New & Used Records (439 W Hastings Street, 604 683 3344) will cater to hip hop cravings, while Scrape Records (17 W Broadway Street, 604 877 1676) is devoted strictly to the hard stuff. In addition, the city supports two cavernous music stores dedicated to classical music. Downtown, check out Sikora's Classical Records (432 W Hastings Street, 604 685 0625); in Kitsilano, head to the Magic Flute (*see p134*) – and if you're not sure which version of *Die Gotterdammerung* is for you, don't be shy: both are staffed by underemployed but friendly musicians.

A&B Sound

556 Seymour Street, between Dunsmuir Street & W Pender Street, Downtown (604 687 5837/www. absound.ca). All city-centre buses. **Open** 9.30am-6pm Mon-Wed, Sat; 9.30am-9pm Thur, Fri; 11am-5pm Sun. **Credit** AmEx, MC, V. **Map** p249 L3.
This superstore features two floors of compact discs in addition to DVDs and home electronics. The prices are staggeringly cheap, with some new releases actually marked down below the wholesale cost.

West Coast chic. **Caban**. *See p132.*

Magic Flute

2203 W 4th Avenue, at Yew Street, West Side (604 736 2727/www.magicflute.com). Bus 4, 7. **Open** 10am-6pm Mon-Sat; noon-5pm Sun. **Credit** AmEx, MC, V. **Map** p251 F6.

A unique store specialising in classical, choral, jazz and world music. The staff, often musicians, know their stuff so it's worth asking their advice about purchases. Listening stations are available in order for you to preview your purchases.

Zulu Records

1974 W 4th Avenue, at Maple Street, West Side (604 738 3232/www.zulurecords.com). Bus 4, 7. **Open** 10.30am-7pm Mon-Wed; 10.30am-9pm Thur, Fri; 9.30am-6.30pm Sat; noon-6pm Sun. **Credit** AmEx, MC, V. **Map** p251 F6.

One could easily lose an afternoon in Zulu. Separate areas are dedicated to new CDs and vinyl, while an upstairs loft is filled with an excellent selection of used CDs. Also on offer are an abundance of listening stations and a couple of vintage video games.

Opticians

Bruce Eyewear

219 Abbott Street, at Water Street, Gastown (604 662 8300/www.bruceeyewear.com). Bus 4, 7. **Open** 10am-6pm Mon-Sat; noon-5pm Sun. **Credit** AmEx, MC, V. **Map** p249 M3.

This design-forward Gastown shop is also a licensed optometrist, so you can actually see through those new Dior shades you just bought.

Eyes On Burrard

775 Burrard Street, at Robson Street, Downtown (604 688 9521/www.eyesonline.com). Bus 2, 5, 22. **Open** 10am-6pm Mon-Wed; 10am-8pm Thur-Sat; noon-7pm Sun. **Credit** AmEx, MC, V. **Map** p249 K3.

A massive designer selection and long service track record have kept this place on the map for years. **Other locations:** Eyes On Twelfth, 1493 W 12th Avenue (604 732 8812).

Pharmacies

Semperviva Holistic Health Centre

2608 W Broadway, at Trafalgar Street, West Side (604 739 1958/www.semperviva.com). Bus 9, 17, 99. **Open** 10am-7pm Mon-Fri; 9.30am-6pm Sat; 11am-6pm Sun. **Credit** AmEx, MC, V. **Map** p250 E6.

Whether it's organic insect ointment or an emergency cold sore cure, this is where to find it.

Shopper's Drug Mart

1125 Davie Street, at Thurlow Street, West End (604 669 2424/www.shoppersdrugmart.ca). Bus 6. **Open** 24 hours daily. **Credit** AmEx, MC, V. **Map** p248 J3.

All the basics, all at decent prices, and, most importantly, available at all the hours God gives. **Other locations:** 2302 W 4th Avenue (604 738 3138); 885 W Broadway (604 708 1135).

Photography

Leo's Camera Supply

1055 Granville Street, between Helmcken Street & Nelson Street, Downtown (604 685 5331/www.leos camera.com). Bus 4, 6, 7, 10, 16, 17, 50. **Open** 9am-5pm Mon-Fri; 10am-4pm Sat. **Credit** MC, V. **Map** p249 K4.

Professional shooters shop here, but they'll still sort out all of your plebeian photographic needs.

London Drugs

710 Granville Street, at W Georgia Street, Downtown (604 448 4802/www.londondrugs.com). All city-centre buses. **Open** 8am-10pm Mon-Sat; 10am-8pm Sun. **Credit** AmEx, MC, V. **Map** p249 K3.

The one-hour developing service is high quality, and the computer department is known for its deals. **Other locations:** throughout the city.

Shoes

Dayton Boots

2250 E Hastings Street, at Nanaimo Street, East Vancouver (604 253 6671/www.daytonboots.com). Bus 10, 16, 135. **Open** 10am-5pm Mon-Wed; 10am-6pm Thur-Sat. **Credit** MC, V.

Wondering where Johnny Depp got those black leather boots he's always wearing? Bingo. Loggers wore them first, then film crews and eventually the stars themselves. Now people shop from all over the world via the website, but the original factory is still here on the gritty downtown Eastside.

Gravity Pope

2205 W 4th Avenue, at Yew Street, West Side (604 731 7673/www.gravitypope.com). Bus 4, 7. **Open** 10am-9pm Mon-Thur; 10am-7pm Fri, Sat; 11am-6pm Sun. **Credit** AmEx, DC, MC, V. **Map** p251 F6.

With the most far-ranging selection in the city, this is the best stop for funky flats, cowboy boots, bejewelled Birkenstocks, leather clogs, espadrilles, or whatever else is causing a fuss this season.

Intra-Venus

1072 Mainland Street, at Helmcken Street, Yaletown (604 685 9696/www.intra-venus.com). Bus 15. **Open** 10am-6pm Mon-Wed; 10am-7pm Thur, Fri; 11am-7pm Sat; noon-5pm Sun. **Credit** AmEx, MC, V. **Map** p249 K4.

Cool trainers are the mainstay here, but you'll also find funky heels from the likes of Miss Sixty. **Other locations:** Bionic, 3065 Granville Street (604 731 9688).

John Fluevog

837 Granville Street, at Robson Street, Downtown (604 688 2828/www.fluevog.com). All city-centre buses. **Open** 11am-7pm Mon-Wed, Sat; 11am-8pm Thur, Fri; noon-5pm Sun. **Credit** AmEx, MC, V. **Map** p249 K3.

A local legend, Fluevog's been cobbling since the 1980s, when high school girls wore his black pointy flats and street punks donned his 12-eyelet boots.

Clothes to cover your **TNA**. *See p125.*

From chunky to funky and then back again, he's stayed true to his streetwise edge, which has earned him a global following with stores in London and New York, as well as this, the original. **Photo** *p136.*

Cobbler

Quick Cobbler
923 Denman Street, at Haro Street, West End (604 682 6354/www.quickcobbler.com). Bus 5. **Open** 8am-5pm Mon-Sat; closed Sun. **Credit** AmEx, MC, V. **Map** p248 H3.
Quick and cobbler. Two words that ring like music in the ear when your heel has broken and you're on your way to the airport.

Spas

Skoah
1011 Hamilton Street, between Nelson Street & Helmcken Street, Yaletown (604 642 0200/toll free 1-877 642 0200/www.skoah.com). Bus 15. **Open** 11am-8pm Mon-Fri; 10am-7pm Sat, Sun. **Credit** AmEx, MC, V. **Map** p249 K4.
Specialising in facials, ranging from a quickie ($30) to an extreme ($150), this modern spa does away with whale music and fountains in favour of ambient techno and elite service. Men will feel as at home as women in the clean, serene environment.

Spruce Body Lab
1128 Richards Street, at Helmcken Street, Yaletown (604 683 3220/www.sprucebodylab.com). Bus 15. **Open** 10am-7pm Mon-Wed; 10am-8pm Thur, Fri; 10am-6pm Sat, Sun. **Credit** MC, V. **Map** p249 K4.

The polished concrete, designer furniture and soundproof massage rooms are all great. But the professionally certified massage therapists (unlike the beauty school graduates that you're likely to find working at most spas) mean you may just get the best rub-down of your life.

Sport & outdoors

Comor
1090 W Georgia Street, at Thurlow Street, Downtown (604 899 2111/www.comorsports.com). Bus 2, 5, 22. **Open** 10am-6pm Mon-Wed; 10am-9pm Thur, Fri; 10am-7pm Sat; 11am-6pm Sun. **Credit** AmEx, MC, V. **Map** p249 K3.
All the major equipment labels under one roof – especially good on snowboarding and skiing gear.

Mountain Equipment Co-op (MEC)
130 W Broadway, between Manitoba Street & Columbia Street, West Side (604 872 7858/ www.mec.ca). Bus 9, 99. **Open** *July-Sept* 10am-9pm Mon-Fri; 9am-6pm Sat; 10am-5pm Sun. *Sept-June* 10am-7pm Mon-Wed; 10am-9pm Thur, Fri; 9am-6pm Sat; 11am-5pm Sun. **Credit** MC, V. **Map** p252 M7.
This giant store stocks virtually everything you could require to be at one with the great outdoors – from camping and cycling gear to canoes and carbines. You need to be a member (it's $5 for a lifetime) but the prices here are a fraction of what you would be paying in the UK. The staff are knowledgeable and interested, and there's an invaluable noticeboard with used items for sale and people looking for others to join them on treks, ranging from the heart of the great white north to a weekend in Cypress Park.

John Fluevog. See p134.

Sigge's

*2077 W 4th Avenue, at Arbutus Street, West Side
(604 731 8818/1-877 731 8818/www.sigges.com).
Bus 4, 7.* **Open** phone or check website for details;
closed 16 Apr-31 Aug. **Credit** MC, V.
Map p251 F6.

You'll find all the main cross-country paraphernalia
and brands here (Salomon, Fischer, Atomic, etc) in
this family-owned and operated speciality cross-
country ski shop. The staff are great and will put
you in touch with the right people and point you in
the right direction. The store also offers ski lessons
and trips to Manning Park.

Tattoos & piercing

West Coast Tattoo Parlour
and Museum

*620 Davie Street, between Granville Street &
Seymour Street, Downtown (604 681 2049/www.
westcoasttattoo.com). Bus 4, 6, 7, 10, 16, 17, 50.*
Open noon-6pm Tue-Sat. **No credit cards.**
Map p248 J4.

A tattoo is a surprisingly popular Vancouver souvenir – maple leafs being the most popular. Get
yours done here (alongside clients who fly in from
around the world for intricate work) if you're sober.

Tobacconists

La Casa Del Habano

*980 Robson Street, at Burrard Street, Downtown
(604 609 0511). Bus 2, 5, 22.* **Open** 10am-7pm
Mon-Wed; 10am-9pm Thur-Sat; noon-6pm Sun.
Credit AmEx, DC, MC, V. **Map** p249 K3.

Selling exclusively Cuban cigars, this haven for the
stogie smoker offers a luxurious smoking lounge,
monthly seminars on choosing cigars to suit your
mood and advice on pairing them with wines and
spirits. With the price of cigars ranging from $3 to
$70, anyone can indulge in a puff.

Vancouver Cigar Company

*1093 Hamilton Street, at Helmcken Street, Yaletown
(604 685 0445/www.vancouvercigar.com). Bus 15.*
Open 9am-10pm Mon-Wed; 9am-midnight Thur-Sat;
11am-6pm Sun. **Credit** AmEx, MC, V.
Map p249 K4.

These approachable guys will fix you up with a
great cigar. They are open late and offer a wonderful lounge and patio for your after dinner puff.

Toys

Kids Market

*1496 Cartwright Street, Granville Island (604 689
8447/www.kidsmarket.ca). Bus 50.* **Open** 10am-6pm
daily. **Credit** varies. **Map** p248 H5.

Toys, books and a play area. Heaven.

Travellers' needs

Communications

Kinko's

*789 W Pender Street, at Howe Street, Downtown
(604 685 3338/www.kinkos.ca). All city-centre buses.*
Open 24 hours. **Credit** AmEx, MC, V.
Map p249 L3.

Should you decide to start publishing an alternative
'zine while you are here, line up with the others to
format, print and copy your materials at 4am.
Other locations: 1900 W Broadway (604 734 2679).

Shipping

Mailboxes Etc

*280 Nelson Street, at Mainland Street, Yaletown
(604 608 6681/www.mbe.ca). Bus 15.* **Open** 8.30am-
6pm Mon-Fri; 10am-4pm Sat. **Credit** AmEx, MC, V.
Map p249 K4.

And all the paper and packaging you might need.
Other locations: throughout the city.

Arts & Entertainment

Festivals & Events	**138**
Children	**142**
Film	**146**
Galleries	**150**
Gay & Lesbian	**155**
Music & Nightlife	**159**
Performing Arts	**167**
Sport & Fitness	**173**

Features

The best Festivals	138
Water babies	145
The Vancouver International Film Festival	148
The best Galleries	150
All-comers	158
The songlines	160
Gig hopping	165
Bright sparks	168
Strike the pose	177
Powder play	180

Festivals & Events

At the first sight of sun, Vancouverites head outside to celebrate.

While summer boasts the lion's share of festivals, hardly a week goes by without something happening somewhere. We list the major festivals and events, but it's always worth checking the local press, like the *Georgia Straight*, or www.tourismvancouver.com or www.bcpassport.com/festivals.html, to see what's going on when you arrive.

Spring

Vancouver Sun Run
Starting line at W Georgia Street between Burrard Street & Thurlow Street, Downtown (604 689 9441/ www.sunrun.com). All city-centre buses. **Map** p249 K3. **Date** 23 Apr 2006; late Apr 2007.
The most popular 10km (6 mile) run in Canada takes place on the third Sunday in April and includes a mini 2.5km (1.5 mile) route for under-12s and those not up to the full course.

Vancouver Marathon
BC Place Stadium, Downtown (604 872 2928/ www.adidasvanmarathon.ca). Bus 15. **Map** p249 L4. **Date** 7 May 2006; early May 2007.
Fancy a whistlestop tour of the city? The marathon usually starts at BC Place then heads off through False Creek and Gastown, round Stanley Park, over to Kitsilano and back again.

International Children's Festival
Vanier Park, off Whyte Avenue, West Side (604 708 5655/www.childrensfestival.ca). Bus 2, 22. **Map** p248 G4. **Date** 15-22 May 2006; May 2007.
Easily spotted by its signature red and white striped main tent, the children's festival attracts circus acts, musicians and theatre companies from around the world. Each year, two days are Francophone, with all performances in French. Popular with school groups, but families can still buy tickets. Tickets are available from Ticketmaster (*see p161*).

Cloverdale Rodeo & Country Fair
6050A-176th Street, Surrey (604 576 9461/www. cloverdalerodeo.com). Bus 395 from SkyTrain Surrey Central. **Tickets** $7-$25. **Date** 19-22 May 2006.
An hour's drive from downtown, this is the biggest rodeo west of the Calgary Stampede. If you have qualms about steer wrestling and bronco breaking, the adjacent country fair has the usual attractions.

Victoria Day Long Weekend
Date 22 May 2006; 21 May 2007.
The official start of summer: outdoor swimming pools open and barbecues are dusted off.

Summer

Bard on the Beach Shakespeare Festival
Vanier Park, off Whyte Avenue, West Side (604 737 0625/www.bardonthebeach.org). Bus 2, 22. **Open** *Box office* 9am-5.30pm or showtime daily. **Tickets** $16-$28.50. **Credit** MC, V. **Map** p248 G4. **Date** June-Sept.
Bard on the Beach used to be just a popular success. Now it has respect. The festival programmes four shows in two tents (520 seats and 240 seats) in a beautiful park on English Bay with the beach, water, city and mountains all as a backdrop, and sells over 90% capacity during a four-month run. For 2006: *A Midsummer Night's Dream* and *Measure for Measure* on the main stage, and *The Winter's Tale* and *Troilus and Cressida* on the small. **Photo** *p139*.

International Dragon Boat Festival
Creekside Park, East Vancouver (604 688 2382/ www.adbf.com). Bus 3/SkyTrain Main Street-Science World. **Date** 16-18 June 2006; mid June 2007.

The best Festivals

Bard on the Beach
Shakespeare-on-sea. *See above.*

Chinese New Year
Eat, drink and dance with the dragons as the lunar year turns over. *See p141.*

HSBC Celebration of Light
The biggest international fireworks competition in the world. *See p140.*

Vancouver Folk Music Festival
Release your inner hippie. *See p139.*

Vancouver International Film Festival
16 days and over 300 films from more than 50 countries. *See p141.*

Vancouver International Jazz Festival
Chill out while the world's best toot their horns. *See p139.*

Vancouver Pride Parade
The gay ghetto's annual bash. *See p140.*

Arts & Entertainment

'The rude sea grew civil at her song.' **Bard on the Beach Shakespeare Festival**. *See p138.*

The spectacle, spread over three days, of competitive racing in traditional Chinese dragon boats is memorable. Some 2,000 participants get wet, win races and continue an ancient Chinese method of celebrating the summer solstice. It's not all about boats, however: the park throngs with children's entertainers, activity tents, live music and food stalls. Weekend tickets include entrance to Science World.

Vancouver International Jazz Festival

Various venues (604 872 5200/www.jazzvancouver. com). **Tickets** $12-$59. **Credit** AmEx, MC, V. **Date** late June.

Some 40 venues around the city are involved in one of Vancouver's most impressive music festivals. 2005's line up alone featured local girl Diana Krall, Terence Blanchard, The Bad Plus, Roy Haynes, Bill Frisell, Daniel Lanois and Evan Parker. A number of restaurants host gigs and there are also free outdoor events – the opening street party in Gastown is a favourite. Jazz aficionados planning to attend a number of performances can save money by investing in a festival pass that saves you 15%-45% of the face value of the ticket.

Canada Day

Canada Place, Downtown (604 775 8025/www. canadadayatcanadaplace.com). All city-centre buses. **Map** p249 L2. **Date** 1 July.

Those Vancouverites who own an island summer house, tend to depart for it on Canada's birthday; most everyone else fires up the barbecue. Official celebrations take place in the Canada Place exhibition centre which is filled with lumberjack shows, mechanical bucking broncos, bouncy castles and the like. Check local press for details of other events.

Dancing on the Edge

Various venues (604 689 0929/www.dancingonthe edge.org). **Date** 6-15 July 2006; July 2007.

Two weeks of contemporary dance from international and local companies. The festival features work by both established and emerging choreographers.

Vancouver Folk Music Festival

Jericho Beach Park, West Side (604 602 9798/ www.thefestival.bc.ca). Bus 4. **Tickets** *weekend pass bought by 18 June* $100; *weekend pass bought between 19 June-14 July* $125; *weekend pass at the gate* $135; *Fri night* $40; *Sat, Sun* $60. **Credit** MC, V. **Map** p250 A5. **Map** p250 A5. **Date** 14-16 July 2006; 13-15 July 2007.

Marking its 29th year in 2006, the folk festival is the most direct route to Vancouver's hippie spirit. Even if you don't buy tickets to enter the open-air site, you should make the trip out to Jericho Beach which, for the three days of the festival, turns into Woodstock-on-sea. Joss sticks, tie-dye and other hippie paraphernalia are sold from makeshift stalls that line the edge of the beach, while families and stoners chill out on the sand listening to the music wafting over them. 2005 ticket holders were treated to Waylon Jennings, Iris DeMent, Buck 65 and many more.

Illuminaires Lantern Festival

Trout Lake, at Victoria Drive & E 15th Avenue, East Vancouver (604 879 8611/www.publicdreams.org). Bus 20/SkyTrain Broadway. **Date** late July.

Arts & Entertainment

Vancouver goes up in flames. **HSBC Celebration of Light**.

A free community project that creates a magical sight on a warm summer's night as hundreds of people gather to walk around Trout Lake carrying lit paper lanterns of all shapes, sizes and designs while music is piped through the trees. Lantern workshops take place earlier in the month.

Powell Street Festival

Oppenheimer Park, W Cordova Street, between Dunlevy Avenue & Jackson Avenue, East Vancouver (604 739 9388/http://powellstfestival.shinnova.com). Bus 4, 7. **Date** late July.

The free annual celebration of Japanese Canadian culture has everything from dance to martial arts to traditional tea services – with plenty of theatre, music and art of both local and international origin.

HSBC Celebration of Light

English Bay, West End and West Side (www.celebration-of-light.com). All city-centre buses. **Date** late July-early Aug.

The biggest international fireworks competition in the world takes place over four nights spread across a fortnight at the height of summer, and practically the whole city turns up to watch. Roads and bridges are closed and it's impossible to park, so walk to your nearest vantage point. English Bay, Kitsilano beach and Vanier Park have good views, but be sure to find a spot early. Kick-off time is 10pm, when the whole bay becomes illuminated by the most fantastic pyrotechnics fired from a barge. **Photos** *above*.

Vancouver Pride Parade

Beach Avenue & Denman Street, West End (604 687 0955/www.vanpride.bc.ca). Bus 6. **Map** p248 G2. **Date** 29 July 2006; 6 Aug 2007.

Pride is a major Vancouver event. Clubs and bars put on special events (see local press for details), there are stalls, stages with live performances, tea dances and any number of beer gardens. The parade, which travels along Denman Street and Beach Avenue, is a major spectacle, with ever more elaborate floats, drag queens done up to the nines and hundreds of people in the mood for a party.

PNE (Pacific National Exhibition)

E Hastings Street & Renfrew Street, East Vancouver (604 253 2311/www.pne.bc.ca). Bus 10, 16, 135. **Tickets** phone for details. **Date** mid Aug-early Sept.

Dog shows, daredevil motorcyclists, duck races – the Pacific National Exhibition is a slightly hokey tradition in British Columbia geared towards all the family. Younger children especially love it, while truculent teenagers can let off steam at the next-door funfair, Playland (*see p144*). It's reachable by a (fairly long) direct bus from downtown but if you decide to drive, look out for local residents on the road waving cardboard signs – they want to rent you their parking spot for the day.

Festival Vancouver

Various venues (604 688 1152/www.festival vancouver.bc.ca). **Tickets** $13-$69 through Ticketmaster (*see p161*). **Date** first two weeks Aug.

Two weeks of all things beautiful so long as they're properly musical, thus no rap or rock: orchestral, choral and operatic as well as chamber music and even some jazz. Festival Vancouver is a relative newcomer on the city's scene and the focus is generally split between one composer and the music of a particular country and includes both national and international performers.

Wooden Boat Festival
Granville Island, West Side (604 688 9622/www.
vcn.bc.ca/vwbs/interest.htm). **Map** p248 H5. **Bus** 50.
Date late Aug.
Wooden boat enthusiasts show off their extraordi-
narily detailed vessels at this testament to craftsmanship. There are also facilities for children to
build and sail toy boats, and live performers sere-
nade festival goers with sea shanties. All this plus
rowing, sailing and canoeing races in Alder Bay.

Autumn

Vancouver Fringe Festival
Granville Island, West Side (604 257 0350/www.
vancouverfringe.com). **Bus** 50. **Tickets** $3-$12.
Credit AmEx, MC, V. **Map** p248 H5.
Date 7-17 Sept 2006; Sept 2007.
The tourist mecca of Granville Island is about as far
as you can get from 'fringe' Vancouver but what the
festival lost in grit it has made up for in audience
since moving from Commercial Drive a few years
back. The shows, programmed in island theatres,
rehearsal spaces and tents plus off-site works
around the city, do strong business. The quality
index would make for a line graph as jagged as the
Coastal mountain range but strong local performers,
touring acts and showcase stars make for a great
festival. Advance tickets go on sale by mid August.

Canwest Comedy Fest
For listing and review, *see p171.* **Date**
18-24 Sept 2006; Sept 2007.

Vancouver International Film Festival
For listing and review, *see p148* **Vancouver**
International Film Festival.
Date late Sept-mid Oct.

International Writers and Readers Festival
Various venues (604 681 6330/www.writersfest.
bc.ca). **Tickets** $12-$15. **Credit** MC, V. **Date**
17-22 Oct 2006; Oct 2007.
Literary giants share the stage with new writers in
this hugely popular celebration of the written word.
The week is made up of readings, poetry slams,
workshops, the annual celebrity spelling bee and
special events for children. Past guests have included Margaret Atwood, Julian Barnes, Alice Munro,
Vikram Seth, JK Rowling and Peter Carey.

Vancouver Snow Show
Canada Place, Downtown (250 370 2983/www.
vancouversnowshow.com). All city-centre buses.
Tickets $10; $5-$8 concessions; free under-6s; $25
family. **Map** p249 L2. **Date** late Oct.
Everything you need to hit the slopes under one roof
plus much, much more in this annual three-day trade
exhibition. From heavily discounted new gear, to
second-hand and a ski and board swap-shop, there
are bargains aplenty to be found.

Winter

Festival of Lights
Van Dusen Gardens, 5251 Oak Street, at W 37th
Avenue, West Side (604 878 9274/www.vandusen
garden.org). **Admission** $5.50; $2.25-$3.75
concessions; free under-6s. **Bus** 17. **Date** Dec.
The always spectacular gardens become simply
magical in the run-up to Christmas when 20,000
fairy lights are draped through the trees .

Carol Ship Parade of Lights
Various locations along the waterfront
(604 878 8999/www.carolships.org). **Date** Dec.
As the festive season approaches, the boats in False
Creek and Coal Harbour are bedecked with lights,
some hosting onboard carol services, others just sailing around to add a twinkle to the night sky. On
peak evenings, more than 80 crafts turn out.

Polar Bear Swim
Sunset Beach, English Bay, West End (www.city.
vancouver.bc.ca/parks/events/polarbear). **Bus** 6.
Map p248 G3. **Date** 2.30pm New Year's Day.
Just ten hardy souls braved the waters of English
Bay on New Year's Day 1920 – the first ever Polar
Bear Swim in Vancouver. In 2005, some 1,600 peo-
ple registered to take part, and a whole lot more
found themselves overcome with the urge to strip
off and take the plunge.

Annual Bald Eagle Count
Along Sea-to-Sky Highway, Squamish (604 898
3333/www.brackendaleeagles.com). **Date** early Jan.
From December to February, literally thousands of
bald eagles congregate to feast on dead or dying
salmon in the Cheakamus Valley. The highest concentration of birds is from mid December to mid
January, with the annual count taking place the first
Sunday in the new year. The count draws visitors
from all over the world.

Chinese New Year Festival
Various locations, Chinatown (www.vancouver
chinatown.ca). **Bus** 3, 4, 7. **Date** Jan or Feb.
Held on the first Sunday of the Lunar New Year,
these celebrations are understandably extensive
given Vancouver's population. The traditional
parade in Chinatown is a big draw, but check local
press for other events and don't forget to practise
saying 'Gung hay fat choy'. Happy New Year!

PuSh International Performance Festival
Granville Island, West Side (604 709 9973/www.
pushfestival.ca). **Tickets** $14-$58. **Credit** MC, V.
Bus 50. **Date** 10 Jan-4 Feb 2006; Jan 2007.
Entering its fourth season in 2006, the PuSh Festival
is the best current expression of Vancouver's theatrical ambitions. A smartly curated set of hand-
picked shows from Europe and across Canada
mingle with new work by local hotshots, along with
play readings, a cabaret and, on occasion, even a
Kronos Quartet concert for good measure.

Arts & Entertainment

Children

It's playtime.

Vancouver is great for kids. If it's sunny – and it is, sometimes – there are parks and beaches aplenty, plus two wonderful open-air swimming pools (*see p178*), while snow brings the best excuse to go play on the mountains. And the rest of the time? Well, there are enough first-class indoor attractions to keep the tykes amused. Vancouver is also replete with day camps during school holidays – offering everything from skiing and snowboarding in the winter, to kayaking in the summer, with arts and drama classes year-round. Summer camp listings are at www.bcparent.com.

BABYSITTING

Most of the big hotels will arrange babysitting for you, but if you need to organise it yourself, Nannies On Call (604 734 1776, www.nannies oncall.com) has a good reputation.

Indoor attractions

Cliffhanger Climbing Gym

106 W 1st Avenue, at Manitoba Street, West Side (604 874 2400/www.cliffhangerclimbing.com). Bus 3. **Open** noon-11pm Mon-Fri; noon-9.30pm Sat, Sun. **Rates** $15-$17/day. **Credit** MC, V. **Map** p249 M5.
With over 1,100 sq m (12,000 sq ft) of 12m (40ft) vertical surfaces, Cliffhanger is an ideal place for your budding Spider-man (or woman) to begin their training in webslinging. Children from 5-17 can take part in scheduled programmes or drop-in sessions and they have sessions for brave adults too.

CN IMAX

For listings, *see p149*.
From the spectacle of space to the mysteries of the ocean floor, this bigger-than-life movie experience is always a good choice on a rainy day. There are usually four or five different films to choose from.

HR MacMillan Space Centre

1100 Chestnut Street, at Whyte Avenue, West Side (604 738 7827/www.hrmacmillanspacecentre.com). Bus 2, 22. **Open** 10am-5pm Tue-Sun. **Admission** $13.50; $5-$10.50 concessions; free under-5s. **Credit** AmEx, MC, V. **Map** p248 G4.
Housed in the same hat-shaped building as the Vancouver Museum, the Space Centre is a small but well thought out attraction that appeals most to school-age children. Much of this interactive exhibit utilises computer screens, where budding astronauts can practise skills such as planning an interplanetary research mission, landing the Space Shuttle or launching rockets. Hourly presentations

in the lecture theatre on diverse science-related subjects move at a clip and are 'performed' by actors, so never feel stodgy, and the Virtual Voyage full-motion simulator is not to be missed. Younger children will enjoy the specially commissioned Music With Marnie show in the top-floor planetarium, which also puts on laser shows to music.

Kids Market

1496 Cartwright Street, Granville Island (604 689 8447/www.kidsmarket.ca). Bus 50. **Open** 10am-6pm daily. **Credit** varies. **Map** p248 H5.
A two-level shopping mall with everything your child could want, the Kids Market even has pint-sized doorways (don't worry, there are regular openings as well). Highlights include Knotty Toys, a store dedicated to old-fashioned wooden playthings that also stocks a mean *Thomas the Tank Engine* selection, and Kites and Puppets with its beautiful collection of both. Upstairs there are separate (pay for) play areas for toddlers and older kids where they can tumble in ball pits, paint ceramics or get their video games fix. There's also a fast food eatery, the Hairloft Princess Spa for little girls who adore all things glittery, and Everything Wet, a good place to stock up on swimsuits and raingear.

Maritime Museum

1905 Ogden Avenue, at Chestnut Street, West Side (604 257 8300/www.vancouvermaritime museum.com). Bus 2, 22. **Open** *June-Aug* 10am-5pm daily. *Sept-May* 10am-5pm Tue-Sat; noon-5pm Sun. **Admission** $10; $7.50 concessions; free under-5s; $20 family. **Credit** AmEx, MC, V. **Map** p248 G4.
The main attraction here is the *St Roch*, the first vessel to have navigated the Northwest Passage in both directions. Regular guided tours follow a short video presentation which details the history and the hardships of the journey and those brave men who made it. The crew quarters are on view, and make for a sharp contrast between the officers and the regular men. But even those hardships pale next to the accommodation provided for the ship's Inuit guide: he slept in a tent on deck, with his large extended family and pack of huskies. The dogs were fed with walrus meat. Elsewhere, there are a lot of model ships on display, some interesting photos detailing Vancouver's development as a port, and a good interactive discovery area for children, that is very welcome on a wet day. Outside, take a look at the *Ben Franklin* submersible – a craft that was found rotting in a scrapyard, before being lovingly restored – and the collection of heritage boats at the nearby dock. Note: as of late 2005, the museum was discussing expansion and possible relocation.

Vancouver Aquarium Marine Science Centre.

Roundhouse Community Centre

181 Roundhouse Mews, at Pacific Boulevard and Drake Street, Yaletown (604 713 1800/www. roundhouse.ca). Bus 17. **Open** 9am-10pm Mon-Fri; 9am-5pm Sat, Sun. **Admission** free. **Map** p249 K5.
On the site of the former Canadian Pacific Railway's switching yard, the community centre houses the original Engine 374 that pulled the first passenger train into Vancouver in 1887. Train-obsessed small fry can clamber into its cabin and be the driver.

Science World

1455 Quebec Street, at Terminal Avenue, East Vancouver (604 443 7443/www.scienceworld.bc.ca). Bus 3/SkyTrain Main Street-Science World. **Open** 10am-5pm Mon-Fri; 10am-6pm Sat, Sun. **Admission** $14.50; $10 concessions; free under-4s; $49 family. *With one Omnimax film* $19.50; $15 concessions; free under-4s. **Credit** AmEx, MC, V. **Map** p249 M5.
Impossible to miss, the huge silver golf ball that is Science World is a significant part of the Vancouver skyline. Once you've finished marvelling at it and the perpetual motion ball sculpture just outside the entrance, a day's worth of activities await inside. Filled with fun interactive exhibits, Science World is broad enough to capture the imagination of most children. From the age-split area where kids are encouraged to get physical, to the more bucolic nature section, the mind-bending metal puzzles, hourly whiz-bang science shows and Omnimax theatre with its wraparound screen, they have to try really hard to be bored. There's a White Spot on site that will satisfy the hungriest child's burger cravings and a picnic area overlooking False Creek.

Storyeum

142 Water Street, between Cambie Street & Abbott Street, Gastown (604 687 8142/www.storyeum.com). Bus 4, 7. **Open** 10am-5pm daily. **Admission** $21.95; $15.95-$18.95 concessions; free under-5s. **Credit** AmEx, MC, V. **Map** p249 M3.

Opened to much fanfare in 2004, this historical pageant is aimed squarely at the tour bus crowd. To reach the exhibit proper you descend beneath the street in one of the world's largest passenger lifts and exit into a mock-up of a pre-colonial landscape. Then the fun begins: hokey dramatisations walk you through 130 years or so of the history of British Columbia. The backdrops are quite impressive, but the writing is worthy of a school revue. School children (8-12) are likely to enjoy it, but if the audience is near capacity – which is 100 – it's best to come back for a later show. You'd only go once – and that's why it's pushed hard to tourists.

Vancouver Aquarium Marine Science Centre

For listings, *see p63*.
A real hub in Stanley Park, the aquarium is endlessly fascinating to young and old alike. Outdoors you can watch the regular dolphin, sea lion and beluga whale shows, not to mention fall in love with everyone's favourites, the adorable sea otters. Inside, the local BC tanks are as interesting as the tropical exhibits, with a camera-shy octopus, beautiful jellyfish and sea horses, and plenty of coldwater critters. Downstairs there's a play area and underwater viewing room to watch the belugas. The outdoor café serves surprisingly good food – just be careful where you sit: the left side facing the whale enclosure is only for those who don't mind getting splashed. Very busy during summer. **Photo.**

Vancouver Aquatic Centre

1050 Beach Avenue, at Thurlow Street, West End (604 665 3424). Bus 4, 7, 10, 16, 17, 50. **Open** 6.30am-4.15pm, 7-9.40pm Mon-Fri; 8am-1pm, 5-9pm Sat; 10am-9pm Sun. Closed August. **Rates** $4.50; $2.50-$3.40 concessions. **Credit** MC, V. **Map** p248 H4.
A 50m (164ft) pool with shallows at either end, the aquatic centre is roomy enough to accommodate

serious swimmers and silly splashers alike. There's nothing flashy here, though various types of floats and inflatable rings are provided. A warmer beginners' pool offers respite and refuge for those with younger children (under-8s).

Vancouver Art Gallery SuperSunday

For listings, see p56.
Every third Sunday in the month, from noon to 5pm, the VAG opens its doors to school-age kids eager to get hands-on about art. It's a great afternoon, filled with everything from screen printing and working with clay, to making mobiles and watching dance performances. Activities are varied to connect with current exhibitions. It's very popular, especially on rainy days, but you do book in for popular activities on arrival, so queuing is not usually an issue. The gallery's café (see p89) is a nice spot to rejuvenate yourself – particularly in summer when the patio overlooking Robson Street is open.

Vancouver Museum

1100 Chestnut Street, at Whyte Avenue, West Side (604 736 4431/www.vanmuseum.bc.ca). Bus 2, 22. **Open** 10am-5pm Tue, Wed, Fri-Sun; 10am-6pm Thur. **Admission** $10; $6-$8 concessions; free under-4s. **Credit** AmEx, MC, V. **Map** p248 G4.
The museum is currently undergoing a major refit, but a part of the permanent exhibition devoted to the city's history will reopen in spring 2006. The full display is not expected to be on view until 2008.

Vancouver Public Library

350 W Georgia Street, between Homer Street & Hamilton Street, Downtown (604 331 3603/ www.vpl.ca). All city-centre buses. **Open** 10am-9pm Mon-Thur; 10am-6pm Fri, Sat; noon-5pm Sun. **Admission** free. **Map** p249 L4.
The central Library Square branch offers a well-stocked children's section downstairs, with multimedia computer stations, listening stations, internet access, a toddler play area and a preschool learning centre, all free. If you want to borrow any items a $25 visitor's card will allow that.

Outdoor fun

Capilano Salmon Hatchery

4500 Capilano Park Road, off Capilano Road, North Shore (604 666 1790). No buses. **Open** Nov-Mar 8am-4pm daily. Apr, Oct 8am-4.45pm daily. May, Sept 8am-7pm daily. June-Aug 8am-8pm daily. **Admission** free.
A government-owned fish farm, the hatchery is designed to help stem the depletion of salmon stocks. The education centre allows you to learn about the life cycle of the salmon, view the fish in various stages of growth, and follow the process from the hatchery to the river and reintegration into the wild. October is the best time to see the salmon leap the fish ladders. You'll need a car to get here.

Capilano Suspension Bridge & Park

For listings, see p81.
A pricey tourist attraction in the trees, this spectacular swinging bridge across a canyon also offers a treetops trail and other activities.

Children's Farmyard and Miniature Railway

Stanley Park, West End (604 257 8531). Bus 19. **Open** varies, call for information. **Admission** Railway or Farmyard $5; $2.50-$3.75 concessions. Bright Nights (Railway and Farmyard) $7; $4 concessions. Ghost Train (Railway and Farmyard) $8.50; $5 concessions. **Credit** MC, V. **Map** p63.
A popular double attraction inside Stanley Park where children can pet goats, sheep, pigs and other assorted farm animals – as well as the odd reptile and llama – before taking a 15 minute train ride through the forest. The miniature engine is a replica of the one that pulled the first transcontinental passenger train into the city in 1886. In the run-up to Hallowe'en, the railway operates at night, decked out as a ghost train, the surrounding forest decorated with a different ghoulish theme every year.

Lynn Canyon

For listings, see p81.
Another suspension bridge – this time free – in a park with plentiful trails and picnicking areas.

Maplewood Farm

405 Seymour River Place, off Old Dollarton Highway, North Shore (604 929 5610/www.maplewood farm.bc.ca). Bus 211. **Open** Oct-Mar 10am-4pm Tue-Sun. Apr-Sept 10am-4pm daily. **Admission** Regular farm days $3.50; $2 concessions. Special events $5; $4.50 concessions; $18.25 family. **Credit** MC, V.
With some 200 farm animals, milking displays, pony rides and a large canopied area for stroking and feeding the rabbits, this North Shore attraction (once a working farm) is always popular. There are themed events tied to seasons and holidays.

Nat Bailey Stadium

4601 Ontario Street, at 33rd Avenue, West Side (604 872 5232/www.canadiansbaseball.com). Bus 3, 15. **Open** 1pm afternoon game; 7pm evening game. **Rates** $8-$20. **Credit** MC, V.
This 6,500-seater open-air stadium is the home of the family-friendly Canadians baseball team.

Playland

2901 E Hastings Street, at Renfrew Street, East Vancouver (604 252 3583/www.pne.ca). Bus 10, 16, 135. **Open** May-Sept phone for details. Fright Nights 14-31 Oct 6-11pm daily. **Admission** $24.95. Fright Nights $20. **Credit** AmEx, MC, V.
All the fun of the fair, with a roller-coaster, Ferris wheel and some 35 other gravity-defying rides. A bus ride out of town, Playland opens from Easter through the summer, combining with the PNE (see p140) in late August and reopening for a couple of weeks in October as the Hallowe'en themed Fright Nights. Admission includes unlimited rides and discounted tickets can be purchased at 7-11, Safeway and Shoppers Drug Mart stores.

Water babies

When the heat begins to rise, the city's water parks are a great way to cool little bodies down. **Granville Island** boasts North America's largest and is a watery paradise indeed with its fake fire hydrants, spray guns and large water slide. For those who prefer dry pursuits, there's an adjacent decent-sized sand-filled playground and plenty of shady trees for picnics. It's on Cartwright Street, between the Information Centre and False Creek Community Centre.

Just past Lumberman's Arch, next to the Seawall, **Stanley Park**'s water playground includes a mini cave as well as a walk-through dryer. There's scant grass for

parents to sprawl on and the bike traffic can make journeys to the loos a bit treacherous at times, but there's a handy ice-cream stand and a takeaway serving hot dogs and fish and chips nearby.

Minimalism is the key in **Coal Harbour**, where the park at the end of Bute Street is basically water jets springing out of concrete. Despite its lack of apparent child-pleasing colour and gadgets, the children love it; here it's all about simply getting drenched with no messing about. To add to its attractions (for parents at least), it's overlooked by the Mill Marine Bistro (1199 W Cordova Street, 604 687 6455, www.millbistro.ca).

Further afield

About an hour's drive from Downtown is the **Greater Vancouver Zoo** (5048 264th Street, Aldergrove, 604 856 6825, www.gvzoo.com), where a free 15-minute safari bus will take you inside the North American enclosure to view bear, bison, elk and wolves up close. The daily lion and tiger feeding at 1pm is also popular. However, in 2005, the zoo was listed for sale, so check details before venturing there.

Close enough to the zoo to make a combined visit, **Fort Langley Historic Site** (23433 Mavis Avenue, Fort Langley, 604 513 4777, www.pc.gc.ca/lhn-nhs/bc/langley) was one of the Hudson's Bay Company's original fur-trading posts and is now a government-run museum with costumed guides. The heritage

village of Fort Langley is just two blocks away and the surrounding **Fraser Valley** offers plenty of trails (*see p190*).

Closer to town, **Burnaby Village Museum** (6501 Deer Lake Avenue, Burnaby, 604 293 6500, www.burnabyvillagemuseum.ca) also employs costumed guides to talk you through this replica early 20th-century village. Watch the blacksmith at work, discover the history of the local newspaper or catch a silent film, before heading into the ice-cream parlour.

Just before the BC Ferries terminal at Tsawwassen, **Splashdown Park** (4799 Nulelum Way, 604 943 2251, www.splashdownpark.ca) is open from June to September and offers water slides of various heights, angles and speeds, plus a gentler area for small children, and volleyball courts and picnic areas.

Film

Welcome to Brollywood.

In June 1913, the British Columbia Moving Pictures Act established a provincial censor for the first time. By October, the American studios were issuing complaints about his severity. One peculiar bone of contention was the depiction of the Stars and Stripes – anathema to the censor. The following year, he banned 50 reels of film for this reason – an infringement surpassed only by many instances of licentious behaviour.

It is safe to say that this honourable gentleman would not be well pleased by British Columbia's subsequent cinematic history: years of stagnation, followed by rapid industrial growth dominated by American capital.

Today, the film industry ranks alongside timber and tourism as one of BC's biggest businesses. But if you were asked to list memorable home-grown BC movies, the fingers of one hand might suffice: *The Grey Fox* (1982); *My American Cousin* (1985) and *Kissed* (1997) are the first to come to mind.

Vancouver in the movies is like one of those ubiquitous character actors whose name and face become familiar from repeated sightings, even if you're not entirely confident you could put the two together. The city pops up in all manner of places, but it hardly ever appears as itself. *The X Files* shot here for its first five seasons, but Vancouver only got star billing in the final episode, when the production team had a ball including all the giveaway road signs, mounted policemen and moose which they'd been hiding for years. Then they moved back to LA. San Francisco, Los Angeles, Seattle, New York, Boston, London, Hong Kong – Vancouver has played them all.

It's ironic that one of the world's most spectacular cities is typecast as an anonymous cinematic backdrop – Nowheresville, USA – on its website the BC Film Commission boasts about the area's chameleon-like qualities: 'Skyscrapers, mean streets, mountains, marinas – Vancouver is every great city in the world rolled into one.' (Yup, even the squalid Downtown Eastside has its civic uses; ready-made deprivation for the likes of *Catwoman*.)

In the late 1970s the provincial government aggressively courted Hollywood with tax breaks and industry services ten to 20 years before most of North America wised up. The famous 'Hollywood North' tag was coined as early as 1982. (Californians prefer a less flattering label: 'Brollywood'.) This provincial support has generally fallen under the umbrella of the department of tourism, although as movies become more computer-generated, it's hard to see how such films as *I, Robot, X-Men* and *Fantastic Four* will help to attract visitors.

Employing some 30,000 locals and bringing in $800 million in 2004 alone, the investment has paid off in mean economic terms, but Hollywood is an inconstant partner. The competition has intensified. Toronto now vies with Vancouver for the 'Hollywood North' tag (precipitating a dizzy tax-inducement spiral) and with the US dollar falling against its Canadian counterpart the studios are as likely to choose Prague, Sydney or London for their bigger blockbusters.

That's left Vancouver with an unfortunate reputation as a haven for cheapjack and DTV productions; Hollywood's cast-offs. In the last couple of years the roll call is undistinguished: *Catwoman, Elektra, Are We There Yet?, White Chicks, Alone in the Dark, Scooby Too, Superbabies: Baby Geniuses 2, Scary Movie 3* and *Blade Trinity*, for starters.

If you're looking for landmarks, your best bets are the 1986 Mel Gibson, Goldie Hawn thriller *Bird on a Wire* (which relocates the Harbour Centre Tower, Gastown and the BC Hydro Building to Detroit); the scenic Ted Danson, Isabella Rossellini romance *Cousins* (1989); and especially 1994's *Intersection*, which has the rare distinction of actually being set in British Columbia (Richard Gere's architect works in Gastown and counts the UBC Museum of Anthropology among his designs). The best of a poor bunch is undoubtedly Robert Altman's 1971 Western *McCabe and Mrs Miller*, set in fictional Presbyterian Church but shot in West Vancouver and presenting a credible picture of the Pacific Northwest in the Gold Rush days.

These days BC filmmakers turn out more than two dozen features annually, even if they've yet to make a mark on the international stage. Victoria-bred Atom Egoyan and local boy-made-good Michael J Fox had to get out of town to find their respective niches. In the field of interactive games design though, Vancouver is a world player. Years of Hollywood colonisation has made this fertile ground for reimagining cyber space.

Cinephile paradiso. **The Vancity Theatre**. *See p148.*

CINEMAS

Vancouver isn't particularly well served for cinemas – gone are the days when Granville Street boasted ten cinemas within five blocks. Today most locals watch their movies at home or in suburban multiplexes like the (relatively grand) Silvercity Riverport (14211 Entertainment Boulevard, Richmond, 604 277 5993, www.famousplayers.com), which also houses an IMAX screen and adjoins an entertainment complex, aquatic centre etc. Nevertheless, a couple of recent additions to the downtown scene hope to buck the trend: the **Paramount Vancouver** on the corner of Smithe and Burrard is a showcase for Hollywood blockbusters and 'techno zen' design, while the **Vancity Theatre** aims to provide experimental, avant-garde and international repertory programming.

TICKETS AND INFORMATION

The local press carries daily cinema listings with disposable critical commentary. The *Vancouver Sun* and the *Georgia Straight* try to be comprehensive, and the *Globe and Mail* publishes a Vancouver arts supplement (*Seven*) with the paper every Friday. Online, www.cinemaclock.com provides a search engine for films and/or venues, with trailer links and occasionally useful user reviews, but you will have to phone or go to the exhibitors' websites to prebook.

Art house, repertory & second run

Denman Cinema

1737 Comox Street, at Denman Street, West End (604 683 2201/www.denmancinema.com). Bus 6. **Screens** 1. **Admission** *Double bills* $6; $4 concessions. *Tue* $4. **No credit cards**. **Map** p248 H2.
Handily placed should that trip to Stanley Park be rained off, Denman is a comfortable, discount second run mainstream movie theatre.

Hollywood

3123 W Broadway, at Balaclava Street, West Side (604 738 3211/www.hollywoodtheatre.ca). Bus 9, 17. **Screens** 1. **Admission** *Double bills* $4 Mon; $6 Tue-Sun; $3.50 concessions. *Matinées* $5.
No credit cards. **Map** p251 C6.
Tucked away in Kitsilano, the Hollywood celebrated its 70th birthday in 2005. Remarkably, it's been owned and operated by the same family, the Farleighs, throughout that time. The programming, as the name might suggest, is strictly studio Hollywood second run.

Pacific Cinematheque

1131 Howe Street, between Helmcken Street and Davie Street, Downtown (604 688 3456/www. cinematheque.bc.ca). Bus 4, 7, 10, 16, 17, 50, N9, N10, N17. **Screens** 1. **Admission** $8.50; $7 concessions. *Double bills* $10.50; $9 concessions. *Annual membership* $3. **No credit cards**. **Map** p248 J4.

The city's old stalwart rep theatre, the Cinematheque has raised its game of late with the Vancity Theatre opening nearby. Expect auteur retrospectives, seasons celebrating contemporary national cinemas and remastered prints of classic films. In vintage rep style, you'll also get cramped, uncomfortable seating and only adequate sight-lines.

Ridge Theatre

3131 Arbutus Street, at W 16th Avenue, West Side (604 738 6311/www.ridgetheatre.com). Bus 16. **Screens** 1. **Admission** $8; $5 concessions. *Tue* $6; $4 concessions. *Double bills* $7; $4 concessions. **No credit cards. Map** p251 F8.
With the most iconic theatre awning in the city (complemented with a bowling pin from the alley next door), the Ridge is a characterful rep house a ten-minute taxi ride from Downtown. Opened in 1950, it retains most of its original features, including a balcony fitted with an enclosed 'crying room' for infants. A change of ownership in late 2005 may bring with it a change in programming, so phone or check the website before setting off. **Photo** *p149*.

Vancity Theatre

Vancouver International Film Centre, 1181 Seymour Street, at Davie Street, Yaletown (604 685 0260/www.vifc.org). Bus 4, 7, 10, 16, 17, 50, N9, N10, N17. **Screens** 1. **Admission** $9.50; $7.50 concessions. *Membership* $2. **Credit** V. **Map** p248 J4.
A spin-off from the successful Vancouver International Film Festival, which operates it, the Vancity Theatre opened in early 2006 after a brief trial run during the festival. It promises the most adventurous repertory programming in the city. The state of the art 175-seat theatre puts comfort over

commerce: double arm rests, spacious leg room, excellent sight-lines – and a balcony. Cinephiles will think they've died and gone to heaven. **Photo** *p147*.

Mainstream & first run

Cinemark Tinseltown

Third floor, 88 W Pender Street, at Abbott Street, Chinatown (604 806 0797/www.cinemark.com). Bus 10, 16, 20, N20, N35. **Screens** 9. **Admission** $10.50 Mon-Thur; $11.50 Fri-Sun; $6.50 concessions. *Matinées* $6 Mon-Fri; $7 Sat, Sun. **Credit** AmEx, MC, V. **Map** p249 M3.
Located on the third floor of an under-utilised mall on the western edge of Chinatown, the Tinseltown is a 9-screen multiplex which only merits a mention here for Cinemark's mildly adventurous programming. Mainstream fare is mixed up with a sprinkling of indie, subtitled and Canadian flicks.

Fifth Avenue Cinemas

2110 Burrard Street, at W 5th Avenue, West Side (604 734 7469/www.allianceatlantiscinemas.com). Bus 4, 7. **Screens** 5. **Admission** $12; $7 concessions. *Tue* $7.50. *Matinées* $9 Mon-Fri; $10 Sat, Sun. **Credit** AmEx, MC, V. **Map** p251 G6.
Operated by Alliance Atlantis, the Fifth is a cosy five screen venue specialising in left-field indie and art-house film. It even has a cappuccino bar – though the Elysian Room Tea House around the corner is a better spot for leisurely movie chat.

Granville Cineplex Odeon

855 Granville Street, between Robson and Smithe Streets, Downtown (604 684 4000/www.cineplex.com). All cross-city buses. **Screens** 7. **Admission** $8.95. **Credit** AmEx, MC, V. **Map** p249 K3.

The Vancouver International Film Festival

Canada's big three film festivals all jostle in the (hopefully) clement post-summer period: Toronto in early September, Montreal a week later, and Vancouver's 16-day movie marathon spanning the end of the month and continuing through into the first two weeks of October. The **Vancouver International Film Festival** (604 685 0260, www.viff.org) may be the least glamorous of the trio, but it is often the most enjoyable, with a relaxed, friendly atmosphere and a committed, adventurous crowd attending.

Festival director Alan Franey steers wide of Hollywood, reasoning that his job is to showcase international art cinema, political documentaries and independent films that would not otherwise reach this part of the

world. Such a course may have alienated a number of North American distributors, but has proved a hit with the local audience – so much so that the festival has been encouraged to establish the Vancouver International Film Centre and Vancity Theatre to present this kind of work for the other 50 weeks of the year.

Reflecting the city's ethnic mix, VIFF has built up an especially strong international reputation for its East Asian section, Dragons & Tigers, programmed by British critic Tony Rayns and with an enviable track record for talent-spotting. Here you'll quite possibly find the art-house stars of the future, even if the rest of the fest is strictly a celeb-free zone. For further details see www.viff.org.

The most iconic cinema awning in the city. **The Ridge Theatre**. *See p148.*

There were once ten cinemas within five blocks on Granville, but this is the last remaining downtown cinema. Commonly known as the 'Granville 7', it's conveniently located between Robson and Smithe and unlike the Paramount, it boasts THX sound.

Paramount Vancouver

900 Burrard Street, at Smithe Street, Downtown (604 630 1407/www.famousplayers.com). Bus 1, 2, 22, 98. **Screens** 9. **Admission** $10.95. **Credit** AmEx, MC, V. **Map** p248 J3.

A big, spanking new, nine-screen multiplex, the Paramount opened in 2005 with a rave review from U2 (who had been invited in to see a sneak preview of *Kingdom of Heaven* there). The cinema is touted for its 'techno-zen' interior (an attractive indoor waterfall is complemented with cheesy fusion decor and the usual odiferous junk food counters) and is therefore an appropriate venue in which to consume most mainstream Hollywood blockbusters.

Park Theatre

3440 Cambie Street, at W 18th Avenue, West Side (604 709 3456/www.parktheatre.info/). Bus 15. **Screens** 1. **Admission** $9; $7-$8 concessions. *Tue and matinées* $7. **Credit** AmEx, MC, V. **Map** p246 C4.

Built in 1940 but fully refurbished in 2005, this independently run neighbourhood single screen cinema continues with its commitment to art-house films of the middlebrow school, such as *North Country*.

IMAX

Alcan OMNIMAX Theatre

Science World, 1455 Quebec Street, at Terminal Avenue, Downtown (604 443 7453/www.science world.bc.ca). Bus 3, 8, 19, 22/SkyTrain Main Street-Science World/Aquabus. **Screens** 1. **Admission** $11.25; $9 concessions. **Credit** MC, V. **Map** p249 M5.

Even if you're jaded with IMAX screens, the all-enveloping sphere of the OMNIMAX is quite special, making excellent use of one of the city's biggest, most characteristic and most photographed landmarks, the golf ball-like protuberance that is the Science World dome (*see p143*). The screen itself is an extraordinary 27m (89ft) in diameter and five storeys high, while the resulting image is three times larger than 70mm and ten times larger than the standard 35mm print you normally see in theatres.

CN IMAX Theatre

201-999 Canada Place, between Howe Street and Burrard Street, Downtown (604 682 4629/www.imax.com/vancouver/). All cross-city buses/SkyTrain and Seabus Waterfront. **Screens** 1. **Admission** $11.50; $9.50-$10.50 concessions. **Credit** AmEx, MC, V. **Map** p249 L2.

The menu here tends to be nature on the big big screen, sometimes in 3-D, and the occasional IMAX blow-up of standard Hollywood blockbusters.

Galleries

The West Coast is the best.

Despite being a small city, Vancouver boasts a surprisingly rich array of artistic talent. But its size is reflected in a gallery scene that betrays a modest economy and a populace with other fish to fry. Nor is this unique: most of the gallery action in the world is limited to a few cities – New York, London, Berlin, Los Angeles and perhaps a handful of other spots. These days, however, much of the commercial activity takes place in art fairs, a calendar-based, peripatetic scene that has come to replace New York or London as the focus of the art world. Basel Art Fair, Basel Miami, Frieze (London), FIAC (Paris) and ARCO (Madrid) are where the art and money change hands these days. Meanwhile the Biennales, of which Venice remains queen with São Paulo, Sydney and Lyon the princesses aspiring to her throne, are where new reputations are made.

Still, Vancouver is an ambitious town, and its art scene towers over the rest of Canada like a Douglas fir over a sumac. If you came to see the biggest names that contemporary art in Vancouver has to offer, however, you might want to head back to the airport. Although Jeff Wall, Rodney Graham and Stan Douglas, perhaps Vancouver's most famous trinity of artists, all have work in the permanent collection of the Vancouver Art Gallery, they only show regularly with their galleries in New York, London or elsewhere in Europe. But wait. Turn around again, and go to South Granville, the heart of the gallery scene in Vancouver. Grab a coffee and walk around – it's a pleasant corner of the city and eminently viewable in a couple of hours. Once you've had your fill of the commercial spaces, downtown is the place for artist-run galleries.

Most galleries in Vancouver can be divided into simple categories. The tradition of lyrical landscape, a Canadian speciality exemplified by the Group of Seven and Emily Carr, remains strong in many of the galleries in South Granville. Aboriginal art, both Northwest Coast wood-carving and Inuit stone sculpture, is well represented, especially in that tourist ghetto, Gastown. Vancouver also has a solid tradition of artist-run spaces, of which the Western

▶ For more on **West Coast Art**, see pp26-32.

The best Galleries

For Northwest Coast aboriginal art
Douglas Reynolds Gallery (see p154).

For Inuit art
Marion Scott Gallery (see p152).

For photography
Monte Clark Gallery (see p154).

Non-commercial space
Contemporary Art Gallery (see p151).

For contemporary art
Catriona Jeffries Gallery (see p152).

Front, slightly isolated in East Vancouver, is the original. Contemporary, Access, Or and other galleries carry on this tradition, showing local and international artists in a supportive, non-commercial environment. But to really take the pulse of the artistic life of the city, visit the cluster of young, commercial galleries that show the work of Vancouver's best young artists: Tracey Lawrence Gallery, Monte Clark Gallery and, most importantly, Catriona Jeffries Gallery, the hottest spot in the city.

Downtown

Art Beatus
108-808 Nelson Street, at Howe Street (604 688 2633/www.artbeatus.com). Bus 4, 6, 7, 10, 16, 17, 50. **Open** 10am-6pm Mon-Fri; calling ahead is advisable. **Credit** AmEx, MC, V. **Map** p249 K4.
Art Beatus shows some of the biggest names in Chinese art – along with a handful of other Asian artists. China's creative entrepreneurs have kept pace with their economic counterparts over the last few years and two spaces in Hong Kong (and Vancouver's own large Chinese population) help Art Beatus to maintain strong links to the motherland.

Buschlen-Mowatt Gallery
1445 W Georgia Street, between Broughton Street & Nicola Street (604 682 1234/www.buschlen mowatt.com). Bus 5. **Open** 10am-6pm Mon-Sat; noon-5pm Sun. **Credit** AmEx, MC, V. **Map** p248 J2.

Catriona Jeffries Gallery. *See p152.*

One of the commercial engines of the city's art world, Buschlen-Mowatt has been plying a lucrative trade since 1979. The gallery flogs the kind of stuff that could happily fill a boardroom or a hotel lobby: big, colourful paintings and grand, imposing sculptures. A sister establishment in Palm Desert, California, should tell you all you need to know about their well-heeled, perma-tanned clients.

Contemporary Art Gallery

555 Nelson Street, between Seymour Street & Richards Street (604 681 2700/www.contemporary artgallery.ca). Bus 4, 6, 7, 10, 16, 17, 50. **Open** noon-6pm Wed, Fri, Sat; noon-8pm Thur; noon-5pm Sun. **Credit** MC, V. **Map** p249 K4.

Probably the leading non-profit gallery in the city, the Contemporary boasts ample space, a good budget and shrewd curators. Scott MacFarland, Brian Jungen and other rising stars of the local scene have shown here recently. The exhibition schedule is matched by a series of talks and lectures, often by visiting artists and critics. The opening nights are among the best attended in Vancouver.

Gastown

Access Artist Run Centre

206 Carrall Street, at Water Street (604 689 2907/ www.vaarc.ca). Bus 4, 7. **Open** noon-5pm Tue-Sat. **No credit cards. Map** p249 M3.

The name says it all: a space for collaborative projects and artist-organised exhibitions. 'Cyclops Dreams: Artists' Books, Comics and Zines' is the name of a recent show, and gives you a hint of the kind of things that get shown here.

Artspeak

233 Carrall Street, between Water & Cordova Streets (604 688 0051/www.artspeak.ca). Bus 4, 7. **Open** noon-5pm Tue-Sat. **Credit** MC, V. **Map** p249 M4.

Just down the street from the Access Centre, you'll find Artspeak, another dynamic non-profit space. Expect to find work that is experimental, formally innovative and most likely politically engaged.

Centre A Asian Art

2 W Hastings Street, at Carrall Street (604 683 8326/www.centrea.org). Bus 10, 16, 20. **Open** 11am-6pm Tue-Sat. **No credit cards. Map** p249 M3.

A non-profit space dedicated to Asian art and culture. Ken Lum, one of a cluster of Vancouver artists who has achieved an international following, is the vice president of a board of directors that heads up a strong administrative and curatorial team. Backed by a decent level of funding, Centre A has been able to create an excellent programme, with shows such as 'Charlie Don't Surf: 4 Vietnamese American Artists'. A new 465sq m (5,000sq ft) space, with library and screening room, should make this one of the more dynamic spots in Vancouver.

Helen Pitt Gallery

102-148 Alexander Street, between Main Street & Gore Avenue (604 681 6740/www.helenpitt gallery.org). Bus 4, 7. **Open** noon-5pm Tue-Sat. **No credit cards. Map** p249 N3.

Artist-run since 1975, the Helen Pitt Gallery is an important venue for non-commercial and experimental performances and exhibitions. Youngsters, recent graduates, artists whose work has yet to be gobbled up by the art business – you'll find them all exhibiting here, often collaboratively.

Inuit Gallery of Vancouver

206 Cambie Street, at Water Street (604 688 7323/ www.inuit.com). Bus 10, 16, 20. **Open** 10am-6pm Mon-Sat; 11am-5pm Sun. **Credit** AmEx, DC, MC, V. **Map** p249 L3.

Located in Gastown since 1979, the Inuit Gallery of Vancouver is a good place to take a quick look at Canadian aboriginal art from the west coastal or arctic regions. Immense soapstone sculptures jostle for space with cedar masks and contemporary design pieces by West Coast aboriginal artist Stevie Smith and architect Sabina Hill (non-native). Jewellery and prints are also available for purchase. If it has been a while since you heard Vivaldi's *Four Seasons*, drop in here: easy listening classical music creates the unwelcome mood of a souvenir shop.

Marion Scott Gallery

308 Water Street, at Cambie Street (604 685 1934/ www.marionscottgallery.com). Bus 10, 16, 20. **Open** 10am-6pm Mon-Sat; 11am-5pm Sun. **Credit** MC, V. **Map** p249 L3.

Established in 1975, Marion Scott Gallery is the best space in Vancouver for Inuit art. Unlike most galleries that show native Canadian art, which resemble production lines with rolling stock selected for swift turnaround, Marion Scott Gallery holds carefully researched and presented exhibitions. Part of their programme is to focus on art 'less for ethnographic content and more for its aesthetic merit'. Always worth a look, the gallery is also starting to show work by non-aboriginal artists.

Spirit Wrestler Gallery

8 Water Street, at Carrall Street (604 669 8813/ www.spiritwrestler.com). Bus 10, 16, 20. **Open** 10am-6pm Mon-Sat; noon-5pm Sun. **Credit** AmEx, DC, MC, V. **Map** p249 M3.

Spirit Wrestler Gallery takes in a range of work from aboriginal traditions, from Inuit to Maori and West Coast. However, the relatively small gallery makes the display a bit higgledy-piggledy, with the end result that you sometimes have a Maori wood carving, all toothy-grinned and glaring, facing down an Inuit stone sculpture as if it were invading its turf. Some interesting stuff nonetheless, with a selection not unlike the Inuit Gallery. Don't miss the jewellery and small objects downstairs.

West Side

Atelier Gallery

2421 Granville Street, at W 8th Avenue (604 732 3021/www.ateliergallery.ca). Bus 10, 16, 17. **Open** 11am-5pm Tue-Sat. **Credit** MC, V. **Map** p251 H6.

A well-established presence on Granville. It might sound cruel to say that the Atelier Gallery exhibits nice stuff to show on your wall, but it's true, and it's not a bad reputation to have. Landscapes and drawings by local artists feature strongly, and a lot of it is worth a second look. Royal Art Lodge, the Winnipeg gang, show here, and their work is a madcap blend of whimsy and anguish.

Bau-Xi Gallery

3045 Granville Street, between W 14th Avenue & W 15th Avenue (604 733 7011/www.bau-xi.com). Bus 10. **Open** 10am-5.30pm Mon-Sat; noon-4pm Sun. **Credit** AmEx, MC, V. **Map** p251 H7.

One of the oldest galleries on Granville Street, Bau-Xi has been exhibiting local artists, mostly from the lyrical landscape tradition, since 1965. Competent, decorative and lovely, you can find some terrific stuff here, but it's unlikely to set your heart racing.

Bjornson Kajiwara Gallery

1727 W 3rd Avenue, between Pine Street & Burrard Street (604 738 3500/www.tag.bc.ca). Bus 4, 7. **Open** 11am-6pm Tue-Fri; 11am-5pm Sat. **Credit** AmEx, MC, V. **Map** p251 G6.

Just up the road from Tracey Lawrence Gallery, Bjornson Kajiwara is a relatively new space that shows a mix of youngish artists whose work, though fresh and contemporary, is not quite as avant-garde as their neighbour's. Displays by painter Mark Neufeld, recent winner of the prestigious Joe Plaskett award, are worth checking out.

Catriona Jeffries Gallery

3149 Granville Street, between W 15th Avenue & W 16th Avenue (604 736 1554/www.catriona jeffries.com). Bus 10. **Open** 11am-5pm Tue-Sat. **No credit cards.** **Map** p251 H8.

Catriona Jeffries is Vancouver's most important contemporary gallery and one of a handful in the city – perhaps the only one – to boast an international reputation. Legendary father figure Ian Wallace shows here, as do a host of younger artists who can boast growing worldwide reputations: Brian Jungen, Ron Terada, Myfanwy Macleod, Damian Moppet and Geoffrey Farmer. If you want to find out what Vancouver's next generation of ambitious artists are up to, a trip here is a must. Plans are afoot to change locations, so call before you visit. **Photo** *p151.*

Charles H Scott Gallery

1399 Johnston Street, Granville Island (604 844 3809/information line 604 844 3811/http://chscott. eciad.bc.ca). Bus 50. **Open** noon-5pm Mon-Fri; 10am-5pm Sat, Sun. **Credit** MC, V. **Map** p251 H5.

The gallery for the Emily Carr Institute of Art and Design that shows work by international artists as well as the annual graduation show. An academic and non-commercial agenda means that they can feature artists from far-flung parts of the world whose work would otherwise be impossible to see.

Diane Farris Gallery

1590 W 7th Avenue, at Fir Street (604 737 2629/ www.dianefarrisgallery.com). Bus 10, 16, 17. **Open** 10am-5.30pm Tue-Fri; 10am-5pm Sat. **Credit** AmEx, MC, V. **Map** p251 G6.

Diane Farris has been selling international and local artists just off Granville since 1984. The gallery's star artist, however, is unquestionably Dale Chihuly, the Washington State-based glass man whose gooey, biomorphic sculptures in riots of intense colour grace two of London's grandest foyers: the

Dale Chihuly at **Diane Farris Gallery**.

Victoria & Albert Museum, and Claridge's Hotel (in the tearoom actually). Conservative, mid-career local painters also show here. **Photo** *p153*.

Douglas Reynolds Gallery

2335 Granville Street, between W 7th Avenue & W 8th Avenue (604 731 9292/www.douglasreynolds gallery.com). Bus 10, 16, 17. **Open** 10am-6pm Mon-Sat; noon-5pm Sun. **Credit** AmEx, MC, V. **Map** p251 H6.

Douglas Reynolds is the best place in the city to find top-notch Northwest Coast native art. If you want to see work by Robert Davidson, Bill Reid or other masters of the ovoid, Douglas Reynolds offers the best selection outside UBC's Museum of Anthropology. Besides the masks and totems, the jewellery counter is a highlight, with exquisite work in silver and gold, some of it surprisingly affordable. The gallery also exhibits and sells rare historical carvings.

Douglas Udell Gallery

1558 W 6th Avenue, between Granville Street & Fir Street (604 736 8900/www.douglasudellgallery.com). Bus 10, 16, 17. **Open** 10am-6pm Tue-Sat. **Credit** MC, V. **Map** p251 H6.

Douglas Udell Gallery is a bit of a rattle bag: lots of established Canadian artists along with a few from abroad, and it also carries a significant amount of secondary market, so you can pick up anything from a Picasso to a Dempsey Bob. American Caio Fonseca's abstracts and Tony Scherman's chunky encaustic paintings are both highlights.

Equinox Gallery

2321 Granville Street, at W 7th Avenue (604 736 2405/www.equinoxgallery.com). Bus 10, 16, 17. **Open** 10am-5pm Tue-Sat. **Credit** AmEx, MC, V. **Map** p251 H6.

The elder statesman of Vancouver's gallery scene, Equinox has been dealing big names from abroad and local favourites since the early 1970s. These days, expect to find paintings by veterans Gathie Falk and Gordon Smith as well as thought-provoking sculptures and installations by Liz Magor.

Heffel Gallery

2247 Granville Street, between W 6th Avenue & W 7th Avenue (604 732 6505/www.heffel.com). Bus 10, 16, 17. **Open** 10am-6pm Mon-Sat. **Credit** MC, V. **Map** p251 H6.

More an auction house, Heffel Gallery maintains an exhibition space and is probably the best place in the city to see the historical Canadian landscape: Group of Seven, EJ Hughes and others are often shown. Tiko Kerr, a painter of wobbly local landscapes that are a bit too easy on the eye and mind, can also be seen here. Check the website for temporary displays and the twice-yearly auctions.

Monte Clark Gallery

2339 Granville Street, between W 7th Avenue & W 8th Avenue (604 730 5000/www.monteclark gallery.com). Bus 10. **Open** 10am-6pm Tue-Sat. **Credit** AmEx, MC, V. **Map** p251 H6.

You may have heard that Vancouver is a city that breeds conceptual photographers, documenters of the everyday and artists who like to point their lens at busted buildings or empty landscapes. Don't believe it? Come to Monte Clark Gallery. Here you'll find Roy Arden, Scott Macfarland, Howard Ursuliak and other artists whose work bears superficial resemblance to that of Jeff Wall. This is also the best space in Vancouver for photography, but in addition you'll find a selection of painters and other artists. Monte Clark also has a space in Toronto, and is one of the most-respected galleries in Canada.

State Gallery

Upper floor, 1564 W 6th Avenue, between Granville Street & Fir Street (604 632 0198/www.state-gallery.com). Bus 10. **Open** 11am-5pm Wed-Sat. **Credit** MC, V. **Map** p251 H6.

State Gallery was founded in 2001 and has since become a space to watch. Alongside an interesting, if erratic, exhibition schedule, showing mostly recent grads from local art schools, the gallery hosts lectures and, as befits an ultra-contemporary spot, a 'Project Space'. Check out Natasha McHardy's chewing gum paintings – that's the medium, not the subject – and Aaron Plant's superbly eerie series of photographs of playgrounds at night.

Tracey Lawrence Gallery

1531 W 4th Avenue, at Fir Street (604 730 2875/ www.traceylawrencegallery.com). Bus 4, 7. **Open** 10am-5pm Tue-Sat. **Credit** AmEx, MC, V. **Map** p251 G6.

A relatively new kid on the block, the Tracey Lawrence Gallery has big ambitions. The chances are it will have the finances to realise those ambitions since they make most of their sales – about 80% – to clients outside Vancouver at the big international art fairs. If Monte Clark has taken up the Wall tradition, Rodney Graham's presence can be felt here. Tim Lee is probably their hottest artist, and others include Shannon Oksanen, Jeremy Shaw and Torontonian Kelly Mark. Photography, installation, video – you name it, they show it, as long as it's fresh, witty and preferably with a satirical edge.

East Side

Western Front Gallery

303 E 8th Avenue, at Scotia Street (604 876 9343/ www.front.bc.ca). Bus 3. **Open** noon-5pm Tue-Sat. **Credit** MC, V. **Map** p252 N6.

Vancouver's original artist-run centre, the Western Front Society has been an essential part of the city's cultural scene for a generation. Many of Vancouver's biggest names passed through these low-rent doors before becoming commercially successful. Along with exhibitions, media arts and performance (a Vancouver speciality), 'The Front', as it is affectionately called, also boasts an in-house magazine and runs a new music programme, so you can enjoy the soothing sounds of, say, the Nihilist Spasm Band, after enjoying some cutting-edge art.

Gay & Lesbian

Follow the rainbow to Vancouver's gay mecca.

Even the bus shelters are pinky and perky on **Davie Street**.

Walk along Davie Street in Vancouver's West End and you will be in no doubt that you have arrived at a gay mecca. From Burrard Street to Denman Street, rainbow banners, fuchsia-painted bus shelters and same-sex couples walking hand in hand are emblems of pride in this 'gaybourhood'.

The Davie Village Business Improvement Association (DViBIA) (411-1033 Davie Street, 604 696 0144, www.davievillagebia.com) has played a large part in the development of gay owned and operated businesses. Don't be fooled by Vancouver's laid-back reputation: this is a city that rallies hard to ensure equal rights for all its citizens. This was one of the first provinces in North America to legalise gay marriage (announced in June 2003 and finally ratified federally in the summer of 2005). Now, same-sex couples in British Columbia can get married with the same rights and benefits as any heterosexual couple. Even if you're not a citizen of BC you can still get married here. A marriage licence from the Office of Vital Statistics (604 660 2937, www.vs.gov.bc.ca/marriage) can be obtained for $100. Add

another $150 if you wish to be married by a gay clergyman – or woman – and voila! You are now officially recognised as married in Canada.

Of course, as soon as it became legal to marry, one gay couple felt it necessary to test the new legislation by filing for divorce. When the case came before the courts, Justice Laura Gerow ruled that the section of BC's Divorce Act, which defined spouses as 'a man and a woman', needed to be changed to 'two persons'. This ruling allowed BC's first gay divorcees to legitimise the dissolution of their relationship.

While many lesbians live and work in the West End, Commercial Drive is where the 'girls' are. If the curious mixture of old-world Italian culture sharing sidewalk space with the lesbian community doesn't intrigue you, perhaps a chance encounter with a star from locally shot television series *The L-Word* – Jennifer Beals or Pam Grier, for instance – is reason enough to plan a picnic in Grandview Park.

Whether you're gay, bi or transgendered, there's really no place in the city that isn't friendly to some extent. For a free guide to businesses that are gay owned or gay run, ask for the *Guide to Vancouver* brochure at Little Sister's Book & Art Emporium (1238 Davie Street, 604 669 1753, www.littlesistersbook store.com). Little Sister's has the largest selection of gay and lesbian publications, as well as a used books section, stickers, cards, T-shirts, sex toys, videos and DVDs. It's also worth checking out the LGBT Centre (1170 Bute Street, 604 684 5307, www.lgbtcentre vancouver.com) for a directory of gay professionals in Vancouver.

If you arrive in summer, don't miss the annual **Queer Film & Video Festival** (early August, www.outonscreen.com) and the **Vancouver Pride Parade** (first weekend in August, www.vanpride.bc.ca, *see p140*).

MEDIA & PUBLICATIONS

Vancouver's only gay and lesbian paper, *Xtra West* (www.xtra.ca) has an exhaustive classified section including club listings and other services. Also available is the *Lesbian Quarterly*, a community newsletter. On the internet, www.gayvan.com is a valuable up-to-the-minute tourist resource.

Accommodation

When in Vancouver, follow the rainbow! The West End offers a wide selection of hotels, hostels and B&Bs to suit everyone's fancy. You'll find several five-star hotels listed in the *Pink Pages* (www.pinkpagesnet.com) that are considered gay friendly, but be aware that this does not necessarily mean that the other guests are. You're best off finding a gay-owned and operated business to ensure a fun stay.

Nelson House Bed and Breakfast (977 Broughton Street, 604 684 9793 or toll free 1-866 684 9793, www.downtownbandb.com, $68-$198, MC, V) is located in the heart of the West End, only a few blocks from Stanley Park. Built in 1907, this three-storey character home is cosy and affordable, with themed bedrooms from Hollywood and the Raj to lumberjacks.

Just off the Drive is A Place at Penny's B&B (810 Commercial Drive, 604 254 2229, www. pennysplacevancouver.com, $65-$175, V) where discreet and professional female lodgings have been offered for over 30 years. It's so exclusive that you have to call Penny directly – there is no front desk. Each apartment boasts Persian carpets over hardwood floors, spacious bedrooms and full kitchens and it's mere blocks from parks, outdoor markets, cafés and Vancouver's thriving lesbian community.

Grandmother's house was never like this. The West End Guest House (1362 Haro Street, 604 681 2889 or toll free 1-888 546 3327, www.westendguesthouse.com, $95-$255,

AmEx, MC, V) is a lovingly restored heritage house in the heart of the gay ghetto. Your inner diva will warm to the antique furnishings, parlour with fireplace, and sundeck facing a well-tended garden. The proprietors also manage Inn Penzance (1388 Terrace Avenue, North Vancouver, 604 681 2889, www.inn penzance.com) which is recommended for same-sex couples staying on the North Shore.

Bars & clubs

Cruising

The Dufferin Pub

900 Seymour Street, at Smithe Street, Downtown (604 683 4251/www.dufferinhotel.com). All city-centre buses. **Open** noon-2am Mon-Thur, Sat; noon-3am Fri; noon-midnight Sun. **Admission** free. **Credit** AmEx, MC, V. **Map** p249 K4.

An afternoon watering hole for the old-school crowd. Comfortable and cosy, the Dufferin is an alternative to the flashy leather bar scene. The tavern next door has games and a pool table. Mostly men, no-frills decor and a fabulous weekend drag show.

Numbers

1042 Davie Street, between Burrard Street & Thurlow Street, Downtown (604 685 4077/www. numbers.ca). Bus 2, 6, 22, N6. **Open** 9pm-2am Mon-Thur; 9pm-4am Fri, Sat; 8pm-2am Sun. **Admission** free-$5. **No credit cards. Map** p248 J4.

Vancouver's 'cruisy dance bar', this multi-level dance club with a pub-style feel boasts pool tables, dartboards, video games and dancing. Men, men and more men of all ages enjoy the drink specials and weekly events. A good place to get hooked up at the end of the night. There is a $5 cover charge Fri, Sat after 10.30pm.

The PumpJack

1167 Davie Street, between Thurlow Street & Bute Street, West End (604 685 3417/www.pumpjack pub.com). Bus 6, N6. **Open** 1pm-midnight Mon-Thur; 1pm-3am Fri, Sat; 1pm-1am Sun. **Admission** free. **Credit** MC, V. **Map** p248 J3.

Once upon a time, Doll and Penny's Restaurant was the most popular eaterie on Davie Street. When the original owners updated the kitschy decor they kept the restaurant's casual, easygoing vibe firmly in place. Renovated and renamed, the PumpJack is undoubtedly the best spot on the strip for cruising. Drop in Friday or Saturday nights and enjoy the scenery before clubbing.

Dancing

Celebrities

1022 Davie Street, between Burrard Street & Thurlow Street, Downtown (604 681 6180/ www.celebritiesnightclub.com). Bus 2, 6, 22, N6. **Open** phone for details. **Admission** free-$10. **Credit** MC, V. **Map** p248 J4.

The best mixed dance club in town. It's newly renovated, boasts a large dance-floor and a state-of-the-art lighting and sound system. A different crowd of all ages can be found here every night in this straight/gay/ bi/curious entry point in to the gay community and fetish scene. The cover charge varies according to the events.

Lotus Sound Lounge
455 Abbott Street, at W Pender Street, Downtown (604 685 7777/www.lotussoundlounge.com). Bus 10, 16, 20, N20, N35. **Open** 10pm-2am Mon-Thur; 10pm-3am Fri, Sat. **Admission** $5-$12. **Credit** AmEx, MC, V. **Map** p249 M3.
This is the place to go to for tasty beats, innovative sounds and a mostly mixed (straight/gay/bi) crowd. Venture downstairs to meet, dance and play with Vancouver's hottest dykes at Lick Club (www.lick-club.com), a women-run, women-only nightclub that hosts a large roster of talented female DJs.

Odyssey
1251 Howe Street, between Davie Street & Drake Street, Downtown (604 689 5256/www.theodyssey nightclub.com). Bus 6. **Open** phone for details. **Admission** free-$7. **Credit** V. **Map** p248 J4.
Boys will be boys, thank goodness. Flirty vibes, great music and a spacious dance floor that offers plenty of hiding places from the abundant chicken hawks. Odyssey attracts a younger crowd, mostly men who enjoy the outdoor patio for smoking and cruising and the best Sunday night drag show in town. For those wanting to keep their visits quiet, there is a discreet back door entry/exit. The cover charge varies; call ahead for information.

Relaxing

The Fountainhead Pub
1025 Davie Street, between Burrard Street & Thurlow Street, Downtown (604 687 2222/www. thefountainheadpub.com). Bus 2, 6, 22, N6. **Open** 11am-midnight Mon-Thur, Sun; 11am-2am Fri, Sat. **Credit** MC, V. **Map** p248 J4.
The first gay-owned and operated pub on Davie Street. A casual, unpretentious spot equipped with all the amenities: electronic dart boards, pool tables, pub food and a wide selection of beer on tap. A popular place for weekend brunches.

Oasis Pub
1240 Thurlow Street, between Davie Street & Burnaby Street, West End (604 685 1724/www. theoasispub.com). Bus 2, 6, 22, N6. **Open** 3.30pm-midnight Mon-Thur, Sun; 3.30pm-1am Fri, Sat. **Credit** MC, V. **Map** p248 J4.
Light and airy, this elegant piano bar with a baby grand boasts the widest selection of Martinis anywhere in Vancouver. Lush, tropical plants lend something of a Polynesian feel to the surroundings. Go for the friendly waiting staff, drink specials and excellent nouvelle cuisine. The entrance is at the back and up the stairs. There's a cover charge for live entertainment Wednesday to Sunday.

Odyssey is no drag.

Restaurants & cafés

Café Deux Soleils
2096 Commercial Drive, between E 5th Avenue & E 6th Avenue, East Vancouver (604 254 1195/www. cafedeuxsoleils.com). Bus 20/SkyTrain Broadway. **Open** 8.30am-midnight daily; sometimes closes early. **Main courses** $5-$10. **Credit** V. **Map** p252 Q6.
The lesbian brunch spot on the Drive has a hippie vibe and a bi/lesbian/experimental crowd.

Delaney's Coffee House
1105 Denman Street, at Nelson Street, West End (604 662 3344). Bus 6. **Open** 6am-11pm Mon-Fri; 6.30am-11pm Sat, Sun. **Credit** V. **Map** p248 H2.
The hottest cruising spot on Denman Street, this is the place to show off a buff body and a summer tan.

The Elbow Room Café
560 Davie Street, between Richards Street & Seymour Street, Downtown (604 685 3628/www. theelbowroomcafe.com). Bus 4, 6, 7, 10, 16, 17, 50. **Open** 8am-4pm daily. **Main courses** $3-$12. **Credit** AmEx, MC, V. **Map** p248 J4.

This modestly sized café garnered a reputation for sass and sarcasm when it opened in the early 1980s. The waiters are not above scolding you for taking too long to order or for leaving something uneaten on your plate, so don't be naughty, eat your greens.

Hamburger Mary's

1202 Davie Street, at Bute Street, West End (604 687 1293/www.hamburgermarys.ca). Bus 6, N6. **Open** 8am-3am Mon-Thur; 8am-4am Fri, Sat; 8am-2am Sun. **Main courses** $7-$15. **Credit** AmEx, MC, V. **Map** p248 H3.
Every strip needs a late-night respite for the weary and wasted at the end of the evening. This is also a regular weekend brunch spot for the gals.

The New Mekong

1414 Commercial Drive, at Kitchener Street, East Vancouver (604 253 7088). Bus 20. **Open** 11am-3pm, 5-9pm Mon-Fri; noon-10pm Sat; noon-9pm Sun. **Main courses** $8.95. **Credit** AmEx, MC, V. **Map** p247 E4.
A favourite lunch spot and hangout for many lesbians on the Drive. A table by the window is recommended for girl watching in the 'hood.

Sugar Daddies

1262 Davie Street, between Bute Street & Jervis Street, West End (604 632 1646). Bus 6. **Open** 11am-2am Mon-Fri; 10am-2am Sat, Sun. **Main courses** $9-$13. **Credit** MC, V. **Map** p248 H3.

Sugar Daddies is part gay sports bar and part Martini lounge, with three large screens for watching queer television in between screenings of those strapping young athletes doing their thing.

Bath houses

Fahrenheit 212

1048 Davie Street, between Burrard Street & Thurlow Street, Downtown (604 689 9719/www. f212.com). Bus 2, 6, 22, N6. **Open** 24 hours daily. **Admission** *Rooms* $15-$30. *Membership* $3 for 3 days; phone for more details. **Credit** MC, V. **Map** p248 J4.
Three different room sizes, lockers, snack bar, fully stocked weight area, 12-man jacuzzi enclosed steam room, and a second hotter, more intimate steam room. There's also an adult video room with leather couches and a fireplace to keep you warm. Men only.

M2M

1210 Granville Street, at Davie Street, Downtown (604 684 6011/www.M2Mplayspace.com). Bus 4, 6, 7, 10, 16, 17, 50. **Open** 24 hours daily. **Admission** *Rooms* $18-$25. *Membership* $3 for 3 days. **Credit** MC, V. **Map** p248 J4.
A fairly hardcore leather and Levi's crowd enjoy at M2M a well-equipped play space with public and private rooms, slings, lockers, group showers and a deluxe steam room too. Men only.

All-comers

Up for a walk on the wild side? Vancouver's fetish scene has much to offer kinky visitors, from neophytes to hard-core BDSM players.

Most fetish events have a strict dress code and if you're not suitably attired you will in all likelihood be turned away. PVC, leather, latex, lingerie, formal period dress, rubber, full uniform, cross-dressing, fantasy, real kilts for men, pyjamas, fur, etc are all welcomed. Blue jeans are a definite no-no, as are business suits and street clothes. Make sure you carry picture ID at all times.

If you're new to the scene, check out **Fetish Lite** (555 Davie Street, www.Fetish Lite.com). It was created as a crossover to the underground scene for the novice, but seasoned players attend as well. Visit website for dates, times and location. **Body Perv Social Club** (Lotus Hotel, 455 Abbott Street, www.bodyperv.com) is held on the last Saturday of every month. This is the original play party in Vancouver that started it all, over 10 years ago. Strict dress code. $7-$14. **Sin City** (23 W Cordova Street, www.gothic.bc.ca/sincity) takes place at Club 23 every second

Saturday of the month. The biggest fetish party in Vancouver, this multi-level club offers three floors of entertaining action, an outside patio, large dancefloor and well-equipped dungeon for BDSM play. Come see, be seen, dance, play and have a blast. The Vancouver Dungeon Monitor Team (DM) supervises to ensure all BDSM play abides by house safety rules. Doors open at 9pm, but arrive at least a half hour early – queues are long and you might not get in until midnight or later. The strict dress code is enforced. Admission ranges from $7 to $10.

BIO play parties are held the first weekend of every month (778 885 5463, www. VancouverDungeon.com and www.BIO entertainment.com), featuring an hour-long free workshop from 8pm, followed by a Vancouver DM team-moderated play party. No alcohol and no dress code in effect, although most participants usually dress 'fetishy'. A very discreet place to come and play: to attend, you must get your name on the guest list by contacting BIO prior to the event. The doors open at 7.30pm. $15.

Music & Nightlife

Where music reaches the end of the line.

A suitable setting for Orpheus. **Orpheum.** *See p162.*

Rock & folk

Hemmed in by an ocean, border crossing and mountains, Vancouver's musicians could be forgiven for succumbing to an isolationist mentality. Yet a close-knit, creative community forming various informal collectives has sparked an exciting live music renaissance. It's now presumed that any given musician will ply his trade in at least two bands; the industrious will balance three or four acts. An inevitable effect of this cross-pollination has been an abundance of diverse bands that defy simple classification. A guitar player might lend his talent to both a country and a punk act. Invariably, the influence of one project will be reflected in the other and as a result Vancouver bands are rarely recipients of one-word descriptions. Instead, most are categorised via a multitude of hyphens (space-country-rock, for example) or protracted analogies. The communal dynamic has also resulted in greater sustainability for local bands. Members are free to come and go, and the music evolves in accordance with the personnel shifts.

During the nadir of the mid '90s, when dance culture ran rampant and many of the city's venerable live venues changed formats or simply closed their doors, only musicians with a survivor's spirit and DIY ethic persisted. The release of the New Pornographers' *Mass Romantic* in 2000 proved a turning point. With members culled from various notable Vancouver bands, the Pornographers stormed the international indie rock scene. Their success illustrated the viability of the 'collective' approach to music and hinted at the heights a local band might ascend to. More recently, Black Mountain supported British heavyweights Coldplay on a North American tour. Band lynchpin Steve McBean is a veteran of countless bands for more than a decade now. It's difficult to envision a scene survivor more deserving of widespread recognition.

International accolades have also been afforded to the likes of art-rockers Destroyer, sullen darlings the Organ and punk troubadour Geoff Berner. Meanwhile, Ladyhawk, the Doers, Kids These Days, Sparrow, Fond of Tigers, the Book of Lists and Bend Sinister are all vying for the title of 'best live band' in the city. Mint Records are the leaders among Vancouver's many independent record labels. They count scholarly P:ano, country chanteuse Carolyn Mark and sophisticated Young & Sexy among their artists. The city boasts a vibrant roots and folk community highlighted by the Be Good Tanyas, Veda Hille and Rodney DeCroo & The Killers. Those looking for something with more of an edge might want to lend a bleeding ear to Golden Phoenix, S.T.R.E.E.T.S. and Raking Bombs. On the hip hop front, Josh Martinez, No Luck Club and McEnroe stand out. In the field of avant-garde electro, Primes and Secret Mommy are both worthy of attention. Finally, Rumbletone and Sealed With A Kiss are two of the premier promoters in the city. Their names on a gig poster are a mark of quality.

Classical & opera

When it comes to the classical music scene in Vancouver it's worth remembering that the city's largest, oldest and most opulent concert hall, the **Orpheum Theatre**, started life in 1927 as a vaudeville house. These days, Vancouver's roots as a frontier logging town may be submerged beneath a layer of low-fat latte foam, but in many ways it remains a city at the edge of the musical wilderness. While there is a serviceable symphony orchestra and opera company, programming for these larger organisations tends to err on the populist side. What Vancouver lacks in depth of tradition, though, it makes up for in innovation on a

smaller scale: it's through Vancouver's specialised music societies and small- to mid-sized ensembles that the most adventurous music and, frequently, the most luminous talents, are to be heard. Of particular note is the vibrant choral music scene, which counts heldentenor Ben Heppner as its most esteemed alumnus. Vancouver is also distinguished by an intimate but internationally networked community of players and composers who straddle the classical/jazz divide. The fusion of new music, classical influences from Europe and Asia, improv, and free jazz gives the city's highbrow music scene a New World flavour.

To the disappointment of Vancouver arts organisations, 2005 saw the construction of a $50 million civic arts complex put on hold as the downtown waterfront site earmarked for the project was reassigned to the Vancouver Trade and Convention Centre. Still, the city has committed to seeking an alternative space in time for the Winter Olympics in 2010: in the works are plans for an 1,800-seat concert hall, 450-seat studio theatre and outdoor performance plaza.

TICKETS AND INFORMATION

Free publications such as the *Georgia Straight* and *WestEnder* (released Thursday every week) offer listings and features concerning the local music scene and touring acts. You can also consult www.livemusicvancouver.com, which provides venue programmes and links to bands' websites. Many club shows involving local acts don't sell advance tickets. Instead, a cover

The songlines

A plethora of small- and mid-sized choral groups sets this city's classical music community apart: many of Canada's best choirs call Vancouver home. Of particular note are four internationally recognised chamber ensembles that offer diverse repertoires, vibrant, polished sound, and emotively rich, musically exacting performances: the **Vancouver Chamber Choir** (604 738 6822, www.vancouverchamberchoir.com), **Phoenix Chamber Choir** (604 986 7520, www. phoenixchamberchoir.bc.ca), baroque specialists **Vancouver Cantata Singers** (604 730 8856, www.cantata.org) and the youthful 12-voice **Musica Intima** (604 731 6618, www.musicaintima.org). Musica Intima's conductorless, musically inventive concerts in particular epitomise Vancouver's fresh approach to classical music making.

The larger, semi-professional men's choir, **Chor Leoni** (604 999 6153, www.chorleoni. org), and women's choir, **Elektra** (604 833 1255, www.elektra.ca), perform less challenging and more populist fare. Vancouver's largest singing group, the 160-voice **Bach Choir** (www.vancouverbach choir.com) stages a stentorian sing-along *Messiah* in the 2,900-seat Orpheum Theatre each Christmas season; at the other end of the size and volume spectrum, the men's and women's **Scholae of Christ Church Cathedral** (690 Burrard Street, 604 682 3848, www. cathedral.vancouver.bc.ca) alternate weekly to present an a cappella candlelight compline service each Sunday night at 9.30pm. Smells and bells, and eight- to ten-voice polyphony provide a profoundly meditative close to the musical weekend.

charge is simply paid at the door. For a relatively small city, Vancouver does a commendable job of luring top flight touring talent. And, in contrast with their previous behaviour, Vancouver's concert-goers now flock in large numbers to see touring performers and local bands. It's not uncommon for these shows to sell out well in advance. Tickets for such events can be purchased through Ticketmaster (604 280 4444, www.ticketmaster.ca or for classical, Ticketmaster Artsline, 604 280 3311) and from their outlets at the Pacific Centre Mall, 633 Granville Street, at W Georgia Street, Downtown or the Tickets Tonight booth, tourist information centre, 200 Burrard Street, at Canada Place, Downtown. They are, however, known for their service charges. Record stores such as Zulu (*see p134*) and Red Cat (*see p133*) often carry slightly less expensive tickets for many of the same shows. These shops also double as sources for insider information as they're often staffed by either musicians or individuals closely tied to the music community.

Two websites provide comprehensive links and listings for classical and jazz performance in Vancouver: www.vancouverjazz.com is up and running while www.classicalvancouver. com is slated to launch in November 2005.

Chan Centre. *See p162*.

Music societies

Early Music Vancouver
604 732 1610/www.earlymusic.bc.ca.
Early Music brings together high-profile visiting artists such as Sequentia and Musica Antique Köln with local groups including the Burney Ensemble (604 727 8532, www.burney.ca), and the Pacific Baroque Orchestra (604 215 0406, www.pacificbaroqueorchestra.com). Their fine, plush, fully-staged summer productions of baroque opera for Festival Vancouver (604 688 1152, www.festivalvancouver.bc.ca) have merited international recognition.

Vancouver New Music
604 633 0861/www.newmusic.org.
Vancouver New Music is one of Canada's major presenters of cutting-edge sonic art and electro-acoustic music. Regular-season concerts plus a yearly New Music Festival showcase the likes of Pan Sonic, Laurie Anderson and Philip Glass, together with newly commissioned Canadian works ranging from multimedia sound installations to modern opera.

Vancouver Recital Society
604 602 0363/www.vanrecital.com.
The most significant force in Vancouver's classical music scene, the Vancouver Recital Society (RCS) presents established and emerging talents in concerts year-round. Artistic Director Leila Getz has a reputation for identifying rising luminaries before

they become stars elsewhere: Vancouverites were treated to the voice of Cecilia Bartoli in 1992, when the diva had yet to perform in New York.

Performing groups

Vancouver Opera
604 683 0222/www.vancouveropera.ca.
Solid talent, resplendent costumes and the only people in town to bring you your dose of Puccini: that's Vancouver Opera. Modern classics, such as Robert Lepage's production of *Erwartung* and *Bluebeard's Castle*, occasionally hit the boards – but the typical fare is traditional opera, traditionally staged.

Vancouver Symphony Orchestra
604 876 3434/www.vancouversymphony.ca.
Affable Music Director Bramwell Tovey's hard-working symphony presents 140 accessible concerts each season, with everything from flamenco dancers to Broadway show tunes spicing up the Bach and Beethoven. Free Symphony in the Park concerts at Stanley Park let you picnic while you listen.

Venues

Short of larger theatres, Vancouver's principal venues tend to serve double duty, housing all kinds of musical performance and often theatre too. The Queen Elizabeth Theatre, for example, is home to the Vancouver Opera and Ballet British Columbia, but you are just as likely to find Brian Wilson playing here, or a theatrical event. On the plus side, you're quite likely to find a major name playing in a more intimate venue than would be the case elsewhere.

Stadiums/Theatres

Phone or check the local press for ticket prices and opening times for the following.

Chan Centre for the Performing Arts

6265 Crescent Road, at East Mall, University of British Columbia (604 822 2697/www.chancentre. com). Bus 4, 17, 99. **Open** *Box office noon-5pm Mon-Sat; noon-intermission performance days.* **Admission** *$10-$50.* **Credit** AmEx, MC, V.
The cylindrical, zinc-panelled exterior of the Chan Centre is striking, but it's the sonorous interior of the Chan Shun Concert Hall that has thrilled Vancouver audiences since it first opened in 1997. The Chan has impeccably clear acoustics that make the 20-minute trek through the traffic to the far west side of Vancouver well worth the effort: it's by far the best place for a discerning ear to listen to classical music in this city. **Photo** *p161.*

GM Place

800 Griffiths Way, between Expo Boulevard and Pacific Boulevard, Downtown (604 899 7889/www. generalmotorsplace.com). Bus 17, 22, 50, N8, N19/ SkyTrain Stadium-Chinatown. **Credit** AmEx, MC, V. **Map** p249 L4.
If you really must see the likes of U2 or Green Day, this will be the place to do it. While popular opinion states that the 21,000-seat arena (built in 1995) betters its brethren in terms of sound and comfort, it's still ideally suited for sporting events.

Orpheum

884 Granville Street, at Smithe Street, Downtown (604 665 3050/www.city.vancouver.bc.ca/theatres/ orpheum/orpheum.html). All city-centre buses. **No credit cards. Map** p249 K4.
Once the largest theatre on North America's Pacific Coast, this is an incredible venue for a live rock show. While unassuming from the exterior, inside its vaulted ceiling, ornate chandelier and gilded decor often rival stage performers for the audience's attention. The Orpheum is the permanent home of the Vancouver Symphony Orchestra but the room's acoustics lend themselves well to any style of music, though a lack of resonance means it's not great for soloists and smaller choirs. For these lower volume performances, try to sit centre balcony, just behind the dress circle, for the best sound. **Photo** *p159.*

Pacific Coliseum

100 N Renfrew Street, between McGill Street & E Hastings Street, East Vancouver (604 253 2311/ www.pne.ca). Bus 4, 10, 135, N16, N35. **No credit cards.**

Cavernous, cold and outdated, the 17,000-seat arena still has the odd concert bone thrown its way. All told, it's the live equivalent of listening to an album using tin cans for speakers.

Queen Elizabeth Theatre

600 Hamilton Street, at W Georgia Street, Downtown (604 665 3050/www.city.vancouver. bc.ca/theatres/qet/qet.html). Bus 15, 17, N19/ SkyTrain Stadium-Chinatown. **No credit cards. Map** p249 L4.
Built in 1959 by the City of Vancouver, the Queen E is the home of Vancouver Opera and Ballet British Columbia (604 732 5003, www.balletbc.com). Its somewhat uneven acoustic is augmented by a good sound system, but rock shows struggle to create any real atmosphere. Large enough to house 2,900 people, theatre staff don't seem to be at their best in handling them once they arrive.

Bars & clubs

The majority of the city's venues are located in the downtown core, Gastown or downtown East Side. With the possible exceptions of the Asbalt, Railway Club and Yale, venues in Vancouver don't have 'regular' patrons. The audience makeup and resulting ambience are largely dictated by the bands that are playing and the crowd they draw. The music scene is still in flux and smaller venues have a habit of changing formats on a whim, so consult local listings before venturing out.

Asbalt

769 E Hastings Street, at Hawks Avenue, East Vancouver (604 764 7865/www.asbalt.com). Bus 10, 16, 20, N20, N35. **Open** *11am-1am Mon-Sat; 11am-midnight Sun.* **Admission** *free-$8.* **No credit cards.**
Booked by eminent promoter wendythirteen, this 250-capacity venue has picked up the crusty gauntlet laid down by the sorely missed Cobalt. If you like your alcohol cheap and your music blistering, this is the room for you. Indie rock acts can also be found here and the venue boasts theme nights such as karaoke (albeit with a live backing band). While the club is situated in one of the city's seedier districts, the patrons are almost always hospitable.

Brickyard

315 Carrall Street, between E Hastings Street & E Cordova Street, Gastown (604 685 3922). Bus 3, 4, 7, 10, 16, 20, N20, N35. **Open** *11am-1am Mon-Thur, Sun; noon-2.30am Fri, Sat.* **Admission** *free-$15.* **No credit cards. Map** p249 M3.
Perpetually on the brink of extinction but never quite slipping over, the Brickyard somehow survives. Brimming with untapped potential, the bar primarily books local metal, rock and punk bands of middling quality. However, due to its relatively large size, touring bands or some of the more credible local talent are occasionally drawn to the venue.

Where legends are made. **Commodore Ballroom**.

Candy Bar & Grill

2066 Kingsway, at Victoria Drive, East Vancouver (604 877 1066). Bus 7, 19, 20, 25, N19, N20. **Open** 11am-2am Mon-Sat. **Admission** free-$5. **No credit cards**. **Map** p252 R10.

Until recently a greasy spoon diner, the Candy Bar has ascended the ranks of scenester hangouts. Set well away from the city's other music venues, its unique two-room set up – a lounge up front with live music space in the rear – and taste-making indie showcases make this a haunt worth investigating.

Commodore Ballroom

868 Granville Street, between Robson Street & Smithe Street, Downtown (604 739 7469/www.hob. com/venues/concerts/commodore/). All city-centre buses. **Open** phone for details. **Admission** $10-$50. **Credit** AmEx, MC, V. **Map** p249 K4.

Located in the heart of downtown, the Commodore is the music scene's crown jewel and a truly world-class facility. Having recently celebrated its 75th birthday, the 1,200-capacity venue has a renowned history and has staged early career shows by seminal bands such as Talking Heads, the Clash and Nirvana. As such, its closure for two years in the '90s marked the darkest hour for live music in the city. A $3.5-million makeover later it was relaunched in 1999, although the redevelopment robbed the room of much of its charm. The most regrettable sacrifice was the room's trampoline-like sprung hardwood floor. Nevertheless, it remains the principal destination for all varieties of high-calibre touring acts and rightfully so. The room's sound system is excellent and its layout offers an abundance of vantage points.

Lamplighter

210 Abbott Street, at Water Street, Gastown (604 681 6666/www.thelamplighter.ca). Bus 3, 4, 7. **Open** noon-2am daily. **Admission** free-$15. **Credit** AmEx, MC, V. **Map** p249 M3.

Already distinguished by the fact of being Vancouver's oldest bar, the Lamplighter nonetheless wallowed for decades as an anonymous watering hole before finally being refurbished in 2004. The changeover also witnessed the recruitment of a new promoter/booker with a taste for inventive talent irrespective of musical style. Since then, the stylish 200-capacity venue has welcomed a wide variety of high-calibre local and touring bands to its compact stage. A Friday night at the Lamplighter is one of the city's surest bets to ensure you start the weekend with a smile on your face. Furthermore, the venue features various theme nights (hip hop, karaoke and house) throughout the week.

Marine Club

573 Homer Street, between W Pender Street & Dunsmuir Street, Downtown (604 683 1720). Bus 3, 17, 20, N19, N35. **Open** 2pm-2am Mon-Sat; 4pm-midnight Sun. **Admission** free-$10. **No credit cards**. **Map** p249 L3.

The Marine Club makes up for its many shortcomings with an abundance of character. Amid dated decor consisting of nautical memorabilia, the small 'private' club (you'll be buzzed in at the door) boasts a barely adequate stage, shoddy bathrooms, expensive liquor and dilapidated furniture. Nevertheless, it possesses an intangible charm that keeps modest-sized crowds coming back.

Not for trainspotters. **Railway Club**.

Media Club

695 Cambie Street, at W Georgia Street, Downtown
(604 608 2871/www.themediaclub.ca). Bus 15, 17,
N17/SkyTrain Stadium. **Open** phone for details.
Admission free-$20. **Credit** MC, V.
Map p249 L4.
The Media Club has made a strong bid to establish
itself as a premier small venue (150 capacity) in the
city. The results have been mixed. A variety of promoters keep the room teeming with an array of
bands, including some 'name' touring acts, every
night of the week. But an undersized sound system
and barely raised stage don't always befit the calibre of guests. This can result in a disinterested audience whose nattering drowns out the performers.

Pat's Pub

403 E Hastings Street, between Dunlevy Street and
Jackson Street, East Vancouver (604 255 4301/www.
patspub.ca). Bus 3, 10, 16, 20, N20, N35. **Open**
9am-11pm Mon-Sat; 11am-9pm Sun. **Admission**
free-$10. **No credit cards**.
Despite being completely devoid of ambience or any
of the other traits commonly found in a quality
venue, tiny Pat's Pub occasionally serves up some
of the city's most influential showcases of local talent. On the right night, every hipster in Vancouver
will be present and accounted for.

Pub 340

340 Cambie Street, at W Hastings Street, Downtown
(604 602 0644). Bus 3, 4, 7, 10, 16, 20, N20, N35/
SkyTrain Stadium. **Open** 9am-2am Mon-Thur;
9am-2am Fri; 11am-2am Sat; 11am-midnight Sun.
Admission free-$12. **Credit** MC, V. **Map** p249 L3.

An unambitious, lower rung venue, Pub 340 rarely
receives any attention from influential promoters.
So, more often than not, the 110-capacity room is
host to local high-volume rock and punk acts recognisable only to their friends and family. However, to
its credit, the bar does boast friendly staff and a variety of food and drink specials.

Railway Club

579 Dunsmuir Street, at Seymour Street, Downtown
(604 681 1625/www.therailwayclub.com). All city-
centre buses. **Open** noon-2am Mon-Thur; noon-3am
Fri; 2pm-3am Sat; 4pm-midnight Sun. **Admission**
$5-$20. **Credit** AmEx, MC, V. **Map** p249 L3.
Let's not be mealy mouthed about this: the Railway
Club is the finest small venue in Vancouver. Its supposed capacity listing of 175 will surprise many a
regular patron. On a busy night (of which there are
many), the upstairs hangout is crammed wall-to-
wall with sweaty gig goers. Featuring three rooms,
two miniature railroads and a kitchen that stays
open late, the club has been in operation since the
1930s and is steeped in local lore. A collection of ami-
cable employees produce a neighbourhood pub
ambience. Always eager to champion roots, folk and
solo artists, the venue is also open to touring and
local indie acts. There's a drunken sing-along the
first Monday in the month.

Red Room

398 Richards Street, between W Cordova Street and
W Hastings Street, Downtown (604 687 5007). All
city-centre buses/SkyTrain Waterfront. **Open** phone
for details. **Admission** $10-$30. **Credit** AmEx, MC,
V. **Map** p249 L3.

Relatively new to hosting live music, the Red Room is still learning the ropes. Indicatively, they ran out of beer during their first show. However, the room's size (400-capacity) and sound quality ensure that it'll continue to be used for prominent touring acts.

Richard's On Richards

1036 Richards Street, between Nelson Street and Helmcken Street, Yaletown (604 687 6794/www. richardsonrichards.com). Bus 20, all city-centre buses then 5min walk. **Open** phone for details. **Admission** $12-$35. **Credit** AmEx, MC, V. **Map** p249 K4.

Be warned that a trip to Richard's will afford you an encounter with some of the most insufferable staff in the city. Some of the employees seem genuinely aggrieved that a live music show is denying them their regular dance crowd. Sadly, they are a necessary evil. The 400-capacity venue regularly welcomes major touring acts from every genre. Sound quality is near perfect and the room's horseshoe design and balcony make for an intimate atmosphere. However, once the show is over, prepare to be unceremoniously herded towards the exits by a burly bouncer.

Yale

1300 Granville Street, at Drake Street, Downtown (604 681 9253/www.theyale.ca). Bus 4, 6, 7, 8, 10, 16, 17, 50, N17. **Open** 11.30am-2am Mon-Thur, Sun; 11.30am-3am Fri, Sat. **Admission** free-$30. **Credit** AmEx, MC, V. **Map** p248 J4.

This 225-capacity bar pledges, 'If they're legends, they've played the Yale.' It's possible that the term 'legends' is being used rather liberally. However, it remains the only room in the city committed to booking blues artists on an ongoing basis. With live music every night, it's often the sole recourse for fans of traditional R&B.

Jazz venues

In Vancouver's cosy jazz world, a sprinkling of performance venues throughout the city support an intimate scene heavily influenced by the free jazz of late-era John Coltrane. Free jazz and improv bigwigs perform here to small houses of enthusiasts: Vancouver plays low-key host to many of the same talents that sell out Amsterdam's Icebreaker and the Knitting Factory in New York. Local names to watch for include Coat Cooke and the NOW Orchestra, Francois Houle, John Korsrud, Peggy Lee and Dylan van der Schyff; along more traditional lines, Oliver Gannon, Brad Turner and Sharon Minemoto are standouts. Each summer, the Coastal Jazz and Blues Society (604 872 5200, www.coastaljazz.ca) puts on a two-week jazz festival ranging from mainstream to free jazz.

1067

1067 Granville Street, at Helmcken Street, Downtown. Bus 4, 6, 7, 10, 16, 17, 50, N6, N9, N10, N17. **Open** 10.30pm-late Fri, Sat. **Admission** $6. **No credit cards**. **Map** p248 J4.

If you can find it, the cavern-like space at 1067 (off the westward alley behind Granville Street) is a beatnik throwback that provides long, sometimes smoky evenings of everything from electro-acoustic honk-and-squeak to dazzlingly adept bebop.

Cellar

3611 W Broadway, at Dunbar Street, Kitsilano (604 738 1959/www.cellarjazz.com). Bus 7, 9, 17, 99, N9, N17. **Open** 8pm-midnight Mon-Wed; 7pm-midnight Thur-Sun. **Admission** free-$20. **Credit** AmEx, MC, V. **Map** p250 B6.

More traditional jazz notes by some of Vancouver's best, including Brad Turner and Seamus Blake, are heard at the Cellar, a restaurant and jazz club with sets six nights weekly at 8.30 and 10pm.

O'Doul's

1300 Robson Street, at Jervis Street, West End (604 661 1400/www.odoulsrestaurant.com). Bus 5, N6. **Open** 6.30am-3pm, 5pm-1am Mon-Sat; 6.30am-3pm, 5pm-midnight Sun. **Admission** free-$10. **Credit** AmEx, MC, V. **Map** p248 J2.

Gig hopping

As interest in live music has returned in Vancouver, a stark reality has become apparent: there's a glaring shortage of quality, dedicated venues in the city. As a result, it's common practice for touring bands to be booked at nightclubs. When such shows fall on a Friday or Saturday, the venue often institutes an early start time in order to have the band off the stage by 10.30pm. That way, they're still able to usher in their regular dance crowd. This practice can leave a concert-goer wondering how to occupy the latter hours of the night. Fortunately, local bands rarely take to the stage before 10pm. Therefore, it's become customary among city scenesters to accept the staggered show times and double book themselves for any given night. For example: after watching a touring band at Richard's on Richards, one can still make it to the Lamplighter early enough to catch sets by a couple of Vancouver acts. As the cover charge for local bands rarely exceeds $8, moving from venue to venue is not impossible. Eavesdrop on locals and you're bound to hear the question posed: 'What show were you at before this?'

Arts & Entertainment

Fabulous food and accomplished cool jazz on Vancouver's downtown shopping street, with Sharon Minemoto's smooth, understated trio featured every Monday at 8pm.

Rime

1130 Commercial Drive, between William Street and Napier Street, East Vancouver (604 215 1130/www. rime.ca). Bus 20, N20. **Open** 5pm-1am Mon-Fri; noon-1am Sat, Sun. **Admission** $5-$10. **Credit** AmEx, MC, V.

This small restaurant is the most talked-about new venue in Vancouver, serving up live music almost every afternoon and evening, along with cheap and delicious Turkish cuisine; its programming includes some of the best improv and free jazz around.

Rossini's Kitsilano

1535 Yew Street, at Cornwall Avenue, Kitsilano (604 737 8080/www.rossinis.bc.ca). Bus 2, 22, N22. **Open** 11am-1am. **Admission** free. **Credit** AmEx, MC, V. **Map** p251 F5.

You'll have to cut through the haze generated by the smouldering glances of amorous patrons at this fortysomething pick-up spot, but the reward is consistently good mainstream jazz.

Nightclubs

While Vancouver has spawned only a handful of international DJs, including house heavyweights Luke McKeehan and Tyler Stadius, the city's club scene is very much DJ driven, with true clubheads stepping out only when their fave drum 'n' bass whiz is playing. Vancouver also regularly attracts touring DJs; the most popular take over Commodore Ballroom or pack out Sonar. For more club happenings, check Clubvibes (www.clubvibes.com), ClubZone (www. clubzone.com) or the *Georgia Straight*.

Dance clubs along Granville Street draw a weekend crowd of flashy rowdies. Looking for company? Cruise Caprice Night Club (965 Granville Street, 604 685 3288), Bar None (1222 Hamilton Street, 604 689 7000), Au Bar (674 Seymour Street, 604 648 2227), SkyBar (670 Smithe Street, 604 697 9199). Meanwhile, for their commitment to progressive music, courteous staff and cool clientele, herewith, five choice clubs for your boogie-down pleasure:

Atlantis

1320 Richards Street, at Pacific Boulevard, Yaletown (604 662 7707/www.atlantisclub.net). Bus 4, 7, 10, 16, 17, 50, N9, N10, N17. **Open** phone for details. **Admission** $8-$12. **Credit** MC, V. **Map** p248 J5.

This colossus of a club boasts a $1.5-million light system, VIP area and eight bars – one for each drink! The lavish visuals alone are worth the trip: the dancefloor is embedded with lights and surrounded by video screens featuring sultry imagery.

International Gold Fridays unites all races and cultures for an urban music party spun by the allstar likes of Flipout, Hedspin, P-Luv and more.

Lotus Sound Lounge

455 Abbott Street, at W Pender Street, Downtown (604 685 7777/www.lotussoundlounge.com). Bus 10, 16, 20, N20, N35. **Open** 10pm-2am Mon-Thur; 10pm-3am Fri, Sat. **Admission** $5-$12. **Credit** AmEx, MC, V. **Map** p249 M3.

On Fridays this subterranean club fills with young creatives sweating their week's worries away in a dark but friendly environment. Lotus is known for progressive house and techno but Tuesday's Automatic is Vancouver's premier drum 'n' bass night – and still going strong after five years. A bonus: should you get bored, you can always check out Lick, a womyn-friendly scene, and Honey, all chandeliers and red velvet (and mod music on Fridays!) – both residing in the same hotel as Lotus.

Shine

364 Water Street, at Richards Street, Gastown (604 408 4321/www.shinenightclub.com). Bus 3, 4, 7, 50, N20, N35. **Open** 10pm-2am Mon-Wed, Sun; 9pm-2am Thur; 10pm-3am Fri, Sat. **Admission** $8-$12. **Credit** AmEx, MC, V. **Map** p249 L3.

Another venue which offers nightly genre specials (the pinnacle of which is Saturday's Big Sexy Funk). Shine attracts talented DJs. The vibe is more flirt party to great music than globally-conscious club action. From soul to breaks, this sleek, double room sounds fresh and looks great with its crowd of young, happy people. Nice staff, good drink prices.

Sonar

66 Water Street, at Abbott Street, Gastown (604 683 6695/www.sonar.bc.ca). Bus 3, 4, 7, 50, N20, N35. **Open** phone for details. **Admission** $10-$15. **Credit** MC, V. **Map** p249 M3.

Audiophiles will appreciate the sound system in this two-room Gastown institution, where some of the finest spinners in town play different flavours every night and host guests on the international circuit on an almost weekly basis. A fave venue for breakdance crews, the floor often gives way to headspinners circled by cheering b-boys and girls.

Tokyo Lounge

350-1050 Alberni Street, between Burrard Street & Thurlow Street, Downtown (604 689 0002/www. tokyolounge.ca). Bus 2, 5, 22, 98, N6, N22/SkyTrain Burrard. **Open** phone for details. **Admission** $5-$10. **Credit** MC, V. **Map** p249 K3.

A swanky, second-floor room with stars on the ceiling and, you guessed it, an Asian aesthetic, Tokyo Lounge's labyrinth of make-out nooks, er, cosy booths, and warm red lighting make it a great chill out place. Which isn't to say that All Good Thursdays can't get crazy as DJ Physik and Blaze rule with dancehall and hip hop. Fridays, TL hosts Get Up, Get Down, an easygoing funk party. Drink specials and girls-in-free are good enough reasons to arrive early and beat the queues.

Performing Arts

Look to the fringe for the best in theatre, dance and comedy.

Is it a bird? Is it a plane? No, it's **boca del lupo**'s *The Perfectionist. See p170.*

Theatre

The Vancouver theatre scene – like the rest of the city – is still under assembly. But it has momentum. The building blocks were set in place a mere 40 years ago with the foundation of the Playhouse and Arts Club theatres. The 1970s and '80s saw the formation of a handful of companies that remain major players. And in the last ten years independent innovators have remapped the theatre landscape.

There are gaps, but at least the theatre scene now feels like a reflection of the city. Vancouver has the writers, directors and producers to explore its underbelly as well as dissect the glittering, glass covered, modern surface.

Despite this, theatrical folk are always battling with a perception that their performances are in a losing battle with the natural beauty that surrounds the city. How can *Waiting for Godot* contend with mountain biking down Grouse Mountain? Well, the way to do it is to either seal yourself off from the distractions, or embrace them by creating trippy environmental work. The **Electric Company**, **boca del lupo** and director Kendra Fanconi have all been especially successful in the creation of site-specific works.

Meanwhile, the major employers – **Arts Club**, the **Playhouse** and Bard on the Beach – retain the city's senior talent and give some breaks to emerging artists. Collectively, they create a half-dozen of the best shows in a given season but maintain their position as much through hefty marketing, corporate sponsorship and the weight of their history.

Commercial theatre, however, has had a rough ride as the number of touring productions (which usually land at the Queen Elizabeth Theatre) have dropped off in recent years. The short history of the former Livent venue (now known as the **Centre in Vancouver for the Performing Arts**) offers a crude case study in the realities facing extended-run commercial theatre in a city large enough to support it but too culturally fragmented to create and sustain the critical mass of audience necessary for such ventures.

As far as theatre companies go, there are still no mid-sized troupes in Vancouver, although **Touchstone Theatre** comes close. There are half a dozen companies that should be at this level but their efforts have been stymied by a lack of investment at all levels of government. The result is that the action is happening at small theatre level with companies that produce plays in venues of 100-250 seats.

One of those is a local gem known as the **Vancouver East Cultural Centre**, just off Commercial Drive. The 'Cultch' hosts a savvy programme of local companies, national and international touring productions, as well as dance and music events. Another is the **Firehall Arts Centre** near Gastown, which presents a similar mix minus the international work, and which has been instrumental in creating a forum for First Nations theatre and issues relating to the city's troubled Downtown East Side. The PuSh International Performance Festival (*see p141*) is a new player on the scene, bringing a mid-winter spark to the performing arts with a smart collection of international, national and local shows.

In 1997, five small, established companies formed the See Seven subscription series in order to share resources. It's become the best deal in town for well-crafted, cutting-edge contemporary theatrical work. The founders, **Felix Culpa**, **Pi Theatre**, **Ruby Slippers**, **Rumble Productions** and **Western Theatre Conspiracy**, form the foundation of a sharply curated line-up along with regulars such as the Solo Collective and emerging bright lights like Theatre Replacement, Horseshoes& Handgrenades, Screaming Flea and Section 8. See www.seeseven.bc.ca for the current line-up.

As in any arts scene, the quality varies widely from company to company and season to season. There is no shortage of variety, though, and any time you visit there are sure to be at least a couple of shows in town creating some excitement or controversy.

Festivals

Festivals

Vancouver's theatre scene is augmented by three important festivals; the popular **Bard on the Beach Shakespeare Festival** occupies two large tents in Vanier Park through the summer months (*see p138*); the **Vancouver Fringe Festival** stages nearly 100 shows at the beginning of September (*see p141*); and the **PuSh International Performance Festival** brings an ambitious mix of productions to the city in January (*see p141*).

TICKETS AND INFORMATION

Most performances are at 8pm Tuesday to Saturday with 2pm matinées Saturday and/or Sunday and (at the Arts Club and Playhouse) on Wednesdays. Tuesday evening is often a half-price or pay-what-you-can performance. Many shows can be seen for $12 and tickets in Vancouver tend to max out at about $65.

Individual box office information is provided here by venue but most companies sell some tickets through **Ticketmaster** or **Festival Box Office**. Check for half-price tickets to many theatre productions (and other entertainment events) at the Tickets Tonight booth in the Touristinfo Centre near Canada Place (Plaza level, 200 Burrard Street, 604 684 2787, www.ticketstonight.ca. Open 10am-5pm Tue-Sat. Credit MC, V).

Reviews and previews appear regularly in print and online in the daily *Vancouver Sun and Province* as well as the weekly *Georgia Straight, Westender and Courier* and the

Bright sparks

Any new show by the **Electric Company** (604 253 4222, www.electriccompanytheatre.com) is an event. The company creates innovative work that's utterly charming and accessible – a mix of innocence and daring that is quite prototypically West Coast and very much Vancouver. The tight-knit team of Kim Collier, Jonathan Young, Kevin Kerr and David Hudgins graduated from Vancouver's Studio 58 in the mid 1990s and immediately had a hit with their first production, *Brilliant (The Blinding Enlightenment of Nicola Tesla)*. The stylish show featuring song, tap and judicious use of video in a story about the electricity innovator managed to maintain dramatic focus even while making an explanation of the difference between AC and DC enormously entertaining. *Brilliant* seemed to mark a generational shift in the Vancouver

theatre scene as both like-minded artists and competitors suddenly became more ambitious and audiences more responsive.

As the darlings of the community, Electric Company quickly gained status – and funding – as a creative team and as individual artists. They've rarely disappointed. Kevin Kerr won the Governor General's award for *Unity 1918*, premiered by Touchstone Theatre and subsequently produced across the country. Young is a busy actor and playwright. Collier recently directed a film adaptation of *The Score*, an Electric Company play dealing with ethical issues in genetics. Expectations are extremely high for *Studies in Motion: The Hauntings of Eadweard Muybridge* (2006) – but the Electric Company always sets the bar high and ordinarily sails over with consumate style and panache.

Friday edition of the *Globe & Mail*. UBC theatre professor and *Province* critic Jerry Wasserman posts valuable upcoming notes and a review archive at www.vancouverplays.com.

Student rush tickets are similar to standby tickets, but sold only to those with student ID.

Festival Box Office

1402 Anderson Street, Granville Island (604 257 0366/toll free 1-888 777 0366/www.festivalbox office.com). **Open** 10am-7pm Mon-Fri; 11am-7pm Sat. **Credit** AmEx, MC, V. **Map** p248 H5.

Ticketmaster

Pacific Centre, 700 W Georgia Street, Downtown (604 280 3311/www.ticketmaster.ca). **Open** 9am-7pm Mon-Fri; 8am-6pm Sat; noon-6pm Sun. **Credit** AmEx, MC, V. **Map** p249 K3.

Venues

Arts Club Theatre

1585 Johnston Street, Granville Island (box office 604 687 1644/www.artsclub.com). **Bus** 50. **Open** *Box office* 10am-showtime. **Tickets** $26-$60; $18.50 student rush. **Credit** AmEx, MC, V. **Map** p248 H5.
The Arts Club operates three venues, programming its own productions at the Stanley Industrial Alliance Stage, the Granville Island Stage and the Revue Stage, which is also home to Vancouver TheatreSports League (*see p171*).

Centre in Vancouver for the Performing Arts

777 Homer Street, between Robson Street & W Georgia Street, Downtown (604 602 0616/www.centreinvancouver.com). **Bus** 17. **Open** *Box office* two hours prior to showtime. **Tickets** $30-$60. **Credit** AmEx, MC, V. **Map** p249 K3.
So much trouble in so few years. Designed by Moshe Safdie, the 1,850-seat, $27million venue opened as the Ford Theatre in 1995, part of Garth Drabinsky's chain for Livent musicals. It closed in 1998 as Livent's financial troubles had Drabinsky spending more time with lawyers than artists. The Ford remained dark until a quartet of Hong Kong-born, Denver-based doctors, the Law bothers, bought the joint for the firesale price of $7 million. Dennis Law's idea was to wow Vancouver's Asian audiences and the regular theatregoer by creating 'action musicals': spectaculars steeped in (mainly) Chinese tradition, with dance, music and martial arts all lit up by the centre's state-of-the-art technology. But so far, the expected hit hasn't materialised. Law has said that the prime patch of downtown real estate might have to be sold for residential or commercial redevelopment if the box-office receipts don't improve.

Firehall Arts Centre

280 E Cordova Street, at Gore Avenue, East Vancouver (604 689 0926/www.firehallartscentre.ca). **Bus** 4, 7. **Open** *Box office* 9.30am-5pm Mon-Fri and one hour prior to show. **Tickets** $12-$26. **Credit** AmEx, MC, V. **Map** p249 N3.

Built in 1906, Vancouver's first fire station was transformed into one of Vancouver's busiest venues in 1982. The centre's theatre productions lean towards social issues and the venue has been instrumental in developing work by First Nations playwrights such as Drew Hayden Taylor.

Granville Island Stage

For listings, *see left* Arts Club Theatre.
The Arts Club was originally a loose collection of like-minded artists running a converted downtown gospel hall in the 1960s and '70s. Director Bill Millerd deftly moved it to touristy Granville Island in 1979 and then boosted prestige further with the conversion of the beautiful 1930-vintage Stanley Theatre in 1998. Today the Arts Club is Vancouver's unrivalled theatre machine. However, quality is still erratic, lurching from exquisitely designed and acted showpieces to under-rehearsed clunkers. One writer to watch for is Morris Panych (*7 Stories*, *Vigil*), who also directs with set designer and life partner Ken McDonald. Shows by this duo are must-see. Programming tends to contrasts: the populist with plays so elitist even the authors don't understand them. Thus 2006 saw shows ranging from Disney's *Beauty and the Beast* to Beckett's *Waiting for Godot* (directed by Panych). The Stage boasts the Arts Club Backstage Lounge, one of the city's best waterfront outdoor patios, featuring a solid line-up of live music in the evenings, beer specials and pub food.

Pacific Theatre

1440 W 12th Avenue, at Hemlock Street, West Side (604 731 5518/www.pacifictheatre.org). **Bus** 9, 10. **Open** *Box office* 1-6pm Tue-Fri and one hour prior to show. **Tickets** $17-$28; $8-$21 concessions. **Credit** MC, V. **Map** p251 H7.
Pacific Theatre, a 125-seat alley configuration in the basement of Holy Trinity Anglican Church, programmes work focused on ethical and spiritual issues by emerging locals as well as literary greats like CS Lewis and Athol Fugard.

Queen Elizabeth Theatre

For listings, *see p162*.
Home to Ballet BC, Vancouver Opera, touring theatre productions and occasional rock shows, the QET has a wide proscenium stage in the modern civic style of the late 1950s. It is planning a major redevelopment to create a more intimate audience chamber with improved acoustics and sight-lines.

Stanley Industrial Alliance Stage

2750 Granville Street, at W 12th Avenue, West Side. Bus 10. **Open** *Box office* Show days only 4.30-8.15pm Tue, Thur, Fri; noon-8.15pm Wed, Sat; 11am-4pm Sun. **Credit** AmEx, MC, V. **Map** p251 H7.
See above Arts Club Theatre & Granville Island Stage.

Vancouver East Cultural Centre

1895 Venables Street, at Victoria Drive, East Vancouver (604 251 1363/www.vecc.bc.ca). **Bus** 20. **Open** *Box office* one hour prior to show. **Tickets** $12-$22. **Credit** AmEx, MC, V.

The most committed audience in the city come to the Cultch. The former Unitarian church, built in 1909, has been a 250-seat theatre, dance and music venue since 1973. Executive director Duncan Low arrived to save the place from financial ruin in the mid '90s and now programmes an ambitious collection of touring shows and top-of-the-line independent work. Your best bet for quality programming.

Companies

boca del lupo
604 684 2622/www.bocadellupo.bc.ca.
If you're here in the summer boca del lupo's brilliantly inventive free shows under and in Stanley Park's arboreal cover (some scenes are, literally, up in the trees) should be near the top of your tour itinerary. A highly regarded company. **Photo** *p167*.

NeWorld Theatre
604 602 0007/www.neworldtheatre.com.
Theatre that crosses cultural divides with humour, music, smart writing and inventiveness. NeWorld's adaptations, from Persian folk tales to James Fagan Tait's hit retrofit of *Crime and Punishment*, and the hilariously scathing satire *The Adventures of Ali & Ali and the Axes of Evil*, have brought the company national attention and due respect at home.

Pi Theatre
604 872 1861/www.pitheatre.com.
Formed as Pink Ink in 1984, the company became Pi Theatre in 1999 under artistic director Del Surjik. Expect polished English-language versions of Quebecois plays and world stage works.

Playhouse Theatre Company
Playhouse Theatre, 600 Hamilton Street, at Dunsmuir Street, Downtown (604 873 3311/ www.vancouverplayhouse.com). Bus 17/SkyTrain Stadium. **Open** *Box office* three hours prior to show. **Tickets** $24-$59; $18 student rush. **Credit** AmEx, MC, V. **Map** p249 L4.
For 42 years the Playhouse produced a balanced programme of classics, recent hits from the world stage and Canadian plays – the traditional mandate of the nation's regional theatres. In its prime the Playhouse had a 12-show season. In an attempt to set the theatre company apart from the Arts Club, artistic director Glynis Leyshon last year made the politically fraught move to refocus on plays written since 1950. The deficit battle continues with the season shrunk to five plays, including two one-person shows in the 2005/06 season (*The Syringa Tree* and *I Am My Own Wife*). Still, Playhouse shows are usually well-directed and designed, with casts featuring the finest national and local talent.

Ruby Slippers
604 602 0585/www.rubyslippers.ca.
Diane Brown produces smart, stylish productions of work by local playwrights as well as international hits such as Lisa Loomer's *The Waiting Room*.

Rumble Productions
604 662 3395/www.rumble.org.
Catchily billed as Vancouver's 'all terrain theatre vehicle', this baby's an energy-efficient hybrid with plenty of power left over to burn. The programme travels from a refined *Hedda Gabler* through to stylish contemporary works about Vancouver such as Aaron Bushkowsky's *Soulless*. The company is currently in transition as guiding light Norman Armour moves on to the PuSh Festival, but Rumble shows are essential viewing.

Theatre la Seizieme
604 736 2616/http://atfc.ca/seizieme.
The theatre for Francophones and Francophiles. Seizieme produces highly regarded French-language theatre for adults and children. The 100-seat theatre in the French Cultural Centre (1565 W 7th Avenue, at Granville Street) is also used by independents.

Touchstone Theatre
604 709 9973/www.touchstonetheatre.com.
A cornerstone of the scene for 30 years, Touchstone produces 'essential Canadian plays' such as Kevin Kerr's *Unity 1918*, which won the Governor General's award (the nation's top play prize) in 2002. Well-produced, quality shows.

Western Theatre Conspiracy
604 878 8668/www.conspiracy.ca.
Artistic producer Richard Wolfe makes it his business to premiere critically lauded new work from the world stage that won't make it to the larger theatres, such as *Mojo*, *Closer* and *Blue/Orange*. Conspiracy also puts on some original works, the dystopian *Omniscience*, for example, tapping currents in international politics and culture.

Theatre for young audiences

Green Thumb Theatre (604 254 4055, www.greenthumb.bc.ca), **Axis Theatre** (604 669 0631, www.axistheatre.com) and **Theatre la Seizieme** all create world-class shows for children, focusing most of their attention on school tours but all presenting shows in theatres from time to time. The Axis mime-and-mask show, *The Number 14*, which turns up regularly at the Arts Club, is must-see for all ages, as is any show by the **Leaky Heaven Circus** (604 488 0003, www.leakyheaven.com), which usually performs at the Vancouver East Cultural Centre.

Carousel Theatre
604 669 3410/www.carouseltheatre.ca.
Carousel Theatre produces full-length plays, with high production values, focusing on children's classics like *Peter Pan*, *Treasure Island* and *The Wind in the Willows* – do you notice a watery theme to the productions? The company regularly packs the Waterfront Theatre on Granville Island.

Arts & Entertainment

Comedy

Vancouver comedy booms and busts, but the core scene consistently grows in strength and popularity. Stand-up and sketch improv are the bedrock but there is great overlap with the theatre and the spoken-word scenes. The *Georgia Straight* is the only publication that covers comedy, so consult the free weekly to determine the current hotspot.

Canwest Comedy Fest

604 683 0883/www.vancouvercomedyfest.com. Most performances at Yuk Yuk's (*see below*) and other downtown clubs. **Dates** 18-24 September 2006.
Canadian media behemoth Canwest signed on as the big name sponsor and eased the pains of the former Vancouver International Comedy Festival in 2005. With the necessary money on board the festival then took a big step upwards – the schedule ran wider and deeper with more famous names like Stephen Wright, Mike Wilmot and Scott Thompson, the rising stars of the US talk-show circuit.

Lafflines

26 4th Street, at Columbia Street, New Westminster (604 525 2262/www.lafflines.com). SkyTrain Columbia. **Shows** 9pm Thur; 9.30pm Fri; 8pm & 10.30pm Sat. **Tickets** $5-$15. **Credit** AmEx, MC, V.
A quick ride from Downtown on the SkyTrain gets you out to this popular suburban comedy club. The acts on show tend to feature Grade A locals such as Roman Danylo and rising stars from the American circuit, trying out audiences north of the border.

Urban Well

1516 Yew Street, at Cornwall Avenue, West Side (604 737 7770/www.urbanwell.com). Bus 2, 22. **Shows** *Improv* 9pm Mon. *Standup* 7.30pm & 10pm Tue. **Tickets** $7. **Credit** AmEx, MC, V.
Map p251 F5.
A hot little room just a few steps from Kitsilano Beach features Monday and Tuesday night comedy events made popular over the years by former host Brent Butt. Robin Williams has been known to parachute in to blast through new material when he's shooting a movie in Vancouver. The Tuesday stand-up set is where many performers test out new material, giving the night more of an edge than you might find at the comedy clubs.

Vancouver TheatreSports League

Arts Club Theatre's New Revue Stage, 1601 Johnston Street, Granville Island (604 738 7013/ www.vtsl.com). Bus 50. **Shows** 8pm, 10pm & 11.45pm Fri; 11.30am, 1pm, 8pm, 10pm, 11.45pm Sat; 11.30am, 1pm Sun. **Tickets** $7-$16.50. **Credit** AmEx, MC, V. **Map** p248 H5.
TheatreSports' shows – such as *The Imprentice* – do boffo box office. The company has something for all tastes, from Instant Improv's Saturday and Sunday matinées to Friday and Saturday late-night Extreme Improv. Second Thursday of each month is Girls' Night Out, featuring an hour of girl-on-girl improv.

Yuk Yuk's

Century Plaza Hotel, 1015 Burrard Street, at Helmcken Street, Downtown (604 696 9857/www. yukyuks.com). Bus 2, 22. **Shows** 8.30pm Tue-Thur; 8pm & 10.30pm Fri, Sat. **Tickets** $5-$15. **Credit** AmEx, MC, V. **Map** p248 J4.

Yuk Yuk's.

'Art is hidden by its own perfection.' **Dance Centre**.

High-profile comics like Mike Wilmot and Emo Philips make Yuk Yuk's their Vancouver stop, so this is the town's top comedy shop. There's a corporate feel about the place – it's part of Mark Breslin's chain – but even shows early in the week approach capacity. Dinner packages available. **Photo** *p171*.

Dance

While Terpsichore, the Classical muse of dance, has inspired many in Vancouver, fans of the professional dance scene may become frustrated seeking out regular performances to attend. The best source for weekly listings is the *Georgia Straight*, but if you're planning ahead, check out upcoming events at www.thedancecentre.ca. Established in 1986, the **Dance Centre** offers resources, information, teaching programmes, and even some political muscle to BC dance companies, choreographers, dancers, artists and the public. In 2001 it found a splendid new home in a seven-storey glass structure designed in collaboration with Arthur Erickson. Classes, workshops and performances take place in six two-storey studios (677 Davie Street, 604 606 6400, pictured). The Dance Centre also houses the biennial Dance in Vancouver event (the next one is due in the autumn of 2007) and the informal Discover Dance! noon dance sessions, one Thursday every month except

December, from September to May (check the website for details). The centre is home to more than 20 dance companies, among them **Judith Marcuse Projects** (604 606 6425, www. judithmarcuseprojects.ca), which has a long history of collaborating with artists like William Gibson and the late Toni Onley.

Ballet BC (604 732 5003, www.balletbc. com) is the leading company in town, and under the leadership of dancer/choreographer John Alleyne (artistic director since as far back as 1992) they have established a strong reputation for creating innovative contemporary ballet. The BBC's annual danceAlive! season runs from September through April, with three or four performances from their repertoire each month at the company's base, the Queen Elizabeth Theatre (*see p162*). Tickets are available through Ticketmaster.

Among numerous festivals in the dance calendar, the highlights are the Vancouver International Dance Festival (604 662 7441, www.vidf.ca), in March, and Dancing on the Edge Festival (604 689 0691, www. mcsquared.com/edge), in early July.

If you want to dance, not watch, the **Harbour Dance Centre** (3rd Floor, 927 Granville Street, 604 684 9542, www.harbour dance.com) is an accessible training and teaching facility which offers drop-in classes at all levels, seven days a week.

Arts & Entertainment

Sport & Fitness

From boards and blades to skis and sails, sport is anything but tame in British Columbia.

Within easy, sweat-free reach of Vancouver is a natural playground of skiing, windsurfing, hiking, boarding, sailing, skating, blading, kayaking and running opportunities. No surprise then that Vancouverites are obsessed (come rain or shine) with the great outdoors.

As a result you'll meet some of the fittest people you've ever seen here. After all, workouts are preferred to a session in the pub and being asked to do the Grouse Grind (*see p85*) is occasion to break out your running shoes rather than your prophylactics.

Even the most hardened loafers will find the locals' enthusiasm hard to resist. This young and vibrant city is deftly geared to keeping fit. Paths set up for cycling, blading and walking strategically hug the waterfront for miles and more organised runs (the Marathon and Sun Run) are so scenic you're almost oblivious to the pain. Beaches are rarely just for lounging, with posts crying out for games of volleyball, outdoor swimming-pools and even the odd yoga class, *see p177* **Strike the pose**.

Eastern Canadians often dismiss the west as the land of 'lotus eaters'. No insult, really – maybe Vancouverites have sussed out life's priorities. Remember, you will need to add taxes to most prices in BC and for rentals you need a credit or debit card as a deposit and photo ID (passport/driving licence).

Land sports

Beach volleyball

Posts are put up on beaches between Kitsilano and Locarno/Spanish Banks on the West Side and downtown at English Bay in the summer. Turn up with a ball and a net (lifeguard stations will loan them with ID deposit) and it's first come, first served. Many Vancouverites chill out with a game and a barbecue after work, so expect to wait. There is a league, so some courts will be in use on set nights. Try www.vancouvervolleyball.com for drop-ins.

▶ For more on **sport and the outdoors**, see pp81-85.

Cycling

See *p229* and *p84* **Downhill racers**.

Golf

Carved out of a rainforest, Vancouver's courses are so beautiful they might put you off your swing. See www.vancouverparks.ca for information on courses in or near the city. Most offer lessons and equipment to hire.

Gleneagles Golf Course
6190 Marine Drive, at Orchill Road, West Vancouver (604 921 7353). Bus 250, 257. **Open** dawn-dusk daily. **Rates** $20/9 holes. **Credit** AmEx, MC, V.
Obviously named by a homesick Scot, this Gleneagles is one of the oldest courses in the city and worth the trip out to West Vancouver for the backdrop of mountains with ocean out in front.

Stanley Park Pitch and Putt
Lagoon Drive, Stanley Park, near Beach Avenue entrance (604 681 8847/www.vancouverparks.ca). Bus 6. **Open** *Nov-Feb* 9am-dusk daily. *Mar-Oct* 7.30am-dusk daily. **Rates** $11/18 holes; $3/putting green. **Credit** MC, V.
Leave your woods behind for this popular spot in Stanley Park as the 18 holes are a maximum of 100 yards and it's free of anything approaching the word 'hazard'. Just turn up (there's no advance booking), and it's first come, first served (weekends are busy). Hungry? Try the Fish House restaurant (*see p99*).

University Golf Club
5185 University Boulevard, between Blanca Street & Acadia Road, University of British Columbia (604 224 7799/www.universitygolf.com). Bus 4, 17. **Open** dawn-dusk daily. **Rates** $60-$70/18 holes; $6/75 balls driving range. **Credit** AmEx, MC, V.
An 18-hole course in the Pacific Spirit Park, barely a quarter hour from downtown. The University Golf Club is a great public course and driving range that's been a city institution since 1929. It's good for all levels of play and lessons are available.

Gyms

Vancouverites take image seriously and train hard. Whether you're in for an intense spinning class or a chill-out yoga session, there will always be plenty of eye candy to distract you. On the 'Wet Coast', gyms are essential – but if it's sunny you'll find them deserted.

Arts & Entertainment

Cypress. *See p176.*

Sweat Co

*736 Richards Street, at W Georgia Street, Downtown
(604 683 7938/www.sweatcostudios.com). All city-
centre buses.* **Open** 8am-8pm Mon-Thur; 8am-7pm
Fri; 8am-2pm Sat. **Rates** $7.50. **Credit** AmEx, MC,
V. **Map** p249 K3.
For those who like their gyms small and more intimate, Sweat Co is well-equipped.

YWCA

*535 Hornby Street, between Dunsmuir Street &
W Pender Street, Downtown (604 895 5777/www.
ywcavan.org). All city-centre buses.* **Open** 6am-10pm
Mon-Fri; 8am-5.30pm Sat, Sun. **Rates** $16/day.
Credit MC, V. **Map** p249 K3.
A day's membership will give you access to the Y's
state-of-the-art facilities in a central location.

Hiking & camping

Hiking

Pacific Spirit Park

*W 16th Avenue, between Camosun Street & SW
Marine Drive, University of British Columbia (GVRD
parks office 604 224 5739/www.gvrd.bc.ca/parks/
PacificSpirit.htm). Bus 25.*
If you want a taste of north-west wilderness within
easy reach of Vancouver, Pacific Spirit Park is one
option. Part of the University Endowment Lands,
the park is far less touristy than its city cousin,
Stanley. Enormous trees tower over 54km (34 miles)
of hiking trails criss-crossing one another. On a bike
or in the saddle? There are 38km (24miles) of trails
dedicated to producing a vertical dirt track down
your back, or really aching thighs. Maps are found
at the various entrances to the park.

Camping

Porteau Cove Provincial Park

*25 miles north of Vancouver on Highway 99 (604
986 9371). 16 walk-in campsites available (some
ocean-fronted), only five minutes from the car park;
44 vehicle-accessible sites.* **Rates** Walk-in $10/party/
night. *Vehicle* $22/party/night. **Credit** MC, V
(Nov-Apr payment by cash only).
Camping is a popular weekend activity with locals.
To guarantee a space for any campsite within BC,
it's best to call the Campground Reservation Service
on 604 689 9025. Most reservations can be made up
to 3 months in advance and no later than 2 days
before your arrival date (www.discovercamping.ca).

Ice-skating

Ice-skating is huge in Vancouver, so there
was outrage when the free rink at Robson
Square between Howe and Hornby was closed.
Outdoors in the winter you can always skate at
the top of Grouse Mountain (*see p84*). How you
get there is up to you.

West End Community Centre

*870 Denman Street, at Barclay Street, West End
(604 257 8333/www.westendcc.vancouver.bc.ca).
Bus 5.* **Open** *Oct-Apr* 9am-10pm Mon-Thur; 9am-
9pm Fri; 9am-5pm Sat; 10am-5pm Sun. Closed May-
Sept. **Rates** $4.40/hour; $2.50 skate rental. **Credit**
MC, V. **Map** p248 H2.

In-line skating

Vancouverites swap skates for Rollerblades in
the summer. There's a vibrant skating culture
here and undoubtedly the most beautiful route
is around the seawall, through Stanley Park and
on to Yaletown, False Creek, past Science World
and on to Granville Island. The rule is to go
anti-clockwise around the park and there are
pictures of bladers and bikers on one side of the
path to separate them from the walkers on the
other. Nice theory, although it does not always
work and you need to keep your wits about you.
The etiquette is to generally pass on the left and
before you do, shout out 'on your left' so they
know you're coming. As for what to wear, you'll
see people naked apart from Speedos and skates
through to those dressed in full body armour
(helmet, knee, elbow and wrist pads).
   Speed freaks and experts might find the
Seawall a frustrating ride what with all the –
often cheerfully oblivious – walkers, strollers
and bikers, so either head there early or late
to avoid the dawdlers, or for a real challenge
check out the North Shore's Lower Seymour
Conservation Reserve (formerly the Seymour
Demonstration Forest) for the Seymour Valley
Trail, which is ten kilometres (six miles) long
(604 990 0483, www.gvrd.bc.ca).

Bayshore Rentals

*745 Denman Street, between Robson Street
and Alberni Street, West End (604 688 2453/
www.BayshoreBikeRentals.ca). Bus 5.* **Open** 9am to
dusk daily. **Rates** *Roller blades* $5/hour; $13.50/four
hours; $18.50/8 hours. *Protective pads* $1/day. *Helmet*
free. **Credit** AmEx, MC, V. **Map** p248 H2.

Jogging & running

There are countless routes of all levels of
difficulty: the Seawall around Stanley Park
and beyond (*see above*); the Pacific Spirit Park
(*see left*); and the Grouse Grind (*see p84*) for
something a hell of a lot more challenging.

Sun Run

www.sunrun.com.
Held on the third Sunday of April, this long-established 10km (6 mile) run seems to involve the whole
city. Most participants (and there are about 50,000)
are named in time order in the *Vancouver Sun* newspaper, the main sponsor, which also has four months
of training schedules to get you in the mood.

Arts & Entertainment

Vancouver International Marathon

604 872 2928/www.vanmarathon.ca.
Staged on the first Sunday of May, this is run on breathtaking routes across the city.

Mountain biking

After the snow, the local mountains test your mettle on the bike. It's easy to see why it's the law to wear a helmet if you're biking, so swallow your vanity and put one on. Skinny tyres not recommended on any routes. *See also p84* **Downhill racers**.

Cypress

Cypress Bowl, Cypress Bowl Road, West Vancouver (604 926 5612/www.cypressmountain.com). Cypress Mountain Shuttle Bus at Lonsdale Quay $15 return; $10 concessions; phone 604 419 7669 for details. **Open** *Summer* 10am-6pm daily (phone for details). **Rates** *lift* $32; *bikes* $39-$79; *full armour set* (helmet, shin and elbow pads) $20. **Credit** AmEx, MC, V.
Cypress Mountain is the largest on the North Shore. That leaves plenty of room on its flanks for a mountain bike park and some serious trails. **Photo** *p174.*

Pacific Spirit Park

For listings, *see p175.*

Rock climbing

Vancouver has a good reputation for rock climbing. And for the real thing nothing beats the Chief in Squamish – the largest granite outcrop in the world – about an hour north of Vancouver along the Sea-to-Sky highway (www.chiefguide.com).

Cliffhanger Indoor Rock Climbing Centre

106 W 1st Avenue, at Manitoba Street, West Side (604 874 2400, www.cliffhangerclimbing.com). Bus 3. **Open** noon-11pm Mon-Fri; noon-9.30pm Sat, Sun. **Rates** $15-$17/day. **Credit** MC, V. **Map** p249 M5.

Skateboarding

Skaters are celebrated in Vancouver, with the city council providing well-respected spaces for their tricks and general practice.

Vancouver Skate Plaza

Under the Georgia Viaduct at the intersection of Union & Quebec Streets & Expo Boulevard, Downtown. Bus 10, 20, 135/SkyTrain Main Street-Science World. **Map** p249 L4.
With its ramps, rails and steps, it's no wonder that skateboarders are dubbing the city's recently opened street-style park the best this side of LA.

Skiing

See p180 **Powder play**.

Tennis

The city is home to some 180 free courts, in varying conditions. The 15 popular Stanley Park courts have been recently resurfaced, and other good ones include Kitsilano Beach Park and Queen Elizabeth Park. The rules for these courts are: from the moment you turn up to wait for a court, the players have no more than 30 minutes left. If queuing doesn't appeal, head for the courts at Jericho Beach Park (by the Jericho Youth Hostel, *see p48*), which are far less crowded. You can book some well-maintained courts at Stanley Park ($5 per 30 minutes in summer, although they are actually free until 3pm during the week – you pay between 3pm and dusk. Book on 604 605 8224.)

Watersports

Vancouverites love mucking around on and beside the water and are always keen to try out new sports such as kite surfing as well as the old favourites – sailing, fishing and diving. Many people relocate here from around the world just for the ease of boating to the myriad islands that pockmark the Pacific.

Boating

Kayaking

Ecomarine Kayak

Jericho Sailing Centre Association, 1300 Discovery Street, West Point Grey (604 222 3565/www. ecomarine.com). Bus 4. **Open** *3 May-25 Sept* daily (phone for details). **Rates** $33/2 hours single kayak; $45/2 hours double kayak. $69 lessons/3 hours. **Credit** MC, V.
Second location: *Granville Island, next to the boatyard (604 689 7575). Bus 50/Aquabus Granville Island.* **Open** daily (phone for details).
Third location: *English Bay in the historic Bath House, at Denman Street & Davie Street, West End (604 685 2925). Bus 6.* **Open** *30 Apr-3 Sept* daily (phone for details).

Speedboats

Granville Island Boat Rentals

1696 Duranleau Street, Granville Island (604 682 6287/www.granvilleislandboatrentals.com). Bus 50/ Aquabus Granville Island. **Open** 10am-7pm daily. **Rates** $35-$45/hr (plus gas, insurance and taxes); $500 credit-card deposit. **Credit** AmEx, MC, V.
For petrolheads, decent speedboats can be hired here by the hour. Easy throttle-system and they'll chuck in a map of all the rocks to avoid and where to head. The driver must be 25 or older and hold a motor vehicle licence. They don't rent out fishing gear themselves, but can arrange for a guide and gear.

Yachts

Cooper Boating
1620 Duranleau Street, Granville Island (604 687 4110/1-888 999 6419/www.cooperboating.com). Bus 50/Aquabus Granville Island. **Open** *June-Aug* 8am-6pm daily. *Sept-May* 9am-5pm daily. **Rates** $341-$1,607/5 days. **Credit** AmEx, MC, V.

For longer charters and bigger boats, this is a good firm. If you're not confident about sailing (or you're feeling lazy), you can rent a skipper (from $250/day).

Mac Sailing
Jericho Sailing Centre Association, 1300 Discovery Street, West Point Grey (604 224 7245/www.mac sailing.com). Bus 4. **Open** *May, Sept* noon-5pm daily. *June-Aug* 9am-6pm daily. **Rates** Sailboats $25-$45/hour. **Credit** MC, V. **Photo** *p179.*

Fishing

Depending on the time of year and where you are in British Columbia, salmon is the catch of choice. There are five main types (sockeye, coho, chinook, pink and chum). A non-resident licence for freshwater fishing is around $15 a day ($30 for eight); saltwater is $8 a day ($35 for five). Fishing is governed by the Recreational Fishing (Pacific Region) department; for current licences information call 604 666 5835 (8.30am-4.30pm) or log on to www.pac.dfo-mpo.gc.ca where you'll find the whole gamut of recreational fishing regulations, seasons, and area openings and closures, including ones caused by red tides and paralytic shellfish poisoning. While you'll see the odd fishermen

Strike the pose

Forget stuffy yoga studios – there's nothing like a bit of omming on the beach. Head to **Kitsilano**, **Jericho** or **Sunset** in the summer months and you are likely to spot some downward-dogging and sun salutations supervised by teachers sporadically holding drop-in classes. Simply roll out your mat (or borrow one), and you'll find the outdoor yoga session is in a league of its own: a Pacific breeze to keep you cool and an unrivalled view. Such is the popularity of yoga that, even if you are in the most contorted pose, fellow beach aficionados hardly give you a second look. Drop-ins usually last an hour to an hour-and-a-half, are held after work (most start at 6pm to catch the last of the rays) and payment is by donation (usually around $8). For the taste of outdoor yoga but in a more formal arrangement, check out Outdoor Yoga at the Showboat (power yoga for all levels, www.vancouveryoga.com), by Kitsilano Beach Pool on Tuesday and Thursday 6-7.40pm, and Saturday 9-10.40am (drop-ins $10).

There are myriad types of yoga on offer: power, hot, zen, hatha, etc. If yoga in 90-degree heat ('hot yoga') is your bag, then the Bikram's Yoga College of India has three locations in Vancouver (Cambie: 2893 Cambie Street, 604 876 9642; Kitsilano: 2681 W Broadway, 604 742 3830; and the West End: 1650 Alberni Street, 604 662 7722, www.bikramyogavancouver.com). It's hardcore, but very addictive and each studio offers numerous classes throughout the day, from 6am until 8.15pm. Be sure to leave yourself a bit of time afterwards to cool down. (Drop-ins: $20, which includes two classes.)

For the more hippie, earth-mothery yoga venue, try a session at the friendly Prana Yoga & Zen Centre (1083 Cambie Street, 604 682 2121, www.pranayoga.com, $16/day drop-in; $59 unlimited month). Lululemon (*see p125*) is a brand synonymous with yoga. It's also a great place to hear of courses from staff who practise what they sell. *Namaste.*

on Jericho pier and Sunset Beach, people normally take to boats or go further up the coastline (Howe Sound is popular). Licences are sold at tackle stores throughout the city.

Scuba diving

It's a little known fact that Vancouver is a world leader in creating artificial reefs (old ships specially scuppered to provide a suitable habitat for reef forming organisms) and plenty of divers head this way to see the corals' creations off Vancouver Island (the *Saskatchewan* and *Cape Breton* near Nanaimo; log on to www.artificialreef.bc.ca for details). Closer to Vancouver, smaller ships sunk as training wrecks by the Artificial Reef Society of BC can be found at Porteau Cove Park (http://wlapwww.gov.bc.ca/bcparks/explore/parkpgs/porteau.htm#parkmap) on the Sea-to-Sky highway, and the area is better suited to people not experienced with West Coast currents. It is a diver-friendly park with showers and changing-rooms. Also on the divers' radar are Howe Sound and Indian Arm, which are both magnets for underwater enthusiasts. Both can get crowded in the tourist season. Whytecliff Park in West Vancouver (bus 250) offers a classic dive called 'the Cut' with a wall that goes down hundreds of feet and some 200 species of marine life. A general rule is that all divers must watch for the currents.

Diving Locker
2745 W 4th Avenue, between Macdonald Street & Stephens Street, Kitsilano (604 736 2681/ www.divinglocker.ca). Bus 2, 4, 7, 22, 44. **Open** 10am-6pm Mon-Fri; 9.30am-5.30pm Sat; 9.30am-4pm Sun. **Rates** *Full equipment package* $100/day (certified divers only). **Credit** AmEx, MC, V. **Map** p250 D6.

Great Pacific Diving
1236 Marine Drive, at Pemberton Avenue, North Vancouver (604 986 0302/www.greatpacific.net). Bus 239. **Open** 9.30am-6pm Mon-Sat; 9am-5pm Sun. **Rates** *Full equipment package* $55/day (certified divers only). **Credit** MC, V.

Swimming (outdoor pools)

Kitsilano Pool
2305 Cornwall Avenue, at Yew Street, Kitsilano (604 731 0011). Bus 2, 22, 44. **Open** *Mid May-mid June* noon-8.45pm daily. *Mid June-early Sept* 7am-8.45pm daily. *Sept* 7am-7.15pm daily. **Admission** $4.50. **Credit** AmEx, MC, V. **Map** p251 F5.
A saltwater pool (Canada's largest), divided in half between a play area and swimmers going in an anti-clockwise direction (the lifeguards will set you right if you try swimming against the flow). It's an excellent place for families to hang out.

Second Beach Pool
Stanley Park Drive, West End (604 257 8371). Bus 6. **Open** *Mid May-mid June* noon-8.45pm daily. *Mid June-end July* 10am-8.45pm daily. *End July-mid Sept* 7am-7pm daily. **Admission** $4.50. **Credit** AmEx, MC, V. **Map** p63.
This freshwater pool has plenty of lanes and slides and the location could scarcely be better.

Windsurfing

Windsure Windsurfing
Jericho Sailing Centre Association, 1300 Discovery Street, West Point Grey (604 224 0615/www.windsure.com). Bus 4. **Open** *Apr-Oct* 9am-8pm daily. **Rates** *Windsurf hire* $17.55/hr (includes wet suit and lifejacket). *Lessons* $49/2hr intro group lesson. *Introduction to kiteboarding* $89/hr. **Credit** AmEx, MC, V.

Spectator sports

To be honest, most of Vancouver's home teams are pretty average, although that doesn't stop the locals rooting for them. The notable exception is the hockey team, the Canucks, which offers a high-octane performance with the all-important and highly entertaining sin bin for naughty players. The team has also been contenders for the holy grail of their sport: the Stanley Cup. Don't expect to see any basketball in the city: the Vancouver Grizzlies relocated to Memphis a few years back. For tickets, go through Ticketmaster (604 280 4400, www.ticketmaster.ca) or Coast to Coast (1-866 800 2828, www.coasttocoasttickets.com), although some venues sell them at the door.

Baseball

Nat Bailey Stadium
4601 Ontario Street, at 33rd Avenue, West Side (604 872 5232/www.canadiansbaseball.com). Bus 3, 15. **Open** 1pm afternoon game; 7pm evening game. **Tickets** $8-$20. **Credit** MC, V.
The Vancouver Canadians are the city's team in the Single-A Northwest League – against seven other groups – playing out of the dinky ballpark at Nat Bailey Stadium. The regular season is from June to September. At around the 7th inning stretch (out of 9), the spectators go through the mysterious ritual of standing and stretching to music.

Football

BC Lions
BC Place Stadium, 777 Pacific Boulevard, between Griffiths Way & Terry Fox Way, Downtown (604 589 7627/www.bclions.com). Bus 15/SkyTrain Stadium. **Open** 7pm kick-off. **Tickets** $25-$65. **Credit** AmEx, MC, V. **Map** p249 L4.

Mac Sailing. *See p177.*

Of course, we're not talking British soccer – or real American Football either for that matter. BC Lions is Vancouver's team in the Canadian Football League with various differences to the way the game is played in the United States. Still, the Lions have won the national competition, the Grey Cup, four times, the last victory being as recently as 2000.

Horse racing

Hastings Park
Renfrew Street, at E Hastings Street, East Vancouver (604 254 1631/toll free 1-800 677 7702/www.hastingsracecourse.com). Bus 4. A complimentary courtesy shuttle runs every 30mins between the racecourse and Renfrew Street & E Hastings Street, and to Renfrew SkyTrain Station on live race days only (5pm Fri and 11.30am Sat, Sun). **Open** 9am-11pm daily; on nights when it broadcasts live racing from Hong Kong to 3am. **Rates** *Admission* free. *Minimum bet* $2. **No credit cards**. This is no Epsom, but it has to be one of the prettiest racecourses in the world. It's free, with thoroughbreds flat-racing on Saturdays and Sundays from April until November (and Friday nights from June to September), with the first gallop at 1.25pm until between 5pm and 6pm depending on the number of races on a given day (usually between eight and ten). Friday night races start at 6.25pm and end from 9.30pm to 10.30pm. Not everyone is here for the live horses, however; Hastings Park also televises races from across North America and around the world and it's common for people to come here and not venture out to the track at all.

Powder play

Once summer's over, Vancouverites eagerly look north and anticipate the first dusting of snow on the local mountains. The three areas (**Cypress**, **Grouse** and **Seymour**) each offer enough for a day's fun in the snow within a half hour of downtown. All provide terrain for skiing, boarding and snowshoeing and, on Cypress, cross-country skiing. Thanks to great floodlights the runs are open until around 10pm seven days a week during the main season. Many people zoom up after work and have a season pass for a specific night. The mountains are not on a par with Whistler but what they lack in long and fulfilling runs, they make up for in stupendous vistas – some of the sea, some of the city. With Cypress comes a view of the Lions from the Sky chair, or of Mount Baker, Bowen Island and the city from the Panorama run. The peak is set to host the snowboarding and freestyle skiing competitions of the 2010 Olympics, so it's about to undergo a makeover with a new quad chair and eight new ski trails (www.winter2010.com). There are quite a few black diamond runs (the most difficult) but they're short. Generally, the three mountains are a great place to learn with plenty of blue and green runs. Snowshoeing is also popular. It takes next to no time to pick up the technique (you basically walk) and the treks are well marked. There's less of the hassle factor of skiing/boarding too: strap on the high-tech snowshoes and off you go. And don't forget the snow tubing parks for the kids. If you're around in the third weekend in October, check out the Vancouver Snow Show (www.vancouversnowshow.com).

Cypress Mountain
Cypress Provincial Park, Exit 8 off Highway 1, West Vancouver (604 926 5612/Snow & shuttle phone 604 419 7669/www.cypress mountain.com). Shuttle bus from Lonsdale Quay SeaBus. **Open** phone or see website for details. **Rates** *Shuttle* $15 round-trip. **Tickets**

Ice hockey

Canucks

GM Place, 800 Griffiths Way, at Pacific Boulevard, Downtown (604 899 7469/604 899 7444/www. canucks.com). SkyTrain Stadium. **Open** Face-off 7pm. **Tickets** $30-$100. **Credit** AmEx, MC, V. **Map** p249 L4.

Remember to call it just plain 'hockey'. After a disastrous 2004-2005 season with no NHL (National Hockey League) because of lock-outs and strikes, now it seems it's all 'Go, Canucks, Go' in Vancouver. The team are thrilling to watch, with a hard and fast puck over the three time periods. The atmosphere is generally a lot politer and less frenzied than a British football crowd. The team play in the NHL season from September until April and tickets go quickly.

Soccer

Whitecaps Football Club

Swangard Stadium, at Kingsway & Boundary Road, Burnaby (604 669 9283/www.whitecapsfc.com). SkyTrain Patterson. **Open** Games start 7pm. **Rates** $14-$22/game. **Credit** AmEx, MC, V.

Previously known as the 86ers, the Whitecaps play soccer (our football) in retro jerseys in the USL A-League championship. The team came third in the USL First Division in 2005. Meanwhile, the women's team went two places better, topping the Western Conference that same year. Women's football has found much greater acceptance and a much wider fan base in North America, so it's worth catching a match. Men's games run from the end of April to mid-September, women's from May to the end of July.

$42.06-$45.79/day downhill; $15.89/day cross-country; $8.41/day snowshoeing; $12.63-$14.95/2 hr snow park. **Lessons** $40/2 hour drop-in lesson; $72 including lift; $102 with lift & equipment rental; $65/hour private lessons. **Rentals** *Downhill equipment* $38 (skis, boots & poles, or snowboard &

boots). *Clothing rentals* $24. *Cross-country equipment* (skis & poles) $17.47. *Snowshoeing equipment* $23.18. **Credit** AmEx, MC, V.

Grouse Mountain

6400 Nancy Greene Way, North Vancouver (604 984 0661; snow report 604 986 6262/ www.grousemountain.com). Bus 232, 236. **Open** 9am-10pm daily. **Rates** *Lift tickets* $42; free-$32 concessions; $110 family. *Downhill lessons* $33/hour drop-ins; $66/hour private; $99/hour semi-private (2 people). **Rental rates** *One-day ski or snowboard package* $39 (jacket and trousers: $25). *Snowshoes* $15. **Credit** AmEx, DC, MC, V. **Map** p253 Z1. Grouse boasts a 91m (300ft) half pipe for snowboarders, snowshoe trails, a mountain top ice rink, and the Observatory fine dining restaurant with a fabulous view of the city. It's probably best to head up via the Skyride cable car although of course there is the Grouse Grind for the super fit (*see p85*).

Mount Seymour

1700 Mount Seymour Road, North Vancouver (604 986 2261/www.mountseymour.com). Shuttle bus from Lonsdale Quay SeaBus. **Open** 9.30am-10pm Mon-Fri; 8.30am-10pm Sat, Sun. Closed Apr-Dec, exact dates depending on snow. *Snowtube park* 10am-6pm Mon-Thur, Sun; 10am-8pm Fri, Sat. **Rates** *Lift tickets* $36/$19-$25 concessions. **Credit** MC, V. There's a shuttle service 7 days a week in season (24-hour snow report 604 718 7771). Some people use the 10km (6mile) snowshoe trails for cross-country skiing.

Trips Out of Town

Getting Started   184
Excursions   188
Victoria &
    Vancouver Island   195
The Okanagan   207
Whistler   213

Features

On the ocean wave   185
Sea to sky   191
Thar she blows!   199
Spa around   204
Grape expectations   210
Seeking powder   221
Bro-speak: lessons in the
    local lingo   222

Maps

Trips out of Town   186
Victoria   196
Okanagan   209
Whistler   217

Kelowna. *See p207*.

Getting Started

So far away, so close.

Ferry to Bowen Island.

British Columbia is nearly four times the size of Great Britain. It's 1,300 kilometres (808 miles) long (north-south), and 700 kilometres (435 miles) wide. Nestled in the south-west corner, the city of Vancouver is about as central to the province as Exeter is to the UK. Yet, more than three quarters of BC's four million population live either in the Greater Vancouver Lower Mainland region or on neighbouring Vancouver Island – so there's an awful lot of wilderness left over to explore in the hinterlands.

Those characteristics that make British Columbia so attractive – the wild coast, dotted with bare, rocky outcrops large and small; the mountain ranges, thick forests and glacier-fed rivers and lakes – have protected much of the province from development. But don't worry: 20,000 tourism-related businesses exist to help you make the most of it.

There are two trips that almost all visitors to Vancouver make: the mountain resort of **Whistler** (*see p213*) is just 120 kilometres (75 miles) north of the city and **Victoria**, BC's provincial capital, is a couple of hours away by ferry, or 30 minutes by float plane (*see p195*).

When they want to get away for the weekend, Vancouverites flock to the Gulf Islands, of which there are dozens. In the summer, the **Okanagan** (*see p207*) is another popular rural retreat about five hours drive to

the east. With some planning, adventurers can venture into the wilds of sea kayaking with whales, skiing off-piste, watching grizzly bears, or ranching in cowboy country. All is possible.

But even if you only have time to get a flavour, there is enough on the city's doorstep to serve as a microcosm for the rest of BC. You can hike in Manning Park; bathe in the hot springs at Harrison; visit Bowen Island, just a 20-minute ferry ride from West Vancouver, or take a scenic flight in a seaplane. And an afternoon is all you need to get up close and personal with the killer whales that make their home in the southern gulf waters.

GETTING AROUND

British Columbia has relatively few major highways. The basic choice is east/west or north/south. From Vancouver you can take Highway 99 north to Horseshoe Bay and Whistler, or south to the ferry terminal at Tsawwassen and the United States (Seattle is a 225-kilometre/140-mile drive; factor in another 30 minutes at the border). Or you can take Route 1, the Trans-Canada Highway, which runs east by way of the Fraser Valley and Kamloops, through the Rockies to Calgary, and all the way to Newfoundland (7,821 kilometres; 4,860 miles).

Pacific Coach Lines (604 662 8074, www. pacificcoach.com) runs a cheap daily shuttle service to Vancouver Island, as does **Greyhound** (604 482 8747, www.greyhound.ca). Greyhound also runs a bus north to Whistler and to Seattle. **TransLink** (604 953 3333, www.trans link.bc.ca) operates bus routes to the ferry terminals at Horseshoe Bay and Tsawwassen, and a comprehensive cheap public transport system throughout the Lower Mainland.

BC Ferries (toll free 1-888 223 3779, www. bcferries.com) connects the mainland with the larger Gulf Islands. You are recommended to book in advance for peak holiday periods and to check in at least 30 minutes prior to departure time – longer at weekend peaks. Tsawwassen, an hour south of Vancouver, is the best port for Victoria; Horseshoe Bay is a quicker route to Nanaimo and the north of Vancouver Island. Seaplanes flying out of Coal Harbour are another option and are an experience in their own right (*see p191* **Sea to sky**). **Helijet** (604 270 1484, www.helijet.com) also provides a Vancouver-Victoria service, at $179 one way.

British Columbia is not well served by rail, and to catch a train down the west coast to San Francisco, you will first need to go to Seattle.

Although transport between large urban centres is relatively straightforward, to really explore British Columbia you will need to rent a car – a small four door can be as cheap as $30 a day, plus taxes. Petrol prices rocketed by up to 20 per cent in 2005, but are still a fraction of those in the UK. (For car rental services, *see p229*.) In the winter months, driving conditions in the north can be treacherous, but snow is rarely a problem on the Lower Mainland.

TOURIST INFORMATION

The **Tourism Vancouver Touristinfo Centre** at the Plaza level, 200 Burrard Street (near Canada Place) has a free reservation and information service and offers some discounts. Despite the name, it covers all of British Columbia. It's open 8.30am-5pm Mon-Sat (604 683 2000, www.tourismvancouver.com).

TELEPHONE CODES

When calling long distance from Vancouver, you will need to dial 1 before the area code. That includes numbers beginning 604 that aren't in the local Vancouver area.

On the ocean wave

One of the most enjoyable ways to see Vancouver's architecture, parks and beaches is by boat. Within paddling distance of the city harbours, boaters can see beaches, cafés and cityscape along False Creek and English Bay, survey the industry of an international port in Burrard Inlet, dock at markets on Granville Island and Lonsdale Quay, and appreciate just how enormous Stanley Park really is. You are advised to steer clear of the Lions Gate Bridge, though, where the currents can be dangerous. Kayaks and canoes are available from **Ecomarine Kayak** (*see p176*).

Getting away from the city, Indian Arm is a 30-kilometre (19-mile) fjord on the North Shore. The most popular launching site is Deep Cove, a pretty village a 30-minute drive over the Second Narrows Bridge (*see p81*). Here you can begin to appreciate the beauty and diversity of BC's shores – and probably see a seal or two. **Deep Cove Canoe and Kayak Rentals** (604 929 2268, www.deep covekayak.com) will rent a single kayak for $28-$32 for two hours, or $56-$60 a day, and also offer lessons. Reservations are recommended. **Lotus Land Tours** will pick you up from your hotel and throw in a salmon beach barbecue for $149 a head (604 684 4922, www.lotuslandtours.com). Although

you can kayak any time of year, March to October is the most clement season.

If paddle power sounds too much like hard work, **Vancouver's Harbour Cruises Ltd** (North Foot of Denman Street, 604 688 7246, www.boatcruises.com) offers a narrated tour of the harbour as well as a popular dinner cruise. You can get your hands on a sailboat for as little as $25 an hour at **Mac Sailing**, at the Jericho Sailing Centre in West Point Grey (1300 Discovery Street, 604 224 7245, www.macsailing.com). **Blue Pacific Yacht Charters** (1519 Foreshore Walk, Granville Island, toll free 1-800 237 2392, www.bluepacificcharters.ca) specialises in sail and large boat charters, which can be rented by the week. A five-sleeper powerboat goes for $2,500, while $5,600 will get you a 17-metre (55-foot) mahogany sailboat. The company also offers customised scuba dive vacations. At **Bonnie Lee Boat Rentals** (104-1676 Duranleau Street, Granville Island, 604 290 7447, www.bonnielee.com), you can rent a four-seater speed boat for $60 per hour. Nearby **Granville Island Boat Rentals** (1696 Duranleau Street, 604 682 6287, www.granvilleislandboatrentals.com) offers a similar deal.

Trips Out of Town

Trips Out of Town

Clendinning
Prov. Park

Mt Tinniswood

Duffey
Lake

Pemberton
Ice Cap

Pemberton

Nairn Falls

Stein River

Stein Valley
Prov. Park

LILLOOET RANGE

Skihist Mtn
2944m

Callaghan
Lake P. Park

99

Lillooet
Lake

Whistler
(p216)

Blackcomb
(p217)

Mehatl Creek
P. Park

Whistler Ski Resort

Elaho River

Jervis Inlet

Squamish River

Garibaldi
Prov. Park

Nahatlatch River

Golden
Ears
Prov. Park

Tantalus
P. Park

Brackendale
(p215)

Squamish
(p215)

Spipiyus
P. Park

Britannia
Beach
(p215)

Tetrahedron
Park

99

Harrison
Lake

Sechelt

Lions
Bay

Mt Seymour
Park

Pinecone
Burke
P. Park

Pitt
Lake

Stave
Lake

Harrison
Hot Springs
(p190)

Gibsons

Horseshoe Bay
Bowen Island
(p188)

West Vancouver

North Vancouver

Indian
Arm
Park

Port Moody

Coquitlam

Haney

Chilliwack

Nanaimo

VANCOUVER

Burnaby

7

Mission

STRAIT OF GEORGIA

New Westminster

See pp246-247

Langley
Fort Langley
(p190)

Cultus
Lake

Richmond
Steveston (p189)

Surrey

1

Abbotsford

See p209

Valdes
Island

Ladner

Delta

Tsawwassen

White
Rock

Aldergrove

Mt Baker
3285m

Ladysmith

Gulf
Islands
Galiano
Island
(p205)

Blaine

Chemainus

Mayne
Island
(p205)

5

Saltspring
Island
(p205)

Pender
Island
(p205)

Saturna
Island
(p205)

Orcas
Island

Bellingham

Lake
Whatcom

Duncan

1

Sidney

San
Juan Island

Lopez
Island

Lummi
Island

Salish
Bay

9

20

Butchart
Gardens

17

Sedro Wooley

VICTORIA
(p195)

See p196

Whidbey
Island

5

Sooke

20

530

Dungeness
Spit

Oak Harbour

Camano
Island

Arlington

Port Townsend

Excursions

Into the great wide open.

Day Trips

Bowen Island

A mini-paradise of mountains, rainforest and lakes, the 52-square-kilometre (20-square-mile) **Bowen Island** is just nine kilometres (5.5 miles) across the water from West Vancouver and 20 minutes by ferry. A tourist magnet since the early 1900s, Bowen still has the peace and tranquillity of a different age. Nearly half the island is forest, with abundant trails for walking, biking and horseback riding. (Although the ferry takes cars, most visitors prefer to leave their vehicle at Horseshoe Bay.)

A great day trip might include stocking up on picnic supplies at the **Ruddy Potato**, hiking through Crippen Park woods to Killarney Lake and then back to Snug Cove for a sup of local-brewed beer at **Doc Morgan's Inn & Pub** before dinner at **Blue Eyed Mary's**.

Daytrippers can rent bicycles from the **Bike Rentals Place** and add more distance to the itinerary, including a trip to **Artisan Square** (www.artisansquare.com). Featuring a dozen galleries and studios for weaving, pottery, jewellery, yoga and dance, a handful of shops and two cafés, this little village reflects the creative flare of Bowen's substantial artistic community: Silver Fern Florist is a beautiful flower shop, built right into the mountainside.

Bike Rentals Place

Union Steamship Marina parking lot, next to ferry terminal (604 999 7462/www.thebikerentals place.com). **Open** *Summer only* 11.30am-5pm Sat, Sun and holidays; by reservation only Mon-Fri.

Ruddy Potato

201-3 Dorman Road (604 947 0098/www.ruddy potato.com). **Open** 9am-7.30pm Mon-Thur, Sat; 9am-8.30pm Fri; 9am-6.30pm Sun. **Credit** MC, V.

Silver Fern Florist

D17 547 Artisan Lane (604 947 0070/www. silverfernflorist.com). **Open** 10am-5pm Mon-Sat; 11am-5pm Sun. **Credit** MC, V.

Where to eat & stay

Many come to Bowen Island just to stroll along the boardwalk and have dinner in Snug Cove. The aforementioned Blue Eyed Mary's offers the finest dining on the island, from chef Carol Wallace, formally of Vancouver's acclaimed Bishop's. **Tuscany Wood Oven Pizza** has a patio but it's classier inside, where smoked wild salmon pizza and southern Italian dishes are expertly prepared. **Bowen Island Pub** also serves pizza (including the Roadkill Special: ham, Italian sausage, bacon and pepperoni) as well as burgers appropriately deemed Big Kahunas, and the usual pub fare.

There are no hotel, motel or camping operations on Bowen, but plenty of B&Bs and some cabins to rent. Check www.bowen-island-bc.com/directory/accommodations.html for listings, and note that in the summer, many places insist on a two-night minimum stay.

Blue Eyed Mary's

433 Trunk Road (604 947 2583). **Open** *Apr-Sept* 5-9pm Wed-Sun. *Oct-Mar* 5-9pm Thur-Sun. **Main courses** $16-$26. **Credit** MC, V.

Bowen Island Pub

479 Bowen Trunk Road (604 947 2782/www.bowen pub.bowenisland.org). **Open** noon-1.30am Mon-Sat; noon-12.45am Sun. **Main courses** $6.25-$14.95. **Credit** MC, V.

Doc Morgan's Inn & Pub

Union Steamship Marina (604 947 0808/www. steamship-marina.bc.ca). **Rates** $100-$200. 2 night minimum stay May-Oct. **Open** *Restaurant* 11am-midnight Mon-Thur, Sun; 11am-1am Sat, Sun. Closed Christmas Day and first three weeks in January. **Main courses** $15-$20. **Credit** AmEx, MC, V.

Tuscany Wood Oven Pizza

451 Government Road (604 947 0550/www.tuscany pizza.com). **Open** *June-early Sept* 5-9.30pm daily; 10am-2.30pm Sat, Sun brunch. *Sept-May* 5-9.30pm Wed-Sun. **Main courses** $10.95-$18.95. **Credit** MC, V.

Getting there

Ferries run from Horseshoe Bay (the journey from downtown via Highway 99 north over Lions Gate Bridge takes 15 minutes). Ferries run approximately one an hour and the crossing takes 20 minutes. Pre-book during peak periods.

BC Ferries

Horseshoe Bay (toll free 1-888 223 3779/www.bc ferries.com). Bus 250, 257. **Rates** *to Bowen Island* $6.25-$6.50/passenger; $3.25 5-11s; free under-5s; $18-$20.50/passenger vehicle. **Credit** AmEx, MC, V.

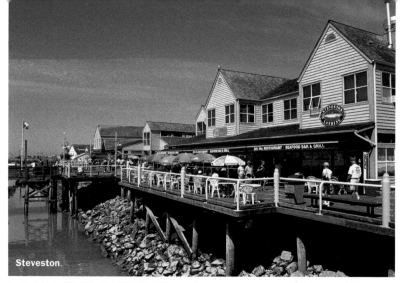
Steveston.

Tourist information

Take the first right after leaving the ferry for the **Visitors Info Centre** (604 947 9024, www.bowenisland.org) and pick up a *Bowen Island Guide*, which lists accommodation, restaurants, cafés, kayak rentals, ferry and water taxi information, and a brochure, *Things to See or Do on Bowen*.

Steveston

Strolling past the brick storefronts and boardwalk bistros, it's easy to presume that Steveston was assembled just for tourists. In fact, the 100-year-old fishing village is very much a working town, home to the largest fishing fleet in Canada – more than 600 vessels. That's not to say they don't take kindly to visitors: in the summertime, Steveston's shops and restaurants are packed, and the fishing boats line up at the pier to sell fresh fish straight out of the net. You can go whale watching from here, although if you're heading out to Vancouver Island it has better options (*see p199* **Thar she blows!**).

But the town centre is more than just fish and kitsch. Like much of the greater Vancouver area, Steveston's heritage is diverse and at times controversial. A substantial population of Japanese immigrants settled here at the turn of the 20th century, but their stay was marred first by a devastating fire that levelled their neighbourhood, then by forced internment during World War II. For a peek at Steveston's Japanese roots, head to the **Murakami Visitor Centre**, part of the **Britannia Heritage Shipyard**, on the southern end of Railway Avenue. The complex consists of ten buildings,

four of them restored: canneries and boatyards dating back as far as 1885. These are the finest surviving examples on the BC coast of a way of life essential to the development of the province. You may also find volunteers restoring old wooden boats using traditional craft methods. Murakami House was built on stilts over the marsh, and features artefacts from the Murakami family, two parents and ten children, who lived there from the early 1930s to 1942 (when Japanese immigrants were interned).

Other immigrant groups, including the British, Europeans and most recently Chinese, found a happier life in town, and their continuing influence is seen in the storefronts on Moncton Street, Steveston's main thoroughfare. The latter group also made their mark with an imposing Buddhist temple (just east of town on Steveston Highway), which was constructed in the 1970s and houses an impressive Chinese classical garden.

Steveston is proud of its fishing history. Though all but one of its 15 working canneries are now gone, the **Gulf of Georgia Cannery** remains in operation, offering tours and a lively account of the town's signature profession. For another taste of small town history, head back to Moncton Street for the unmistakably small town **Steveston Museum and Post Office** – and post a letter home as you soak up the local culture. Just up the road from the cannery is Garry Point Park (entrance at the corner of 7th Avenue and Moncton Street), an open field abutting rocky beaches that give the locals some respite from the summer heat. At the eastern end is a small Japanese garden, and a fisherman's monument – a 4.6-metre (15-foot) sculpture of a needle used to mend fishing nets. The park also serves as entry point to a five-kilometre (three-mile) seafront dyke trail, popular with walkers and bikers alike.

Back in town, there are a surprising diversity of dining options, including Greek, Indian, Japanese and even Mexican. But fish and chips is the signature dish in Steveston, with a half-dozen restaurants offering it.

One of the best is **Pajo's**, which operates from a floating platform, just a stone's throw from the arriving fishing fleet. The fish (your choice of cod, halibut, or the local fave, salmon) is coated in a light, almost tempura-style crispy batter, and the chips are just crispy enough. For a more traditional option, try **Dave's Fish and Chips**, in the centre of town, where the batter is thick, the cod is light and flaky, and the beer selection is generous (Pajo's isn't licenced). Back on the water, the **Charthouse** offers solid sit-down fare, with an emphasis on local seafood and lovely views of the wharf.

Britannia Heritage Shipyard

5180 Westwater Drive, at Railway Avenue (604 718 8050). **Open** *May-Sept* 10am-6pm Tue-Sun. *Oct-Apr* noon-4pm Sat; 10am-2pm Sun. **Admission** free.

Gulf of Georgia Cannery

12138 4th Avenue, at W Chatham Street (604 664 9009/www.pc.gc.ca/gulfofgeorgiacannery). **Open** *May, June, Sept* 10am-5pm daily. *Apr, Oct* 10am-5pm Mon, Thur-Sun. *July, Aug* 10am-6pm daily. **Admission** $6.50; $3.25-$5.50 concessions; free under-6s; $16.25 family. **Credit** AmEx, MC, V.

Steveston Museum and Post Office

3811 Moncton Street, at 1st Avenue (604 271 6868). **Open** 9.30am-1pm, 1.30-5pm Mon-Sat. **Admission** free.

Where to eat & drink

Charthouse

200-3866 Bayview Street, at 2nd Avenue (604 271 7000). **Open** 11am-10pm daily. **Main courses** $6.95-$39.95. **Credit** MC, V.

Dave's Fish and Chips

3460 Moncton Street, at 3rd Avenue (604 271 7555). **Open** 11am-8pm daily. **Main courses** $7-$15. **Credit** MC, V.

Pajo's on the Wharf

Floating platform, at Bayview Street & 3rd Avenue (604 272 1588/www.pajos.com). **Open** *16 May-15 Sept* 11am-8pm daily (weather permitting). *16 Sept-15 May* phone ahead for hours. **Main courses** $2.59-$11.29. **No credit cards.**

Getting there

Steveston is 25 minutes from downtown. Take Highway 99 south (down Oak Street), then turn left on to the Steveston Highway to No. 1 Road and follow that south to Steveston.

Alternatively, take the 491 bus from Burrard Station (rush hour Mon-Fri only), or the 98 B-Line from Burrard Station to Richmond Centre and transfer to 401, 402, 407 or 410.

Tourist information

Steveston Visitor Kiosk

Moncton Street & 3rd Avenue (Tourism Richmond 604 271 8280/www.steveston.bc.ca). **Open** *21 May-30 June, Labour Day-30 Sept* 10am-6pm Fri-Sun. *1 July-Labour Day* 10am-6pm daily.

The Fraser Valley

It's an hour's drive east along the Trans-Canada Highway (Route 1) before the city landscape gives way to the farming flatlands of the Lower Mainland, and another hour until the road weaves into the Cascade Mountains beside Hope. From here, the road forks eastward to Manning Park or north along the canyon walls of the Fraser River. Either choice makes for a terrific day trip, with any number of destinations along the way. If you have time for a longer trip, Manning Park is en route to the Okanagan Valley, and the northern route affords a roundabout journey to Whistler, popularly known as the Circle Trip.

Fort Langley

One of the province's earliest European settlements, **Fort Langley National Historic Site** is a reconstructed Hudson's Bay Company trading post where costumed interpreters give visitors a feel for pioneer life. The surrounding village, not to be confused with fast-sprawling Langley town, is charming and filled with galleries, bookstores and quality coffee houses. Langley's pastoral countryside is an equal delight, for its horses, hot air balloon rides and even the odd winery. If you have children, the trip is easily combined with a visit to Vancouver's zoo, 35 kilometres (22 miles) from the city (*see p145*).

Harrison Hot Springs

Only 90 minutes from Vancouver, **Harrison Hot Springs** has been a favourite getaway for city folk ever since prospectors first discovered its mineral hot springs in the 1850s. Harrison quickly became British Columbia's finest resort, and today the Harrison Hot Springs Resort & Spa – and its famous Copper Dining Room – attracts a loyal family crowd. In addition to fishing and boating on its 64-kilometre (40-mile) lake, Harrison offers hiking, cycling, camping and an amazing sand sculpture competition,

Sea to sky

Unless you happen to live in one of the apartments that overlook Coal Harbour – in which case you're likely to begrudge the regular gnat-like drone – the sight of a seaplane coming in over Stanley Park, gracefully banking in front of Grouse Mountain before coasting to a stop on the calm waters of the Burrard Inlet is a Vancouver image you'll cherish. And the residents have little to complain about. Float planes have been built and harboured on this spot since 1915, long before any of the apartment blocks went up (and 16 years before Vancouver had its own airport).

In aviation's infancy the float plane (a plane with pontoons rigged under the fuselage) was considered the safest option for a flight over any body of water, but by 1927, when Charles Lindbergh crossed the Atlantic in a landplane, the writing was on the wall for the less aerodynamic model. Yet BC's cluster of remote coastal communities have kept the seaplane busy in this part of the world, and **Harbour Air** – which operates a weekday commuter run between Vancouver and Victoria, Vancouver and Nanaimo, and Vancouver and the Gulf Islands – is the largest all-seaplane airline in the world.

Harbour Air maintains single pilot DeHavilland float planes which went out of

production in the mid 1960s, but which remain the most successful seaplanes ever built. The Beaver seats six passengers, the Otter up to 14. **West Coast Air** runs a similar daily service between Vancouver and Victoria, also with the DeHavilland Beaver and a slightly larger Twin Otter aircraft. Both companies offer boarding at Coal Harbour (the terminal is at 1075 W Waterfront Road, two blocks west of Canada Place) or at Vancouver Airport (South Terminal) and fly to Inner Harbour, Victoria for $109 one-way (currently with a $5 fuel surcharge). Both also offer a range of enticing tours and private charters to the Sunshine Coast, coastal mountains and glaciers, and the Gulf Islands, at approximately $250 per person, depending on the size of your party.

Harbour Air

1075 W Waterfront Road, Downtown (604 274 1277/www.harbour-air.com). **Open** 6am-10pm Mon-Thur; 7am-7.30pm Fri-Sun. **Credit** AmEx, MC, V.

West Coast Air

1075 W Waterfront Road, Downtown (604 606 6888/www.westcoastair.com). **Open** 6.30am-7pm daily. **Credit** AmEx, MC V.

Trips Out of Town

held annually during the second week of September. At nearby **Harrison Mills**, sights include the 1906 Kilby General Store and Rowena's on the River, a refurbished heritage home turned elegant B&B. Rowena's River's Edge Restaurant is a great pit stop, especially when combined with a round of golf at the adjoining Sandpiper Golf Club. Garden enthusiasts should include a visit to David Minter Gardens; it's a stunning showcase of 22 themed gardens spread over 11 hectares (27 acres) with two restaurants on site.

Beyond Hope

Nearer to Hope are two detours: **Bridal Falls** where water tumbles down 122 metres (400 feet) on the face of Mount Cheam, and the **Othello Quintette Tunnels**. Built between 1911 and 1916 as the last leg of the Kettle Valley Railway, they are a Herculean feat of engineering.

By and large, **Hope** itself is a pretty, pass-through community, though its two dozen or so chainsaw carvings encourage a few Kodak moments. Outdoor adventurers will likely head to **Manning Park** for activities that range from easy-to-hike interpretive trails (some are wheelchair accessible), to fishing, canoeing and skiing. The Okanagan Valley is another couple of hours' drive from here.

River rafters, however, will head north past Hell's Gate towards **Lytton**. This is where the Thompson river converges with the Fraser

(BC's longest), and you can raft both. The spring snow melt creates furious whitewater in the tall, narrow canyons. (Try Kumsheen Raft Adventures for top choice, 250 455 2296, www.kumsheen.com).

For many folks though, driving through the canyon to **Hell's Gate** is reward enough; this is where the Fraser River surges some 200 million gallons of water through a 35 metre (110 foot) gorge. That's the volume of Niagara Falls, doubled! The Hell's Gate Airtram takes visitors on a gentle 150-metre (500-foot) descent from the highway, into the gorge, where it hovers over the gushing water before continuing to the patio and restaurant on the other side.

If you've time, drive on to **Lillooet**, an historic community that marks Mile 0 of the Cariboo Trail which, in the 1800s, took miners north to the goldfields. It's also where Highway 99 turns west for an achingly beautiful drive towards Pemberton and 'the back door' into Whistler. Just be sure your vehicle has good brakes; the mountain inclines are very steep and it's not a drive to be done in winter.

Fort Langley National Historic Site
For listings, *see p145*.

Hell's Gate Airtram
43111 Trans Canada Highway, Boston Bar (604 867 9277/www.hellsgateairtram.com). **Open** 2006 *13 Apr-18 May; 5 Sept-14 Oct* 10am-4pm daily. *19 May-4 Sept* 9.30am-5.30pm daily. **Admission** $15; $9-$12 concessions; free under-5s. **Credit** MC, V.

'From space, the planet is blue... the territory not of humans, but of the whale.' See p189.

Minter Gardens

52892 Bunker Road, Rosedale (office 604 792 3799/gift shop & admissions 604 794 7191/ restaurants 604 794 7044/www.mintergardens.com). **Open** *Apr, Oct* 10am-5pm daily. *May, Sept* 9am-5.30pm daily. *June* 9am-6pm daily. *July, Aug* 9am-7pm daily. **Admission** $13.95; $8.95-$11.95 concessions; free under-5s. **Credit** MC, V.

Where to stay, eat and drink

The usual suspects are scattered through the Fraser Valley but there are some good restaurants in Langley Village and Harrison. The eateries at Minter Gardens and Hell's Gate are surprisingly good.

Harrison Hot Springs Resort & Spa

100 Esplanade Avenue (604 796 2244/www. harrisonresort.com). **Open** 7am-9pm daily. **Main courses** $5-$35 (patio fare to fine dining). **Rates** $129-$250. **Credit** AmEx, MC, V.

Lakeview Restaurant

150 Esplanade, Harrison Hot Springs (604 796 9888). **Open** 10.30am-7pm daily. **Main courses** $5-$12 (fish & chips). **Credit** V.

River's Edge Restaurant

Rowena's on the River, 14282 Morris Valley Road, Harrison Mills (toll free 1-800 661 5108/www. rowenasinn.com). **Open** 8am-9pm daily. **Main courses** $7-15 lunch; $14-$24 dinner. **Rates** $125-$250. **Credit** MC, V.

Getting there

By car take the Trans-Canada Highway 1 east out of Vancouver and just keep going. As you near Hope, there are signs for Harrison, Minter Gardens and other detours. Fill up at Hope, and continue heading East on Highway 3 to Manning Park or take the Trans-Canada north through the Fraser Canyon.

Tourist Information

Lytton Tourist Information

400 Fraser Street, Lytton (250 455 2523/ www.lytton.ca). **Open** 9am-5pm Mon-Sat.

Expeditions

Few places in the world offer the diverse nature of British Columbia, and visitors to Vancouver should plan at least a couple of days to explore the great outdoors. Sure, you can do it on the fly – rent a car, toss in camping supplies and head for your choice of woods, water or mountains. But for those who plan ahead, here are some choice, once-in-a-lifetime BC experiences ranging from $164,000 a week to $12 a night.

Backcountry huts

Amid the mighty ranges of BC's Rocky and Selkirk Mountains is a series of self-service backcountry huts operated by the **Alpine Club of Canada** (403 678 3200, www.alpine clubofcanada.ca). Ranging in size from cabins that sleep six, to chalets with bunks for 20, they are well supplied for cooking, heat and light.

Bill Putnam Hut in the Selkirks is renowned for its epic powder skiing. Surrounded by towering, Gothic-looking peaks, the two-storey lodge is more like a wilderness palace than a hut and comes complete with a wood-fired sauna – a luxury on crisp winter nights. A helicopter ferries groups of up to 20 people from Golden, BC. Most days start with expeditions up majestic peaks and end with a long ski down to the hut. Nicknamed Fairy Meadow, this hut sees near capacity year-round, so book early.

For summer hiking, **Elizabeth Parker Hut**, in Yoho National Park, is surrounded by trails through cathedral-like rainforest of cedar and hemlock. Visitors arrive here for a chance to spot wolf, cougar, deer, elk, moose, mountain sheep, and bears. You'll also find streams of salmon and trout. This hut can be used as a base for a trip to the **Abbot Pass Hut**, an all-stone cabin at almost 3,000 metres (10,000 feet).

Reservations are required at all huts, most of which range from $12 to $30 per person, per night. In winter high-season Bill Putnam Hut costs $725 per person, per week, including helicopter; book a year in advance.

Fishing

BC offers superb fishing and a stay at a remote floating lodge can transform the catch of the day into a metaphor for how nature interconnects. Framed by mountains and accessible by boat or float plane only, **Blackfish Lodge** (206 789 1229, www. blackfishlodge.com), on the north-east coast of Vancouver Island, is a place of seclusion, contemplation and some of the choicest salmon, trout, steelhead and halibut fishing on the continent. The cabin's laid-back owners, Chris and Hannah Bennett, have lived at the lodge for 16 years and share a vast, intuitive knowledge of fishing in the rivers, lakes and protected ocean waters that surround their comfortable cedar cabin. Your stay is tailored to your schedule: they'll take you whale-watching or sea kayaking, lead you to hiking trails, and cook meals whenever you want. Chris is an accomplished fly fisherman and fine teacher, who's happy to introduce novices to the art. Freshwater spots are located about a half-hour boat ride from the lodge and require moderate

Trips Out of Town

hikes. Once there, though, you're rewarded with enchanting scenery and great fishing.

Rates for the lodge (capacity: six) range between $550 (April or October) and $700 (July, August) per person per night, including food, drink (beer, soft drinks, and wine), and guide fees, and do not include air transport to the lodge. Also recommended: **King Pacific Lodge** (www.kingpacificlodge.com).

Sea kayaking

In the northern wilderness of BC, grizzlies are found in larger, more accessible numbers than perhaps anywhere else on earth. Several tour operators offer trips to observe these powerful animals. **Coast Mountain Expeditions** (250 285 2823, www.coastmountainexpeditions.com) combines a sea kayak tour with the chance to see grizzly bears and meet First Nations people.

The expedition begins at Quadra Island (near Campbell River on Vancouver Island) with kayaking practice and the first night at a lodge. Three days of kayaking and camping brings you to PapKnach River camp, home of the Xwemahlkwu people. Up to 50 bears gather within ten kilometres (six miles) of the camp in the peak autumn season, when salmon return to the river, and viewing takes place both from platforms and your kayak. After two days getting to know grizzlies and the local culture – accommodation is in simple bunkhouses and all meals are taken with the First Nations people, learning about their customs and traditions – a boat will pick you up for the return journey. Paddling averages five hours per day in single or double kayaks, for a maximum of ten fit participants. Cost for the week is $1,525.

Operating in the Johnstone Strait further north up the coast of Vancouver Island – the famous Inside Passage – **Northern Lights Expeditions** (toll free 1-800 754 7402, www.seakayaking.com) offers day and week-long sea kayaking itineraries, including whale and grizzly watching, based at lodges, camping, or from the *Spirit Bear* yacht, at approximately US$250 per night. No previous kayaking experience is necessary; the northern lights themselves are a potential bonus.

Heli-skiing

The beauty of heli-skiing is that it allows exceptional experiences in the wilderness without the hassle of hiking long hours to reach vast virgin slopes and lodges. After each descent, a chopper takes skiers back up to the peaks and, at day's end, they can be sauna-bound in minutes. If you are a strong, very experienced skier, able to ski on all types

of terrain and in all snow conditions (not only powder), then you are ready for heli-skiing. But it doesn't come cheap.

Canadian Mountain Holidays (toll free 1-800 661 0252, www.cmhski.com) offers groups week-long adventures, including lodge accommodation, meals, specially designed heli-skis, experienced guide and helicopter for approximately $1,000 per night. (Want to lose the group? A private week at their Valemount lodge goes for a cool $164,000). Also recommended: **Mike Wiegele Heli-Skiing** (www.wiegele.com).

Ranching

Picture a working cowboy ranch in the middle of tranquil wilderness. Now, add a luxury spa, gourmet food and luxurious accommodation. If a galloping horse ride is best followed by deep, Thai massage, then **Echo Valley Ranch and Spa**, near Kootenay, BC (toll free 1-800 253 8831, www.evranch.com) is ideal.

Key elements make the experience spectacular. First is the location: mountains to the east; the near desert conditions of the Fraser Canyon to the south; grasslands to the west; and countless lakes of the Cariboo plateau to the north – all within an eight-kilometre (five-mile) radius. This near-mythological paradise offers adventures galore, including 'flight-seeing' in the ranch's Cessna, mountain-climbing, fly-fishing and white-water-rafting.

The words 'gourmet cuisine' and 'cowboy' rarely rub shoulders, but the Echo Valley Ranch offers outstanding food – virtually all grown or raised on its own organic farm.

The ranch is 400 kilometres (250 miles) north of Vancouver, in the Cariboo Region of BC. Capacity is 26 people; prices range from around $2,000 per week in low season to $5,000 for the full-service Thai spa experience.

For a more authentic western ranching adventure, the **Flying U Ranch** (250 456 7717, www.flyingu.com) claims to be Canada's oldest guest ranch. Situated on the shores of Green Lake, BC (a five hour drive from Vancouver), the Flying U remains true to wild frontier customs. At this 'working cattle ranch' you are assigned a horse and expected to care for it during your stay. You learn to square dance, drink at the Longhorn Saloon, shop at the General Store and sleep in wood stove-heated 1920s log cabins. If there's a 'living museum' ambience about the ranch, it's because it was founded in 1886. Prices are $140-$160 per adult per night, with a three day minimum stay, with reductions for children and in low season. You'll find similar experiences at **Crystal Waters Guest Ranch** (www.crystalwatersranch.com).

Victoria & Vancouver Island

Wild seas and high teas.

It wouldn't be unreasonable to think that Vancouver, the biggest city in BC, would be its capital. Nor to expect it to be sited on Vancouver Island. But no. Vancouver sits firmly on the edge of the continental mainland, while Victoria, the provincial capital, lies south-west across the Strait of Georgia on Vancouver Island. The island itself stretches 454 kilometres (282 miles) along the western coast of BC, with Victoria tucked away in its far south-eastern corner. With a population of 750,000 in an area the size of England and a capital in Victoria that predates its brash cousin across the water, this is one trip out of town that any visitor to Vancouver should consider making.

Victoria

British Columbia's provincial capital, **Victoria**, has the look and feel of Vancouver's maiden aunt: old-fashioned and decorous, with a somewhat faded charm. Things were not always this way. Located on the southern tip of Vancouver Island (diplomats put a dink in the 49th Parallel to keep the city in Canadian territory), Victoria was prized by the British for its natural harbour, clement weather and fertile hinterland. (For much the same reasons, ten Lekwammen villages were dotted along the shore of what is now Greater Victoria.)

The Hudson's Bay Company established its local headquarters here in 1843. 'Fort Victoria' prospered during the 1850s and '60s – the gold rush years – when it became both an essential staging post and an administrative centre. In 1866 it was the obvious capital for the newly minted province; the Parliament Buildings were completed in 1897.

By the 1920s the city's lustre was beginning to fade. Across the Strait of Georgia Vancouver was eclipsing it in importance as a port and, with the Canadian Pacific Railway ending there, as a train terminus. However, Victoria remained undaunted. In place of industrial expansion, the town cultivated its British heritage, preserving the turn-of-the-century architecture that was demolished or allowed to fall into disrepair and disrepute in Vancouver.

Along with the buildings, certain manners and customs were also preserved: high tea at the Fairmont Empress Hotel (or 101 less formal tea rooms) for example. British visitors may find the 'olde England' accoutrements twee and chintzy, and the city isn't about to shake its retirement community atmosphere, but at least it stands in sharp relief to the sprawling strip malls that dominate the North American urban landscape. A contained, walkable town that makes the most of its waterfront and the mildest climate in Canada, Victoria is a congenial spot to recharge your batteries for a day or two before (or after) venturing into the wilds of Vancouver Island.

Sightseeing

Attracting a seemingly unstoppable flood of tourists, Victoria has devised more attractions than many cities twice its size. Many of these are quite dispensable, or at best of limited appeal. Unless there is a pressing need to escape the rain, you won't want to spend much more than an hour in the Art Gallery, Craigdarroch Castle, Crystal Gardens, the Maritime Museum, Miniature World, the Pacific Undersea Gardens, the Royal London Wax Museum, the Victoria Butterfly Museum or the Bug Zoo... at least most are priced accordingly.

Victoria's appeal stems not from these estimable cultural institutions, but from its ambience and environment. Its heart is centred on the Inner Harbour and the Old Town behind it – a relatively compact area easy to cover on foot. Horse-drawn carriage tours and open-topped double-decker buses will expand your horizons just a little to take in the pleasant borough south of downtown towards Ogden Point, a man-made breakwater with beautiful views looking across the Juan de Fuca Strait towards the Olympic Mountains and the US.

The Inner Harbour is dominated by two Francis Rattenbury buildings: the **Parliament Buildings** at 501 Belleville Street (250 387 3046) and the **Fairmont Empress Hotel** at 721 Government Street (250 384 8111, www.fairmont.com/empress).

Trips Out of Town

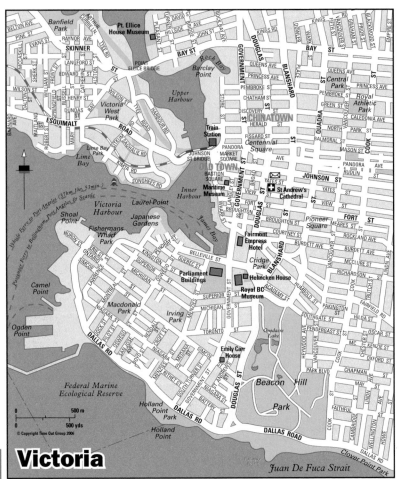

Victoria

Rattenbury was just 25 years old when he won the commission to design the provincial legislature in 1893. An Englishman from Leeds, he had recently arrived in Victoria; it is thought that the pen name under which he entered the competition helped his cause: 'A BC Architect'. The Parliament Buildings are grand, with six fortress-like turrets facing the harbour and a rotunda at the centre. Free guided tours are available (every 20 minutes in summer; hourly in winter) but the legislature is best seen at night, when more than 3,000 light bulbs give it a fairy land glow – a tradition which dates from its opening in 1897, when the lights were a Diamond Jubilee tribute to Queen Victoria.

Rattenbury also undertook several commissions for the Canadian Pacific Railway, of which the most famous is the Empress Hotel. A variation on the CPR French chateau style, the seven-storey Empress is more imposing even than the Parliament Buildings from which it takes its turrets. Inside it's just as opulent, with lounges and lobbies in the Edwardian Imperial style. Expressly designed to transform the Inner Harbour causeway built on reclaimed mudflats into a tourist-friendly beauty spot, the Empress fulfilled its brief.

Among Rattenbury's other buildings, the best known are the Crystal Gardens and Montreal Bank in Victoria; the Roedde House in Barclay Square, Vancouver (*see p56*); and the original courthouse building – now the Art Gallery – in Vancouver.

Despite his success, the architect was ostracised in British Columbia after he divorced his wife and remarried the twice-divorced Alma Pakenham, 30 years his junior. He took Alma back to England in 1930, but four years later, in an affair that scandalised and fascinated the nation, he was clubbed to death by Alma's lover, the 17-year-old chauffeur George Stoner. Although Alma was acquitted, she stabbed herself through the heart after Stoner was sentenced to hang, but the young man later had his sentence commuted to life imprisonment.

Between the Empress and the Parliament Buildings, but off to the side on the corner of Belleville and Government, the **Royal BC Museum** is the city's cultural jewel. The collection goes back to the 19th century, but the current building was opened in 1968, with a new foyer added in 1996.

Tucked away in the shadow of the south-east corner of the complex, Heritage Court encompasses Thunderbird Park, a cedar longhouse and carving shed alongside a thicket of totem poles; and Helmcken House, Victoria's oldest surviving dwelling, a simple log cabin dating back to 1852. A few blocks further south you find the **Emily Carr House**, which takes fashions forward to the early 1870s.

Strolling north up Government Street into the Old Town, take a peek in at **Roger's Chocolates** (913 Government Street) for the original art nouveau interior. Roger's have been making and selling chocolate here since World War I. The aroma alone is worth the detour, although it would be a shame not to taste too. Speaking of which, **EA Morris** at number 1110 is a splendidly tangy tobacconist.

Munro's Books at 1108 Government Street is a relatively new tenant for the 1909 Royal Bank. It's handsomely designed, with Doric columns before a recessed arched entrance and, although the interior decoration is austere, it's been sensitively restored and makes an impressive setting for this fine bookstore. The warehouses on Wharf Street are also well preserved, many dating from the 1860s.

Bastion Square is the site of the original Fort Vancouver, and a successful example of civic regeneration. Hard to believe now, with its sidewalk cafés, street entertainers, craft stalls and gas lamps, but for 50 years this was a car park. The **Maritime Museum** on the east side of the square has all manner of seafaring paraphernalia, though again, it's the building itself – BC's Supreme Court for most of its lifetime – which is more impressive. It's another Rattenbury design, this one dating to 1889.

Market Square, a couple of blocks north of Bastion, is another recovered public space that maximises access to restored many 19th century storefronts and restaurants. Retail wise, you'll find souvenir shops competing with Scottish, Irish and English knits, and outdoor equipment specialists.

Chinatown, a block north on Fisgard Street, has also been restored, although you won't find the opium dens, brothels and gambling joints which earned it the nickname 'Forbidden Town' in the 1880s. This was Canada's first Chinatown, and more than 15,000 immigrants passed through here in the wake of the gold rush. **Fan Tan Alley**, between Fisgard and Pandora Streets, is said to be the narrowest street in the whole of North America.

Roger's Chocolates.

Victoria Harbour Ferries (453 Head
Street, 250 708 0201, www.victoriaharbour
ferry.com) runs small boats on a daily schedule
(every 12-15 minutes in summer) to half a dozen
stops along the Inner Harbour. Tickets are $4
for a short harbour hop ($2 for under 12s) and
$16 ($14 seniors; $8 children) for the 45 minute
Harbour Tour or 55 minute Gorge Cruise.

Fisherman's Wharf – west of the US
customs office on Belleville Street, and a stop
on the Harbour Ferry route – is a pretty marina
of houseboats and yachts. You can buy fresh
fish here, or sign up for whalewatching
excursions with the legendary Captain Ron
(*see p199* **Thar she blows!**).

Butchart Gardens

Butchart Gardens, 21 kilometres (14 miles)
north of Victoria on Highway 17, are the city's
most heavily marketed attraction. Begun in
1904 by the wife of RP Butchart, a local cement
pioneer, the gardens fill 20 hectares (50 acres)
of the former limestone quarry. An organised
tour mecca, the gardens are overcrowded in the
summer; the best times to visit are as soon as
the doors open (before the buses make it in from
either the ferry or the city), or late afternoon,
when the crowds have dispersed. Summer
evenings see classical concerts and fireworks
displays on the lawns. The gardens themselves
are stuck in a timewarp, with gaudy displays of
begonias, dahlias and annuals planted with
little sensitivity to colour or texture. The best
areas are the Japanese garden – though this is
a pale imitation of the real thing – and the bog
garden, a quieter wooded area off to the side
of the centrepiece sunken garden. High tea is
available, and a fairly snooty affair it is too,
despite the endless tour groups. The gift shop,
shelves sagging with flowery china hats,
puppies and pigs, sums up the appeal.

Butchart Gardens

*800 Benvenuto Avenue, Brentwood Bay (toll free
1-866 652 4422/www.butchartgardens.com).*
Open 9am-dusk daily (later on fireworks evenings).
Admission $12-$23; $2.50-$11.50 children.
Credit AmEx, MC, V.

Emily Carr House

*207 Government Street (250 383 5843/www.emily
carr.com).* **Open** May, Sept 11am-4pm Tue-Sat;
June-Aug 11am-4pm daily. **Admission** $5; $3.50
6-18s; free under-6s; $15 family. **Credit** MC, V.
The birthplace of the artist and writer has been
painstakingly restored to the way it would have
looked in 1871. Note that the paintings here are
reproductions, for the real thing head to the otherwise undistinguished Art Gallery of Greater
Victoria, at 1040 Moss Street (250 384 4101,
www.aggv.bc.ca) or *see p27* and *p56*.

Fisherman's Wharf.

Maritime Museum

28 Bastion Square (250 385 4222/www.mmbc.bc.ca).
Open 16 Sept-14 June 9.30am-4.30pm daily. 15 June-
15 Sept 9.30am-5pm daily. **Admission** $8; $3-$5
concessions. **Credit** AmEx, MC, V.

Royal BC Museum

*675 Belleville Street (250 356 7226/www.royalbc
museum.bc.ca).* **Open** 9am-5pm daily. **Admission**
Museum $12.50; $8.50 concessions; free under-5s.
Museum & IMAX film $21; $16.95-$18.20
concessions; $5 under-5s. **Credit** AmEx, MC, V.
The Royal BC, with its three permanent galleries, is
the most visited museum in Canada. The First
Peoples Gallery has an array of Kwakwaka'wakw
ceremonial masks (a *son et lumière* exhibit provides
some keys to deciphering the iconography); carvings, models, a longhouse, and some extraordinary
early 20th-century footage of native ceremonies.

In the Modern History Gallery you can board a
partial replica of George Vancouver's HMS
Discovery from the 1790s, join the gold rush, or
explore the streets of turn of the century Victoria.
It's a similar mix to Vancouver's Storyeum, without
the poor actor/narrators.

If you have children, the Natural History Gallery
on the second floor is a must-see, with its artfully

rendered dioramas of BC ecologies (augmented with subtle atmospheric effects) and – the museum's undisputed prize – a life-size woolly mammoth. He's one species you are unlikely to meet elsewhere on your journey. This gallery has recently been supplemented with interactive climate-change models and exhibits. The museum's IMAX theatre is an extra charge with your admission.

Where to eat & drink

As you might expect of a city that gets crammed to the gills with tourists, there are plenty of bad places to eat, many of them in the 'Olde English' pub grub style. If you want to avoid being left with no other choice during high season, make reservations.

For breakfast, **John's Place** (723 Pandora Avenue, 250 389 0711, www.johnsplace.ca,

main courses $5.50-$14.95) is popular for traditional big-portioned American-style diner fare. Sports and music memorabilia line the walls of this noisy, bustling place made homely by the extremely friendly waitresses. An altogether different vibe can be found at **Mo:Le** (554 Pandora Avenue, 250 385 6653, main courses [breakfast & lunch only] $7.95-$13.95), where exposed brick walls and ramshackle furniture make for hipper surroundings. Locals come for plates laden with artful takes on traditional brunch fare.

The **Noodle Box** (626 Fisgard Street, 250 360 1312; 818 Douglas Street, 250 384 1314, www.thenoodlebox.net, main courses $7.50-$13) is a tasty, good value South-east Asian option. Healthy fare with pizzazz can be found at **Rebar** (50 Bastion Square, 250 361 9223, www.rebarmodernfood.com, main courses

Thar she blows!

Playing Ahab is one of BC's most popular tourist activities. Not that you'll see sperm whales. But there are plentiful orcas (also known as killer whales – though strictly speaking they're part of the dolphin family), and you could see Pacific grays, humpbacks and minke whales. More than 20,000 Pacific grays tour the west coast of Vancouver Island en route for the Bering Straits in March and April; 40 to 50 will stay in the area through the summer. All return to Baja California from October to December. Seals, dolphins, otters and sea lions are all relatively common.

What you'll see depends to some extent on where you set off from. You can sign up for tours in Granville Island, Vancouver, but the nearest whale boats actually depart from Steveston, the fishing village about 25 minutes south of downtown. From there, the expedition will last a minimum of three hours and possibly as long as five.

Victoria offers a greater choice of boats and shorter journey times: there are three pods of orcas (about 100 animals) resident year round in the Juan de Fuca Strait. In addition, between May and October up to 30 smaller pods of transient orcas pass through this neighbourhood. The orcas range about 160 kilometres (100 miles) a day, but you're unlikely to have to spend more than three hours in the boat. Tour operators here routinely guarantee sightings – which means that if the pods are too far away for comfort, or if the weather conditions aren't conducive, they won't go out. (Cancellations are by no

means uncommon.) In any case, if the forecast is for wind and rain, it's probably best to come back another day.

Boats are not allowed to run motors within 100 metres (330 feet) of the whales, and it is illegal to chase or drive the pods – however contact is often much closer than that, as an experienced captain will let the craft drift into the orcas' route. Although the time you spend face-to-fin with a whale will only be a matter of minutes, most people treasure this brief proximity to seven tonnes of blubber.

When choosing a tour, the deciding factor has to be the type of craft. In Victoria, the market leader is **Prince of Whales**, operating ten open-air zodiac boats (toll free 1-888 383 4884, www.princeofwhales.com, rates $75-$85 three hour tour; $65 under-18s). The zodiacs offer plenty of splash, if that's what you're after, but limited room to move and only five have toilet facilities. Covered boats are more comfortable, but less of a thrill – and higher passenger numbers cut down your access to the skipper. We recommend **SeaKing Adventures** (Fisherman's Wharf, Pier 4, 250 381 4173, www.seaking.ca). Captain Ron has been running whale tours for ten years and fished these waters for 25 years before that. His customised motorboat offers wrap-around seating for parties no larger than 12. It's a small business with the personal touch. Chances are you'll see a harbour seal before you even leave Fisherman's Wharf. In high season expect to pay about $80 plus tax or $55 for children younger than six.

Temptation in the **Temple**.

$6.95-$13.95), where a few fish options fill out a modern vegetarian menu supported by a made-to-order juice bar.

Much is made of high tea in Victoria, but if you're going to do it, just go the whole hog and reserve at the **Fairmont Empress Hotel** (721 Government Street, toll free 1-800 441 1414, 250 384 8111, www.fairmont.com/empress, afternoon tea from $30-$50) where finger sandwiches and scones have been a fact of life for almost a century. (Note: no ripped jeans, short shorts or jogging pants.) It's not cheap though. A curry in the Bengal Lounge is an alternative as long as you're over 19.

Canada's oldest brewpub, **Spinnakers Gastro Brewpub** (308 Catherine Street, 250 386 2739, www.spinnakers.com, main courses $10-$21), serves upscale pub food using local produce and free range meat.

Café Brio (944 Fort Street, 250 383 0009, www.cafe-brio.com, main courses $12-$28) receives widespread praise for its French and Italian-inspired cooking, but on our most recent visit we were disappointed by a couple of the dishes (one just didn't come together properly while the other's saltiness rendered it inedible) and complacent service. Still, it's packed every night, so we may have been unlucky.

A trendier space can be found at the **Temple** (525 Fort Street, 250 383 2313, www.thetemple.

ca, main courses $8-$21), a rare example of an old building sporting a modern wardrobe – including a furry wall and a bed. An extensive cocktail and wine list accompanies a smart, locally sourced menu of small plates and more substantial dishes. Home-made pâté served with a slick of fruity olive oil, rye bread and fruit compote, lamb cutlets on minted pea purée and a light as air blackberry Napoleon all hit the spot. Later on, DJs turn up the sounds.

For reliably good French country cooking, **Brasserie L'École** (1715 Government Street, 250 475 6260, www.lecole.ca, main courses $18) is everyone's favourite for moules, steak frites, local trout, braised duck legs and the like.

A short trip across the Johnson Street Bridge will bring you to English Inn & Resort's award-winning **Rosemeade** restaurant (429 Lampson Street, toll free 1-866 388 4353, 250 388 4353, www.englishinnresort.com, main courses $26-$30), where the elegant decor combines with sophisticated cuisine, beautifully presented in dishes such as a fish hot pot in a miso broth.

Where to stay

Though it is crammed with hotels and B&Bs, Victoria in the summer months is even more crowded with visitors. Finding a decent room at an affordable price can be a challenge and you'd be crazy to come without making a reservation. If you do find yourself without a room go to the **Tourism Victoria Visitor Info Centre** (*see p202*), or call their reservation hotline on 1-800 663 3883. Off-season rates plummet and there's usually a deal for the asking. Check www.tourismvictoria.com for up-to-date listings or www.bestbnbvictoria.com for the best B&Bs.

There's no getting away from the **Fairmont Empress Hotel** (721 Government Street, toll free 1-800 441 1414, 250 384 8111, www.fairmont.com/empress, doubles $179-$449), the number one landmark of Victoria's inner harbour. If you can afford the cost, give in to temptation, or, even better, push the boat out for one of the Gold rooms.

Victoria takes pride in its old English charm, sometimes to a fault. If you're after more up-to-date elegance, the **English Inn & Resort** (429 Lampson Street, toll free 1-866 388 4353, 250 388 4353, www.englishinnresort.com, suites $89-$499) is a luxurious option. Set on two hectares (five acres) of private land, a few minutes water taxi from the inner harbour, its classy rooms and suites provide a tranquil respite from the tourist throng. Its restaurant, the Rosemeade (*see p200*), has been busy picking up accolades and awards and is worth the trip.

For contemporary surroundings on the Inner Harbour, try **Laurel Point Inn** (680 Montreal Street, toll free 1-800 663 7667, 250 386 8721, www.laurelpoint.com, doubles $70-$204). Spacious rooms all have water views, and there's an indoor pool and Japanese garden.

Bed and breakfasts don't come more swish than **Andersen House** (301 Kingston Street, 250 388 4565, www.andersenhouse.com, doubles $78-$275), where modern art vies with the elegant Queen Anne building. Rooms are spacious and beautifully turned out, with soaker tubs or jacuzzis, CD players and complimentary Wi-Fi access.

Off the waterfront, **Swan's Suite Hotel** (506 Pandora Avenue, toll free 1-800 668 7926, 250 361 3310, www.swanshotel.com, suites $119-$359), in an 1880s grain store, offers high-ceilinged lofts decorated with local artworks and with full kitchens.

Isabella's Guest Suites (537 Johnson Street, 250 595 3815, www.isabellasbb.com, suites $150) are two self-contained stylish units in the heart of the Old Town with high ceilings, hardwood floors and claw foot tubs. Breakfast is provided at the downstairs bakery.

If you're on a budget, book well in advance at the ever-popular **Cherry Bank Hotel** (825 Burdett Avenue, toll free 1-800 998 6688, 250 385 5380, doubles $49-$99). The best rooms are in the original 1897 wing – although you may not wish to hear about the three ghosts that come with the territory. The clean, comfortable rooms are without television or phones.

A 20-minute walk from the Inner Harbour, the cheap and cheerful **Surf Motel** (290 Dallas Road, 250 386 3305, www.surfmotel.net, $95-$130 double) offers perhaps the best views in town – of the ocean and distant US mountains. There is also a simple three-bedroom bungalow to rent around the back.

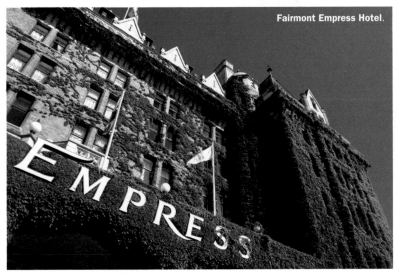

Fairmont Empress Hotel.

Trips Out of Town

Cherry Bank Hotel. *See p201.*

The **Victoria International Youth
Hostel** (516 Yates Street, toll free 1-888 883
0099, 250 385 4511, www.hihostels.ca, dorm bed
$17-$24.28) is the most central hostel, just a few
blocks from the Inner Harbour.

Resources

Hospitals

Victoria General Hospital
*1 Hospital Way (250 727 4212/emergency
250 727 4181).*

Internet

James Bay Coffee and Books
143 Menzies Street (250 386 4700). **Open** 7.30am-
9pm daily. **Rates** $3.25/hour. **Credit** MC, V.

Stain Internet Café
609 Yates Street (250 382 3352). **Open** 11am-2am
daily. **Rates** $3.50/hour. **Credit** AmEx, MC, V.

Police

In an emergency, dial **911**.

Victoria City Police
850 Caledonia Avenue (250 995 7654).

Post office

Main Post Office
*714 Yates Street, between Douglas Street &
Blanchard Street (250 953 1352).* **Open** 8am-5pm
Mon-Fri. **Credit** AmEx, MC, V.

Tourist information

Tourism Victoria Visitor Info Centre
*812 Wharf Street (250 953 2033/www.tourism
victoria.com).* **Open** *1 Sept-15 June* 9am-5pm daily.
16 June-31 Aug 8.30am-7.30pm daily.

Getting there

For ferry information *see p185* and for
seaplanes *see p193* **Sea to sky**. **Air Canada**
(toll free 1-888 247 2262, www.aircanada.com)
and **West Jet** (toll free 1-888 937 8538,
www.westjet.com) operate many daily flights
between Vancouver International Airport and
Victoria International Airport. The prices start
at around $109.

From Swartz Bay Ferry Terminal or
the adjacent Victoria International Airport,
downtown Victoria is 26km (16 miles) by route
17 (the Patricia Bay Highway). The number 70
bus connects Victoria with Schwartz Bay.

Getting around

Ferries from Tsawwassen, about an hour south
of Vancouver, come into Swartz Bay, just 20
minutes from downtown Victoria by Highway
17. To access the north of the island and Tofino
on the west coast, the faster ferry route is from
Horseshoe Bay on Vancouver's North Shore to
Nanaimo, the island's second largest town.

By car

There is only one main artery running south-
north: Route 1 (the Trans-Canada Highway)
continues in Victoria and hugs the east coast
passing through pretty Cowichan Bay, Duncan
('the city of totems'), Chemainus (with its 33 life-
sized murals) and Ladysmith (the birthplace of
Pamela Anderson) before turning into Highway
19 at Nanaimo, 113km (70 miles) from Victoria.

From Nanaimo you can take either Highway
19 or the old, scenic Highway 19A to Campbell
River – the halfway point up the island, 231km
(144 miles) from Victoria, 220km (137 miles)
from Port Hardy on the farthest tip. Campbell
River is also the exit for Highway 28 into the
Strathcona Provincial Park.

By rail

The Malahat (250 383 4324, www.viarail.ca) is
a pleasant and cheap alternative to car or bus.
One train runs each way, daily, from Victoria
to Courtney (and the ski possibilities of Mount
Washington) by way of Nanaimo. The Victoria-
Nanaimo round trip costs as little as $30. Check
the website for schedule and fare alternatives.

Vancouver Island

Vancouver Island is going places. In September 2005 seismologists detected the island had slipped three millimetres towards Japan in the course of just a few days. Comparable tectonic slips occur every 14 months, and are a possible trigger for the long-awaited megathrust earthquake, the 'big one' due to visit this coastline any time in the next two hundred years. Looking on the bright side, this is an island the size of England, with a population of just three quarters of a million (half of them in Victoria). Forest, rock, brush, wetland, lakes and rivers cover 96 per cent of the island. Only four per cent – concentrated in the south-east corner – is farmland, towns, or industrial sites. If and when the big one hits, Vancouver Island will likely take it in its stride.

Undeterred? There are plenty of ways to explore this wilderness. Most of the towns and villages hug the shoreline. Kayaking, canoeing, whale watching, fishing, yachting and diving tour companies are ubiquitous (despite the cold water temperature this is considered one of the best diving areas in the world for its exceptional visibility, rich marine life and a number of artificial reefs). The west coast provides BC's best surfing and storm watching (*see below* **Tofino**). On land, cycling, skiing, hiking and climbing are all readily available in season. Black-tailed deer, elk and black bears are relatively plentiful in the north of the island. Bird watching is another common pursuit, especially during the migration period. More than 1,000 limestone caves have been explored and recorded. The forests include the world's largest yellow cedar and towering spruce, conifers, arbutus trees and Garry oaks. Then there's **Della Falls**. At 440 metres (1,445 feet) these are nearly eight times as high as Niagara – but to get there requires a 34-kilometre (21-mile) boat trip up Great Central Lake, followed by a seven hour, 16-kilometre (10-mile) trek through Strathcona Park (for guided trips, try Ark Resort, 250 723 2657, www.arkresort.com). For more island adventures, *see p205.*

Tofino & the Pacific Rim National Park

Although it was named as early as 1792 after a Spanish explorer, Don de Vincent **Tofino**, it's only since Highway 4 was extended out to land's end in the early 1970s that this Clayoquot village on the western shore of Vancouver Island opened up to the world. Given the location, it's no surprise that the locals tend to be fishermen or loggers. The other main residents are the spiritual descendants of the hippies who journeyed out as far as the road would take them with the coming of the pavement. Environmentalism has been a strong force here ever since, and it's not hard to see why; in fact it's impossible to visit this rugged, windswept coast and not be impressed by nature in all its raw glory.

The Pacific Ocean here is tumultuous – Japan is the nearest port of call 7,456 kilometres (4,633 miles) due west. Long Beach is a jagged 11-kilometre (seven-mile) stretch of white sandy beach framed by rocky outcrops, sitka spruce, dense rainforest and the MacKenzie Range. It's the best spot in Canada for surfers and windsurfers; you can rent boards and wetsuits from Tofino town and Ucluelet 40 kilometres (25 miles) south (with an average summer high of 15 degrees centigrade, 59 degrees Fahrenheit, you will need that wetsuit). Numerous well marked trails provide hiking at all levels of difficulty – the 800-metre (2,625-foot) Bog Trail is wheelchair accessible. The Wickaninnish Centre on Wickaninnish Bay (250 726 4212) provides information, films, exhibits, observation decks with telescopes, and a café, mid March to mid October.

This area gets a lot of rain: 3,000 millimetres (120 inches) a year. The tourism industry has even capitalised on the fiercest of the weather by offering peak prices for storm watching in December through February, when the coast is buffeted by 10-15 storms a month and waves up to six metres (20 feet) high.

The town itself is small, but there are some worthwhile shops and attractions in the vicinity: the **Tofino Botanical Garden** (1084 Pacific Rim Highway, 250 725 1220, www.tofinobotanicalgardens.com) cuts a marked contrast with the Butchart's Victoriana – here you'll find the children's garden, the First Nations garden, and the hippie garden (but no pot, as yet). It's open daily from 9am to dusk, admission is $10, with under-12s free. The **Eagle Aerie Gallery** (350 Campbell Street, at 2nd Avenue, 250 725 3235) is the best known of more than 20 art galleries. And the **Raincoast Interpretive Centre** (451 Main Street, 250 725 2560, www.tofinores.com) is a mine of information about the local ecosystem, with naturalists on site and tours available. It's run by the Raincoast Education Society.

Tofino is a great spot to watch whales – from late February to May you can see pods of Pacific gray whales migrating without even leaving the beach. Up to 50 grays are resident throughout the summer. Increasing numbers of humpbacks are also being spotted on the west coast – expect to pay about $60 for a three

Trips Out of Town

Spa around

A spa break is pure vacation indulgence. So why not indulge?

Urban getaways

The Aerie and Brentwood Bay Lodge & Spa are newsmakers in terms of travel destinations, and both are within a 30-minute drive of Victoria. The **Aerie** (108 Malahat, 250 743 7115, www.aerie.bc.ca, rates $95-$180/ 90 minute treatment, $345-$445 two-night package) is perched atop Malahat Mountain, with views of the coastal peaks and valleys. Combine a visit with a sampling of the resort's acclaimed culinary fare and the entire visit comes near to nirvana. **Brentwood Bay Lodge & Spa** (849 Verdier Avenue, 250 544 2079, www.brentwoodbaylodge.com, rates $80-$175/75 minute treatment, $498-$598 two-night package) lies north of the city. It has an understated, west coast elegance to it and the ocean views come as a restorative interlude to sightseeing.

Island retreats

Although Parksville bustles with visitors in high season, **Tigh-Na-Mara Seaside Resort** (1155 Resort Drive, 250 248 2072, www.tigh-na-mara.com, rates $150-$180/90 minute treatment, $166-$338 two-night package) manages to balance the concept of adult retreat with family togetherness. Its centrepiece is the two-storey Grotto Spa, a large mineral pool set in an oasis of ferns, rocks and waterfalls. **Kingfisher Oceanside Spa** (4330 Island Highway South, toll free 1-800 663 7929, 250 338 1323, www. kingfisherspa.com, rates $110-$150/90 minute treatment, $339-$369 two-night package) in Courtenay, is near Vancouver and Victoria and a terrific alternative to the more pretentious spas elsewhere. However, with 22 treatment rooms, a steam cave, sauna, hot tub and outdoor heated pool, the spa is more than capable of absorbing everyone with comfort and ease.

hour whale-watching voyage. All the local tour operators also offer bear-watching from the boat, and most are more than happy to do a tour to the geothermal springs, where natural pools are supplied by a hot waterfall. It's well worth the six-and-a-half-hour trip.

Where to eat

If anything, the standard of dining in Tofino is superior to that in Victoria. The **Pointe** at the Wickaninnish Inn (Osprey Lane, Chesterman Beach, 250 725 3100, www.wickinn.com, main courses $13-$46, doubles $220-$440) is the one they all try to measure up to. The signature Wickaninnish potlach is a deep, delectable dish of local seafood; the chocolate symphony is sheer decadence on a plate. Reservations are recommended all year round for dinner, but the restaurant is also open for breakfast and lunch.

The vibe at **Shelter** (601 Campbell Street, 250 725 3353, www.shelterrestaurant.com, main courses $16-$36) is just as classy, but it's a more relaxed affair. Its cosy, contemporary interior includes an open fire and an open kitchen. Local organic ingredients are treated with the respect they deserve, letting natural flavours take prominence; the double thick cured pork chop with mashed potatoes is great.

SoBo (1084 Pacific Rim Highway, 250 725 2341, www.sobo.ca, main courses $5-$10) is the cult upstart. It all began with a purple catering truck (and lunch is still 'at the truck') but their travelling days are behind them, and now chef Rick Moore also stuffs his killer fish tacos ($5.25) at the Tofino Botanical Garden café. The name is short for 'sophisticated bohemian' and that pretty well sums up the menu too.

If you fancy a more hippie experience, head to the **Common Loaf Bakery** (180 1st Street, 250 725 3915, main courses $4-$8) for pizza, soups, curries, good coffee and wholemeal baked goods. And it's licenced.

Where to stay

The **Wickaninnish Inn** (see left) is the top spot here for its superb location on a rocky promontory. The rooms – all with views – have double soaker tubs next to floor-to-ceiling windows, and the luxury suites range from family-orientated lofts to the romantic canopy room, with fairy lights twinkling in the ceiling.

The **Long Beach Lodge Resort** (1441 Pacific Rim Highway, 250 725 2442, www.long beachlodgeresort.com, doubles $169-$319) is another high-end treat, with similar amenities to the Wickaninnish Inn, but with the option of a lodge room or one of their 12 spacious two-bedroom cottages.

A good mid-price option is the rustic **Middle Beach Lodge** (Mackenzie Beach Road, 250 725 2900, www.middlebeach.com, doubles $110- $135), where you choose between rooms in the

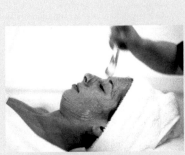

The westerly wilds
Ancient Cedars Spa, at Wickaninnish Inn in Tofino (*see p204*, rates $150-$170/90 minute treatment, $555-$842 two-night package), is geared to well-heeled spa-goers. Windows look onto the crest of ocean-splashed rocks, making the spa experience all the more mesmerising during the storm season. The ultimate west coast spa experience must be at the **Healing Grounds**

Spa & Wellness Centre. Located at Clayoquot Wilderness Resort (toll free 1-888 333 5405, www.wildretreat.com, rates $180-$210/90 minute treatment, $2,800-$3,800 three-day package), a 20-minute boat ride from Tofino, this indoor-outdoor spa offers fern shaded massage decks alongside intimate treatment rooms. The outdoor, waterfall-fed pool and steamy cedar hot tubs are an added bonus. Set aside half a day and plan to include lunch.

oceanfront lodge, or self-contained cabins on the beach. No telephones or televisions make sure you really do get away from it all.

You can camp for $20 to $41 at **Bella Pacifica Resort & Campground** (250 725 3400, www.bellapacifica.com) two miles south of Tofino near Mackenzie Beach. Or check out the accommodation section of www.tofinotime.com for a range of houses to rent and B&Bs.

Tourist information

The **Tofino Visitor Info Centre** (Pacific Rim Highway, 250 725 3414, www.tofinobc.org) is eight km (five miles) out of town and open 10am-4pm; phone for winter hours. www.tofinotime.com and www.longbeachmaps.com have good listings, maps and advice.

Getting there

By car

To reach Tofino from Vancouver, take the BC Ferry from Horseshoe Bay to Nanaimo, drive north on Highway 19. Take exit 60, about 30km (19 miles) north of Nanaimo, onto Highway 4 for a scenic but twisty 180km drive by way of Port Alberni. Cathedral Grove, just past Cameron Lake, is a worthy stop: a strip of old growth forest where 800-year-old Douglas firs tower 70 metres (230 feet).

By plane

Plane charters can knock four hours off the five hour ferry/drive from Vancouver to Tofino. **Craig Air** (toll free 1-877 866 3466, www.craigair.com) charges $153 one way.

By bus

Tofino Bus (toll free 1-866 986 3466, www.tofinobus.com) runs a direct express service from Victoria to Tofino and Ucluelet daily, picking up from Hostelling International, 516 Yates Street at 8.15am, and Ocean Backpackers Inn, 791 Pandora Avenue, fifteen minutes later. The trip takes five hours and costs $53.50 one-way/$102 return.

The Southern Gulf Islands

Idyllic in landscape and rustic in character, the Southern Gulf Islands are a favourite getaway for urbanites seeking quiet, pastoral havens. While some 300 islands sprinkle British Columbia's southern coastline, the majority are picturesque rock formations or wilderness reserves visited only by boaters. The larger islands, however, support substantial communities – artists, city escapees and folks

Trips Out of Town

who live to the beat of a different drummer. Getting there via **BC Ferries** (toll free 1-888 223 2779, www.bcferries.com) is half the fun.

Salt Spring Island

www.saltspringtoday.com.
The largest of the Gulf Islands (pop.10,000), **Salt Spring** is where west coast temperate rainforest meets English countryside. Sheep graze on grassy hills, deer meander freely, and gardens are filled with foxgloves, shasta daisies and other wild flowers. **Ganges** is 'island central' and home to numerous shops, galleries and restaurants, including the award-winning **House Piccolo** (108 Hereford Avenue, 250 537 1844, www.housepiccolo.com, main courses $26-$34) and the more casual, local hangout, **Moby's Marine Pub** (124 Upper Ganges Road, 250 537 5559, main courses $6.50-$12.50). More than 150 inns and B&Bs make staying longer easy. **Hastings House** (160 Upper Ganges Road, toll free 1-800 661 9255, 250 537 2362, www.hastingshouse.com, doubles $390-$490) is the hot spot for the well heeled, world weary traveller, but you need to reserve at least six months in advance. At the other end of the scale, **Ruckle Provincial Park** (Beaver Point Road, 250 539 2115, campsite $14) is the in-place for campers and hikers. While on Salt Spring, be sure to take the self-guided art studio tour, following a trail of potters, weavers, glass blowers and painters and try to include the Saturday market in Ganges.

Galiano Island

www.galianoisland.com.
Galiano is the second largest island, yet has only 1,000 residents, and although it's the shortest ferry ride from Vancouver, it has managed to retain a distinctly hippie ambience. Galiano is also regarded as the prettiest of the Gulf Islands in terms of its log-strewn beaches, windswept coastlines, parks, views and abundant wildlife, including more than 130 species of bird and many rare and protected plants. Naturalists and eco-orientated visitors love the place. Most commercial activity is located in and around Sturdies Bay where the ferries dock. In fact, one of the island's nicest inns, **Galiano Inn and Madrona Del Mar Spa** (134 Madrona Drive, toll free 1-877 530 3939, 250 539 3388, www.galianoinn.com, closed Dec-Mar, doubles $125-$249), is within a few minutes' walk of the ferry queues. Travel north, and the landscape of this long, skinny island gives way to lush forests, meadows and magnificent parks: two of particular note are **Montague Harbour** and **Dionisio Point**.

Mayne Island

www.mayneislandchamber.ca.
Mayne Island's compact size and shape make this an ideal day trip. If you're a cyclist, Mayne is also the easiest island to manoeuvre around. There are a few tough climbs but you're rewarded with plenty of beaches, bays and vistas to explore. Among the best are Campbell Bay for its swimming and sculpted sandstone cliffs, Horton Bay for its quaint boat harbour and Piggott Bay for its wide, sandy beach. The hub of the community is Miner's Bay, so named in the mid 1800s for the Vancouver Islanders who made it their overnight stop before rowing across the Georgia Strait, en route to the Cariboo gold fields. Here's where to find **Springwater Lodge** (C-27 Miners Bay, 250 539 5521, www.springwaterlodge.com, main courses $7-$15), one of BC's oldest watering holes, plus an 1896 gaol (now a museum), and a multi-purpose agricultural hall that doubles as a cinema, bingo hall and community theatre. Groceries, liquor and kayak rentals (www.maynekayak.com) are here, also. An unexpected delight is the fairly new Japanese Memorial Garden at Dinner Bay, a stone's throw from the island's choicest inn, **Oceanwood Country Inn & Restaurant** (630 Dinner Bay Road, 250 539 5074, www.oceanwood.com, set four-course menu $48, doubles $139-$179).

Sailing on...

As the transfer point for inter-island ferries, Mayne is a good base for island-hopping, particularly if you're heading to Pender (www.penderislandchamber.com) or Saturna (www.saturnatourism.com). From Vancouver, however, ferry schedules make it difficult to do these islands justice as a day trip. Stay over, and you'll discover **Pender Island** to be a thriving community of 2,000 residents with diverse B&Bs and sophisticated destinations like **Poets Cove Resort & Spa** (9801 Spalding Road, South Pender Island, toll free 1-888 512 7638, www.poetscove.com, doubles $169-$249). Pender's sheltered anchorages, hidden coves and accessible beaches make it a boater's paradise. Add to this, areas such as Mount Norman and Mount Menzies, both part of the Gulf Islands National Park Reserve, as well as Brookes Point, and you begin to see why Pender Island deserves more than a passing visit. **Saturna Island** is somewhat different, and its 400 homesteaders, while friendly, tend to relish their isolation. Saturna is where you come to truly get away from it all unless you have a day or two to spare stick to the big three, and you won't be disappointed.

The Okanagan

Wine country.

The most populated area of British Columbia outside the Lower Mainland, the Okanagan sits on a Southern Interior plateau. In recent years its wine-making industry has put this picturesque lake region on the international tourism map. Following Highway 97 for 234 kilometres (145 miles) – from Salmon Arm in the north to Osoyoos in the south – you can visit more than 50 wineries, many with Vintner Quality Alliance (VQA) certification. Varietals range from a regional signature pinot gris and other European-style whites, made with grapes grown mainly in the cooler north, to pinot noir, merlot, cabernet sauvignon and other reds from fruit nurtured in the dips and slopes of the central and southern mountains. World-famous ice wines are made from grapes picked mid-winter at precisely minus eight degrees Celsius.

But wine is a relative newcomer here. Since the mid 1800s, when Oblate Father Charles Pandosy planted the first orchard (and vineyard) at a Roman Catholic mission in Kelowna, orchard fruits have been the region's mainstay industry. In fact, tons more apples than grapes are grown up and down the valley, and soft fruits like peaches, plums, apricots and cherries figure prominently among the Okanagan's glorious output.

Add the fact that summers are reliably hot and rainless, and you have a region to which people flock for swimming, boating, fishing and other sports on five almost contiguous lakes and several rivers. Factor in 28 golf courses and innumerable hiking and biking trails, and you have a multifaceted, laid-back recreational paradise. In winter, with cold but relatively dry and sunny weather, full-facility ski resorts at Vernon (Silver Star, www.skisilverstar.com) and Kelowna (Big White, www.bigwhite.com) attract families as well as experienced skiers.

Orientation

Highway 97 runs the length of the Okanagan, with roads to wineries, recreational and wilderness sites branching out along the way. For wine seekers, the region can be divided into north, central and south – each with clusters of wineries and subtly different products. The highest concentrations are near Kelowna, Penticton, and south of Oliver. Major resorts are located in and around Kelowna and Penticton.

Smaller hotels, motels, B&Bs and camping sites can be found the length of the region. Similarly, culinary, cultural and recreational attractions are scattered throughout.

What to see

Kelowna (pop. 150,000) straddles 144-kilometre (89-mile) long Lake Okanagan at mid girth (*pictured p208*). A bit of a sprawl, the city is sited on the east bank, then meanders over on to what's called Westbank. A dozen wineries are found on both sides of the lake, including Mission Hill, Quail's Gate and Cedar Creek.

Calona Vineyards, the granddaddy of Okanagan wineries, opened in 1932 and made plonk well into 1960s. Today it turns out award-winning VQA varietals, as well as beers and spirits. Its downtown winery, open daily year-round, showcases BC wine industry history and the mechanics of big-time beverage production. It has a tasting room too.

For similar insight into the fruit growing industry, visit the Kelowna Land & Orchard Co, in the city's northeast. Covered wagons take visitors on hour-long tours of the 50-hectare (123-acre) working orchard. There's a petting farm, store, restaurant and fine cidery.

Downtown Kelowna boasts an attractive lake front, and a burgeoning cultural district (www.kelownasculturaldistrict.com) with a new arts centre for visitors and working artisans, and galleries, theatres, shops and restaurants. The Laurel Packinghouse is a former fruit-packing facility that now houses the Wine Museum & VQA Wine Shop and the delightful little Orchard Museum that charts the region's development from cattle range to fruit farms using a real apple tree and a 15-metre (50-foot) model railway. Nearby are the Kelowna Museum (470 Queensway Avenue, 250 763 2417, www.kelownamuseum.ca) and Okanagan Military Museum (1424 Ellis Street, 250 763 9292, www.okmilmuseum.ca).

The city's early history is encapsulated at the Father Pandosy Mission (3685 Benvoulin Road, 250 860 8369), a reconstructed mission site operated by the Central Okanagan Heritage Society. For serious walkers and cyclists, the Mission Creek Greenway (www.greenway.kelowna.bc.ca) begins on Lakeshore Drive and wends 16.5 kilometres (10 miles) eastward.

In 2003 a forest fire ravaged the Kelowna region, destroying 12 of 18 wooden trestles along the former Kettle Valley Railway route, a national historic site. They're slowly being rebuilt and the 18-kilometre (11-mile) Myra Canyon cycling and hiking route (www. trailsbc.ca) is open with bypasses.

In and around Kelowna you'll see images of a Loch-Ness-like monster that is known as the Ogopogo. The creature reputedly mainly lurks on the east side of Okanagan Lake, while residing in a cave near Peachland.

Highway 97 runs north through **Vernon**, with historic O'Keefe Ranch (www.okeeferanch. bc.ca) nearby, and **Armstrong**, with several artisan cheese-makers. At Highway 97's extremity (connecting with Highway 1) are the towns of **Salmon Arm** and **Sicamous**, both on Shuswap Lake, renowned for hot-season house boating.

Heading south on 97 from Kelowna, you pass through Westbank, Peachland and Summerland and into **Penticton**. Historically an agricultural hub and watersports mecca, the city of 40,000 has of late acquired a glossier patina thanks to the burgeoning wine industry.

More than a dozen smallish wineries perch along the lovely **Naramata Bench**, lined with orchards and vineyards, to the northeast of the city. The 16-kilometre (ten-mile) Naramata Road, one of BC's best short drives, follows the bench to the lakeside village of Naramata.

Penticton attractions include the permanently moored stern-wheeler SS *Sicamous* (1099 W Lakeshore Drive, 250 492 0403, www.sssicamous.com) and the Kettle Valley Steam Railway, which offers two-hour excursions from nearby Summerland on a ten-kilometre (six-mile) stretch of track constructed between 1910 and 1915.

Sandy beaches bless both ends of the city. On Okanagan Lake in the north there's water-skiing, wind-surfing and boat rentals. Skaha Lake in the south (slightly warmer, some say) offers water slides and firepits for barbecues. A mid-city channel that connects the lakes is reserved for the pastime of rubber-tube floating. Family groups tie the floats together and catch the current. Tubes can be rented. Amusement facilities proliferate throughout town.

Golf is huge in the Okanagan. The most prestigious course in the Penticton region is the 18-hole Penticton Golf and Country Club. Kelowna boasts five courses of similar championship status, including Predator Ridge, Gallagher's Canyon, Harvest, and the Quail and the Bear. Other courses are located as far north as Vernon and south in Osoyoos. Hiking and mountain biking over the sage-covered mountains are increasingly popular.

From Penticton, Highway 97 continues to the southern region where the Okanagan embraces the northern end of the Sonoran desert (which begins in Mexico). Protectors of this unique and endangered desert environment have been struggling to save at least some of it from ever-encroaching vineyards, which also covet the dry heat. So numerous have become the vineyards, with their long, hot growing season, and wineries, that the town of **Oliver** calls itself the 'wine capital of Canada'.

North of Oliver, near the village of Okanagan Falls and Vaseaux Lake (a pristine wildlife reserve), nestle mostly smaller wineries, some with enviable reputations. From Oliver south on 97 stretches the Golden Mile, with big operations like Tinhorn Creek, Gehringer Brothers and Inniskillin. To the east of 97, from just outside Oliver, the Black Sage Road winds along hills said to grow the best red grapes anywhere. Here wineries range from the boutique-like Black Hills to the destination complex called Burrowing Owl. Near the town of **Osoyoos**, nestles Nk'Mip Cellars, operated by the Osoyoos Indian Band. The large complex includes a winery and restaurant, and the Nk'Mip Desert & Heritage Centre, devoted to regional history and ecology with self-guided trails over 20 hectares (50 acres), a reconstructed traditional village and an adopt-a-rattlesnake programme. For those who prefer their wildlife one step removed, the Desert Centre (250 495 2470, www.desert.org), located on 97 north of Osoyoos, offers guided interpretive tours along an elevated boardwalk.

In BC, Highway 3 travels west through the **Similkameen Valley**, an extension of the

Kelowna. See p207.

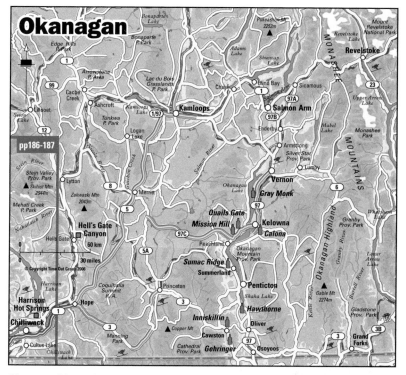

Okanagan with ranching, fruit-growing and increasingly, grape-growing. In summer and autumn fruit sellers populate **Keremeos**, dubbed 'the fruit stand capital of Canada'. From here the 3 becomes the twisty Hope-Princeton, before rejoining the 1 at Hope. Osoyoos to Vancouver is 396 kilometres (246 miles), roughly the same as the distance between Kelowna and Vancouver via the Coquihalla.

Calona Vineyards
1125 Richer Street, Kelowna (250 762 9144/ www.calonavineyards.ca). **Open** 9am-6pm daily. **Admission** *Tour* $5. **Credit** AmEx, MC, V.

Kelowna Land & Orchard Co
3002 Dunster Road, Kelowna (250 763 1091/ www.k-l-o.com). **Open** *Apr-Oct;* tours 11am and 1pm daily; restaurant 11am-3pm daily. **Main courses** $13.95 (lunch). **Admission** $6.50; $3 students; free under-12s. **Credit** MC, V.

Kettle Valley Steam Railway
Prairie Valley Station, 18404 Bathville Road, Summerland (250 494 8422/www.kettlevalley rail.org). **Open** *May-Oct;* phone for details. **Admission** $17; $11-$16 concessions; $60 family. **Credit** MC, V.

Laurel Packinghouse
1304 Ellis Street, Kelowna (250 763 4761/www. kelownamuseum.ca/laurel). **Open** *Wine Museum & VQA Shop* 10am-6pm Mon-Fri; 10am-5pm Sat; 11am-5pm Sun. *Orchard Museum* 10am-5pm Mon-Sat. **Admission** By donation. **Credit** MC, V.

Nk'Mip Desert & Heritage Centre
1000 Rancher Creek Road, Osoyoos (250 495 7901/ 1-888 495 8555/www.nkmipdesert.com). **Open** *May-Oct;* phone or check website for details. **Admission** $7; $5 4-16s; $22 family. **Credit** MC, V.

Penticton Golf and Country Club
Comox Street, off Eckhardt Avenue, Penticton (250 492 8727/www.pentictongolfcc.com). **Open** Phone for tee times. **Rates** $40-$49. **Credit** AmEx, MC, V.

Where to eat & drink

Okanagan wine makers have long out-performed their culinary equivalents, but the restaurateurs have started to catch up. The major centres now have good restaurants serving fresh regional produce and a commendable range of Okanagan (and other) wines. Some larger wineries now run

Trips Out of Town

restaurants – usually with patios and some open all year-round (*see below* **Grape expectations**).

In Kelowna **Bouchons** is a classic French bistro with an 800-bottle wine cellar. Kelowna's **Fresco Restaurant** serves adventurous contemporary cuisine and is generally considered the best in town.

Penticton's **Theo's** is hailed as one of BC's best Greek eateries. The Naramata Heritage Inn's **Rock Oven Dining Room** delivers locally inspired fare, including imaginative pizzas, at lunch and dinner.

In Oliver, the **Toasted Oak Wine Bar** in the VQA complex focuses on fine BC and local fare, while in Osoyoos, casual dining **Wildfire Grill** includes a pleasing courtyard patio.

Bouchons
105-1180 Sunset Drive, Kelowna (250 763 6595/www.bouchonsbistro.com). **Open** 5.30pm-midnight daily. **Main courses** $17.50-$29.50. **Credit** MC, V.

Fresco Restaurant
1560 Water Street, Kelowna (250 868 8805/ www.frescorestaurant.net). **Open** *May-Oct* 5.30pm-late Tue-Sun. *Nov, Dec, Feb-Apr* 5.30pm-late Tue-Sat. **Main courses** $21.95-$48.95. **Credit** AmEx, MC, V.

Rock Oven Dining Room
Naramata Inn, 3625 1st Street, Naramata (250 496 6808/www.naramatainn.com). **Open** *May-Oct* 6pm-late Thur-Sun, reservations advised. **Main courses** multi-course tasting menu $50-$90. **Credit** AmEx, MC, V.

Theo's
687 Main Street, Penticton (250 492 4019/ www.eatsquid.com). **Open** 11am-10pm Mon-Sat; 4-10pm Sun. **Main courses** *lunch* $5.95-$18.95; *dinner* $15-$27. **Credit** MC, V.

Toasted Oak Wine Bar
34881 97th Street, Oliver (250 498 4867/www. winecountry-canada.com). **Open** 11am-10pm Mon-Thur, Sun; 11am-11pm Fri, Sat. **Main courses** *lunch* $7-$12; *dinner* $16-$23. **Credit** MC, V.

Wildfire Grill
8523 Main Street, Osoyoos (250 495 2215). **Open** 11am-2.30pm, 5-9pm Tue-Fri; 5-9pm Sat. **Main courses** *lunch* $6.50-$12.50; *dinner* $8-$21. **Credit** MC, V.

Okanagan accommodation is plentiful and varied (though rarely luxurious). Mid-range resorts are numerous and there are many

Grape expectations

Wineries are so numerous and so varied that choosing standouts is foolish. The following list therefore spans regions, varietals, eateries and access. Many are open year-round, but the hours change, so check ahead. All offer wine tastings and many provide tours.

Getting to **Gray Monk Estate Winery** from Highway 97 north of Kelowna, requires a little map work. But the northern lake setting and crisp, fruity wines enjoyed in the patio restaurant with a sophisticated light meal, make the travel worthwhile.

Mission Hill Winery, whose monastery-like complex with bell tower rises from a hill west of Kelowna, is a worthy destination. The architecture and craftsmanship are one of a kind and the four bronze bells, reminiscent of the owner's European childhood, chime regularly to great effect. While the signature wine is a Bordeaux-inspired Oculus, Mission Hill makes many varietals.

Nearby **Quail's Gate Estate Winery** maintains a stellar reputation not just for its many wines, but also for its historic log house that serves as an intimate tasting room, and the year-round beautifully appointed Old Vines Patio restaurant.

Cedar Creek Estate Winery, sidling up to the lakeshore southeast of Kelowna, keeps a low profile while its wines, particularly whites, garner many awards.

Sumac Ridge Estate Winery is a major producer with an enviable reputation. It's on 97 near Summerland. Along the Naramata

Trips Out of Town

roadside motels. More accommodation is listed on the tourism information websites, *see p212*.

Just outside Kelowna on Okanagan Lake reposes the mid-size, historic (and, in this case, luxurious) **Hotel Eldorado**. The original inn was built in 1926 by the obscure but wonderfully named Countess Bubna Litite of Austria, presumably for Europeans seeking civilisation – today it boasts luxury suites and a fancy spa. The nearby contemporary **Manteo Resort Waterfront Hotel** provides a gorgeous waterfront setting. Both establishments have reputable restaurants to match the standard of accommodation.

A modestly priced option in Kelowna's city centre is the **Royal Anne Hotel**, with a fitness centre and Irish pub on site.

Penticton's elegantly restored **Naramata Heritage Inn & Spa** offers special packages offering wine tours and spa treatments. For something completely different, head from Penticton south to **God's Mountain Crest Chalet** near Summerland, a delightful if slightly eccentric inn perched on a ledge above Skaha Lake. It comes complete with glassed-in temperature-controlled private balconies, swimming pool and hot tub.

God's Mountain Crest Chalet

4898 Lakeside/Eastside Road, at White Gazebo, Penticton (250 490 4800/www.godsmountain.com). **Rates** *Jan-Mar, Oct* $79-$99 queen; $119-$159 suite. *Apr-Sept* $99-$119 queen; $139-$189 suite. **Credit** MC, V.

Hotel Eldorado

500 Cook Road, on the lake, Kelowna (250 763 7500/1-866 608 7500/www.eldoradokelowna.com). **Rates** *Heritage building* $89-$239; *Eldorado Arms* $129-$259 room; $179-$349 suite. **Credit** AmEx, MC, V.

Manteo Resort Waterfront Hotel

3762 Lakeshore Road, Kelowna (250 860 1031/ www.manteo.com). **Rates** $149-$270 room; $175-$330 suite; $275-$580 2 bdrm villa; $320-$620 3 bdrm villa. **Credit** AmEx, MC, V.

Naramata Heritage Inn & Spa

3625 1st Street, Naramata (250 496 6808/ 1-866 617 1188/www.naramatainn.com). **Rates** $116-$284 double/king; $330-$510 suite. **Credit** AmEx, MC, V.

Royal Anne Hotel

348 Bernard Avenue, Kelowna (250 763 2277/ 1-888 811 3400/www.royalannehotel.com). **Rates** $79-$189. **Credit** AmEx, MC, V.

Road a dozen or so well-signposted wineries are young, playful, and turning out commendable wines. They include pioneer Lang Vineyards (2493 Gammon Road, 250 496 5987, www.langvineyards.com); Elephant Island Winery (2765 Naramata Road, 250 496 5522, www.elephantislandwine.com), a crafter of fruit-based wines; and the Red Rooster Winery (891 Naramata Road, 250 492 2424, www.redroosterwinery.com), with an added interest in avant-garde art.

Above Okanagan Falls, reposes **Hawthorne Mountain Vineyard**. The climb up a longish road is well rewarded in the tasting room.

Blasted Church, in the same region, gets its name from the dynamiting of a place of worship in 1929. The wines (and art labels) are worthy of close attention.

South of Oliver on the Black Sage Road, stands the adobe-style **Burrowing Owl Estate Winery**. In a short time this large operation has taken its place among the best producers. The unparalleled hillside setting includes a commendable restaurant with patio.

Serious wine-seekers will set aside time for the majors on the southern stretch of 97. For variety and price a good bet is the long-established **Gehringer Brothers Estate Winery**, which makes more than 20 wines, including a signature ice wine. Another biggie known for its ice wines (among other varietals) is **Inniskillin Okanagan Vineyards**.

Slip eastward through Osoyoos, and you'll find **Nk'Mip Cellars**, recently emerged to dramatic effect from a dry, sage-covered landscape overlooking Osoyoos Lake. This winery was built by the Nk'Mip Indian Band in co-operation with Vincor International and it has already begun to garner a strong reputation for its wines.

Blasted Church

378 Parsons Road, Okanagan Falls (250 497 1125/www.blastedchurch.com). **Open** *May-Oct & Easter weekend* 10am-5pm daily. **Credit** AmEx, DC, MC, V.

Burrowing Owl Estate Winery

100 Burrowing Owl Place, off Black Sage Road, Oliver (1-877 498 0620/www. burrowingowlwine.ca). **Open** *Easter-June, Thanksgiving-Oct* 10am-5pm daily; *July-Thanksgiving* 10am-6pm daily. **Credit** MC, V. ▶

Resources

Canada Post
591 Bernard Avenue, Kelowna (250 868 8480/ www.canadapost.ca). **Open** 8.30am-5.30pm Mon-Fri. **Credit** MC, V.

Kelowna General Hospital
2268 Pandosy Street, between Royal Avenue & Rose Avenue (250 862 4000).

Kelowna Tourism
544 Harvey Avenue, at Ellis Street (250 861 1515/ www.tourismkelowna.com). **Open** 9am-5pm Mon-Fri; 10am-6pm Sat.

Okanagan Wine Country Tours
470C Cawston Avenue, Kelowna (250 868 9463/ 1-866 689 9463/www.okwinetours.com). **Rates** Day trip $130. Half day $55-$65; phone or see website for details and custom bookings. The company also arranges overnight stays and floatplane wine tours starting at $300 per person.

Penticton & Wine Country Chamber of Commerce
553 Railway Street, between Power Street & Eckhardt Avenue (250 492 4103/1-800 663 5052/ www.penticton.org). **Open** 9am-5pm Mon-Fri.

Wine Country Welcome Centre
34881 97th Street, Oliver (250 498 4867/ 1-888 880 9463/www.winecountry-canada.com). **Open** Wine store and gift shop from 10am daily. The complex includes the Toasted Oak Wine Bar & Grill (see p210) as well as a wine store.

Getting there

By car
The principal route from Vancouver to the Okanagan is via highways 1 (the Trans-Canada) and 5 (the Coquihalla) to Kelowna – an almost 400km (250mile) drive of four to five hours. From Calgary, Alberta, Kelowna is 600km (375miles); from Edmonton almost 900km (560miles). Alternately, you can drive highways 1 and 3 (the Hope-Princeton) from Vancouver to Osoyoos (400 km, 250miles).

By air
Kelowna (www.kelownaairport.com) and Penticton (www.cyyf.org) airports are both served by regional carriers; Kelowna also handles direct flights on major airlines from as far away as Toronto. Vehicles can be rented at both airports.

By bus
Greyhound serves all the major centres in the Okanagan (www.greyhound.ca).

▶ **Grape expectations (continued)**

Cedar Creek Estate Winery
5445 Lakeshore Road, Kelowna (250 764 8866/www.cedarcreek.bc.ca). **Open** Wine shop May-Oct 10am-6pm daily; Nov-Apr 11am-5pm daily. Tours May-Oct 11am, 2pm, 3pm daily. **Credit** MC, V.

Gehringer Brothers Estate Winery
Highway 97, at Road 8, between Oliver & Osoyoos (250 498 3537/1-800 784 6304). **Open** June-mid Oct 10am-5pm daily. **Credit** MC, V.

Gray Monk Estate Winery
1055 Camp Road, Okanagan Centre (250 766 3168/1-800 663 4205/www.graymonk.com). **Open** Apr-June, Sept, Oct 10am-5pm daily; July, Aug 9am-9pm daily; Nov-Mar 11am-5pm Mon-Sat. **Credit** AmEx, MC, V.

Hawthorne Mountain Vineyard
Green Lake Road, Okanagan Falls (250 497 8267/www.hmvineyard.com). **Open** Year round daily, phone for details. **Credit** MC, V.

Inniskillin Okanagan Vineyards
Road II, Oliver (250 498 6663/www.inniskillin.com). **Open** Nov-Apr 10am-5pm daily; May-Oct 10am-6pm daily. **Credit** MC, V.

Mission Hill Winery
1730 Mission Hill Road, Westbank (250 768 6448/www.missionhillwinery.com). **Open** 9.30am-5pm daily. **Credit** AmEx, MC, V.

Nk'Mip Cellars
1400 Rancher Creek Road, Osoyoos (250 495 2985/www.nkmipcellars.com). **Open** phone for tour schedule. **Credit** MC, V.

Quail's Gate Estate Winery
3303 Boucherie Road, Kelowna (250 769 4451/1-800 420 9463/www.quailsgate.com). **Open** 9am-6pm daily. Phone for tour schedule. **Rates** Tours $5. **Credit** MC, V.

Sumac Ridge Estate Winery
17403 Highway 97N, Summerland (250 494 0451/www.sumacridge.com). **Open** Tours May-Oct 10am-3pm daily; Nov-Apr phone to reserve. **Rates** Tour and tasting $5; tutored tasting $10. **Credit** AmEx, MC, V.

Whistler

Peak skiing, snowboarding and mountain biking.

When the winter Olympics comes to Vancouver in 2010, they will be co-hosted with Whistler, the purpose-built ski town 120 kilometres (75 miles) to the north. Rated one of the top winter sports resorts in the world, Whistler is establishing itself as a summer destination too, with hiking, canoeing, white water rafting and the best mountain biking in North America.

Whistler's development continues to accelerate in the run-up to the Olympics. If you want to escape into the wilderness, by all means bypass Whistler and pitch your tent deep in Garibaldi Provincial Park. But if, on the other hand, you want to savour BC's mountains, lakes and forests, don't object to letting a gondola take the strain and fancy sampling some of the best dining in the country while you're at it – all within a breathtaking two-hour drive of Vancouver – then you need look no further.

Sea-to-Sky Highway

Locals are rightly proud of Route 99, the Sea-to-Sky Highway from Vancouver to Whistler, that affords spectacular viewpoints over the city, Howe Sound and the coastal mountain range.

To get to it, take W Georgia Street, through Stanley Park and over the Lions Gate Bridge.

In the run-up to the Olympics, Highway 99 is getting a $600 million upgrade that will supposedly knock an hour off the journey time. While the engineers blast their way through the mountains, current journeys are often disrupted by between five and 30 minutes.

Unless you are staying in Whistler Creekside (a couple of miles from the main village) you are unlikely to require a car in Whistler, especially in winter, when the focus is squarely on the Whistler-Blackcomb slopes and free shuttle buses constantly circle the perimeter of the village. However, in the summer months a car opens up several worthwhile destinations en route. (Though please note that overnight parking is at a premium and hotels take advantage of this, adding $12-$20 a night to your bill.)

Fifty kilometres (31 miles) from Vancouver, **Britannia Beach** (population of 300) is a hippiefied outpost skirting the **BC Museum of Mining**, which features an on-site tour of a now spent copper mine with giant machinery and a descent into one of the old tunnels. The mine is

EVERYTHING YOU NEED
FOR THE
PERFECT BREAK

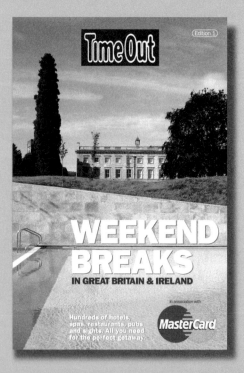

a National Heritage Site and the museum is a good example of a community rehabilitating a toxic industrial relic. The site is a favourite with moviemakers: among its screen credits, *We're No Angels*, *This Boy's Life* and *Insomnia*.

Britannia Beach also offers an art gallery/shop featuring local Salish paintings, carvings and jewellery and a couple of quite decent, unpretentious food joints. The Mountain Woman Take Out, in a converted bus, does good fish and chips, poutine and burgers at rock bottom prices.

Twelve kilometres (seven miles) further up the road, **Squamish** marks the halfway point. From the road, this is a typical North American pitstop: gas, burgers and more of the same. Explore a little deeper and this First Nations municipality affords enough activities to boast it's 'the outdoor capital of Canada'. Rock climbers flock here to tackle the Stawamus Chief – a 652 metre (2,139 foot) granite outcrop with more than 200 climbing routes – and windsurfers come to pit themselves against the strong winds that gust across Howe Sound. 'Squamish' means 'Mother of the winds'.

If you're looking for food or a place to stay in Squamish, your best bet is the Howe Sound Inn & Brewing Company (37801 Cleveland Avenue, 604 892 2603, www.howesound.com, main courses $8.99-$14.99, doubles $95-$105), a microbrewery which comes with 20 simply furnished but attractively priced rooms and the best dining in town.

In this vicinity you'll also find the **West Coast Railway Heritage Park** (Government Road, Squamish, 604 898 9336, www.wcra.org), **Shannon Falls** and **Alice Lake** (a popular campsite and picnicking spot 13 kilometres/eight miles north of Squamish; www.alice lakepark.com). **Brackendale** is a must-see if you're here between the months of November and February, when literally thousands of bald eagles converge to feast on the even greater numbers of salmon that die in the Squamish river after the spawning season. There is a viewing platform along Government Road (*see p141*).

BC Museum of Mining

Highway 99, Britannia Beach (toll free 1-800 896 4044/www.bcmuseumofmining.org). **Open** *May-Thanksgiving* 9am-5.30pm daily. *Thanksgiving-May* 9am-4.30pm daily (some exhibits and gift shop closed in winter). **Admission** *Summer* $14.98 adults; $11.75 concessions. *Winter* $6. **Credit** AmEx, MC, V.

Whistler Village

A large bronze plaque on the floor of Whistler's shoebox of a museum tells the story of the ski resort's development. In the 1960s, an IOC representative surveyed the area and proclaimed it 'one of the best sites in North America to meet all criteria for an Olympic bid'. Roads and lifts were subsequently built, and in February 1966, **Whistler** – until then known as London Mountain with a local population of 25 people – commenced operation. Apparently locals had called the mountain Whistler for years, allegedly 'because of the shrill whistle made by the Western Hoary Marmots who lived among the rocks'. Three failed bids to host the winter games were a source of frustration, losing to Sapporo in 1972, Innsbruck in 1976 and Lake Placid in 1980. It will have taken 44 years when Whistler finally achieves its goal and hosts the 2010 Winter Olympics.

Plans to develop a town centre began in the late 1970s on a site that was then the community garbage dump but which today commands some of the highest prices in Canadian real estate. According to the Canada Mortgage and Housing Corporation, the average price of a Whistler home is over a million dollars, making it the most expensive municipality in the country. If you're after a $20-million mansion, come and get it. But if you need rental accommodation more in line with your salary, you're likely out of luck, or in for a long wait – currently three years.

Zero help, not to mention hope, is available to the thousands of seasonal workers from Australia and the UK who fly here each November in search of work and a place to live for the season. In 2003, one local home owner was prosecuted after taking rent from 70 tenants who were found living sardine-style in the crawl-spaces of his single-dwelling home. Not much has changed since, and the problem isn't expected to ease until after 2010 when the facility built for Olympic athletes will be handed down, and converted into staff housing.

Nevertheless, Whistler/Blackcomb remains an irresistible magnet for snow hounds. For one thing, it is a good bet for North America's longest ski season. In 2004/5, the resort stayed open for 198 days from late November to early June. And if at the end of the season you're still dying for snow, the Blackcomb Glacier is open through the summer with various specialised ski and snowboard camps. In fact, the latest visitor numbers show that summer outstrips winter in popularity by almost a half a million people. A newly developed mountain bike park is the principal draw but Whistler's freshwater lakes, parks for picnicking, bear watching, camping and hiking are increasingly appealing to travellers of a more modest budget.

Occasionally, visiting foreigners are under the impression that they have landed smack in the middle of the Rockies when, actually, Whistler and Blackcomb are part of the much more climatically-temperate Coast Mountain Range – the Rocky Mountain Range is further to the east, running through Banff, Alberta. The area is considered to be part of British Columbia's rainforest. The average winter alpine temperature rarely dips below minus five degrees centigrade (23 degrees Fahrenheit). Compare that to Sunshine Village in Banff at minus 12 degrees centigrade (ten degrees Fahrenheit), and you're looking at one layer of clothing less at least. The 'rainforest' aspect can make for worrisomely wet village weather but more often than not the prodigious precipitation means powder at the top. Whistler's average snowfall is a towering nine metres (30 feet).

Navigating the village can be a challenge. Bear in mind that the Upper Village (at the foot of Blackcomb) is a five minute walk from the more developed Lower Village. (Whistler Creekside is a quieter, self-sufficient resort with its own gondola, but it's five minutes' drive from the dining options of the Lower Village.) Most stores and restaurants face inward along a zigzag pedestrian mall of identikit faux-alpine architecture that some locals describe as the 'Disneyland of the North'. Parking is scarce and the no-car zone means that taxis can't always deliver to the door of the restaurant you've booked. Luckily, what will never be lost to you are the mountains in front: Whistler to your right; Blackcomb to your left.

Skiing

Whistler's greatest feature is its offer of two distinct, fully operating mountains sitting side by side. Growing tired of the resort's terrain is almost inconceivable. There is simply too much ground – 2,800 hectares (7,000 acres), 200 trails, 33 lifts. To think that you can cover it in a week's stay is akin to believing you can do the Louvre in a 20-minute run-through. The bonus is, whatever ticket you purchase, from a day pass to a season pass, is valid on both mountains so theoretically yes, you could ski Whistler in the morning and Blackcomb in the afternoon. But on this debate it's best to take the locals' advice: pick a mountain and stick with it for the day, if for no other reason than the travel-time on lifts between mountains wastes valuable skiing time. Intrawest plans to connect the two mountains with a new $50 million, 4.4 kilometre (2.7 mile) gondola

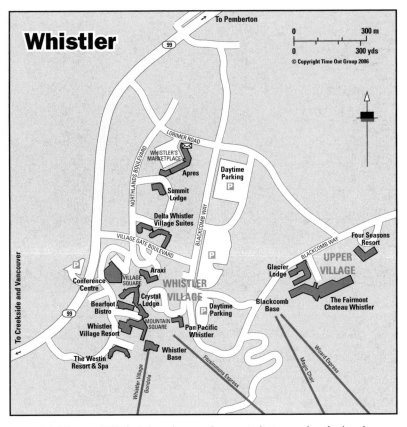

Whistler

To Pemberton

99

| 0 | | | | 300 m |
| 0 | | | | 300 yds |

© Copyright Time Out Group 2006

LORIMER ROAD

WHISTLER'S
MARKETPLACE

NORTHLANDS BOULEVARD

Apres

Daytime
Parking
P

Summit
Lodge

Delta Whistler
Village Suites

BLACKCOMB WAY

VILLAGE GATE BOULEVARD

P

Four Seasons
Resort

BLACKCOMB WAY

UPPER
VILLAGE

Glacier
Lodge

To Creekside and Vancouver

P

Araxi

VILLAGE
SQUARE

WHISTLER
VILLAGE

Conference
Centre

Crystal
Lodge

Bearfoot
Bistro

99

MOUNTAIN
SQUARE

Whistler
Village Resort

P

Daytime
Parking

Pan Pacific
Whistler

Blackcomb
Base

The Fairmont
Chateau Whistler

The Westin
Resort & Spa

Whistler
Base

Whistler Village
Gondola

Fitzsimmons Express

Magic Chair

Wizard Express

suspended 415 metres (1,360 feet) above the valley floor, but that dream won't become a reality before 2007/8 at the earliest. Until then, the question remains open: which mountain to choose? Locals love them both. Here are a few insider tips to help you make your decision.

Blackcomb vs Whistler

In general, boarders prefer Blackcomb. It is the newer of the two developments, the result of which is a better-designed fall line – a good fall line means fewer flat patches to traverse. Traversing is anathema to boarders who have to unbuckle from their boards and trudge across the flats. By contrast, Whistler's infamous nickname is 'Traverseler'; wide flat patches are not uncommon.

That said, on days of massive, fresh snowfall, powder addicts of both ski and snowboard persuasion invariably head to Whistler where

the opportunity to scoop lap after lap of untouched high alpine powder is greater. And pay attention here because this is the top, big secret among locals: Harmony Chair and Peak Chair on Whistler are the fastest, most direct lines to the good stuff on a powder day. Sure, Blackcomb's bowls of Ruby, Diamond, Sapphire and Garnet offer some of the best, steep, avalanche-controlled powder in the world but here's the deal: they take two chairlifts to get to. You don't have time for this. 'Whistler for freshies. Blackcomb for leftovers.' Remember this old chestnut, and you're on the right track.

Note: when you're queuing at the Peak chair on Whistler, look to your right at the long cliff band known as the Waterfalls, and further along, the famous rocky outcropping known as Air Jordan. You'll be able to see, live, one of the sport's most dangerous attractions: skiers and boarders lined up like lemmings to throw themselves off cliffs from life-threatening

heights. They're insane but it's fun to watch. Oh, and if you're a beginner and it's a powder day, the locals have this to say, with all due respect: 'Take a lesson or go shopping.' For beginners powder's like death by quicksand.

Whistler Mountain's other big plus is the sun. Sol crests Whistler before illuminating Blackcomb. A Fresh Tracks ticket (extra $18) allows you on the lifts early to load up with scrambled eggs and bacon at 7.15am while watching the sun rise in the Roundhouse at the top of Whistler. Apart from Seventh Heaven, most of Blackcomb doesn't see sun until 11am.

Not that this should deter you from Blackcomb. For a start, Seventh Heaven is the Shangri-la of mountain vistas. Frequently, when the village is enveloped with fog and rain, the chairlift ascent through the clouds is like a new day. You're literally lifted through a ceiling of cloud into an ear-popping altitude of blue sky and airplane-like views. Likewise, the intermediate skier should not miss a chance to cruise and conquer Blackcomb's glacier. The glacier is within bounds, patrolled and avalanche controlled, yet the short hike in makes it feel like serious, backcountry terrain.

Also on Blackcomb, treat yourself to the resort's best lunch at **Crystal Hut**, with its wood-burning oven, roasted salmon and chicken, and dessert waffles. But arrive before noon. The Crystal Hut is the cutest log cabin, and packs out early. In fact, wherever lunch is concerned, arrive early or late, avoiding the

madness of noon to two o'clock. Don't bother skiing to the base for lunch, either. Lift traffic is at its worst at the bottom. As mountain employees say: 'Go high and stay high'.

Beginners

For the Very First Time Beginner, there's really no better experience than Whistler Mountain. Ski school meets at mid-station, which means you get to take the gondola like a normal person, elbow to elbow with the gnarliest of experts. You've travelled to the big leagues, after all. Who wants to be ostracised at the bottom on the bunny hill beside the pavement? However, ski instructors also warn that Blackcomb's many narrow roads are a hazard to first time beginners, whose newly learned stopping skills may not be sufficient to ensure they don't disappear over the road's far lip.

For the more experienced beginner (able to ski green runs solo) either mountain is a great choice. You'll find long, cruisey trails beginning at every lift, from top to bottom (with the exception of the two T-bars on Blackcomb, which are designated intermediate). A team of 80, friendly, red-jacketed 'Mountain Hosts' patrol the slopes to answer questions and provide directions. They also 'police' the lift lines, although European visitors, used to the chaos of continental queuing patterns, might wonder why anyone needs to regiment the orderly skiers waiting their turn.

Children

Whistler is a great place for children to learn to ski and snowboard. Programmes start for three-year-olds and continue up to 18. If your children are tiny and just beginning, then the bunny hill at the base of Blackcomb is probably the best (they won't have to negotiate the Gondola as well as all the equipment that, even at three, they are expected to carry themselves). Small groups start off making pizza slices (snow ploughs), learn to stop, and sing their ABC's while standing on the 'magic carpet' (a conveyor belt that takes them back up the slope). If they get too tired, or upset, they can adjourn from the slopes and play inside the adjoining nursery. Fives and up will prefer Whistler, where they travel halfway up the mountain for lessons. (Tip: kit your child out with their skis, boots, helmet, etc the night before they start – it can be really overwhelming for them otherwise.)

Groups are organised first by age (three and four; five and six; seven to 12; 13-18) and then by ability; snowboarding lessons are only available for six years and up. Choose between three and five day adventure camps, where your child stays with the same instructor all week, or book individual days. Lunch and snacks are included.

Whistler Kids

Toll free 1-866 298 9690/www.whistlerblackcomb.com. Prices for lesson, lift and rentals range from $126-$167 (increasing with age) per day. If you're travelling off-season check the dates for half price 'Whistler Days'. Day care is available for babies and toddlers aged three-48 months at $98 per day. Advance booking is recommended.

Lift prices

Prices fluctuate throughout the season from early pre-Christmas to spring, according to the basic economic laws of supply and demand. For instance, a one-day lift pass in December's busy period, 2004, cost $72. The same ticket in April, with fewer people and superior conditions, was $45. Best to check online at www.whistler blackcomb.com/tickets/winter for latest pricing.

Summer

Whistler now attracts more visitors in the summer months than during the ski season – in fact this area has been pulling Vancouverites north for some backwoods adventure since the 1920s, when the trip involved ferry, rail and horse travel (and you still got change from $5).

While some things may have changed in the intervening 85 years, the mountains remain the main attraction, and the Whistler Village Gondola remains the quickest way to climb to 1,830 metres (6,000 feet) (a single ride costs $25; $20 concessions; $7 7-12s; free under-7s). You can snack at the Roundhouse Lodge and choose between a dozen mountaintop trails, ranging from an easy 30-minute stroll to a 21-kilometre (13 mile) trek back to the village via Singing Pass. Even in August there is still snow on the peaks, and you are advised to stick to the prescribed trails. More adventurous souls can try mountaineering, glacier walking, rap jumping (abseiling head downwards from Whistler peak) or horseback and all terrain vehicle (ATV) tours.

There are more hiking and cycle trails down in the valley, along with such gentle pursuits as golf, canoeing and kayaking on Alta Lake, and fishing. At the base of Blackcomb in the Upper Village a kids' adventure zone includes a bungee trampoline, a 315-metre (1,033-foot) luge, a maze, a climbing wall, a human gyroscope, pony rides, and even a flying trapeze – open to all-comers, early June to October.

Several local tour operators also offer white-water rafting. The rafting itself is a fun day out – with tremendous scenery to enjoy on the calmer stretches – but do be aware that it takes about two hours each way to reach the rapids on the Elaho river.

Go to www.tourismwhistler.com for further information and links.

Bears

It is by no means uncommon to see bears in Whistler. These are black bear, not grizzly. If you keep your distance the bear will likely do the same. If it's a close encounter, back off slowly, facing the animal, speaking in a normal voice. If you're face-to-face, waving a large stick and screaming is in order – as is climbing the nearest tree (although the bear may follow you up). In an effort to minimise serious human/bear contact (usually necessitating killing the beast) various measures are implemented involving electric fences and closing areas to humans. If you are planning to do some independent hiking or camping, it would be an idea to read up on guidelines regarding the storing and cooking of food and other measures to prevent unwelcome ursine contacts; www.bearsmart.com is a good place to start. Although bear walks are available, sightings are not guaranteed. The tours take you through their typical habitats – both woodland and alpine meadow – pointing out food sources and old hibernation dwellings. It makes for a pleasant walk and you'll learn a lot, but you're just as likely to spot a bear in the parking lot.

Mountain biking

Despite the body armour mountain bikers wear (crash helmets, gloves, goggles, elbow and knee pads are absolutely *de rigueur*), and despite the vertiginous trails and jumps they throw themselves down, the sport itself is relatively easy to pick up. As in any other kind of cycling, you regulate your speed with the brake. Unlike conventional cycling, you'll rarely be troubled to pedal; gravity does the work for you. The trick of it is to steer with your eyes. Look down at the ground and that's where you'll end up. Instead, keep your eyes fixed on the route ahead – spotting the best line on corners and through obstacles natural and man-made – and your bike will follow. That's the theory anyhow.

What Hawaii is to surfboarders, Whistler has become to 'free riders'. The sport was more or less invented on Vancouver's North Shore, but Whistler has the chairlifts. When your bike weighs about 20 kg (50 lbs) that makes a big difference. There are now more than 200 kilometres (124 miles) of lift-serviced bike trails on Whistler-Blackcomb catering to all levels of expertise and attracting 100,000 visitors a year.

Whistler Mountain Bike Park

(604 932 3434/toll free 1-866 218 9690/www. whistlerblackcomb.com/bike). **Open** *May-Oct* (phone for exact dates) 10am-5pm daily. **Rates** $41/day; $36/day 13-17s; $21/day 10-12s. *Bike and armour rental* approx $120/day. **Credit** AmEx, MC, V.

Zip trekking

You might be forgiven for thinking zip trekking is a children's adventure playground ride scaled up for adults. It involves harnessing yourself to a high tension steel cable and a pulley, then launching from one of five tree-top platforms that stud Fitzsimmons Creek in the valley between Whistler and Blackcomb mountains. The ziplines range between 24 and 335 metres (80 and 1,100 feet) in length, and, depending on your weight, you could reach speeds of up to 72 kilometres per hour (45 miles per hour). Part thrill ride, part bird's-eye-view nature trail, the zip trek lasts two-and-a-half hours.

Ziptrek Ecotours

Carleton Lodge, Whistler Village (604 935 0001/ www.ziptrek.com). **Open** year round; phone for reservations. **Rates** $98 adults; $78 concessions. **Credit** AmEx, MC, V.

Shopping

The 'village stroll' is seemingly designed to get visitors from A to B by way of as many store-fronts as possible. If you're in the market for ski-wear, fleeces and woolly jumpers, you'll be in hog heaven. Roots, Gap and Spirit of the North rub shoulders with countless lesser-known brands. There are two supermarkets in the Lower Village, one in the Marketplace and the other at the Village Square. You will have to go next door to the liquor store to buy alcohol. Cuban cigars, on the other hand, are available in abundance, reminding visiting Americans what they're missing. There is a farmers' market every Sunday in the Upper Village from mid June to early October, 11am to 4pm.

Where to stay

Most tourists will arrive in Whistler on package deals, although the new low-cost flights from Europe to Vancouver are bringing in more independent travellers. Budget rooms are at a premium all year round and virtually unknown in the ski season. A central reservation system (toll free 1-888 403 4727, UK toll free 0800 731 5983, www.whistlerblackcomb.com) is in place for all properties in the area. Prices fluctuate wildly. We have quoted for the cheapest rooms in low and high season.

At the top end, the **Fairmont Chateau Whistler** (4599 Chateau Boulevard, 604 938 8000, www.fairmont.com/whistler, doubles $159-$309) is the granddaddy on the block, an imposing manse-like structure in the quieter Upper Village at the foot of Blackcomb. The cavernous lobby is a sightseeing attraction in itself, and the suites for gold level guests are huge. There are three restaurants, an indoor/outdoor pool with hot tubs, a sauna and eucalyptus steam rooms (swimming outside as the snow falls is a real treat here).

The Chateau has been usurped in the luxury stakes by the nearby **Four Seasons** (4591 Blackcomb Way, 604 935 3400, www.four seasons.com/whistler, doubles $245-$545), completed in 2004, and with an altogether more contemporary feel. A more intimate lobby reflects the hotel's boutique attitude (no conventions here), local art is prominently displayed and the rooms all feature wonderful walk-in slate showers, soaker tubs and L'Occitane products.

In the Lower Village, the **Pan Pacific Whistler Mountainside** (4320 Sundial Crescent, 604 905 2999, www.whistler. panpacific.com, studio suite $119-$389) has the prime location: you can practically step out of your room on to the lifts for either mountain and the pool deck overlooks the lower ski slopes. Rooms are all suites, with picture windows and full kitchen facilities.

If you prefer more independent accommodation, there are apartments, condos

Seeking powder

If you're looking for powder without the crowds and lift queues, consider some of these alternatives.

Callaghan Backcountry Ski Lodge (604 938 0616, toll free 1-877 938 0616, www.callaghancountry.com) 20 kilometres (12 miles) north of Whistler, offers ski-touring, snow-shoeing and cross-country skiing in unadulterated backcountry terrain. This is pure wilderness. The lodge is a three-storey Whistler-style cabin with eight private rooms. It sleeps 18 people, that's it. Packages are available for one to six days. Prices include all meals and non-alcoholic beverages. A standard room starts at $530. The developing Callaghan Valley has been chosen as the future site for the 2010 Olympic ski jumping events.

Whistler Heli-Skiing (604 932 4105, www.whistlerheliskiing.com), in operation since 1981, offers day trips from Whistler Village for the intermediate, advanced and expert powderhound. A typical days consists of three runs with descents anywhere from 1,370 to 2,300 vertical metres (4,500-7,500 feet) at a cost per person of $670. The Whistler Heli-Skiing Store is located in the Crystal Lodge (4154 Village Green). The day ends at Buffalo Bill's with a recap of video footage of the day's exploits. All guides are trained in avalanche safety, first aid, mountaineering and rope handling.

Powder Mountain Catskiing (604 932 0169, www.pmsnowcats.com) delivers the same vertical and powder but at prices cheaper than heli-skiing. It's also the perfect solution for the heli-phobic. Bombardier snowcats transport passengers high into the untracked lines of Tricouni Mountain, 20 kilometres (12 miles) south of Whistler. Guests meet at the Southside Deli in Creekside. Cost: $449 per day, per person, which includes breakfast and lunch.

and houses in every price range. On the edge of town in Village North, the **Valhalla** (4375 Northlands Boulevard, toll free 1-877 887 5422, www.whistlerblackcomb.com, doubles $109-$309) offers spacious accommodation for those on a moderate budget. Two bedroom condos, with sofabeds in the living room and full kitchen facilities, are comfortable and well-appointed. Cheaper still, **Glacier Lodge** (4573 Chateau Boulevard, 604 938 3455, www.glacier-lodge.com, doubles $79-$329) in the Upper Village is basic, but well situated. **Le Chamois** (4557 Blackcomb Way, 604 932 4113, www.wild flowerlodge.com/lechamois.html, doubles $125-$250) is a good mid-range choice in the Upper Village, although cooking facilities in some suites consist of a microwave and toaster-oven.

Whistler Creekside has its own gondola and amenities, but it's five minutes drive to the village dining options. At the base of the gondola, **First Tracks Lodge** (2202 Gondola Way, 604 938 9999, www.whistler blackcomb.com, doubles $109-$299) offers plush suites with kitchens good enough that you won't need to eat out every night anyway.

Where to eat

There is no shortage of places to eat – and eat well – in Whistler. Compared to Vancouver, however, it is expensive. With a great location on the Village Square and a reputation to match, **Araxi** (4222 Village Square, 604 932 4540, www.araxi.com, main courses $28-$39) is the place to see and be seen. A large, vibrant room, it includes an excellent seafood bar at the front and a patio (heated in winter) to people-watch. The menu draws from local produce.

Trips Out of Town

The Four Seasons' **Fifty Two 80 Bistro** (4591 Blackcomb Way, 604 966 5280, www.fourseasons.com/whistler, main courses $15-$30), named after Whistler peak's vertical mile, is the newcomer in the local fine dining scene and has been tempting people to the Upper Village for its elegant surroundings, inventive use of regional produce and some exclusively held British Columbian wines. Summer brings a more casual (and affordable) weekly seafood barbecue on the patio.

When asked to nominate the best places in town concierges will instantly rattle off these plus the **Bearfoot Bistro** (4121 Village Green, 604 932 3433, www.bearfootbistro.com, tasting menu $90-$225), for its elaborate multi-course tasting menus, and the **Rim Rock Café** (2117 Whistler Road, 604 932 5565, www.rimrock whistler.com, main courses $18-$36), an unpretentious log cabin specialising in fish and game. But for an upscale meal in more modern surroundings try **Après** (103-4338 Main Street, 604 935 0200, www.apres restaurant.com, main courses $30-$59), where boldly creative dishes are served in a coolly contemporary atmosphere.

You don't have to break the bank to find good food however. Chef Bernard's **Ciao-Thyme Bistro** (1-4573 Chateau Boulevard, 604 932 9795, www.chefbernards.ca, main courses $15-$19) serves breakfast and lunch, then morphs seamlessly into BBK's Pub for dinner. Under either name this Upper Village eaterie ticks all the right boxes: fresh ingredients simply, yet precisely, prepared and at surprisingly reasonable prices from the Chateau Whistler's former executive chef.

In the Lower Village the regular queues outside **Caramba! Restaurante** (12-4314 Main Street, 604 938 1879, www.caramba-restaurante.com, main courses $11.95-$32.95) speak volumes. A wide range of pastas (all available in half portions), pizzas and spit-roasted meats with mashed potatoes hit the spot after a day on the slopes. Or, for an alpine experience from a different continent, make your way to **Bavaria** (101-4369 Main Street, 604 932 7518, www.bavaria-restaurant.com, main courses $18.95-$38.95) in the Village North. The menu fairly sags with hearty schnitzel and *spaetzle*, but the real fun is to be had with the fondues – choose from meat or cheese and finish off with the yummy chocolate.

For lighter fare, there are cafés around every corner. Try **Mogul's Café** (4208 Village Square, 604 932 4845) for excellent coffee and muffins and WiFi access, **Hot Buns Bakery** (4232 Village Stroll, 604 932 6883) for

Bro-speak: lessons in the local lingo

Amped *adjective* – stirred emotionally, aroused, as in: 'Dude, I'm amped. It dumped all night.'

Blower *noun* – snow prized for its fine, arid texture and float-away lightness, as in: 'Dude, it's blower. I'm totally amped.'

Chowder *verb* – to humiliate oneself through human error as in: 'Dude, I totally chowdered that line.'

Dump *noun* – copious snowfall. **Dumped**, **dumping** *verb* – past and present tense of copious snowfall or snow falling during a storm as in: 'Dude, it's dumping. I'm amped.'

Eating it *adverbial phrase* – meaning spectacular fall or crash. **To eat** *verb*, past tense **ate**, as in: 'Dude, he ate it.'

Epic *noun* or *adjective* – referring to a series of great (most likely personal) achievements worthy of lengthy alcohol-induced narration as in: 'Dude, it was epic,' etc and so forth.

Gondubula *noun* – passenger-carrying box-shaped lift in which to smoke a joint.

Gorby *noun* (pl. Gorbies) – derogative reference to novice skier, especially a tourist, derived from G (geek) O (on) R (rental) B (boards).

Poacher *noun* – morally impaired individual involved in the crime of butting ahead in the lift queue.

Scoping lines *adverbial phrase* – to investigate and hunt for, esp. from chairlift, next desirable line or route down the face of the mountain

Shredding the gnar *adjectival phrase* – circa 1999. Current usage is ironic, implying the successful execution of a sick line by a Gorby as in: 'Dude, look! He's shredding the gnar! No wait! He's eating it!'

Sick *adjective* – exceptionally good or unusual; marvellous, superb.

croissants, baguette sandwiches and French style crêpes, **Hotbox Internet + Coffee** (Town Plaza, 604 905 5644, www.hotbox internet.com) where the latte art is as good as the coffee and (quickly sold out) croissants, and don't miss **Ingrid's Village Café** (4305 Skiers Approach, 604 932 7000) for a great selection of veggie burgers, sandwiches and soups.

Nightlife

Nightclubbing with the in-crowd is as simple as the days of the week. For the 19 to 26-year-olds (be sure to bring photo ID or risk being arrested, jailed and fined) here's how it rotates. Monday is **Tommy Africa's** (4216 Gateway Drive, 604 932 6090, admission free-$28). Tuesday is the **Savage Beagle** (4222 Village Stroll, 604 938 3337, admission free-$15). Wednesday is **Buffalo Bill's** (4122 Village Green, 604 932 6613, admission free-$20). Thursday is **Garf's** (1-4308 Main Street, 604 932 2323, admission free-$12). Friday is **Moe Joe's** (4115 Golfer's Approach, 604 935 1152, admission free-$15). Saturday is wherever you can get in (read: a good night for a house party). Sunday is the **Longhorn** (4280 Mountain Square, 604 932 5999) at the base of Whistler Mountain, or the **Boot Pub** (7124 Nancy Greene Drive, 604 932 3338, admission free-$10), depending on your tastes. If you like live punk, the Boot is the place to be Sundays and Mondays, and on four of the other five nights, this institution features stage shows with 'dancing' women taking off all their clothes. Clubs don't start rocking until late, so on nights out, **Merlin's** (Blackcomb Daylodge, Upper Village, 604 938 7700), is a good place to start with the cheapest beer and burgers in town.

For the slightly older crowd the **Dubh Linn Gate** (Pan Pacific, 4320 Sundial Crescent, toll free 1-800 387 3311) serves up live Celtic music and cover tunes in a pub setting.

For the even older, more mellow crowd, the **Mallard Lounge** (4599 Chateau Boulevard, 604 938 8000) at the Fairmont Chateau is all about sofas and fireplaces and scotch on the rocks, and usually someone crooning at the grand piano. Off season: the **Bearfoot Bistro** (*see p222*) throws its annual MasqueRave party ($195 per person) in November. Capacity: 2,000 people. Yes, that's right, the girls serving drinks are only wearing body paint.

Getting there

By car

It takes two hours to drive the 120 kilometres (75 miles) from Vancouver up Highway 99.

By bus

Perimeter (604 266 5386, toll free 1-877 317 7788, www.perimeterbus.com) runs a regular direct express bus service from Vancouver airport to Whistler. There are 11 departures daily throughout the ski season, with seven in the summer, and the bus will pick up from downtown hotels. Tickets are $65 each way and reservations are required. Journey time is approximately three hours.

Greyhound (604 482 8747, www.greyhound. ca) runs seven buses a day from Pacific Central Station, 1150 Station Street, Vancouver for a cost of $31.60. The journey time is two hours and 20 minutes.

By rail

From May 2006 the **Whistler Mountaineer** (604 606 7245, www.whistlermountaineer.com) promises a daily service departing the BC Rail Station at Pemberton Avenue, North Vancouver at 8.30am. Downtown pick ups and a light meal are included in the price, $99 one-way, $179 round-trip. Reservations required.

Tourist information

Tourism Whistler Activity and Information Centre

4010 Whistler Way (604 938 2769/toll free 1-877 991 9988/www.tourismwhistler.com). **Open** 9am-5pm daily.

GET IT OFF YOUR CHEST

Let us know what you think about Time Out guides and you could win ten guides of your choice. We know you've got an opinion – and we want to hear it.

Go to www.timeout/guidesfeedback.com
Every month another reader will win ten city guides of their choice.

Directory

Getting Around	**226**
Resources A-Z	**230**
Further Reference	**238**
Index	**240**
Advertisers' Index	**244**

Features

Travel advice	230
Average temperatures	236

Directory

Getting Around

By air

Vancouver International Airport

604 207 7077/www.yvr.ca.
Vancouver International
Airport is situated on Sea
Island, approximately 10km
(6 miles) south of downtown.
The largest airport on the west
coast of Canada, it's a major
hub for both international and
domestic flights. Besides flights
to other Canadian cities, and a
host of smaller destinations
within British Columbia,
Vancouver International Airport
is particularly convenient for
flights to and from the west
coast of the USA. Anyone
flying from Vancouver to the
US should note that American
customs and immigration
checks must be gone through
before you board the plane.

There are three terminals at
Vancouver International Airport:
the International Terminal
(arrivals are on Level 2, departures
are on Level 3); the Domestic
Terminal (arrivals are on Level
2, departures are on Level 3); and
the South Terminal. The South
Terminal is on the Fraser River
and provides access to seaplane
facilities, helicopter operations
and an array of small plane
airlines that serve destinations
in and around Vancouver,
Vancouver Island and the Gulf
Islands, as well as mainland
British Columbia.

It is estimated that by 2010
21 million passengers a year will
be passing through Vancouver
International Airport.
Consequently, the Airport
Authority has embarked on a ten
year, $1.4 billion development
plan to improve facilities at the
airport. An Airport Improvement
Fee ($5 for passengers travelling
to a destination within British

Columbia or the Yukon, and $15
for all other destinations) is now
being levied to help fund this
development.

There are several means of
getting to and from Vancouver
International Airport. The
quickest and most convenient
is by taxi. 400 licensed taxis
serve the airport on a 24/7 basis,
charging between $25 and $30
(inclusive of taxes) for a trip to
or from downtown.

The airport bus service, or
Airporter (604 940 1707, www.
yvrairporter.com) as it is known,
runs every 20 minutes from 9am
to 7pm, and then every 30 minutes
from 7.15pm to 9.30pm. It calls
at major hotels in downtown,
the Canada Place Cruise Ship
Terminal and the bus depot/train
station. Adult fares are $12 one-
way, $18 return; children $5 single
or $10 return; seniors $9 or $17;
families $24 or $36 return.

Car rental can be arranged on
the ground floor of the Parkade/
Airport Car Park situated opposite
the Domestic and International
Terminals. Hertz, Avis, Budget
and Dollar Rent-a-car all have
offices in the Parkade. Rental cost
will vary according to vehicle size
and length of rental.

For those not in a hurry, or on
a budget, Vancouver city buses
offer the best alternative to the
Airporter and taxi services. Buses
arrive and depart from the Airport
Station Bus Terminal, which is
located near the Delta Hotel. A
connecting service (Route 424)
then transfers passengers to
and from the Ground Level of
the Domestic Terminal. Fares
must be paid in exact change
when boarding the bus. The
standard fare is currently $3.25,
or $2.25 after 6pm weekdays and
all day weekends. Tickets can also
be purchased at the 7-11 store and
the Pharmasave pharmacy, both
of which can be found in the
Domestic Terminal. Popular
routes include the 98 B Line
and Route 496 to downtown

Vancouver, Route 620 to BC
Ferries at Tsawwassen, and
Route C 92 which provides a
connecting service to the
airport's South Terminal.

The City of Vancouver, in
conjunction with TransLink
and its subsidiary RAV Project
Management Ltd (RAVCO), is
about to start construction of a
rapid transit rail link between
Richmond, Vancouver
International Airport and
downtown. Although its primary
role will be to ease commuter
traffic, the rail link will also be
of benefit to air passengers.
The RAV rapid transit line
(www.ravrapidtransit.com) is
scheduled to open by 2009.

Air Canada
Toll free 1-888 247 2262/
www.aircanada.com.

Air Canada Jazz
Toll free 1-888 247 2262/
www.flyjazz.com.

Air Canada Tango
Toll free 1-888 247 2262/
www.flytango.com.

Air France
Toll free 1-800 667 2747/
www.airfrance.com.

Air India
604 879 0271/
www.airindia.com.

American Airlines
Toll free 1-800 433 7300/
www.aa.com.

British Airways
Toll free 1-800 247 9297/
www.britishairways.com.

Cathay Pacific
Toll free 1-800 268 6868/604 606
8888/www.cathaypacific.com.

China Airlines
Toll free 1-800 227 5118/604 682
6028/www.china-airlines.com.

Japan Airlines
Toll free 1-800 525 3663/
www.jal.co.jp/en/.

Lufthansa Airlines
Toll free 1-800 563 5954/604 303 3086/www.lufthansa.com.

Northwest Airlines
Toll free 1-800 225 2525/ www.nwa.com.

Singapore Airlines
Toll free 1-800 663 3046/604 689 1223/www.singaporeair.com.

United Airlines
Toll free 1-800 241 6522/ www.united.com.

WestJet Airlines
Toll free 1-800 538 5696/ www.westjet.com.

By bus

The bus station in Vancouver is located in Pacific Central Station at 1150 Station Street, off Main Street, on the corner of Terminal Avenue. **Greyhound Canada** (604 482 8747, 1-800 661 8747, www.greyhound.ca) operates services across Canada and links Vancouver with Seattle, as well as other cities in the USA.

Pacific Coach Lines (604 662 8074, www.pacificcoach.com) runs buses to Victoria, on Vancouver Island, at 15 minutes to the hour throughout the day. The exact number of buses varies according to the season. Tickets include the ferry crossing. Adults $23.50, children $12, seniors $11.75.

Quick Coach Lines (604 940 4428, www.quickcoach.com) offers a daily shuttle service between Vancouver and Seattle, stopping at Seattle's Sea-Tac airport and Bellingham Airport along the way. Adults $36 one way, $65 roundtrip; seniors $34/$61; children 5-12 $20/$36; students (with ID card) $27/$49.

Amtrak, (1-800 872 7245, 604 585 4848, www.amtrak.com) America's major rail carrier, also runs four buses a day from Pacific Central Station to Seattle. The journeys take between 3-4hrs and depart at 5.45am, 8.45am, 12.30pm and 5.00pm. $25 adult; children 2-15 $12.50 roundtrip.

By rail

VIA Rail (1-888 842 7245, www.viarail.ca) operates from Pacific Central Station. The ticket desk is open daily and luggage can be checked in anytime after 8.30am

on day of departure. Its flagship service, 'The Canadian', departs Vancouver three times a week, (Tue, Fri and Sun), bound for Toronto. The journey takes three days and calls at Jasper, Edmonton, Saskatoon, Winnipeg and Toronto. At Jasper passengers can connect with 'The Skeena', a VIA train that runs north-west through the Rocky Mountains to Prince Rupert on the coast of British Columbia. 'The Skeena' stops for the night in Prince George (accommodation is not included in the ticket) and takes one day to reach Prince Rupert.

Rocky Mountaineer Railtours (1-877 460 3200, 604 606 7245, www.rockymountaineer. com) is a private company that specialises in luxury rail journeys through the Canadian Rockies. Trains depart from Pacific Central Station and take in stops at Whistler, Kamloops, Banff, Jasper and Calgary. High season runs from mid April to mid October, but winter packages are also available.

Amtrak (1-800 872 7245, 604 585 4848, www.amtrak.com) operates one train a day from Pacific Central Station to Seattle. The train leaves at 6pm and the journey takes 4hrs. From Seattle connections can be made for rail destinations across the USA.

By ferry

BC Ferries' (1-888 223 3779, www.bcferries.com) routes range from Prince Rupert, on the north-west coast of British Columbia to Victoria, on the southern tip of Vancouver Island. In between lie the Queen Charlotte Islands, the Gulf Islands (north and south) and the 'sunshine' coastal towns of Vancouver Island and mainland British Columbia. The company runs 35 vessels and has 47 ports of call. BC Ferries operates two main routes in and out of greater Vancouver. Tsawwassen, about an hour's drive south of downtown, is the terminal for ferries to and from Swartz Bay, which in turn is a 30 minute drive from Victoria. Horseshoe Bay, less than half-an-hour's drive north-west of downtown, is the terminal for ferries to and from Nanaimo. The respective crossings take between 1 to 2hrs. During the

summer months there is usually one crossing every hour between 7am and 10pm. The rest of the year the crossings usually run every 2 hours.

The most convenient way for foot passengers to use the ferry service is to book a ticket with one of the bus lines that connect with BC Ferries. The buses depart from Pacific Central Station on a regular basis.

If you are driving to Tsawwassen or Horseshoe Bay be aware that, unless you reserve in advance, during busy periods you may have to watch one or two ferries sail away before getting on board yourself.

By cruise ship

The Vancouver-Alaska cruise route is the third most popular in the world. Some of the biggest and most luxurious liners arrive and depart from the Canada Place and Ballantyne terminals in the Port of Vancouver. The Canada Place terminal is located in the city centre (999 Canada Place) and the Ballantyne terminal is just east of Canada Place (655 Centennial Road) near the Port's container terminals.

There are 13 cruise lines operating 30 ships out of the Port of Vancouver. Details of the cruise lines, their vessels, schedules and fares can be found on the Port of Vancouver website. Go to www.portvancouver.com and then click the Vancouver-Alaska Cruise link in the menu on the left-hand side of the page.

Passengers who require long-term car parking facilities should contact Cruisepark (1-800 665 0050, 604 266 4243, www.cruise park.com) or Citipark (1-866 856 2254, 604 684 2251) for details about long-stay deals.

Public transport

Vancouver has a varied, efficient and well-integrated public transport network operated by the Greater Vancouver Transportation Authority (TransLink).

City buses offer the most effective and comprehensive means of getting around Vancouver. During the daytime there is at least one bus every ten minutes on most routes, and the NightBus service operates at 30-minute intervals, seven days a week, until 3am. Note that you will need the exact fare when making your journey by bus.

The **SkyTrain** is an iconic symbol of Vancouver, but it does not cover enough of the city to be a stand-alone mode of transport. The addition of the Richmond/Airport/Vancouver line and the Coquitlam line in 2009 will go some way to addressing this problem. However, used with the bus service it is a fast, fun and uncrowded way of getting around. Services on the SkyTrain run 5am-midnight Mon-Fri; 6am-midnight Sat; 7am-11pm Sun. The average wait for a train is approximately 4 minutes, but the frequency of the service can range from 2-8 minutes depending on the time of day.

The **SeaBus** offers a very specific service between Waterfront Station in downtown and Lonsdale Quay in North Vancouver. Sailings in both directions occur at 15-30 minute intervals depending on the time of day. The service runs 6am-midnight Mon-Sat; 8am-11pm Sun. The SeaBus service connects with the SkyTrain and buses at Waterfront Station. The crossing takes approximately 12 minutes.

If you begin your journey by bus and plan on making a connection be sure to ask the driver for a transfer to prove you have paid the fare. Tickets for the SkyTrain and SeaBus are available from stations and terminals. Ticket machines accept $5 and $10 bills as well as coins.

Translink information

For àn in-depth guide to public transport in Vancouver visit www.translink.bc.ca or call the information line on 604 953 3333. The *Transportation Services Guide For Greater Vancouver* is a map of bus, SkyTrain and SeaBus routes. It's available from bookstores, convenience stores and tourist information offices. The SkyTrain and SeaBus are wheelchair accessible, but not all city buses provide this service. If you know the bus route you'd like to take contact TransLink for accessibility details.

Fares & tickets

Vancouver is divided into three zones for the purposes of ticketing. The Yellow Zone (Zone 1) covers downtown; the Red Zone (Zone 2) covers the suburbs, and the Green Zone (Zone 3) covers the city's metropolitan districts. Although the majority of visitors will spend most of their time in downtown it should be noted that North Vancouver and Vancouver International Airport are in the Red Zone.

If you will only be making one or two trips a day on public transport a cash fare is your best option. A Zone 1 journey will cost $2.25 adult, $1.50 concession; a Zone 1-2 journey will cost $3.25 adult, $2 concession; and a Zone 1-3 journey will cost $4.50 adult, $3 concession. After 6.30pm an All Zone ticket is $2.25 adult, $1.50 concession. Cash tickets are only valid for 90 minutes, but this is an ample amount of time for any journey you are likely to make on the TransLink system.

If your day is likely to involve using a lot of public transport your best option is a DayPass. It's valid all day and covers all three zones for $8 adult, $6 concession.

An alternative to a DayPass is a book of ten FareSaver Tickets. A book of Zone 1 tickets costs $18; a book of tickets for Zones 1-2 costs $27, and for Zones 1-3 it's $36. Visitors should note that these tickets can only be used up to 6.30pm and, as with cash fares, each ticket lasts a maximum of 90 minutes.

If you are staying in Vancouver for a month, consider buying a Monthly FareCard. They cost $69 for travel in Zone 1; $95 for travel in Zones 1-2, and $130 for travel in Zones 1-3. If you are entitled to a concessionary fare an All Zone Monthly FareCard costs just $40.

DayPasses, FareSaver Tickets and Monthly FareCards are all available from SkyTrain stations, SeaBus terminals and any shop displaying the FareDealer sign.

As a tourist you will be entitled to the concessionary fares if you are a senior citizen or a child between the ages of 3-13. If your children are around the age of 13 it would be best to have some photo ID handy as proof of age. Children under the age of 3 travel free.

SkyTrain

Vancouver's SkyTrain (604 953 3333/www.translink.bc.ca) is the longest automated light rapid transit system in the world. It covers 49km (30 miles) and stops at 32 stations across downtown and the Greater Vancouver area. The system is composed of two lines: the Millennium Line runs from Waterfront Station out towards Burnaby, New Westminster and Coquitlam before looping around the edge of Surrey to take a more southerly route back to Waterfront Station; the Expo Line also runs from Waterfront Station but follows the southerly route of the Millennium Line through Burnaby, New Westminster and then on to King George in Surrey.

As with the SeaBus you do not need the exact fare to purchase a ticket for the SkyTrain but, as with any cash fare, be sure to ask for a transfer if you are making a connection. The longest journey on the SkyTrain system takes approximately 40 minutes, but all TransLink cash tickets are valid for 1 hour so you should have no problem completing your journey within the allotted time frame.

SkyTrain fares vary according to age, the zones you travel in, and the time of day you are travelling. If you plan on using the SkyTrain regularly a book of ten FareSaver tickets, or a DayPass, might be your best option. FareSaver tickets also serve as transfers. Fares range from $2.25 for a single journey in Zone 1, to $36 for a book of ten FareSaver tickets that allow travel across all 3 zones. A DayPass valid for all zones costs $8. Children 4 years and younger travel free, and there are concessions for older children, students and seniors.

Taxis

All taxi firms in Vancouver are regulated by the City of Vancouver and the British Columbia Motor Carrier Commission (604 453 4250). The meter starts at $2.60 and the cost for each successive kilometre is $1.50.

Drivers are not allowed to make unsolicited recommendations regarding hotels and restaurants etc., but if you ask for such information they can then legally impart their local knowledge.

If you think you may have left an item in a taxi call the firm directly.

Black Top & Checker Cabs
604 731 1111.

MacLure's Cabs
604 731 9211.

Vancouver Taxi
604 871 1111.

Yellow Cab
604 681 1111.

Driving

Vancouverites love to complain about the traffic, but save for a couple of main arteries at rush hour (the Lions Gate Bridge, Highway 99 towards the Oak Street Bridge) you are unlikely to encounter anything that visitors from London, New York, LA or Paris would consider even a minor hold up. This city is eminently traversable by car – but you probably won't need one until you explore the North Shore or venture further into British Columbia.

The city speed limit is 50km/h (31mph) unless otherwise specified. In school zones it drops to 30km/h. On the bridges, it rises to 60km/h. On freeways the limit ranges between 80 and 110km/h.

Driving regulations are similar to those in Britain, with the obvious proviso that you drive on the right-hand side of the road. Seat-belts are mandatory. You are obliged to yield to public buses. Keep your eyes out for overhead traffic lights and stop at stop signs. You may turn right on a red light once pedestrians have crossed and it is safe to do so.

Turning left at intersections, vehicles are expected to cross in front of their opposite number.

Pedestrians have right of way at crosswalks and intersections, and outside of the main thoroughfares drivers will generally stop if a pedestrian is even approaching the curb at an intersection.

Breakdown services

Unless your home Automobile Association has a reciprocal arrangement with the Canadian Automobile Association (604 268 5600 or 604 293 2222 for road service) you will need a towing service. In Vancouver, Busters tow trucks are ubiquitous as they're contracted by the city to impound illegally parked vehicles (call 604 685 7246 if your parked car has vanished). But they also offer an emergency road service (604 685 8181, www.busterstowing.com). Alternatives are Mundie's (604 526 9677) and Canuck Towing (604 254 0501).

Parking

Most downtown streets are metered. Expect to pay $2 for 80 minutes – but note that even some metered streets have parking restrictions in the rush hour period. On non-metered streets, park only in the direction of the traffic, and not within six metres (20 feet) of a stop sign or within five metres (16 feet) of a fire hydrant. Park illegally and you will be towed (*see above* Busters). Car parks are common throughout the city. Most ticket machines take credit cards or change. You can pay between $8 and $20 for all-day parking in the downtown area.

Vehicle hire

To rent a car in BC you will have to be 21 years of age (some companies say over 25) and have a driving licence and a credit card. All the major international rental companies have offices in downtown Vancouver and at the airport; in Victoria; and many also have representatives in Whistler. In high season, reserve your vehicle ahead of time. Prices start at about $30 a day. Check whether your travel insurance covers driving before taking out additional coverage.

Alamo
1132 W Georgia Street, at Thurlow Street (604 684 1401/ www.alamo.ca). **Map** p249 K3.

Avis
757 Hornby Street, at W Georgia Street, Downtown (604 606 2869/ www.avis.ca). **Map** 249 K3.

Budget
416 W Georgia Street, at Richards Street (694 668 7000/ www.budget.com). **Map** p249 K3.

Enterprise
585 Smithe Street, at Seymour Street (604 688 5500/www.enterprise. com). **Map** p249 K4.

Hertz
1128 Seymour Street, at Helmcken Street (604 606 4711/www.hertz.ca). **Map** p249 K4.

National
1130 W Georgia Street, at Thurlow Street (604 609 7150/www.national car.ca). **Map** p249 K3.

Thrifty
Century Plaza Hotel, 1015 Burrard Street, at Nelson Street (604 606 1666/www.thrifty.com). **Map** p248 J3.

Cycling

Vancouver is an ideal city for cyclists, with cycle routes alongside the Seawall around the downtown peninsula, Stanley Park and False Creek. TransLink publishes a route map which is available from most bike stores. It is illegal to ride a bike without a helmet, a law which also applies to child passengers. Buses on the North Shore and increasingly elsewhere are equipped to take bikes on racks mounted on the front of the bus. This excellent service is free, and TransLink's website www.translink.bc.ca has details. *See p62* **On your bike** for bike rental stores.

The North Shore, a boat trip away across Burrard Inlet, and Whistler 125 kilometres (75 miles) to the north are both renowned for their mountain bike trails. Victoria, Vancouver Island and the Okanagan Valley are also popular cycling holiday destinations.

Walking

There can't be many cities with such spectacular nature walks in their midst. Stanley Park and the Seawall are obvious places to start, but you can also walk from Kitsilano Beach all the way out to Wreck Beach at the University of British Columbia (approximately 8 kilometres or 5 miles). The Pacific Spirit Park (also known as the Endowment Lands) east of UBC is a wilder alternative to Stanley Park, and there are many good hikes within easy reach on the North Shore.

Directory

Resources A-Z

Addresses

Despite the city's grid-like street patterns, the logic of postal addresses in Vancouver is complicated by the peculiar shape of the downtown peninsula. Street numbers climb 100 per block as you head south from Canada Place pier or west from Carrall Street (in downtown) or Ontario Street (the West Side). East of Main Street the street numbers start to climb again and take on the prefix East. It sounds confusing but once you have cracked the code you can pinpoint any address without the cross-street. Nevertheless, in this book we have listed the nearest cross-streets in the address.

Please note that suite numbers sometimes precede the street number.

Alcohol & age restrictions

The legal drinking age in British Columbia is 19. Minors are allowed in restaurants licenced to serve alcohol, but not in bars, pubs or nightclubs. All licenced establishments are required to ask anyone who appears to be under the age of 25 for two pieces of identification. It is illegal to drink in a public place (such as a park) except in special circumstances (such as a festival). It is illegal to drive with alcohol open or accessible to anyone else in the vehicle (ie you can't have a can of beer on the passenger seat, even if it's unopened).

You also have to be 19 to smoke tobacco. The age of consent is 14. To hire a vehicle you must be 21 although many hire companies will only rent to customers over the age of 25.

Attitude & etiquette

Vancouver is laid-back and easygoing in most things. When it comes to attire, business suits are the exception, not the rule; even formal occasions are casual by European standards. Some Victoria establishments have a dress code, but these are rare on the mainland. Courtesy is very much the norm.

Business

For copying, *see p136.*

Conventions & conferences

Vancouver Convention and Exhibition Centre

Canada Place, Downtown (604 689 8232/www.vanconex.com). All city-centre buses. **Map** 249 L2.

BC Place Stadium

BC Place Stadium, 777 Pacific Boulevard, between Griffiths Way & Terry Fox Way (604 669 2300/ www.bcplacestadium.com). Bus 15/SkyTrain Stadium. **Map** 249 L4.

Couriers & shippers

For shipping, *see p136.*

Purolator Courier

120-1090 W Pender Street, between Burrard Street & Thurlow Street, Downtown (1 888 744 7123/ www.purolator.com). All city-centre buses. **Open** 9am-6pm Mon-Fri. **Credit** AmEx, MC, V. **Map** p249 K2.

Secretarial services

Hunt Personnel

760-789 W Pender Street, at Howe Street, Downtown (604 688 2555/ www.hunt.ca). All city-centre buses. **Open** 7.45am-5pm Mon-Fri. **No credit cards**. **Map** p249 L3.

Translators & interpreters

Able Translations Ltd

1000-355 Burrard Street, between W Hastings Street & W Cordova Street, Downtown (604 646 4888/ www.abletranslations.com). All city-centre buses. **Map** p249 L2.

Consulates

The opening hours of consulates and embassies are, of course, not renowned for being long and flexible, so check before you go. If you require a consulate or embassy not listed below go to www.embassyworld.com and use the simple search facility at the top of the page.

Australian Consulate General

1225-888 Dunsmuir Street, at Hornby Street, Downtown (604 684 1177). All city-centre buses. **Open** 9am-noon, 1-5pm Mon-Fri. **Map** p249 K3.

British Consulate General

1111 Melville Street, at Thurlow Street, Downtown (604 683 4421). All city-centre buses. **Open** 8.30am-4.30pm Mon-Fri. **Map** p249 K2.

Travel advice

For up-to-date information on travelling to a specific country – including the latest news on safety and security, health issues, local laws and customs – contact your home country government's department of foreign affairs. Most have websites packed with useful statistics, advice and background information for would-be travellers.

Australia	**Republic of Ireland**
www.smartraveller.gov.au	http://foreignaffairs.gov.ie
Canada	**UK**
www.voyage.gc.ca	www.fco.gov.uk/travel
New Zealand	**USA**
www.mft.govt.nz/travel	www.state.gov/travel

Consulate General of the People's Republic of China

3380 Granville Street, at W 16th Avenue, West Side (604 736 5188/ http://vancouver.china-consulate.org/ eng/). Bus 10, 98. **Open** 9am-noon, 2-5.30pm Mon-Fri. **Map** p251 H8.

Consulate General of France

1100-1130 W Pender Street, at Thurlow Street, Downtown (604 681 4345). All city-centre buses. **Open** *Visas* 9.30am-noon Mon-Fri. *Citizens* 9am-1pm Mon-Fri or by appointment. **Map** p249 K2.

German Consulate General in Vancouver

Suite 704, World Trade Centre, 999 Canada Place, at Hornby Street, Downtown (604 684 8377). All city-centre buses. **Open** 9am-noon Mon-Fri. **Map** p249 L2.

Consulate General of India

2nd Floor, 325 Howe Street, at W Cordova Street, Downtown (604 662 8811/www.cgivancouver.com). All city-centre buses. **Open** 9am-noon, 3-4.30pm Mon-Fri. **Map** p249 L2.

Consulate of the Republic of Ireland

10th Floor, 100 W Pender Street, at Abbott Street, Downtown (604 683 9233). All city-centre buses. **Open** 9am-noon, 1-4.30pm Mon-Fri. **Map** p249 M3.

Consulate General of Japan at Vancouver

800-1177 W Hastings Street, at Bute Street, Downtown (604 684 5868/ www.vancouver.ca.emb-japan.go.jp). All city-centre buses. **Open** 9am-noon, 1-4.30pm Mon-Fri. **Map** p249 K2.

New Zealand Consulate General

1200-888 Dunsmuir Street, at Hornby Street, Downtown (604 684 7388). All city-centre buses. **Open** 8.30am-4.30pm Mon-Fri. **Map** p249 K3.

Consulate General of the Republic of Singapore

1820-999 W Hastings Street, at Burrard Street, Downtown (604 669 5115/www.mfa.gov.sg/vancouver). All city-centre buses. **Open** 8.30am-12.30pm, 1.30-5pm Mon-Fri. **Map** p249 K2.

South African Honorary Consul

1700-1075 W Georgia Street, at Burrard Street, Downtown (604 688 1301). All city-centre buses. **Open** 8.30am-noon, 1.30-5pm Mon-Fri. **Map** p249 K3.

United States Consulate General

1075 W Pender Street, at Thurlow Street, Downtown (604 685 4311/ www.usconsulatevancouver.ca). All city-centre buses. **Open** 9am-5pm Mon-Fri. **Map** p249 K2.

Consumer

For advice on your rights as a consumer, contact the Business Practices and Consumer Protection Authority of British Columbia (1-888 564 9963, www.bpcpa.ca). Do note that in British Columbia shops are under no obligation to refund your money unless goods are faulty.

Customs

While all the usual checks will be made at Canadian ports of entry the thoroughness of the checks will vary according to your nationality, where you have come from and your general demeanour. If you are arriving from a country with known links to the drug trade, illicit trafficking of immigrants, or ties to Islamist terrorism you should expect closer scrutiny.

It should go without saying, but do not attempt to enter Canada carrying firearms or weapons of any description. Drugs, other than prescribed drugs complete with documentation, should never be brought into the country. The authorities will throw the book at you and sentences can be harsh. Other things to avoid passing through customs with include cultural antiquities, endangered species, meat, fruit and any form of plant material.

You are allowed to enter Canada with 200 cigarettes, 50 cigars, 1.5 litres of wine, 1.14 litres of liquor or 24 cans of beer without having to pay tax. For more information regarding Canada Customs and Immigration call 1-902 432 5608 if you are outside Canada; 1-800 668 4748 inside Canada, or visit www.ccra-adrc.gc.ca/visitors.

British citizens returning to the UK can bring back £145 worth of duty-free goods, and any amount of money they can prove is theirs. For more details of UK Customs and Excise go to www.hmce.gov.uk.

American citizens can return home from Canada with US$800 worth of duty-free goods. For more details of US Customs visit www.customs.ustreas.gov.

Disabled

Vancouver prides itself on its accessibility for people with disabilities. The airport exceeds national and provincial standards for people with hearing, visual or mobility impairments, airport rental car agencies can provide vehicles with hand controls and there are wheelchair accessible taxis (call 604 871 1111 to book). All buses servicing the airport are also wheelchair accessible; within the city, more than 50 per cent have ramps, check with TransLink (www.translink.bc.ca) for details. The SkyTrain and SeaBus are also wheelchair accessible. Wheelchair accessible vans can be rented from Freedom Rentals (604 952 4499, www.wheelchairvanrentals.com) at around $150/day plus tax (cheaper rates available for longer term rentals). If you are driving and have a disabled parking permit, it is valid in Vancouver. If using BC Ferries, ask for parking near the elevators when purchasing tickets; deck areas and washrooms are all accessible. Pacific Coach Lines (604 662 7575, www.pacificcoach.com) offers accessible services between Vancouver and Victoria. Greyhound Canada (604 482 8747, www.greyhound.ca) has lift-equipped services from Vancouver to Kelowna; book 24 hours in advance. If you want to ski, Whistler's Adaptive Ski Programme (1-604 932 3434, www.whistlerblackcomb.com) offers lessons and equipment at all levels of special need. The Canadian government runs its own website (www.access totravel.gc.ca) with details of national and local travel access. For more information contact the British Columbia Paraplegic Association (604 324 3611, www.bcpara.org).

Directory

Drugs

In keeping with many west coast cities Vancouver does have a laid-back vibe and an active drug culture. However, Canada's police and judicial authorities take a very stern line with drug offences, so you would be wise to avoid narcotics while in the country. For more information on Vancouver's relationship with marijuana, *see p79* **Potted history**.

Electricity

Canada operates a 110-volt, 60 cycle electric power supply. Plugs and sockets are two-pronged, so if you are visiting from anywhere except the US you will need a plug adaptor in order to be able to use your electrical appliances from home. Adaptors can be bought from most department stores.

Emergencies

In the event of an emergency that requires police, firefighters or medical assistance call **911**. This service is free from all telephones.

Gay & lesbian

Vancouver is one of the most gay-friendly cities in North America. The Davie Street Village (between Burrard Street and Denman Street) in the West End is a gay mecca, while lesbians tend to congregate around Commercial Drive in East Van. Look out for the free biweekly gay paper, *Xtra West*, in stores and cafés. The Centre (1170 Bute Street, 604 684 6869, www.lgtbcentre vancouver.com) is a valuable community service resource.

Health

Accident & emergency

If you are in a situation that requires an instant response from any of the emergency services dial **911**. It's free from any telephone.

If you develop a non life-threatening medical problem during your stay in Vancouver the Care Point Medical Centre (1175 Denman Street, 604 681 5338) or the Khatsahlano Medical Clinic (2689 W Broadway, 604 731 9187) should be able to help you on a walk-in basis.

For more serious conditions there is Vancouver General Hospital (855 W 12th Avenue, 604 875 4111), St Paul's Hospital (1081 Burrard Street, 604 682 2344), BC Women's Hospital (4500 Oak Street, 604 875 2424), and BC Children's Hospital (4480 Oak Street, 604 875 2345).

If you require more details about health services in Vancouver visit www.vch.ca.

To contact the police department regarding a non-emergency situation call 604 717 3321, or go down to the headquarters at 2120 Cambie Street, at W 6th Street. For more information about the police visit www.vancouver.ca/police.

Contraception & abortion

Options for Sexual Health

Women's Clinic, Vancouver General Hospital, Willow Pavilion, 805 W 12th Avenue, West Side (604 731 4252/www.optionsforsexual health.org). **Open** call for hours and appointment.

Everywoman's Health Centre

210-2525 Commercial Drive, East Vancouver (604 322 6692/www. everywomanshealthcentre.ca). **Open** call for hours and appointment.

Dentists

British Columbia Dental Association

604 736 7202/www.bcdental.org. Provides referral information.

Doctors

Stein Medical Clinic

Bentall 5 Lobby, 188-550 Burrard Street, at W Pender Street, Downtown (604 688 5924/www. steinmedicalclinic.com). **Open** 8.30am-5.30pm Mon-Fri. No appointment necessary. **Map** p249 K2.

Hospitals

The hospitals listed below all have 24 hour emergency departments.

St Paul's Hospital

1081 Burrard Street, at Helmcken Street, Downtown (604 682 2344). Bus 2, 22. **Map** p248 J4.

UBC Hospital & Urgent Care Centre

2211 Wesbrook Mall, between University Boulevard & W 16th Avenue, West Side (604 822 7121). Bus 4, 17, 25, 99.

Vancouver General Hospital

855 W 12th Avenue, at Oak Street, West Side (604 875 6111). Bus 17, 99.

Opticians

See p134.

STDs, HIV & AIDS

Aids Vancouver

1107 Seymour Street, at Helmcken Street, Downtown (604 893 2201/ www.aidsvancouver.org). Bus 4, 6, 7, 10, 16, 17, 50. **Open** 11am-4pm Mon-Fri. **Map** p249 K4.

Downtown Community Health Clinic

569 Powell Street, at Princess Avenue, East Side (604 255 3151). Bus 4, 7. **Open** phone for hours and appointment.

Helplines

Alcoholics Anonymous

604 434 3933 (24 hrs)/ www.vancouveraa.ca.

Crisis Intervention and Suicide Prevention Centre of British Columbia

604 872 3311 (24hr distress line)/ www.crisiscentre.bc.ca.

Narcotics Anonymous

604 873 1018/ www.bcrscna.bc.ca.

Vancouver Rape Crisis Line

604 872 8212.

ID

You need to be 19 to legally purchase alcohol and tobacco. You will be expected to provide two pieces of ID if you are buying alcohol and your age is at all in question. If you're out clubbing, it's a good idea to have ID to hand. When driving you must always carry picture ID.

Insurance

Canada does not provide health or medical services free to visitors, so make sure you have travel insurance in place before you arrive, and carry your documents with you.

Internet

Most Vancouver hotels provide internet access – though the form that access takes varies a good deal, and so does the price.

Internet cafés

Go to http://vancouver.wifimug. org for a directory of coffee shops offering free Wi-Fi access.

Internet Coffee

1104 Davie Street, at Thurlow Street, Downtown (604 682 6668). Bus 6. **Open** 24 hours daily. **Rates** $4/hr. **Credit** MC, V. **Map** p248 J3.

Third Wish Café

309 W Pender Street, at Hamilton Street, Downtown (604 681 8150). All city-centre buses. **Open** 7am-11pm Mon-Sat. **Rates** $4/hr. **Credit** AmEx, MC, V. **Map** p249 L3.

Language

Although Canadian airlines, government offices and cereal boxes are obliged to repeat information in English and French, English is the mother tongue in British Columbia. Mandarin, Cantonese and Punjabi are all more prevalent than French. Canadian English has both English and American inflections: ask for the bill, but go to the washroom. Chips are crisps and fries are chips (except when ordering fish and chips), you walk on the sidewalk and if there's something wrong with your car, it'll probably be under the hood (your luggage goes in the trunk).

Laundry

If your place of accommodation does not have any laundry facilities, and your suitcase is smelling a bit ripe, you can use the Davie Laundromat (1061 Davie Street, 604 682 2717) in the West End of downtown.

Left luggage

CDS Baggage offers storage in the domestic and international arrivals terminal (level 2, pre-security). Rates range from $2-$5 per item per 24 hours. Hours of operation 5am-11pm. CDS also has a baggage storage facility downtown at Canada Place, but the office only opens on cruise ship days (604 303 4500). Almost all hotels will hold your luggage for you on the day of check-out.

Legal help

If you have legal problems during your stay contact your insurers or your national consulate.

Libraries

Vancouver Public Library (350 W Georgia Street, 604 331 3600, www.vpl.ca), is in the heart of downtown. It is the third largest public library system in Canada and has 20 branches across the city. Opening times are 10am-9pm Mon-Thur; 10am-6pm Fri, Sat; noon-5pm Sun. Note that there are no email and telephone services available on Sundays, and that the library will be closed on Sundays of holiday weekends.

Lost property

Airport

If all or any of your luggage has been lost in transit inform your airline straight away. If you have lost or misplaced property in the airport contact the Customer Service Counter on 604 276 6104. It's open 9am-5.30pm daily, on Level 3 of the international departures terminal.

Public transport

If you lose property on Vancouver's public transport system contact TransLink on 604 682 7887. The lost property office is open 8.30am-5pm Mon-Fri and can be found at the Stadium SkyTrain Station, 590 Beatty Street.

Taxis

If you lose anything in a cab call the company itself.

Media

Newspapers & magazines

Vancouver's media is in some need of a good shake-up. The two local newspapers, the broadsheet *Vancouver Sun* and the tabloid *Province,* are both owned by media conglomerate CanWest, which publishes a number of other dailies across Western Canada, the *Victoria Times Colonist* and the *National Post,* and also owns the cable company Global TV. In addition, CanWest has an equal one-third stake in the free daily *Metro,* and owns another freebie, *Dose,* outright. (The third daily freesheet in town is *24 Hours,* which draws on copy from the Sun Media tabloid chain.) CanWest is owned by the Asper family and is generally known for promoting a conservative party line.

An online paper, the *tyee.ca* is a lively union-backed riposte, staffed by disgruntled ex-CanWest writers.

Canada's other national daily, the *Globe and Mail* is perhaps your best bet for serious, relatively unpartisan news coverage, and is making efforts to extend its reach in British Columbia with a daily BC news section and a new BC-centric version of its Friday arts roundup, Seven.

The *Georgia Straight* is the dominant alt weekly in town. Celebrating its 40th anniversary in 2007, the *Straight* is showing signs of its advancing years. It's complacent, baggy, and in dire need of a redesign. Nevertheless its market position is entrenched, and for most consumers of art and entertainment it's the only game in town. (A rival, the *West Ender,* does its best to pretend otherwise.)

For newsprint junkies who can't do without their home town fix, the *New York Times* and European newspapers are fairly easy to get hold of in the downtown area. Try Chapters bookstore at 788 Robson Street, at Howe Street.

Radio & television

Canadian radio and television stations rely heavily on American programming. Canadian radio content requirements, intended to provide more air-time for home-grown artists, actually result in the few Canadian formulaic pop/rock giants that have broken on to the world market being nauseatingly overplayed. The local stations that have evaded this curse are CBC One's news and more station (690 AM), CBC Two's 'Classics. And Beyond' (105.7 AM), Co-op Radio (102.7 FM), and the eclectic university station, CiTR (101.9 FM). The rest are as follows:

Rock and Top 40
94.5FM The Beat Hip hop, R&B
96.9FM Jack FM Contemporary and classic rock
101.1 CFMI Classic rock

Soft rock and other 'adult favourites'
650 AM CISL Oldies
93.7 JR FM New country
Z 95.3 FM Pop

Talk and news
980 CKNW
1130 CKWX All news
1410 CFUN All talk

Where cable television is available, the local and national stations (CBC, CTV, Global, City TV, and Channel M – which stands for 'multi-cultural,' but seems to play a lot of *Law & Order*) are drowned out by the super abundance of the American channels.

The *Vancouver Sun* and the *Province* newspapers carry comprehensive television schedules. The *TV Guide* is at most grocery and drugstores.

Money

There are 100 cents in each Canadian dollar. The one cent piece is a copper colour; the five cent piece (nickel), ten cent piece (dime) and twenty-five cent piece (quarter) are all silver and feature a beaver, a bluenose schooner and a caribou respectively. The one dollar piece (loonie) is a gold colour and the two dollar piece (twoonie) is a two-tone silver and gold colour.

Notes, or bills as they are commonly referred to in Canada, come in denominations of $5 (blue), $10 (purple), $20 (green) $50 (pink) and $100 (brown). It would be wise to avoid $50 and $100 bills due to counterfeit concerns. The Bank of Canada has recently changed the design of its $5, $10 and $20 bills, but the old-style notes are still in circulation and legal tender.

ATMs/ABMs

You should have no problem finding an ABM (automatic bank machine) as they are referred to in Canada. Most banks will have an ABM, and bank operated machines can be found along most streets in downtown Vancouver. Bars, clubs and shops operate private machines, but you will be charged $1-$2 for the convenience of using it. Canadian ABMs are part of the Cirrus, Interac or Plus networks, so visitors should have no problem getting access to their home accounts through these machines. If in doubt check with your bank before travelling. It is also advisable to find out what charges your bank will make for accessing your account from abroad.

Banks

All the banks listed below are downtown branches and can be found on a stretch of West Georgia Street that runs from Burrard Street to Granville Street.

CIBC
1036 W Georgia Street, at Burrard Street (604 665 1472/www.cibc.com). **Open** 9.30am-4pm Mon-Wed; 9.30am-5pm Thur-Fri. **Map** p249 K3. **Other locations**: throughout the city.

Royal Bank
1025 W Georgia Street, at Burrard Street (604 665 6991/www.royal bank.ca). **Open** 9am-5pm Mon-Fri. **Map** p249 K3. **Other locations**: throughout the city.

Scotiabank
650 W Georgia Street, at Seymour Street (604 668 2094/www.scotia bank.com). **Open** 9.30am-4pm Mon-Thur; 9.30am-5pm Fri. **Map** p249 K3. **Other locations**: throughout the city.

TD Canada Trust
700 W Georgia Street, at Howe Street (604 654 3665/www. tdcanadatrust.com). **Open** 8am-6pm Mon-Fri. **Map** p249 K3. **Other locations**: throughout the city.

Bureaux de change

American Express
666 Burrard Street, at Dunsmuir Street, Downtown (604 669 2813/www.americanexpress.ca). All city-centre buses. **Open** 8.30am-5.30pm Mon-Fri; 10am-4pm Sat. **Map** p249 K3. **Other locations**: throughout the city.

Thomas Cook
Pacific Centre Mall, 777 Dunsmuir Street, at Howe Street, Downtown (604 689 3116/www.thomascook.ca). **Open** 9am-6am Mon-Fri; 10am-6pm Sat. **Map** p249 K3. **Other locations**: throughout the city.

Credit cards

Most businesses in Vancouver take Visa, MasterCard and American Express. Some also take Diners Club. With smaller restaurants out of the downtown area it is best to check beforehand. These cards all have toll-free numbers available around the clock if your credit card should be lost or stolen:

American Express
1-800 668 2639.

Diners Club
1-800 663 0284 standard card.
1-800 563 4653 gold card.
1-800 363 3333 silver card.

MasterCard
1-800 307 7309.

Visa
1-800 847 2911.

Tax

When shopping in British Columbia, remember that marked prices do not include sales tax. The Goods and Services Tax is seven per cent and levied by the federal government on almost everything. The Provincial Sales Tax is seven and a half per cent and is applied to almost everything except some groceries and children's clothes.

Accommodation is taxed at ten per cent, as is alcohol.

The good news is that foreign visitors can claim a GST refund on accommodation (up to a month) and on all goods. Only receipts of $50 and over are eligible. Claim forms are widely available in hotels, many shops, and at the airport. These must be returned within 60 days of leaving the country with the original receipts and stamped by Canada customs (who will verify your purchases) before departure. The customs office at Vancouver International Airport is on the Departures level in the US check-in area. For more information call 1-800 668 4748, or check www.ccra.gc.ca/tax/nonresidents/visitors/.

Opening hours

Shops generally open from 9am onwards (downtown doesn't wake up until 10am) and close around 5pm. Some, depending on the type of business, may stay open till 9pm. Banks open at 9am and close at 5pm Monday to Friday although some branches may open Saturday and close Monday. Post offices usually open between 10am and 5pm Monday to Saturday.

Police stations

If the incident is an emergency and requires an immediate response from the police dial **911** free from any telephone. If it's not an emergency ring the police on 604 717 3321. Vancouver Police Department headquarters is at 2120 Cambie Street. See also www.vancouver.ca/police.

Postal services

Posting a standard letter or postcard within Canada costs 50 cents, so long as it weighs 30 grams or less. To the US the cost is 85 cents. If you want to send a letter or card anywhere else it will cost $1.45 up to 30 grams, and $2 between 30 and 50 grams.

Post offices

The main post office in Vancouver (349 W Georgia Street, 604 662 5723, www.canadapost.ca) is open 8am-5.30pm on weekdays. If you only need stamps try a corner shop or pharmacy. Some drugstores and larger stores also contain post office counters (for instance, in the basement of the Hudson's Bay department store, 674 Granville Street, at W Georgia Street, Downtown).

Poste restante/ general delivery

If you need to receive mail while in Vancouver, but do not have a permanent address, it is possible to have it delivered to any post office with a postal code 'care of General Delivery'. You will be required to show at least one form of photo ID before the post office can hand over your mail. All mail must be collected within 15 days.

Religion

Anglican

St Paul's Anglican Church
1130 Jervis Street, at Pendrell Street, Downtown (604 685 6832/www.stpaulsanglican.bc.ca). Bus 6. **Map** p248 H3.

Baptist

First Baptist Church
969 Burrard Street, at Nelson Street, Downtown (604 683 8441/www.firstbc.org). All city-centre buses. **Map** p248 J3.

Buddhist

Universal Buddhist Temple
525 E 49th Street, at St George Street, East Vancouver (604 325 6912). Bus 3, 8.

Catholic

Holy Rosary Cathedral
646 Richards Street, at Dunsmuir Street, Downtown (604 682 6774/http://hrc.rcav.org). All city-centre buses. **Map** p249 L3.

Islamic

Vancouver Mosque
655 W 8th Avenue, at Heather Street, West Side (604 803 7344/www.islamicinfocenter.org). Bus 15, 17. **Map** p249 K6.

Jewish

Temple Sholom
7190 Oak Street, at W 56th Avenue, West Side (604 266 7190/www.templesholom.ca). Bus 17.

Lutheran

Christ Lutheran Church
375 W 10th Avenue, at Yukon Street, West Side (604 874 2212). Bus 15.

United Church of Canada

St Andrew's Wesley Church
1022 Nelson Street, at Burrard Street, Downtown (604 683 4574/www.standrewswesleychurch.bc.ca). All city-centre buses. **Map** p248 J3.

Safety & security

It is important to stress that Vancouver is a safe city. Violent crime is rare, particularly in the tourist areas, but this does not mean you can be complacent about your safety or the security of your belongings.

Burying your head in a street map tends to identify you as the stranger in town, so it's best not to do it. If you really are having difficulty orientating yourself why not pop into a café or a shop and ask directions.

Try not to carry too much cash on your person. It's also a good idea to make a note of the relevant lost/stolen credit card telephone numbers so that you can cancel any cards the moment you notice they are missing.

Women travelling on their own should apply all the usual safety procedures, especially at night. Avoid alleyways, don't take shortcuts across parking lots and keep an eye on your drink when in bars and clubs. Also, if you've been out for the night, get a registered cab back to where you are staying. Public transport can sometimes leave you with a long walk at the end of your journey.

Vancouver's temperate climate makes the city an appealing place for those who are down on their luck. The majority of these people are harmless, but use your discretion, especially at night

Directory

when there are fewer people about and the streets are quiet.

One area of Vancouver that it's best to avoid is East Hastings Street, especially the section between Homer Street and Main Street. Even though it's a relatively small, self contained area, visitors should note that it backs on to Gastown and Chinatown respectively, so be aware which direction you are going in when exploring these popular tourist areas.

Smoking

All indoor spaces in Vancouver were decreed smoke-free by law in 2000. If you want to light up, you're out on the street – not a great prospect in the rainy season. Most restaurants, cafés and bars circumvent the law by way of large, often heated, patios.

Study

Universities

Foreign nationals wishing to study in Canada require a study permit and, depending on their country of origin, may also need a temporary visa. Applications should be made through local Canadian embassies or high consulates.

Simon Fraser University

8888 University Drive, Burnaby (604 291 3111/www.sfu.ca). Bus 135.

Simon Fraser University (SFU) comprises three campuses: the main – designed by Arthur Erickson – sits 20km (12.5 miles) east of downtown, with satellites in the suburb of Surrey and in downtown's Harbour Centre. Known for its progressive approach to learning and strong liberal arts department, it takes around 25,000 students on site.

University of British Columbia

2329 West Mall, West Side (604 822 2211/www.ubc.ca). Bus 4, 17, 44, 99.
The third largest university in Canada, UBC is a highly desirable option for students, both for its excellent academic reputation and its breathtaking setting. The campus includes the Museum of Anthropology, the Pacific Spirit Regional Park, the botanical gardens and Wreck Beach. Bursting at the seams with some 43,000 students, the campus continues to expand rapidly, with new academic and residential buildings popping up fast.

Telephones

Dialling & codes

Vancouver and much of the Lower Mainland (including Whistler) share the area code 604. (Vancouver Island is 250). Although Vancouver businesses often place the prefix in brackets or drop it altogether, you must dial the code no matter where you are calling from. Even though they share the same area code, calls between Whistler and Vancouver are long distance, so you must add '1' before '604'. Toll free numbers

begin with the codes: 800, 855, 866, 877, 888. All must be prefixed with '1'.

International calls

Canada shares the same international dialling code as the US (1). To call Canada from the UK, dial 001 then the number. To dial the US from Canada, dial 1 for long distance, then the ten digit number. To call overseas from North America, dial 011, the country code, then the number (in some cases dropping the initial zero). The country code for the UK is 44, for Australia it's 61, New Zealand 64, Republic of Ireland 353 and South Africa 27.

Making a call

If you can find one, payphones cost 25 cents per local call, and require change. Most hotels offer free local calls from your room, but check charges before phoning long distance. If you are making a number of long distance calls, a dial-in phone card is the cheapest option. These are available from any convenience store for $5, $10 or $20, and translate long distance calls into local.

Operator services

Dial 0 from any phone to speak to an operator (free from payphones). Dial 00 for the international operator.

Telephone directories

To find a number, dial 411 for information from any phone. This service costs 75 cents.

Mobile phones

As in the US, Canada's mobile phone (cellphone) network operates on 1900 megaHertz. This means that, depending on their billing plan, US travellers should be able to use their usual handset (but should check their tariffs for costs). Tri-band phones will work throughout most of North America; quad-bands tend to give some additional coverage but there is still the odd area with no coverage at all. If you have a dual-band phone or your tri- or quad-band phone might not work, contact your service provider to

Average temperatures		
	Avge maximum C/F	Minimum C/F
January	5/42	2/36
February	7/44	4/40
March	10/50	6/43
April	14/58	9/48
May	18/65	12/54
June	21/69	15/59
July	23/74	17/63
August	23/74	17/63
September	18/65	14/58
October	14/58	10/50
November	9/48	6/43
December	6/43	4/39

find out if it has a way around the problem. You could buy a pay-as-you-go phone from around $125 from one of the ubiquitous local carriers (Bell, Fido, Rogers or Telus).

Alternatively you could rent a phone via your hotel or from a private company such as Hello, Anywhere (toll free 1-888 729 4355, www.helloanywhere.com, credit card deposit required), who will deliver a phone to your hotel from about $40 a week.

Faxes

Many convenience stores offer a fax service, as do all copy shops (*see p136*).

Time

Vancouver is located in the Pacific Time Zone and is eight hours behind Greenwich Mean Time. Daylight Saving Time runs from 2am on the first Sunday in April to 2am on the last Sunday in October.

Tipping

Tipping is *de rigueur* in Canada. Everyone from bellhops to cab drivers to hairdressers will expect to receive one. Restaurant and bar staff are paid a lower minimum wage than most workers because they are expected to make up the difference with gratuities. Average tips range between 10-20 per cent depending on the type and quality of service you have received. However, it's worth remembering that if a restaurant adds a service charge to the bill you are under no obligation to leave a tip.

Toilets

Finding a public toilet in Vancouver is about as easy as finding a stand of old growth forest in downtown, so make a point of using the ones available in cafés, restaurants and bars as you go about your day. Note that some toilets, particularly those in cafés and coffee shops, are reserved for customers only and may be locked. If you want to use the toilet and need the key you'll have to buy a drink first.

Tourist information

Vancouver Tourist Info Centre

Plaza Level, Waterfront Centre, 200 Burrard Street, at Canada Place (604 683 2000). **Open** *June-Aug* 8.30am-6pm daily. *Sept-May* 8.30am-5pm Mon-Sat. **Map** 249 L2.
Other tourist information centres can be found at the Canada Place Cruise Ship Terminal, the Ballantyne Cruise Ship Terminal and Vancouver International Airport. If you are driving up to Vancouver from the US there is a Tourist Information Centre at the Peace Arch Border Crossing, Highway 99, Surrey, BC.

Useful websites

www.tourismvancouver.com/visitors.
www.hellobc.com.
www.city.vancouver.bc.ca/visitors.htm.
www.vancouver-bc.com.

Visas & immigration

Citizens of the UK, the US, Australia, New Zealand and Ireland do not require visas to visit Canada. Citizens of other countries can get up-to-date information regarding visa regulations from www.cic.gc.ca/english/visit/visas.html.

The American administration's proposal to bring in passport controls between Canada and the US is a cause of great concern to British Columbia. At present US and Canadian citizens only require ID and a return date to cross the border.

Weights & measures

Canada uses the metric system of weights and measures.

1 centimetre = 0.394 inches
1 metre = 3.28 feet
1 square metre = 1.196 square yards
1 kilometre = 0.62 miles
1 kilogramme = 2.2 pounds
1 litre = 1.76 UK pints, 2.113 US pints

When to go

Climate

In contrast to most of the rest of Canada, Vancouver enjoys a temperate climate not unlike that of the UK. Owing to the ameliorating effect of the surrounding sea, winters are never that cold and summers are rarely oppressively hot. If you like winter sports, Vancouver's close proximity to Grouse Mountain (30 minutes from downtown) makes it an ideal base from which to enjoy these activities. Whistler is only 100km (60 miles) further north. For those who enjoy the sunshine the summer months will give you ample opportunity to get a tan on one of the many beaches that line the Vancouver shoreline. The only climatic drawback to the city is the rainfall, particularly in the winter months. From October through February the average monthly rainfall goes from 115mm/4.5 inches a month to 167mm/6.5 inches in November, *see p25* **Rain city**.

Public holidays

New Year's Day (1 Jan; if a Sun, then holiday is the following Mon); Good Friday (Mar/Apr); Easter Monday (Mar/Apr); Victoria Day (third Mon in May); Canada Day (1 July); BC Day (first Mon in Aug); Labour Day (First Mon in Sep); Thanksgiving (second Mon in Oct); Remembrance Day (11 Nov); Christmas Day (25 Dec); Boxing Day (26 Dec).

Women

Vancouver is generally a safe city and is no less so for women travelling alone who exercise common sense. Avoiding the notorious Downtown Eastside, particularly at night, is – as it is for anyone visiting Vancouver – a good idea.

For a list of helplines, *see p232*.

For extensive links to organisations dealing with women's reproductive and general health see www.womenshealth collective.ca and www.women space.ca for information and links to organisations dealing with equality issues.

Directory

Further Reference

Books

Fiction

Carr, Emily
Klee Wyck; The Book of Small; The House of All Sorts
In the last decade of her life, painter Emily Carr took to writing – and found immediate acclaim. Some commentators rate her literary work higher even than her art.

Choy, Wayson
The Jade Peony; All That Matters
Born in Vancouver in 1939, Choy won acclaim for his 1995 novel *The Jade Peony*, set in Vancouver's Chinatown in the Depression years. *All That Matters* brought the story on to the 1940s – which is also the setting for Choy's memoirs, *Paper Shadows*.

Coupland, Douglas
Generation X; Life After God; Microserfs; Girlfriend in a Coma; Hey Nostradamus!
North Vancouver born and bred (and still resident there), the Gen X novelist and all round art phenomenon revisits his hometown regularly in his fiction (*see p32* **'X' marks the spot**).

Gibson, William
Neuromancer; Mona Lisa Overdrive; All Tomorrow's Parties; Burning Chrome
The science fiction writer who coined the term 'cyberspace' is a long-term Vancouver resident. Although Vancouver rarely appears by name in his fiction, he claims it colours his vision.

Johnson, Pauline
Legends of Vancouver
Born in 1861, Johnson was half English, half Mohawk. A poet and performer, she is remembered today for her collection of Squamish myths, *Legends of Vancouver*, first published in 1911 (*see p64*).

Lee, Nancy
Dead Girls
This 2002 debut is an evocative and provocative collection of stories in response to the murders of at least 27 Downtown Eastside women (and possibly as many as 69) by Robert Pickton.

Lowry, Malcolm
Under the Volcano
The English-born but restless traveller Malcolm Lowry finished his masterpiece while living in a squatter's shack in Dollarton, BC, in the early 1940s.

Munro, Alice
Runaway; Lives of Girls and Women; Hateship, Friendship, Courtship, Loveship, Marriage
The acclaimed short story writer divides her time between Ontario and British Columbia – though Vancouver only gets the occasional look-in in her work.

Taylor, Timothy
Stanley Park
Taylor's 2003 debut novel is based on Vancouver's twin passions: its park and its restaurants. This witty page turner captures the local foodie mores well.

Various
The Vancouver Stories
Published by Raincoast Books in 2005, *The Vancouver Stories* is a collection of tales set in the city that includes work by many of these writers and more besides.

Non-fiction

Atkin, John and Kluckner, Michael
Vancouver Walks: Discovering City Heritage
Twenty eight city strolls with added historical commentary. Michael Kluckner is a painter and historian, and combined these attributes in the book *Vanishing British Columbia*. He also wrote the history chapter in this guide.

Christie, Jack
50 Best Day Trips from Vancouver; Inside Out British Columbia; The Whistler Outdoors Guide
Christie is the 'outdoors' columnist of the *Georgia Straight* and has written numerous guidebooks to the wild places of British Columbia.

Coupland, Douglas
City of Glass
As you'd expect from Coupland, this is an unconventional guide to Vancouver by the prolific novelist and conceptual artist. Published in 2000, *City of Glass* is full of odd, illuminating perceptions.

Gasher, Mike
Hollywood North
A thoughtful analysis of the history of cinema in Brollywood, as sun starved Los Angelinos dub the city.

Grant, Paul and Dixon, Laurie
The Stanley Park Companion
Stunning photographs and lively text characterise this invaluable park guide, which is short on maps but long on smart history and commentary.

Mackie, John and Reeder, Sarah
Vancouver: The Unknown City
A lively, eccentric guide to the city with fascinating anecdotes and titbits. Under her married name, Bancroft, Sarah Reeder wrote the shopping chapter in this guide.

Various
The Greater Vancouver Book
Out of print, but students of
the city should look it up in
the Vancouver public library
or one of the second-hand book
stores: nearly 900 large format
pages of Vancouver history
and anthropology.

Various
Vancouver Cooks
Choice recipes from the most
acclaimed chefs in British
Columbia.

Weyler, Rex
Greenpeace
Authoritative account of the
birth of the ecology movement
in Vancouver (*see p15* **Going
green**).

(*see p15* **Going green**)

Films

The Corporation (2003)
Vancouver filmmakers Mark
Achbar, Jennifer Abbott and
UBC professor of law Joel
Bakan teamed up to make this
polemic about the psychotic
inclinations vested in the
corporate stranglehold.

The Grey Fox (1982)
Probably the best home-grown
movie in BC's history, this was
the fiction feature debut of
Philip Borsos, who died from
leukaemia at 41. It's the true
story of Bill Miner (Richard
Farnsworth), a train robber
who comes to Canada to
continue his trade in the early
days of the 20th century, after
spending 33 years in jail.

Kissed (1996)
Maple Ridge girl Molly
Parker stars in this chilly story
of necrophilia, directed with
some sensitivity by Lynne
Stopkewich.

Ladies and Gentlemen, the Fabulous Stains (1981)
A cult classic which should be
better known, this punk rock
saga stars a young Diane Lane,
Ray Winstone and Laura Dern.

While the setting is
indeterminate in the film, the
movie was shot in and around
Vancouver. Jonathan Demme
co-wrote the script.

McCabe and Mrs Miller (1971)
Set in the fictional town of
Presbyterian Church, this
seminal Robert Altman
western evokes BC in the
Gold Rush era.

My American Cousin (1985)
Sandy Wilson wrote
and directed this sweet
autobiographical film about
a 12-year-old BC girl's
infatuation with her cool
American cousin.

The Sweet Hereafter (1997)
Like many of Victoria-raised
Atom Egoyan's earlier films
the setting is not specified, but
his most successful film was
shot in Merritt and Spence's
Bridge in northern British
Columbia.

That Cold Day in the Park (1969)
Robert Altman's first feature
proper is set in Vancouver –
although it could have been
anywhere. He shot it in Tatlow
Park, on the West Side. Hard
to believe his next movie was
MASH.

Music

The Be Good Tanyas
Blue Horse (2000)
Rustic blues and roots from
BC trio Frazey Ford, Trish
Klein and Sam Parton (plus
Jolie Holland), recorded in a
wooden shack on the outskirts
of Vancouver.

Geoff Berner
Light Enough to Travel
'Wound up drunk again on
Robson Street…' A passionate
indictment of the city's less
enamouring elements from the
cult songwriter/accordionist.

Black Mountain
Black Mountain (2004)
A foreboding masterpiece that
could only have come to birth
amid the overcast gloom of
Vancouver. Front man Stephen
McBean is also the creative
force in Pink Mountaintops
and Jerk With a Bomb.

Destroyer
Thief
Exemplary songwriter Dan
Bejar's unabashedly literary
attempt to romanticise
Vancouver.

Diana Krall
The Girl in the Other Room
(2004)
The most personal album to
date from the Nanaimo-born
jazz singer.

The New Pornographers
Mass Romantic
This album carried the local
scene to safety on the back
of 'Letter From an Occupant'.
AC Newman's indie outfit
are something of a local
supergroup, with contributions
from vocalist Neko Case, and
Dan Bejar of Destroyer.

P:ano
The Den
The next generation is now.
A grand orchestral pop affair
conducted by wunderkind
Nick Krgovich.

Various
Vancouver Complication
(1979/2005)
Recently reissued snapshot
of Vancouver's punk scene,
including DOA, the
Subhumans, the Pointed Sticks
and the U-J3RK5 – featuring
future art stars Jeff Wall and
Rodney Graham.

Websites

www.biv.com.
www.discovervancouver.com.
www.helloBC.com.
www.katkam.ca.
www.vancouver-bc.com.

Directory

Index

Note: page numbers in **bold** indicate section(s) giving key information on topic; *italics* indicate photos.

a

ABMs 234
abortion 232
accident & emergency 232
accommodation 34-48
  bed & breakfasts 34, 43, 45
  best hotels 35
  by price
    budget 39-40, 43, 44, 46-47; *expensive* 37-38, 40-41, 44-45; *luxury* 35-37, 40, 44; *moderate* 38-39, 41-43, 45-46
  camping sites **175**, 194, 207
  gay & lesbian 156
  hostels 47-48
  tax 235
  see also Accommodation index p243
Adams, Bryan 18
addresses 230
age restrictions 230
AIDS & HIV 232
airports & airlines 226
  lost property 233
alcohol 230, 231
  see also bars; microbreweries; wine
Alpine Club of Canada 193
Annual Bald Eagle Count 141
antiques shopping 122
aquariums see zoos & aquariums
Armstrong 208
art 26-32
art galleries *see* galleries
Arts Club Theatre 167, 169
Asian immigration 14, 16, 18, 21, 76-77, 189, 197
ATMs 234

b

B&Bs *see* bed & breakfasts
babysitting services 142
backcountry huts 193
Ballet BC 172
banks 234
Bard on the Beach
  Shakespeare Festival **138**, *139*, 167, 168
bars 113-120
  best 113
  gay & lesbian 156-157
  microbreweries 116
  see also Bars index p243

baseball 178
bath houses, gay & lesbian 158
BC Lions 178-180
BC Place Stadium 19, 21
BC Sports Hall of Fame & Museum 55, 56
beach volleyball 173
beaches 64, 65, 67, 69, *69*, 71, 72, **82**, 203, 206, 208
  nudist 72
beauty shops 122-123
bed & breakfasts 34
beer *see* bars; microbreweries
bicycles & cycling 229
  bicycle hire & purchase 62, 84, 188
  bicycle paths 173
  mountain biking 84, **176**, 207, 208
  Stanley Park 62
bird watching 203
Black Mountain 85
Bloedel Floral Conservatory 74-75
boating *50*, 141, **176-177**, **185**
boca del lupo *167*, 170
books & literature 238-239
  Coupland, Douglas 32
  literary events 141
  shops 123-125
botanical gardens 74-75, 203
boutiques 125-126
Bowen Island 188-189
  ferry *184*, 188
breakdown services 229
Bridal Falls 192
Britannia Heritage Shipyard 189, 190
British Columbia art 27
bureaux de change 234
Burnaby Village Museum 145
bus services 227
  City buses 227-228
  North Shore 81
  Stanley Park 65
  to/from airport 226
  business 230
Butchart Gardens 198

c

cafés *see* restaurants & cafés
Calona Vineyards 209
Campbell, Gordon 19
camping & camping sites **175**, 194, 207
Canada Day 139
Canada Place 55, *57*
Canadian Pacific Railway (CPR) 12, 14, *14*, 18, 55, 56, 69, 72, 143, 195
canoeing *see* kayaking

Canucks 181
Canwest Comedy Fest 141, **171**
Capilano River Regional Park 81
Capilano Salmon Hatchery 144
Capilano Suspension Bridge & Park **81-82**, *83*, 144
Carol Ship Parade of Lights 141
Carousel Theatre 170
Carr, Emily 27, 197, 198
  Scorned as Timber, Beloved of the Sky 27, *27*, 30
  see also Emily Carr College of Art & Design
cars & driving 184, **229**
Catriona Jeffries Gallery *151*, 152
Centre in Vancouver for the Performing Arts 167, 169
Chan Centre for the Performing Arts *161*, 162
chemists 134
children 142-145
  excursions 145
  festivals & events 138
  indoor attractions 142-144
  outdoor attractions 144
  shops
    clothes 126
    mall 142
    toys 136
  theatre 170
  water parks 145
Children's Farmyard & Miniature Railway 144
Chinatown 76
  restaurants & cafés 102-103
Chinatown Night Market 77, **133**
Chinese Cultural Centre 77
Chinese Cultural Centre Museum & Archives 77
Chinese New Year Festival 141
choral groups 160
Christ Church Cathedral 53
Christmas festival 141
churches 235
cinemas 147-149
Circle Trip 190
classical music 160-161
Cliffhanger Gym 142
climate 25, 236, 237
climbing *see* rock climbing
clothes
  dry-cleaner 125
  shops 125-130
Cloverdale Rodeo & Country Fair 138
clubs *see* Music & Nightlife
coach services 184-185, 227

Coal Harbour 53
  water park 145
coffee 92
  see also restaurants & cafés
comedy *see* performing arts
Commercial Drive 78-79
Commodore Ballroom 163, *163*
computer shops 125
consulates 230-231
consumer protection services 231
contraception 232
conventions & conferences 230
Coupland, Douglas 32
couriers 230
credit cards 234
crime 18, 19, 23, 24, 235-236
cruise ships/lines 227
customs 231
cycling *see* bicycles & cycling
Cypress Mountain *174*, 176, 180
Cypress Provincial Park 85

d

Dance Centre 172, *172*
Dance in Vancouver 172
dance *see* performing arts
Dancing on the Edge **139**, 172
David Lam Park *58*, 59
Davie Street 56, 155, *155*
Deep Cove **81**, **84**, 185
Della Falls 203
dentists 232
department stores 121
designer clothes shops 126-128
dialling codes 236
disabled travellers 231
discount shops 122, 128-129
diving 203
doctors 232
dogs 59
Douglas, Stan 30
Downtown *17*, 18, *21*, **53-59**
  accommodation 35-40
  bars 113-116
  galleries 150-151
  restaurants & cafés 88-92
drink *see* alcohol; bars; coffee
Drive, The *see* Commercial Drive
driving *see* cars & driving
Dr-Sun Yat-Sen Classical Chinese Garden 25, *76*, 77

drugs (illegal) 232
  addicts & Four Pillars
    policy 24
  marijuana 23, **79**
  trade 18, 19, 24
dry-cleaner 125

e

eagles, bald 141
Early Music Vancouver 161
East Side 12, 21
  galleries 154
East Vancouver 76-79
  bars 119-120
  restaurants & cafés
    110-112
Electric Company 168
electricity 232
electronics shops 125
embassies 230-231
emergencies 232
Emily Carr College of Art &
  Design 69, 150, 152
Emily Carr House, Victoria
  197, 198
environmental activism **15**,
  18, 203
Erickson, Arthur **54**, 70, 74,
  172
etiquette 230
excursions 184-185, 188-
  194
  map 186-187
expeditions 193-194
Expo 86 18, **19-20**, 21, 55

f

Fairmont Empress Hotel,
  Victoria 195, 201, *201*
False Creek 69
farmers market 133
farms, children's 144
fashion shops 125-130
fauna 65
faxes 237
ferry services 84, 185, 188,
  198, 206, 227
Festival of Lights 141
Festival Vancouver 140
festivals & events 138-
  141
  best 138
  film 148, 156
  gay & lesbian 156
  fetish scene 158
film 146-149
  cinemas 147-149
    IMAX 149
  festivals 148
    gay & lesbian 156
  films set in Vancouver 239
Firehall Arts Centre 168, 169
fireworks 140
First Nations communities
  11, 16, 75, 152, 168, 169
Fisherman's Wharf, Victoria
  198, *198*
fishing **177-178**, 203
  expeditions 193-194
fitness facilities *see* sport &
  fitness

float planes 191
flower shops 130
folk music 159-160
  festival 139
food & drink
  shops & markets 130-131,
    133
  see also alcohol; coffee;
    restaurants & cafés
football 178-180
Fort Langley National
  Historic Site 145, 190
Four Pillars policy 24
Fraser River 10, 11, 12, 192
Fraser Valley 190

g

Galiano Island 206
galleries 150-154
  best 150
gardens, public 25, **74-75**,
  198, 203
Gastown 12, 13, 18, **57-58**
  accommodation 44
  bars 117
  galleries 151-152
  restaurants & cafés
    100-102
gay & lesbian 56, **155-
  158**, 232
  accommodation 156
  bars & clubs 156-157
  festivals & events 138, 156
  marriage 155
  media & publications 156
  restaurants & cafés
    157-158
Generation X 32
gift shops 132
GM Place 55, 162
Golden Mile 208
golf courses **173**, 207, 208,
  209
Graham, Rodney 30
Granville Island **67-69**, 199
  shopping 128
  water park 145
Granville Island Dock *67*, 69
Granville Island Stage 169
Granville Public Market *68*,
  69, 128
Granville Street Bridge 67,
  73
Great Depression 16-17
Greater Vancouver Zoo 145
Greenpeace **15**, 18
Grouse Mountain 85, *85*,
  180-181
Guinness family 82, 84
Gulf of Georgia Cannery 189,
  190
gyms 173-175

h

hairdressers 132
handbag shops 129-130
Harbour Air 191
Harbour Centre Lookout
  Tower 55, *55*, 56
Harrison Hot Springs
  190-192, 193

Harrison Mills 192
Hastings Park 180
hat shops 130
health 232
heli-skiing 194
Hell's Gate 192
helplines 232
hiking 229
  backcountry huts 193
  equipment shops 135-136
  trails 85, **175**, 193, 207,
    208
history 10-18
  Asian immigration 14, 16,
    18, 21, 76-77
  Edwardian Boom 13
  European colonisation 11
  Great Depression 16-17
  maritime activity 16
  Modern Vancouver 17-18
  native communities (First
    Nations) 10-11, 16
  World War I 16
  World War II 16, 17
HIV & AIDS 232
hockey *see* ice hockey
holidays, public 237
Hollyburn Mountain 85
homeless population 18, 19,
  24, 60
Hope 192
horseracing 180
Horseshoe Bay 82, 84
hospitals 232
hostels 47-48
hotels *see* accommodation
houseware shops 132
HR MacMillan Space Centre
  see MacMillan Space
  Centre
HSBC building 53
HSBC Festival of Light 140,
  140
Hughes, EJ 27, 29
Hughes, Howard 40, **48**

i

ice hockey 181
ice-skating 65, 85, **175**
identification 232-233
Illuminaires Lantern Festival
  139-140
IMAX screens 55, 149
immigration 237
in-line skating 175
insurance 233
International Children's
  Festival 138
International Dragon Boat
  Festival 138-139
International Writers &
  Readers Festival 141
internet 233
interpreters 230
Inuit art 152
izakaya restaurants 101

j

jazz music
  festival 139
  venues 165-166

jewellery shops 130
jogging *see* running
Johnson, Pauline 64
Jones, Jay 114

k

kayaking 176, 185, 203
  sea kayaking 193, **194**
Kelowna 207-208, *208*, 210,
  211
Keremeos 209
Kettle Valley Steam Railway
  208, 209
Kids Market 142
Kitsilano 69-73
  beach 69, *69*

l

L'Aubiniere, GM de 27, 30
language 233
laundry 233
leather goods shops 129-130
left luggage 233
legal help 233
lesbian scene *see* gay &
  lesbian
libraries 55-56, 233
Lighthouse Park 84
Lillooet 192
lingerie shops 129
Lions Gate Bridge 64, *64*,
  81, 82, **84**
literature *see* books &
  literature
lost property 233
Lower Seymour
  Conservation Reserve 81
Lynn Canyon Park **81**, 144
Lynn Headwaters Regional
  Park 81
Lytton 192, 193

m

MacMillan Space Centre
  70, **142**
magazines & comics 233
  shops 123
Main Street 76, **77-78**
malls **121-122**, 142
Manning Park 192
Maplewood Farm 144
marathon *see* Vancouver
  International Marathon
marijuana 23, **79**
Marine Building 16
maritime activity 16
Maritime Museum 142
Maritime Museum, Victoria
  197, 198
markets 69, 78, 128, 132-133
Mayne Island 206
measurements 237
media 233-234
  gay & lesbian 156
menswear shops 129
microbreweries 116
Minter Gardens 193
Mission Creek Greenway 207
mobile phones 236-237
money 234

Mount Seymour 180-181
Mount Seymour Provincial
   Park 85
mountain biking 84, **176**,
   207, 208
movies *see* film
Murakami Visitor Centre 189
Museum of Anthropology
   23, *24*, 54, **74-75**, 146
museums & galleries
   anthropology Museum of
   Anthropology 74; *art*
   Vancouver Art Gallery
   56; *Asian immigration*
   Chinese Cultural Centre
   Museum & Archives 77;
   crime Vancouver Police
   Centennial Museum 58;
   history Burnaby Village
   Museum 145; Steveston
   Museum 189, 190;
   Vancouver Museum
   144; *maritime* Maritime
   Museum 142; Maritime
   Museum, Victoria 198;
   science Science World
   143; *sport* BC Sports Hall
   of Fame & Museum 56
music & nightlife
   159-166
   artists 239
   classical & opera 160-161
   gay & lesbian 156-157
   jazz venues 165-166
   live music 165
   music shops 133-134
   music societies 161
   performing groups 161
   rock & folk 159-160
   venues 161-166
Myra Canyon cycling &
   hiking route 208

Naramata Bench 208
Nat Bailey Stadium 144, 178
newspapers 233
nightclubs *see* music &
   nightlife
Nitobe Memorial Garden 75
noodle houses 106-107
North Shore 81-85
   accommodation 45-47
   North Vancouver 81-82
   restaurants & cafés 112
   treks & trails 85
   West Vancouver 82-84
   nudist beach 72

O

Okanagan, The 207-212
   accommodation 210-211
   eating & drinking 209-210
   map 209
   resources 212
   wineries 207, 208,
   210-212
Oliver 208, 210
Olympic Village 21
Olympics 2010 *see* Winter
   Olympics (2010)

opening hours 235
opera music 160-161
opticians 134
Orpheum Theatre *159*,
   160, 162
Osoyoos 208
Othello Quintette Tunnels
   192

P

Pacific Coliseum 162
Pacific National Exhibition
   (PNE) 140
Pacific Rim National Park
   203
Park Royal shopping
   complex 82, **122**
parking 229
Parliament Buildings,
   Victoria 195, 196
Pender Island 206
Penticton 208, 210, 211
performing arts
   167-172
   comedy 171-172
   dance 172
   festivals 139
   theatre 167-170
      companies 170
      festivals **141**, 168
      for children 170
      tickets & information
      168-169
      venues 169
pharmacies 134
photography supplies 134
Playhouse Theatre Company
   167, 170
Playland 144
Plaza of Nations 19
PNE *see* Pacific National
   Exhibition
Polar Bear Swim 141
police stations 235
Port of Vancouver 16, 50
postal services 235
Powell Street Festival 140
Pride parade see Vancouver
   Pride Parade
public holidays 237
public transport 51,
   227-229
   lost property 233
Punjabi Market/Village
   78, 133
PuSh International
   Performance Festival
   141, 168

Q

Queen Elizabeth Theatre
   162, 167, 169
Queer Film & Video Festival
   156

R

radio 234
rafting *see* whitewater
   rafting
Railway Club 164, *164*

railways *see* trains &
   railways
rainfall 25, 237
ranching 194
Rattenbury, Francis 195,
   196-197
record shops 133-134
religion 235
restaurants & cafés 88-
   112
   best 89
   by cuisine
      Aboriginal 93; *African*
      110; *American*
      110-111; *Asian* 111;
      Belgian 89; *Canadian*
      103; *Chinese* 102-103;
      fish & chips 104;
      French 89-91, 94, 99,
      104-105, 112; *fusion*
      91; *Greek* 94-95;
      Indian 101, 105;
      Italian 91, 95, 99, 101,
      105, 111; *Japanese* 91,
      95, 101, 105-108, 111;
      Korean 95, 111; *Latin
      American* 95-96;
      Mexican 101-102, 108;
      Middle Eastern 110;
      seafood 91, 96, 97-99,
      99, 102, 111, 112;
      steaks 92; *Thai*
      99-100, 108;
      Vegetarian 108, 112;
      West Coast 92, 96-97,
      99, 100, 108-109, 112
   budget eating 108
   cafés 88-89, 92-93, 97, 99,
      100-101, 103, 110, 112
   diners 89, 93-94, 103-104
   gay & lesbian 157-158
   tipping 88, 237
   *see also Restaurants &
      Cafés index pp243-244*
Richard Kidd *122-123*, 126
Ridge Theatre 148, *149*
roads *see* cars & driving
Robson Square Law Courts
   54
rock climbing **176**, 203
rock music 159
rollerblading 175
Roundhouse Community
   Centre 143
rowing 61
Royal BC Museum, Victoria
   197, 198
running 61, 85, 173,
   175-176

S

safety 235-236
sailing 177, *179*, 185
Salish Indians 16
salmon 102, 144
Salmon Arm 208
Salt Spring Island 206
Sam Kee Company 77
Saturna Island 206 Science
   World 55
Science World 143
scuba diving 178

security 235-236
SeaBus 228
sea kayaking 193, **194**
secretarial services 230
Seymour mountain *see*
   Mount Seymour
shippers & shipping
   materials 136, 230
shoe shops 134-135
shops & services 121-136
   prices 121
   tax 234-235
Sicamous 208
sights, the best 51
Similkameen Valley 208
skateboarding 176
skiing & snowboarding 141,
   180-181, *180-181*,
   193, 203, 207
   equipment shops 135-136
   heli-skiing 194
SkyTrain 19, **228**
smoking 230, 236
snowboarding *see* skiing &
   snowboarding
soccer 181
Sonoran desert 208
Southern Gulf Islands
   205-206
spas & spa resorts 135,
   204-205
Splashdown Park 145
Sport & Fitness 173-181
   land sports 173-176,
   180-181, 207
   shops 125, 135-136
   spectator sports 178-181
   watersports 176-178
Stanley Industrial Alliance
   Stage 169
Stanley Park 60-65, *60-61*
   cycling & bicycle hire 62
   English Bay 64-65
   map 63
   restaurants & cafés 97-99
   shuttle bus service 51, 65
   water playground 145
STDs 232
Steam Clock 58
Steveston **189-190**, *189*,
   199
Steveston Museum 189, 190
Stó:lo 10-11
Storyeum 58, 143
Strachan Mountain 85
Strathcona 77
study 236
Sun Run *see* Vancouver Sun
   Run
surfing 203
swimming pools 71, 144, 145,
   178

T

tailor 129
tattoos & body piercing 136
tax 121, 234-235
taxis 228-229
Taylor, AJT 84
telephones & dialling codes
   185, 236
television 234

temperatures, average 236
tennis 176
Terada, Ron 30
Entering the City of Vancouver 26
theatre *see* performing arts
Ticketmaster 169
tickets & information
music 160-161
theatre 168-169
transport 228
time 237
tipping 88, 237
tobacco & tobacconists 136, 230, 231, 236
Tofino 203-205
Tofino Botanical Garden 203
toilets 237
totem poles 62, 82
Touchstone Theatre 167, 170
tourist information 185, 237
tours 51
walking 81
toy shops 136
trains & railways 63, 185, 208, 227
miniature 144
see also Canadian Pacific Railway (CPR)
translators 230
transport *see* public transport
Treetops Adventure 82
trips out of town *see* excursions
Trout Lake Farmers Market 133

UBC Botanical Garden 75
UBC Museum of Anthropology *see* Museum of Anthropology
UBC *see* University of British Columbia (UBC)
universities 236
University of British Columbia (UBC) 74, 236
urban regeneration projects 17-18, 21, 50, 59

Vancity Theatre 147, *147*, 148
Vancouver Aquarium Marine Science Centre 61, 63, 143
Vancouver Aquatic Centre 143-144
Vancouver Art Gallery 30, 53, 54, *54*, **56**, 150
SuperSunday 144
Vancouver East Cultural Centre 168, 169
Vancouver Folk Music Festival 139
Vancouver Fringe Festival **141**, 168
Vancouver International Airport 226

Vancouver International Dance Festival 172
Vancouver International Film Festival 141, **148**
Vancouver International Jazz Festival 139
Vancouver International Marathon 138, 176
Vancouver Island 203-206
Vancouver Maritime Museum 70, **142**
Vancouver New Music 161
Vancouver Opera 161
Vancouver Police Centennial Museum 58
Vancouver Pride Parade 140, 156
Vancouver Public Library 55-56, 144, 233
Vancouver Recital Society 161
Vancouver Snow Show 141
Vancouver Sun Run 138, 175
Vancouver Symphony Orchestra 161
Vancouver Trolley Company 51
VanDusen Gardens 74-75
Vanier Park 70
Varley, FH 27, 30
vehicle hire 229
Vernon 208
Victoria 195-202
accommodation 200-202
map 196
restaurants 199-200
Victoria Day Long Weekend 138
vineyards **118-120**, 207, 208, 209, **210-212**
vintage clothes shops 129
visas 237
volleyball 173

walking 229
Stanley Park 61
tours 81
West Side suggested walk 70-71
see also hiking
Wall, Jeff **28**, 30
Wallace, Ian 29-30
water parks 144, 145, *145*
Waterfront Station 55
watersports **176**, 207, 208
weather 25, 236, 237
websites 239
weights 237
West Coast Air 191
West Coast Art 26-32
West End
accommodation 40-43
restaurants & cafés 92-97
West Side 12, 67-75
accommodation 44-45
bars 117-119
galleries 152-154
map 71
restaurants & cafés 103-109
walk 70-71

West Vancouver 82-84
restaurants & cafés 112
Western Front Gallery 154
whale watching 69, 189, *192*, 193, 198, **199**, 203-204
where to stay *see* accommodation
Whistler 21, 184, **213**
Whitecaps Football Club 181
whitewater rafting 192
wildlife 65
windsurfing **178**, 203
wine 118-120
shops 131
vineyards/wineries **118-120**, 207, 208, **210-212**
Winter Olympics (2010) 19, **20-21**, 34, 55, 160, 180
women travellers 237
safety 235
Wooden Boat Festival 141
World War I 16, 63
World War II 16, 17, 189
Wreck Beach 72

yachting 177, 185, 203
Yaletown 58-59
accommodation 44
bars 116-117
restaurants & cafés 99-100
Yale club 165
yoga 125, 177
youth hostels 47-48

zoos & aquariums 63, 143, 145

Accommodation

Barclay House 43, *44*
Blue Horizon 41
Bosman's Hotel 39
Buchan 43
Century Plaza Hotel & Spa 37
Coast Plaza 41
Crowne Plaza Hotel Georgia 37
Days Inn Downtown 38
Dominion 44, *45*
Empire Landmark Hotel 41
English Bay Inn 43
Escape to the Point B&B 45
Fairmont Hotel Vancouver *34*, 35
Fairmont Waterfront Hotel 35
Four Seasons Hotel 35
Granville Island Hotel 44
Horseshoe Bay Motel 46
Hostelling International – Vancouver Central 47
Hostelling International – Vancouver Downtown 38
Hostelling International – Vancouver Jericho Beach 48
Hotel Le Soleil 37

Howard Johnson 39
Hycroft 45
Kingston Hotel Bed & Breakfast 40
Listel Vancouver 40
Lonsdale Quay Hotel 45
Metropolitan 38
Mickey's Kits Beach Chalet 45
'O Canada' House 43
Opus Hotel 44, 46-47, *46-47*
Pacific Palisades Hotel 40
Pan Pacific 37
Riviera Suites Hotel 41
Rosedale on Robson 38
Samesun Backpacker Lounge 48
Sheraton Wall Centre 38, *39*
St Regis 39
Sunset Inn & Suites 43
Sutton Place Hotel 37, *38*
Sylvia Hotel, The *41*, 43
Wedgewood 37
Westin Bayshore 40
Westin Grand 38
YMCA 40
YMCA Hotel 40

Bars

Alibi Room 117
Aqua 1066 113
Atlantic Trap & Grill 113
Bacchus Piano Lounge 113
Bar None 116
Bimini's Tap House 117
Bin 941 113
Bukowski's 119
Café Deux Soleils 119
Cambie Bar & Grill, The 114
Cellar Jazz, The 118
Five Point 119
George *115*, 117
Gerard (Sutton Place Hotel) 114
Ginger 62 Cocktail Den & Kitchen 114
Havana 120
Hell's Kitchen 118
Honey Lounge 114
Irish Heather, The 117, *117*
Lucy Mae Brown 115
Morrissey Irish House 115
900 West Lounge 115
Nu 115
Opus Bar 117
Reef, The 120
Roxy, The 115
SkyBar 115
Soho 117
Subeez 117
Tatlows Broiler Bar 118
Urban Well 119
Whip, The 120
Wild Rice 116

Restaurants & Cafés

Adesso 105
Aurora Bistro 112
Bacchus 89
Beach House at Dundarave Pier 112

Bean Around the World –
    Dundarave 112
Bin 941 92
Bishop's 108
Bistro Pastis 104
Blue Water Café & Raw Bar
    99
Bon's Off Broadway 108
Brioche Urban Baking 100
Brix Restaurant & Wine Bar
    100
C Restaurant 91
Caffé Artigiano 88, 88
Café Crepe 92
Café Luxy 95
Cannery, The 111
Cardero's 96
Cassis Bistro 91
Ch'i 111
Chambar 89
Characters Taverna 94
Cin Cin Ristorante & Bar 95
Cioppino's Mediterranean
    Grill & Enoteca 99
Cito Espresso 99
Coast Restaurant 99, 100
Congee Noodle House 106
Continental Coffee 110
Cook Studio Café 101
Crocodile, Le 94
Cru 109
Delaney's Coffee House 92
Delilah's 96
Diva at the Met 92
Don Francesco Ristorante 91

Earls on Top 96
E-Hwa 101
Elbow Room 89
Elixir Bar & Restaurant 99
Fatburger 93
Federico's Supper Club 105,
    111
Feenie's 103, 103
Fish House in Stanley Park,
    The 97
Foundation 112
Gallery Café 89
Giardino, Il 91
Go Fish 97, 104
Gotham Steakhouse &
    Cocktail Bar 92
Green Village 107
Guu 101
Gyoza King 95
Hal Mai Jang Moi Jib 95
Hamburger Mary's 93
Hamilton Street Grill 100
Hapa 101
Ho Yuen Kee 107
Hon's Wun-Tun House 102
Imperial 106
Incendio 101
Joe Fortes Seafood & Chop
    House 96
Kalvin's Restaurant 107
Kam Gok Yuen 102
Khai Thai To Go 108
Kim Saigon Sandwich Bar
    102
Kintaro Ramen 95

Kirin 106
Kwong Chow Congee Noodle
    House 106
Landmark Hot Pot House
    107
Legendary Noodle 106, 106
Lift Bar & Grill 94, 96
Lillget Feast House 93
Lolita's South of the Border
    Cantina 95
Lumière 104
Margaritas, Las 108
Maurya 105
Mistral 105
Moderne Burger 103
Mondo Gelato 93
Mouse & Bean Café, The
    101
Moustache Café 112
Mui Garden Restaurant 107
Naam, The 108
New Town Bakery &
    Restaurant 102
Norboo's 111
Nu 92, 93
Okada Sushi 91
Only Seafoods Café 108
Parkside 97
Phnom Penh 102
Raincity Grill 97
Reef 110, 110
Régalade, La 112
Rinconcito Salvadoreno 110
Salmon House on the Hill
    112

Samba Brazilian Steak
    House 96
Sapphire South Asian
    Fusion 101
Save-on-Meat 108
Saveur 94
Sea Harbour Seafood
    Restaurant 107
Section (3) 100
Sequoia Grill at the
    Teahouse 99
Shanghai River Restaurant
    107
Shiru Bay: Chopstick Café
    101
Simply Thai 99
Soma 110
Sophie's Cosmic Café 104, 104
Spice Alley 111
Stanley Park Pavilion 97
Stella's Tap & Tapas Bar
    112
Sun Sui Wah 106
Taki's Taverna 95
Templeton 89
Tojo's 105
Toshi Sushi 111
Vij's 105
Watermark 109
West Restaurant 109, 109
White Spot 104
Wild Rice 91
Yuji's Tapas 105
Zakkushi Charcoal Grill 95
Zanzibar Café Bar 110

Advertisers' Index

Please refer to the relevant pages for contact details

timeout.com **IFC**

Where To Stay

Excecutive House Hotel **36**
Kitsilano Cottage By The Sea **36**
Renaissance Hotel **36**

Sightseeing

Vancouver Attractions **52**
Capilano Suspension Bridge **80**
SmartVisit Solutions **80**
Time Out London **86**

Restaurants

timeout.com/restaurants **90**

Shops & Services

Time Out Walks Guides **124**

Trips Out of Town

Time Out Croatia Guide **182**
Time Out Weekend Breaks **214**

Time Out City Guides **IBC**

Place of interest and/or entertainment	■
Hospital or college	■
Railway station	■
Parks	■
River	■
Highway	⊨Ⓐ⊨
Main road	
Main road tunnel	
Pedestrian road	
Airport	✈
Church	✚
Subway station	Ⓜ
Area name . . . . WEST SIDE	
Hotels	❶
Restaurants	❶
Bars	❶

Maps

Greater Vancouver	**246**
Downtown	**248**
West Side	**250**
East Vancouver	**252**
North Shore	**253**
Street Index	**254**
Local transport	**256**

Greater Vancouver

E F G H

Grouse Mountain Skyride
Grouse Mountain Ski Area

Lynn Headwaters Regional Park

Rice Lake

Seymour Skiing & Hiking Area

Mount Seymour Provincial Park

Indian Arm Provincial Park

OYAL BLVD

QUEENS RD WEST

29 TH ST EAST

SHORE

DEEP COVE

Belcarra Regional Park

ARINE DR

13TH ST WEST   13TH ST E

KEITH RD EAST

COTTON RD

BELCARRA

Belcarra Regional Park

Burrard   Inlet

Vancouver Harbour

See p253

SECOND NARROWS BRIDGE

MAIN ST

Burrard   Inlet

BARNET ROAD

INLET DRIVE

McGILL ST

POWELL ST

DUNDAS ST

HASTINGS   STREET

WALL ST

ETON STREET

Confederation Park

HASTINGS STREET

Kensington Park

Burnaby Mountain Park

PRIOR ST   VENABLES ST

Pacific Central Station

CLARK DRIVE

COMMERCIAL DR

VICTORIA DRIVE

NANAIMO STREET

1ST AVE

RENFREW STREET

Rupert Park

GILMORE AVENUE

WILLINGDON AVENUE

CURTIS STREET

HOLDOM AVE

SPERLING AVENUE

BURNABY MOUNTAIN PARKWAY

BROADWAY   EAST
Broadway
12TH   AVE   EAST

Commercial Dr

Renfrew

GRANDVIEW

Rupert

Brentwood Town Centre

LOUGHHEED HWY

Gilmore

Holdom

DOUGLAS

Sperling

BURNABY

GRANDVIEW HWY

1

CANADA   WAY

WINSTON ST

7   Lake City

Production Way

Trout Lake

John Hendry Park

Nanaimo

22ND   AVE

SPROTT   ST

Burnaby Lake Park

CANADA WAY

WINSTON ST

EAST VANCOUVER

See p252

29 TH AVE

RUPERT ST

WILLINGDON AVE

Burnaby Lake

Burnaby Lake Regional Park

FRASER   STREET

3RD   AVE EAST

Joyce

Deer Lake Park

Deer Lake

Robert Burnaby Park

41ST   AVE   EAST

Memorial Park South

VICTORIA   DR

41ST AVE EAST

JOYCE ST

GRANGE ST

Patterson

Metrotown

OAKLAND ST

BURRIS ST

9TH AVENUE EAST

49TH AVE EAST

Central Park

IMPERIAL   STREET

KINGSWAY

Royal Oak

IMPERIAL ST

CANADA   WAY

NEW WESTMINSTER

57TH   AVE   EAST

FRASER   STREET

KNIGHT   STREET

ARGYLE   ST

54TH AVE

KERR ST

CHAMPLAIN CR.

BOUNDARY   ROAD

PATTERSON AVE

ROYAL OAK   AVENUE

IMPERIAL   STREET

RUMBLE   STREET

GILLEY AVENUE

EDMONDS   STREET

KINGSWAY

10TH AVENUE

6 TH STREET

2 ND   ST

Edmond

SOUTHEAST MARINE

KENT   AVENUE

Everett Crowley Park

MARINE DRIVE

MARINE   WAY

Byrne Creek Ravine Park

SOUTHRIDGE DR

BYRE ROAD

20 TH ST

8TH AVE

QUEENS AVE

ROYAL AVE

North   Arm

KNIGHT ST BRIDGE

KNIGHT   STREET

NO. 6 ROAD

BRIDGEPORT ROAD

RICHMOND

QUEENSBOROUGH BRIDGE

22nd St

New Westminster

91

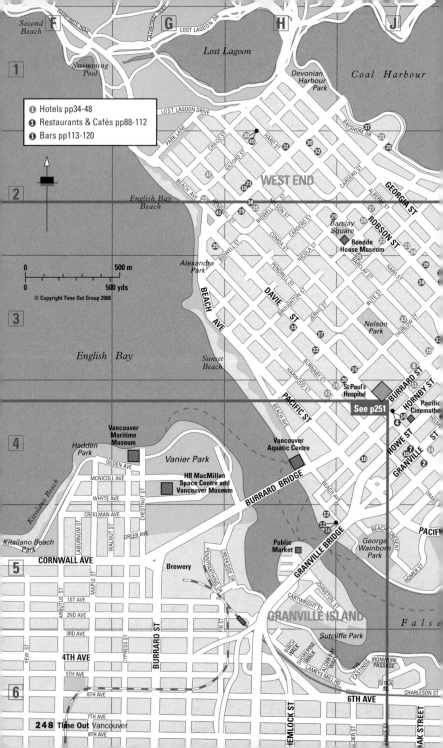

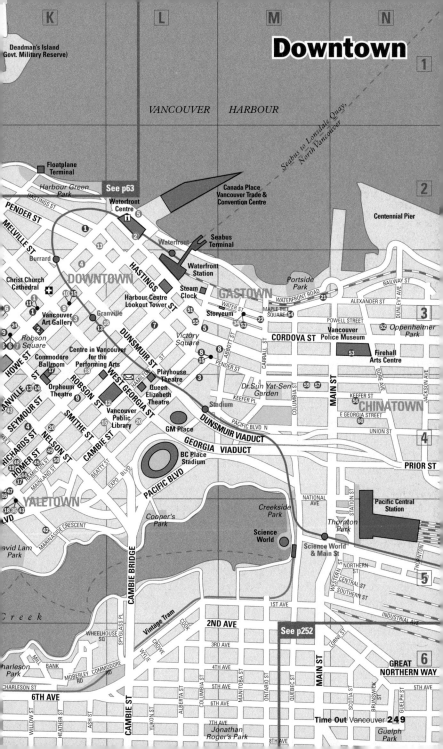

West Side

4

0   500 m
0   500 yds
© Copyright Time Out Group 2006

Jericho Beach

CAMERON AVE

Jean Beaty Park

Margaret Piggot Park

POINT GREY

5

Jericho Beach Park

Waterfront Park

Volunteer Park

To UBC Museum of Anthropology

WALLACE ST

POINT GREY RD

1ST AVE
2ND AVE
3RD AVE

Tatlow Park

MACDONALD STREET

26

77

❶ Hotels pp34-48
❶ Restaurants & Cafés pp88-112
❶ Bars pp113-120

4TH AVE
McBride Park
5TH AVE
6TH AVE

6

ORTONA CR
ANTWERP LANE

GHENT LANE

DUNBAR ST

ALMA STREET

7TH AVE

WATERLOO ST

BLENHEIM ST

TRUTCH ST

BALACLAVA ST

BAYSWATER ST

STEPHENS ST

TRAFALGAR ST

LARCH ST

BROADWAY WEST
WALLACE CR

24

8TH AVE

BROADWAY WEST

70 63 69 64

66

10TH AVE

10TH AVE

KITSILANO DIV

11TH AVE

HIGHBURY ST

WALLACE ST

CROWN ST

Almond Park

DUNBAR DIV

COLLINGWOOD ST

12TH AVE
13TH AVE
14TH AVE

CARNARVON ST

MACKENZIE ST

7

15TH AVE

16TH AVE
17TH AVE

QUESNEL ST

QUADRA ST

PUGET DR

Carnarvon Park

17TH AVE

18TH AVE

DUNBAR STREET

19TH AVE
20TH AVE

GALIANO DR

MACKENZIE ST

MACDONALD STREET

8

21ST AVE
22ND AVE

BLENHEIM STREET

Valdez Park

VALDEZ RD

CROWN STREET

23RD AVE
24TH AVE

Trafalgar Park

OLIVER

KING EDWARD AVE

9

Chaldecott Park

HIGHBURY ST

DUNKIRK ST

26TH AVE

CARNARVON ST

CHALDECOTT ST

ALMA ST

27TH AVE
28TH AVE

MACKENZIE STREET

PUGET DR

HAGGAR

EDGAR ST

250 Time Out Vancouver

29TH AVE

Balaclava Park

East Vancouver

600 m
600 yds

© Copyright Time Out Group 2006

See pp248-249

- ❶ Hotels pp34-48
- ❷ Restaurants & Cafés pp88-112
- ❸ Bars pp113-120

North Shore

Grouse Mountain Skyride
Grouse Mountain Ski Area

❶ Hotels pp34-48
❶ Restaurants & Cafés pp88-112
❶ Bars pp113-120

Grouse Grind Trail

Mosquito Creek

Capilano River Regional Park

MONTROYAL

BLVD

NANCY GREENE WAY

EYREMOUNT DR

SOUTHBOROUGH DR

Capilano Golf and Country Club

STEVENS DR

CREEK RD

EYREMOUNT DR

ROSS

Capilano River

HIGHLAND BLVD

Mosquito Creek

DELBROOK AVE

Hollyburn Country Club

BURLEY DR

Suspension Bridge

EDGEMONT

RIDGEWOOD

DR

CAPILANO ROAD

BLVD

Capilano View Cemetery

QUEENS RD WEST

OSBORNE RD EAST

LONSDALE AVENUE

29 TH ST E

LEWOOD AVE

11TH ST

TAYLOR WAY

Capilano River

MARINE DRIVE

23 RD ST W

23RD ST E

FELL AVE

LARSON

WESTVIEW DR

18TH ST W

18 TH ST E

AVENUE

AVENUE

AVENUE

99

1A

mbleside Park

15 TH WEST

PEMBERTON AVE

MARINE DRIVE

33

32

13 TH ST WEST

13 TH ST E

WELCH ST

3 RD WEST

CHESTERFIELD

LONSDALE

ST GEORGES

3 RD EAST

Lonsdale Market

ESPLANADE EAST

40

First

Narrows

LIONS GATE BRIDGE

PARK DR

STANLEY PARK CAUSEWAY

Beaver Lake

anley Park

LAGOON DR

Lost Lagoon

Coal Harbour

Burrard Inlet

0   1 mile

0   1 km

© Copyright Time Out Group 2006

Street Index

Downtown

1st Avenue - p248 F5/G5 - p249 M5
2nd Avenue - p248 F5/G5 - p249 M5/6
3rd Avenue - p248 F6/G6/H6 - p249 L6/M6
4th Avenue - p248 F6/G6/H6 - p249 L6/M6/N6
5th Avenue - p248 F6/G6/H6 - p249 L6/M6/N6
6th Avenue - p248 F6/G6/H6/J6 - p249 K6/L6/M6/N6
7th Avenue - p248 F6/G6/H6 - p249 K6/L6/M6/N6
8th Avenue - p248 F6/G6/H6 - p249 K6/L6/M6/N6
Abbott Street - p249 M3/4
Alberni Street - p248 H1/2/J2
Alberta Street - p249 L6
Alder Bay Walk - p248 H6
Alder Street - p248 J6
Alexander Street - p249 N3
Arbutus Street - p248 F5/6
Ash Street - p249 K6
Barclay Street - p248 H2/J3
Bayshore Drive - p248 J1/2
Beach Avenue - p248 G2/3/H3/4/J5
Beach Crescent - p248 J5
Beatty Street - p249 K4l3/4
Bidwell Street - p248 G3/H2
Birch Walk - p248 H6
Broughton Street - p248 H3/J2
Brunswick Street - p249 N6
Burnaby Street - p248 H3/4/J4
Burrard Bridge - p248 H4/5
Burrard Street - p248 G5/6/J3/4
Bute Street - p248 H3/4/J2/3
Cambie Bridge - p249 L5
Cambie Street - p249 K4/L3/4/L6
Cardero Street - p248 G2/3/J2
Carrall Street - p249 M3/4
Cartwright Street - p248 H5
Cathedral Trail - p248 G1
Central Street - p249 N5
Charleson Street - p248 J6 - p249 K6
Chestnut Street - p248 G4/5
Chilco Street - p248 G2/H1
Columbia Street - p249 L6 - p249 M3/4
Commodore Road - p249 K6/L6
Comox Street - p248 H2/G2/3/J3
Cook - p249 L5/6
Cordova Street - p249 M3/N3
Cornwall Avenue - p248 F5/G5
Creekside Drive - p248 H5
Creelman Avenue - p248 F5/G5
Crowe - p249 L6
Cypress Street - p248 G4/5/6
Davie Street - p248 G2/H3/J3/4

Denman Street - p248 G2/H1/2
Drake Street - p248 J4/5
Dunlevy Avenue - p249 N3
Dunsmuir Street - p249 K3/L3/4
Dunsmuir Viaduct - p249 L4/M4
East Georgia Street - p249 N4
Expo Boulevard - p249 L4
Fir Street - p248 G5/6
Georgia Street - p248 H1/J2
Georgia Viaduct - p249 L4/M4
Gilford Street - p248 G2/H2
Gore Avenue - p249 N3/4
Granville Bridge - p248 H5/J5
Granville Street - p248 J4 - p249 K3/4/L3
Great Northern Way - p249 N6
Greer Avenue - p248 G5
Guelph Street - p249 N6
Hamilton Street - p249 K4/L3/4
Haro Street - p248 H1/2/J2/3
Harwood Street - p248 H3/4/J4
Hastings Street - p249 K2/L2/3/M3/N3
Heather Street - p249 K6
Helmcken Street - p248 J4 - p249 K4
Hemlock Street - p248 H6 - p249 K4/L3
Homer Street - p248 J5
Hornby Street - p248 J3/4
Howe Street - p248 J4 - p249 K3/4/L3
Industrial Avenue - p249 N5/6
Ironwork Passage - p248 J6
Jackson Avenue - p249 N3/4
Jervis Street - p248 H3/J2/3
Johnston Street - p248 H5/J5
Keefer Place - p249 M4
Keefer Street - p249 M4/N4
Laburnum Street - p248 F5
Lameys Mill Road - p248 H6/J6
Laurel Street - p249 K6
Lorne Street - p249 N6
Lost Lagoon Drive - p248 G1/H1
Main Street - p249 M4/5/6/N4/5/6
Mainland Street - p249 K4
Manitoba Street - p249 M5/6
Maple Street - p248 F4/5/6
Maple Tree Square - p249 M3
Marinaside Crescent - p249 K5
McNicoll Avenue - p248 F4/G4
Melville Street - p249 K2/3
Mill Bank - p249 K6
Moberley Road - p249 K6
National Avenue - p249 M4/5
Nelson Street - p248 H1/2/H2/J3 - p249 K4
Nicola Street - p248 G2/3/J2
Northern Street - p249 N5
Oak Street - p248 J6
Ogden Avenue - p248 F4/G4

Ontario Street - p249 M5/6
Pacific Boulevard - p248 J5 - p249 K5/L4
Pacific Boulevard N - p249 M4
Pacific Street - p248 H3/4/J4
Park Lane - p248 G1/2
Pender Street - p249 K2/3/L3/M3/4/N4
Pendrell Street - p248 G2/H2/J3
Pennyfarthing Drive - p248 G5
Powell Street - p249 M3/N3
Prior Street - p249 N4
Quebec Street - p249 M5/6
Railway Street - p249 N3
Rawlings Trail - p248 F1
Richards Street - p249 K3/4/L3
Robson Street - p248 H1/2/J2/3 - p249 K3/4/L4
Scotia Street - p249 N6
Seymour Street - p249 K3/4/L3
Shorepine Walk - p248 H6
Sitka Square - p248 J6
Smithe Street - p249 K3/4/L4
Southern Street - p249 N5
Spruce Street - p248 J6
Spyglass Place - p249 L6
Station Street - p249 N4/5
The Castings - p248 J6
Thornton - p249 N5
Thurlow Street - p248 H4/J3
Union Street - p249 M4/N4
Walnut Street - p248 F5/G5
Water Street - p249 L3/M3
Waterfront Road - p249 L2/3/M3/N3
West Georgia Street - p249 K3/L4
Western Street - p249 N5
Wheelhouse Square - p249 L6
Whyte Avenue - p248 F4/G4
Willow Street - p249 K6
Wylie - p249 L6
Yew Street - p248 F5/6
Yukon Street - p249 L6

West Side

1st Avenue - p250 B5/C5/D5/E5 - p251 E5/F5/G5
2nd Avenue - p250 B5/C5/D5/E5 - p251 E5/F5/G5/H5
3rd Avenue - p250 B5/C5/D5/E5 - p251 E6/F6/G6/H6
4th Avenue - p250 B6/C6/D6/E6 - p251 E6/F6/G6/H6
5th Avenue - p250 B6/C6/D6/E6 - p251 E6/F6/G6/H6
6th Avenue - p250 B6/C6/D6/E6 - p251 E6/F6/G6/H6
7th Avenue - p250 B6/C6/D6/E6 - p251 E6/F6/G6/H6/J6
8th Avenue - p250 B6/C6/D6/E6 - p251 E6/F6/G6/H6/J6

10th Avenue - p250 A7/B7/C7/D7
11th Avenue - p250 B7/C7/D7/E7
12th Avenue - p250 B7/C7/D7/E7
13th Avenue - p250 B7/C7/D7/E7
14th Avenue - p250 B7/C7/D7/E7
15th Avenue - p250 B7/C7/D7/E7
16th Avenue - p250 A7/B7/C7/D7/E7
17th Avenue - p250 A8/B8/C8/D8/E8
18th Avenue - p250 A8/B8/C8/D8/E8
19th Avenue - p250 A8/B8/C8/D8/E8
20th Avenue - p250 A8/B8/C8/D8/E8
21st Avenue - p250 A8/B8/C8/D8/E8
22nd Avenue - p250 A8/B8/C8/D8/E8
23rd Avenue - p250 A9/B9/C9/D9/E9
24th Avenue - p250 A9/B9/C9/D9/E9
26th Avenue - p250 A9/B9/C9/D9/E9
27th Avenue - p250 A9/B9/C9/D9/E9
28th Avenue - p250 A9/B9/C9/D9/E9
29th Avenue - p250 A9/B9/C9/D9/E9 - p250 G10/H10/J10
Alder Bay Walk - p251 H6
Alder Street- p251 J5/6/7
Alexandra Street - p251 G9
Alma Street - p250 B5/6/7/8/9
Angus Drive - p251 G8
Antwerp Lane - p250 A6/B6
Arbutus Street - p251 F5/6/7/8/9
Balaclava Street - p250 C5/6/7
Balfour Avenue - p251 H8/9/J8/9
Balsam Street - p251 E5/6/7/8
Bayswater Street - p250 D5/6
Beach Avenue - p251 H4/J4/5
Birch Walk - p251 H6
Blenheim Street - p250 C5/6/7/8/9
Brakenridge Street - p251 E9/10

Broadway West - p250 A6/B6/C6/D6/E6
- p251 E6/F6/G6/H6/J6
Burrard Bridge - p251 H4/5
Burrard Street - p251 G5/6/7
- p251 J4
Cameron Avenue - p250 B5
Carnarvon Street - p250 D7/8/9
Cartier Street - p251 H8/9/10
Cartwright Street - p251 H5
Cedar Crescent - p251 F8/G8
Chaldecott Street - p250 A9
Chestnut Street - p251 G4/5
Collingwood Street - p250 B5/6/7/8/9
Cornwall Avenue - p251 E5/F5/G5
Creekside Drive - p251 H5
Creelman Avenue – p251 F5/G5
Crown Street - p250 A7/8/9
Cypress Crescent - p251 F9
Cypress Street - p251 G5/6/7/8/9
Devonshire Crescent - p251 H9/10
Douglas Crescent - p251 J8/9/10
Dunbar Div - p250 B7
Dunbar Street - p250 B5/6/7/8/9
Dunkirk Street - p250 B9
East Boulevard - p251 F8
Eddington Drive - p251 E9/10/F9
Edgar Street - p250 E9/10
Fir Street - p251 G5/6/7
Galiano Drive - p250 C8
Ghent Lane - p250 B5/6
Granville Bridge - p251 H5/J5
Granville Street - p251 H5/6/7/8/9
Greer Avenue - p251 G5
Haggart Street - p250 E9
- p251 E9/10
Hemlock Street - p251 H5/6/7
Highbury Street - p250 B7/8/9
Hornby Street - p251 J4
Hosmer Avenue - p251 F8/G8
Howe Street - p251 J4
Hudson Street - p251 H8/9/10
Johnston Street - p251 H5/J5
King Edward Avenue - p250 A9/B9/C9/D9/E9
- p251 G9/G9/H9
King Edward Avenue West - p251 E9/F9
Kitsilano Div - p250 D7
Laburnum Street - p251 F5
Lameys Mill Road - p251 H6/J6
Larch Street - p250 E5/6/7/8/9
Laurier Avenue - p251 H9/J9
MacDonald Street - p250 D5/6/7/8/9
MacKenzie Street - p250 D7/8/9
Magnolia Street - p251 F9/10
Maple Crescent - p251 F9
Maple Street - p251 F5/6/7/8
Marguerite Street - p251 G9/10
Marpole Avenue - p251 G8/H8
Matthews Avenue - p251 F9/G8/9/H8/J8

McBain Avenue - p251 E9
McMullen Avenue - p251 E9
McNicoll Avenue - p251 F4/G4
McRae Avenue - p251 H8
Montcalm Street - p251 J7/8
Nanton Avenue - p251 G9/H9/J9
Ogden Avenue - p251 F4/G4
Oliver Crescent - p251 E9
Ortona Cr - p250 A6/B6
Osler Street - p251 J8/9/10
Pacific Street - p251 H4/J4
Parkway - p251 F9
Pennyfarthing Drive - p251 G5
Pine Crescent - p251 G8
Pine Street - p251 G5/6/7/8
Point Grey Road - p250 B5/C5/D5/E5
Puget Drive - p250 C8/D8/9
Quadra Street - p250 C8
Quesnel Drive - p250 C8
Selkirk Street – P151 J8/9/10
Shorepine Walk - p251 H6
Spruce Street - p251 H5/6/7
Stephens Street - p250 D5/6
Tecumseh Avenue - p251 H8
The Castings - p251 J6
The Crescent - p251 H8
Townley Street - p251 E9
Trafalgar Street - p250 E5/6/7/8/9
Trutch Street - p250 C5/6/7
Valdez Road - p250 C8/D8
Valley Drive - p250 E8
Vine Street - p251 E5/6/7/8/F9
Wallace Cr - p250 A6
Wallace Street - p250 A7/8/9/B5
Walnut Street - p251 F5
Waterloo Street - p250 C5/6/7
Whyte Avenue - p251 F4/G4
Yew Street - p251 F5/6/7/8/9
York Avenue – p251 E5/F5/G5

East Vancouver

10th Avenue - p252 K7-T7
11th Avenue - p252 K7-T7
12th Avenue - p252 K7-T7
12th Avenue East - p252 N7/O7/P7/Q7/R7
13th Avenue - p252 K7-T7
14th Avenue - p252 K7-T7
15th Avenue - p252 K8-T8
16th Avenue - p252 K8-T8
17th Avenue - p252 K8-T8
18th Avenue - p252 K8-T8
19th Avenue - p252 K8-T8
1st Avenue - p252 M5-T5
20th Avenue - p252 K8-T8
21st Avenue - p252 K9-T9
22nd Avenue - p252 K9-T9
23rd Avenue - p252 K9-T9
24th Avenue - p252 K9-T9
26th Avenue - p252 K9-T9
27th Avenue - p252 K9-T9
28th Avenue - p252 K10-T10
29th Avenue - p252 K10-T10
2nd Avenue - p252 K6-T6
30th Avenue - p252 K10-T10
31st Avenue - p252 K10-T10
32nd Avenue - p252 K10-T10
33rd Avenue East - p252 M10-T11
34th Avenue - p252 N11
35th Avenue - p252 M11/N11
3rd Avenue - p252 K6-T6

4th Avenue - p252 K6-T6
5th Avenue - p252 K6-T6
5th Avenue - p252 N6-T6
6th Avenue - p252 K6-T6
7th Avenue - p252 K6-T6
8th Avenue - p252 K6-T6/R7/S7/T7
Alberta Street - p252 L6/7
Alice Street - p252 R9
Argyle Street - p252 Q10
Ash Street - p252 K6/7/8/9/10
Atlin Street - p252 T9/10
Aubrey Place - p252 N10
Baldwin Street - p252 R10
Balkan Street - p252 N9
Bauer Street - p252 Q6
Beatrice Street - p252 R8/9/10
Brandt Street – p252 S9
Broadway West - p252 K7-T7
Brock Street - p252 S10
Bruce Street - p252 Q10
Brunswick Street - p252 N6/7
Cambie Street - p252 K6/7/8/9/10
Carolina Street - p252 O6/7
Cheyenne Avenue - p252 T10
Clancy Lorange Way – p252 M10
Clarendon Street - p252 S10
Clark Drive - p252 P6/7/8/9
Columbia Street - p252 L6/7/8/9
Commercial Drive - p252 Q6/7/8/9/10
Cook - p252 L6
Copley Street – p252 S8/9
Cotton Drive - p252 Q5/6
Cottrell Street - p252 O5/6/P5
Crowe - p252 L6
Culloden Street - p252 P10
Dinmont Avenue - p252 L9/10
Duchess Street - p252 S10/11/T10
Duke Street - p252 S11/T11
Dumfries Street - p252 Q8/9/10
Durward Avenue - p252 O10
Elgin Street - p252 P9/10
Fleming Street - p252 Q8/9/10
Fraser Street - p252 O6/7/8/9/10
Galt Street - p252 S10
Garden Drive - p252 S6/7/8
Gladstone Street - p252 R8/9/10/11
Glen Drive - p252 P6/7/8/9
Glengyle Street - p252 R9
Gothard Street - p252 S10
Grandview Highway - p252 S7/8/T7/8
Grandview Street - p252 Q6/7/R7/S7
Great Northern Way – p252 N6/O6
Guelph Street - p252 N7
Harriet Street - p252 O10
Heather Street - p252 K6/7/8/9/10
Henry Street - p252 P10
Horley Street - p252 T10/11
Hull Street - p252 R8
Industrial Avenue - p252 N6/7/O6
Inverness Street - p252 P8/9/10
James Street – p252 M10
John Street - p252 N9/10
Kamloops Street - p252 S7/8/9/10

Kaslo Street - p252 T6/7/8/9/10
Keith Drive - p252 P6/7
Kersland Drive - p252 K10/L10
King Edward Avenue - p252 K9-T9
Kingsway - p252 N/O8/P8/9/Q9/R10/S10
Knight Street - p252 P8/9/10
Lakewood Street - p252 R8/9
Lanark Street - p252 Q10
Little Street - p252 R10
Lorne Street - p252 N6
Main Street - p252 M6/7/8/9/10
Manitoba Street - p252 M6/7/8/9
Mannering Avenue - p252 R10
Marshall Street - p252 R8
Maxwell Street - p252 Q8/9
McLean Drive - p252 P6/7/Q6/7
McSpadden Avenue - p252 Q6/R6
Midlothian Avenue - p252 L10
Miller Street - p252 Q9/10
Mohawk Street - p252 P10
Nanaimo Street - p252 S6/7/8/9/10
Nigel Avenue - p252 L9/10
Norquay - p252 S10
Ontario Street - p252 M6/7/8/9/10
Penticton Street - p252 S7/8/9/10
Perry Street - p252 Q9/10
Peveril Avenue - p252 L9/M9/10
Prince Albert Street - p252 O6/7/8/9/10
Prince Edward Street - p252 N6/7/8/9/10
Quebec Street - p252 M6/7/8/9/10
Ravine Street - p252 T10
Ringwood Avenue - p252 O10
Ross Street - p252 P10
Semlin Drive - p252 R6/7
Sidney Street - p252 R9/10
Slocan Street - p252 S10/T6/7/8/9/10
Sophia Street - p252 N6/7/8/9
Spyglass Place - p252 L5/6
St Catherines Street - p252 O6/7/8/9/10
St Lawrence Street - p252 S10
Stainsbury Avenue – p252 R8/9
Stgeorge Street - p252 N6/7/8/9/10
Talisman Avenue - p252 L9
Todd Street - p252 T10
Tupper Street - p252 L8/9
Victoria Div – p252 Q8/R8
Victoria Drive - p252 R6/7/8
Walden Street - p252 N10
Walker Street – p252 S9
Ward Street - p252 T11
Webber Avenue - p252 N9
Welwyn Street - p252 Q8/9/10
Wenonah - p252 R10
Windsor Street - p252 O6/7/8/9/10
Winlaw Place - p252 T8
Woodland Drive - p252 Q5/6/7
Wylie - p252 L6
Yukon Street - p252 L6/7/8/9

Local transport

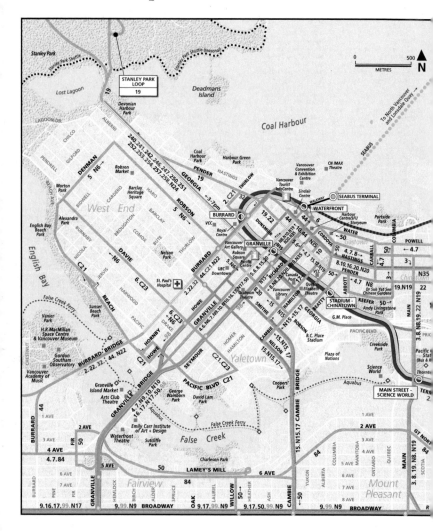